D0221808

Great Problems
of
Philosophy
and Physics
SOLVED?

Bob Doyle
The Information Philosopher
"beyond logic and language"

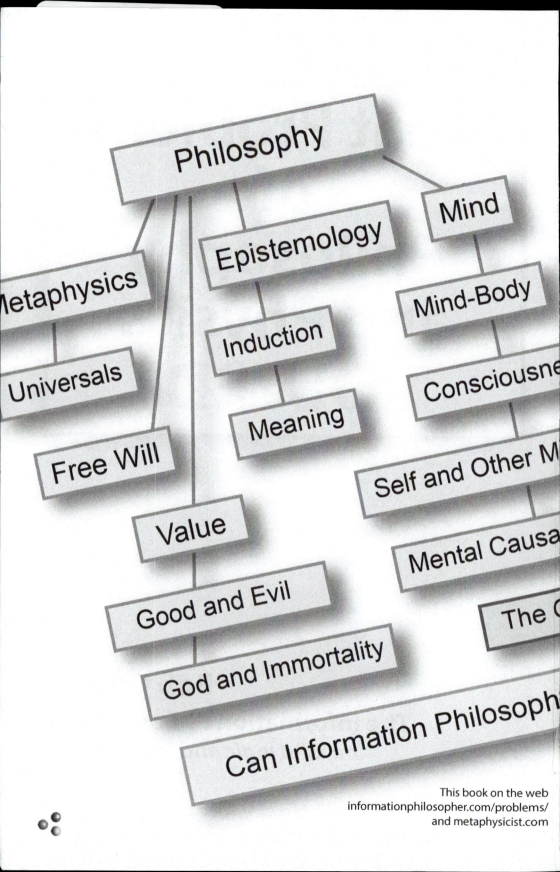

Philosophy

Mind

Epistemology

Metaphysics

Mind-Body

Induction

Universals

Consciousne

Meaning

Free Will

Self and Other M

Value

Mental Causa

Good and Evil

The C

God and Immortality

Can Information Philosoph

This book on the web
informationphilosopher.com/problems/
and metaphysicist.com

Physics

Interpretation of
Quantum Mechanics

Great Problems
of
Philosophy
and Physics
SOLVED?

of Life and Information

elp Solve All These Great Problems?

Bob Doyle

The Information Philosopher

"beyond logic and language"

ST. JOHN THE BAPTIST PARISH LIBRARY
2920 NEW HIGHWAY 51
LAPLACE, LOUISIANA 70068

First edition, 2016

© 2016, Bob Doyle, The Information Philosopher

All rights reserved. No part of this book may be reproduced in any form by electronic or mechanical means (including photo-copying, recording, or information storage and retrieval) without the prior permission of The Information Philosopher.

Publisher's Cataloging-In-Publication Data
(Prepared by The Donohue Group, Inc.)

Names: Doyle, Bob, 1936-

Title: Great problems in philosophy and physics solved? / Bob Doyle, the Information Philosopher.

Other Titles: Great problems - solved?

Description: First edition. | Cambridge, MA, USA : I-Phi Press, 2016. | Includes bibliographical references and index.

Identifiers: ISBN 978-0-9835802-8-7 | ISBN 978-0-9835802-9-4 (EPUB)

Subjects: LCSH: Philosophy--Textbooks. | Philosophy and science--Textbooks.

Classification: LCC BD21 .D69 2016 (print) | LCC BD21 (ebook) | DDC 100--dc23

I-Phi Press
77 Huron Avenue
Cambridge, MA, 02138 USA

Dedication

To the hundreds of philosophers and scientists with web pages on the INFORMATION PHILOSOPHER website.

After collecting and reading their works for the past six decades, I have tried to capture their essential contributions to philosophy and physics, as much as practical with excerpts in their own words.

Special thanks to many who have sent suggestions and corrections to ensure that their work is presented as accurately as possible for the students and young professionals who use the I-Phi website (nearly a thousand unique new visitors every day) as an entry point into some great intellectual problems that they may themselves help to solve in the coming decades.

As a scientist and inventor, the author has contributed some modest tools to help individuals and communities communicate, to share information. So he would like also to dedicate this work to some of the creators of the world's fundamental information-sharing technologies.

Alexander Graham Bell, Alan Turing, Claude Shannon, John von Neumann, Norbert Wiener, Steve Jobs, Tim Berners-Lee, Mark Zuckerberg, Jimmy Wales, Larry Page, Sergei Brin.

Information philosophy builds on the intersection of computers and communications. These two technologies will facilitate the sharing of knowledge around the world in the very near future, when almost everyone will have a smartphone and affordable access to the Internet and the World-Wide Web.

Information is like love. Giving it to others does not reduce it. It is not a scarce economic good. Sharing it increases the *Sum* of information in human minds.

Information wants to be free.

Bob Doyle

Cambridge, MA

September, 2016

Table of Contents

Philosophy

Mind

Epistemology

Metaphysics

Mind-Body

Universals

Preface

Ontology

Consciousne

Free Will

Meaning

Self and Othe

Value

Mental Causa

Good and Evil

God and Immortality

Can Information Philosoph

Preface

If I am right that information philosophy is a new method of philosophizing, if by going "beyond logic and language" it can provide new philosophical insights, it should be tested, applied to some of the great problems in philosophy and the philosophy of science. But what are the great problems?

A survey of several popular textbooks on philosophy produces a remarkable consensus on the problems facing philosophers from ancient to modern times. They typically include metaphysics - what is there?, the problem of knowledge - how do we know what exists?, the mind/body problem - can an *immaterial* mind move the material body?, the "hard problem" of consciousness, freedom of the will, theories of ethics - is there an objective universal Good?, and problems from theology - does God exist?, is God responsible for the evil in the world, what is immortality?

Perhaps the best-known summary of philosophical problems was BERTRAND RUSSELL's *The Problems of Philosophy*, published over a hundred years ago. Other important texts in analytic philosophy were G. E. MOORE's *Some Main Problems of Philosophy* and later A. J. AYER's *The Central Questions of Philosophy*.[1]

Another set of classic problems comes from the philosophy of science, which attempts to use metaphysics, ontology, epistemology, and logic to provide new foundational principles for the sciences. Philosophers of science question the foundations of physics as well as the attempts by some thinkers to *reduce* all sciences to physics. Some philosophers of mind, by contrast, argue for *emergent* properties that cannot be reduced to a "causally closed" world of physics.

Philosophers of biology speculate whether biology can be reduced to physics and chemistry, or whether something else is needed to explain life. We will show that *information processing and communication* is the extra explanatory factor.

---

[1]   A popular recent text surveyed is Feinberg and Shafer-Landau, 2002

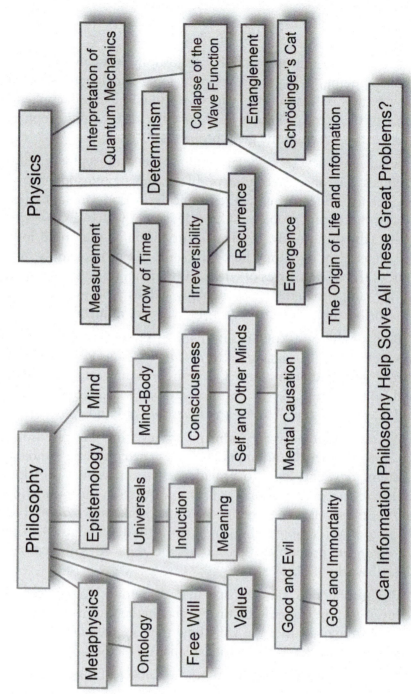

Figure 1. A taxonomy of problems in physics and philosophy.

The figure on the left arranges these great philosophy problems and major problems in the philosophy of physics into a taxonomy showing their relationships.

In the twentieth century, philosophers like LUDWIG WITTGENSTEIN labeled many of our problems "philosophical puzzles." Russell called them "pseudo-problems."

In his *Tractatus Logico-Philosophicus*, Wittgenstein hoped to *represent* all knowledge in words. He saw a proposition as a picture or *model* of reality and that the totality of true propositions is the whole of natural science (or the whole corpus of the natural sciences).[2] In his later work, he and subsequent analytic language philosophers thought many of these problems could be "dis-solved," revealing them to be conceptual errors caused by the misuse of language.

As an aeronautical engineer and architect, Wittgenstein might have explored his idea of dynamical models[3] further. He might have seen that models are a better tool than language to represent the fundamental, *metaphysical* nature of reality. Dynamical interactive models can easily *show* what often cannot be *said*.

Information philosophy goes beyond *a priori* logic and its puzzles, beyond *analytic* language and its paradoxes, beyond philosophical claims of *necessary* truths, to a *contingent* physical world that is best *represented* with *models* of dynamic, interacting information structures, including living things.

Knowledge begins with information in minds that is a partial isomorphism (mapping) of the information structures in the external world. I-Phi is the ultimate *correspondence theory*.

Using the new methodology of information philosophy, many classic problems are now back under consideration as genuinely important, analyzable, and potentially soluble in terms of physical, but *immaterial*, information.

To be sure, where scientists seek solutions, philosophers prefer problems, especially ones that are teachable as problems. But the goal of information philosophy is not to remove a problem from philosophy once it is tentatively solved.

---

2   *Tractatus* 4.01, 4.11
3   *Tractatus* 4.04

Returning to Russell's pioneering text, we can say he simply was wrong when he insisted that

> "questions which are already capable of definite answers are placed in the sciences, while those only to which, at present, no definite answer can be given, remain to form the residue which is called philosophy."[4]

Information philosophy aims to show that philosophical problems should not be reduced to "Russell's Residue."

Although our proposed solutions to dozens of problems are grounded in science, they remain great questions in philosophy that should continue to be taught as philosophy.

What's In The Book

The introductory chapter provides background on the basic concepts of information philosophy - what information is, its relationship to entropy and the second law of thermodynamics, how information is created, why *metaphysical* (non-epistemic) possibilities are needed in order to create new information, the connection between the theoretical *probability* of each possibility and the empirical statistics of *actual* events, how many living things have an *experience recorder and reproducer* (ERR) that stores and recalls information, and why, despite microscopic chaos and ontological indeterminism, the macroscopic world we live in is *adequately or statistically deterministic*, a cosmos that only *appears* to be determined and "causally closed under the laws of nature."

Because information is *immaterial*, it provides insights into many questions regarded as metaphysical. They include being and becoming, causality, chance, change, coinciding objects, composition (parts and wholes), constitution, essentialism, identity (and differences), individuation, modality (counterfactuals), necessity (or contingency), persistence (perdurance and endurance), possibility and actuality, space and time, truth, and vagueness. Much work in recent metaphysics has been an effort to establish metaphysical *necessity*, especially the *necessity of identity*.

By contrast, information philosophy shows the existence of metaphysical *possibilities*. See chapter 2 for some proposed solutions to the questions above and go to **metaphysicist.com** for the rest.

---

4   *The Problems of Philosophy*, 1912, p.155

Chapter 3 explores meta-ontological questions about the existential status of Platonic Forms, such as numbers and other abstract entities.

In chapter 4, we present our two-stage model of free will, which begins with the free generation of random alternatives (new information) followed by a willed decision that is adequately (statistically) determined by our motives and reasons. The chance events in the first stage do not cause our actions, although they are factors in the decision. It is the agent's decision in the second stage that is the cause of the action. Actions are not pre-determined.

Chapter 5 makes the case that, because a formless entity has no utility, information serves as a basis for *objective value*.

In chapters 6 and 7, armed with the value of information, we discuss good, the problem of Evil, God, and information immortality.

Chapter 8 argues that knowledge is created in minds, where it remains embodied in the experience recorder, but may be stored externally in books and the world-wide web.

In chapter 9, we examine the status of attributes and properties.

The problem of induction is connected to deduction and abduction (hypothesis formation) in chapter 10.

Chapter 11 relates the *meaning* of a new experience to the recorded experiences that are played back during the new one.

In chapters 12 and 13, we offer a model of the mind as immaterial information, as "software in the hardware" of the material brain, which we see as a biological information processor.

In chapter 14 and appendix E we analyze consciousness as the interactive exchange of actionable information by the experience recorder and reproducer (ERR) .

We show in chapter 16 how downward mental causation is possible, while bottom-up causal chains that would reduce biology and psychology to physics and chemistry are implausible.

We provide an *interpretation* of quantum mechanics in chapter 17 that minimizes mysteries with *visual models of* what is going on in the quantum world of possibility waves and actual particles.

We show in chapter 18 that unless new information is created, there is nothing for an observer to see and nothing to be measured.

There is no strict determinism and thus no pre-determinism. In chapter 19 we see that the statistical determinism that we have is adequate enough to give us causal control when we need it.

When a particle is located somewhere, the many other possible locations it might have been found (where the wave function was non-zero) simply disappear as possibilities. In chapter 20, we call this the collapse of the *possibilities* function. It is the fundamental unavoidable quantum mystery.

In chapter 21, we disentangle the EPR paradox by showing that we cannot measure one entangled particle without also instantly measuring the second particle, as the two-particle wave function collapses everywhere.

The "transition" from the quantum world to the *appearance* of a classical world (decoherence) occurs when the number of particles is large enough to average over quantum chance. In chapter 22, we see there is only one world, quantum all the way up!

In chapter 23, the puzzle of Schrödinger's Cat is solved by showing that the macroscopic cat is always either dead or alive. Schrödinger's possibilities function gives us only the probabilities that the cat is dead or alive before we look in the box.

Chapter 24 discusses arrows of time (radiation, entropy increase, evolution, history), and the fundamental arrow, the expansion of the universe, which creates all possibilities.

The origin of irreversibility is the random direction of particles after their interaction with radiation. Chapter 25 shows this loss of microscopic path information explains "one-way causality" in the biological and mental realms.

The idea that the universe will ultimately return to its original state is shown in chapter 26 to be wrong.

New information structures created at the biological and mental levels explain how new properties *emerge* that cannot be reduced to lower levels in a "causally closed" physical world. Chapter 27.

In chapter 28, we show that the story of biological evolution is continuous with the evolution of cosmological information structures. Life has evolved to include biological information processing and communications as well as the external storage of information that contains what we call the *Sum* of human knowledge. Living things are dynamic and growing information structures, forms through which matter and energy continuously flow. And it is information that controls those flows!

Appendix A defines information and proposes *dynamical interactive information models* as the best way to teach and to solve problems in philosophy.

In appendix B we show how statistical mechanics calculates the possible positions and velocities for vast numbers of molecules in a gas and proves the famous Second Law of Thermodynamics - that entropy always increases, yet the universe creates magnificent *information* structures, including us!

Appendix C reviews the basic principles of standard quantum physics, which are unfortunately questioned or denied by so many ill-informed philosophers of science.

In appendix D we ask whether chance is *ontological* and real or *epistemic* and the result of human ignorance? We look through Einstein's skeptical eyes to see the origin of ontological chance, without which there would be "nothing new under the sun."

Appendix E describes the *experience recorder and reproducer* (ERR), which stores information about all your past experiences and plays back in the subconscious mind those that resemble something in your current experience.

In appendix F we describe the critical steps in the **cosmic creation process**, which accounts not only for the existence of atoms and molecules, for the formation of galaxies, stars, and planets, and for biological evolution, but also for the "free creations of the human mind" behind our philosophy and our physics.

Appendix G argues that life is coextensive with language, that biology uses a semiotic system of signaling, signifiers, and signifieds. Human language evolved from biological communications.

I hope that you will look at the I-Phi website to explore further work in progress on these great problems in physics and philosophy.

Google Analytics reports that Information Philosopher has tens of thousands of unique visitors each year from all over the world.

I look forward to your emails with critical comments on problems that interest you and your feedback on our web pages for over 300 philosophers and scientists who have worked on these problems.

A Google search for their names often returns links to I-Phi pages on the first results page, alongside those from Wikipedia and the Stanford Encyclopedia of Philosophy.

Wikipedia does not allow original research and each article on the SEP is mostly the work of a single philosopher, with minimal content from original sources. By contrast, I-Phi pages present the work of hundreds of philosophers and scientists, often in their original languages, with downloadable PDFs of their major papers, for scholars without easy online access.

For example, we now have a bilingual *Tractatus*, with indexes in English and German, and a bilingual of Frege's major argument.

Your inputs will help make **informationphilosopher.com** as accurate a resource as possible for twenty-first-century philosophers.

Please also take a look at our new websites devoted to metaphysical problems that we believe are solvable using information philosophy, **metaphysicist.com**, and our case for possibilities - **possibilist.com**.

Bob Doyle

bobdoyle@informationphilosopher.com

Cambridge, MA

September, 2016

How To Use This Book With The I-Phi Website

The content of this book comes primarily from the **Problems** section on the **informationphilosopher.com** website and from our new **metaphysicist.com** site. You will find multiple entry points into the websites from this book, with URLs for the chapters and in many of the footnotes. I hope that you agree that the combination of a printed book and an online knowledge-base website is a powerful way to do philosophy in the twenty-first century.

The **Problems** web page has a right-hand navigation menu to the major problems and left-hand navigation to the hundreds of philosophers and scientists who have contributed to these classic problems in philosophy and physics.

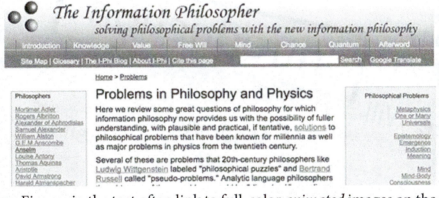

Figures in the text often link to full-color *animated* images on the I-Phi website. All images come from open-source websites.

Names in SMALL CAPS are the philosophers and scientists with web pages on the I-Phi website.

It is not easy to navigate any website, and I-Phi is no exception. Find things of interest quickly with the Search box on every page. Once on a page, a "Cite this page" function generates a citation with the URL and the date you retrieved the page, in standard APA format that you can copy and paste into your work.

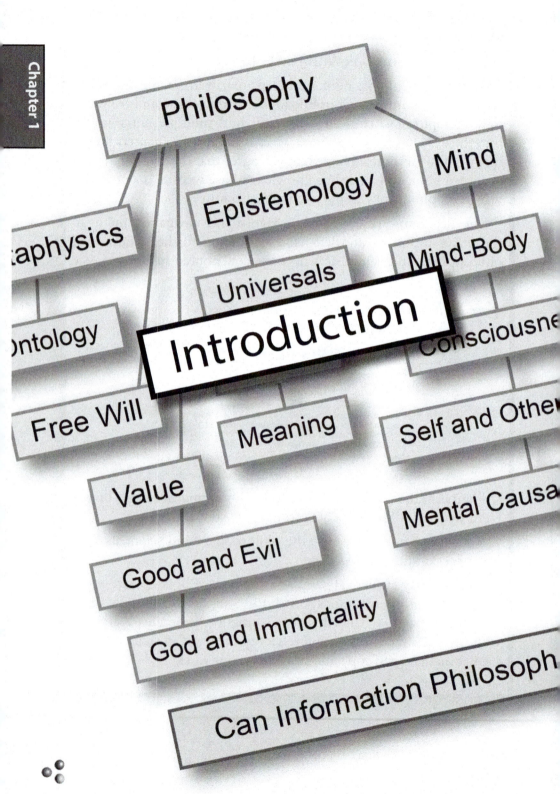

Introduction

Information philosophy is a new methodology for diagnosing and analyzing plausible solutions for several great philosophical problems, many with us since antiquity. It hopes to take philosophy, and the philosophy of sciences like physics and biology, beyond logical puzzles and language games.

The information philosopher proposes information as the preferred basis for examining current problems in a wide range of disciplines - from information creation in cosmology to measurement information in quantum physics, from the emergence of information in biology to its role in psychology, where it offers a solution to the classic mind-body problem and the "hard" problem of consciousness. And of course in philosophy, where failed language analysis can be replaced or at least augmented by the analysis of *immaterial* information content as the basis for justified (if not "true") beliefs and as a ground for objective values.

The immodest goal of information philosophy is to restore philosophy to its ancient role as the provider of first principles to all other systems of thought.

Information philosophy is a *philosophical system,* the first since the nineteenth century, because it makes the somewhat extravagant claim that analysis of the information content, its creation, processing, and communication, can provide profound insight into problems of philosophy, physics and biology that have so far not yielded acceptable solutions.

Just as analytical language philosophy is not the philosophy *of* language, so information philosophy is not the philosophy *of* information, with its focus on the philosophy of computers and the proper uses of information technology.

Information is physical, but it is *immaterial,* and as such, it enters the realm of the *metaphysical*. Information is neither matter nor energy, though it needs matter for its embodiment and energy for its communication. Information is the modern *spirit*.

Although the tagline of information philosophy is "beyond logic and language," the information philosopher uses logic (while noting that logic alone can tell us nothing about the physical world) and of course information philosophy is written in a language, despite the fact that the fundamental ambiguity of words makes precise communication difficult and despite the inability of twentieth-century linguistic analysis to make much progress in philosophy.

As the possible ground for all thought, information philosophy may be a sort of metaphilosophy. Quantitative information comes close to Gottfried Leibniz's ideal ambiguity-free language, though the problem of meaning[1] remains irreducibly contextual.

The strength of information philosophy comes from embracing and incorporating quantitative new knowledge from physics, biology, and neuroscience - but above all, from the fields of information theory and information science.

This raises the bar for young philosophers. In addition to doing clear conceptual analysis of problems and knowing the history of classic philosophical problems, they may now have to master some concepts from quantum mechanics, thermodynamics, molecular biology, neuroscience, and cosmology.

So beyond the words and images in this book, the I-Phi website provides animated visualizations of the most basic concepts that you will need to become an information philosopher.

These visualizations are dynamical and interactive models of what is going on at the most fundamental level of reality. They let us directly *show* concepts that may not be easily *said*.

Some of these concepts are familiar philosophical ones that we hope information will explain more clearly. Some are scientific concepts that every philosopher should know today. Other ideas are novel and unique to information philosophy.

---

1   See chapter 11 for more on the meaning in information.

The New Ideas of Information Philosophy

Here is a quick summary of several key ideas you should know which play major roles in the rest of this book.

1) *Possibilities exist.* Their existential status is problematic, because possibilities are not things, not physical material objects. They belong to the Platonic realm of ideas, an "ideal world" contrasted with the "material world." We will discuss the status of possibilities as a problem in metaphysics. Metaphysicians today defend *necessitism*, especially the necessity of identity. We will defend a *metaphysical possibilism*.

Note that the "possible worlds" of metaphysicians like David Lewis and the "many worlds" of physicists like Hugh Everett III are perfectly deterministic. Actual possibilities mean there is more than one possible future.

2) *Chance is real.* Without chance and the generation of possibilities, no new information can come into the world. Without chance, there can be no creativity. Without the creation of new information, new ideas, the information content of the universe would be a constant - "nothing new under the sun." In such an eliminatively materialist and determinist world, there is but one possible future. Possibilities are metaphysical and chance is ontological.

3) *Determinism is an illusion.* Determinism has had a long and successful history in philosophy and physics, but it is an unwarranted assumption, not supported by the evidence. The material world is quantum mechanical, and ontological chance is the result of quantum indeterminacy. An *adequate* and *statistical* determinism does *appear* when macroscopic objects contain large numbers of microscopic particles so that quantum events can be averaged over.

4) *Knowledge is an isomorphism.* Information *represents* a concept or an object better than an imprecise description in language. Information is the *form* in all concrete objects as well as the *content* in non-existent, merely possible, *abstract entities.* Knowledge is an *information structure* in a mind that is a partial *isomorphism*

(a mapping) of an information structure in the external world. Information philosophy is the ultimate *correspondence* theory.

4) *Beyond language.* But there is no isomorphism, no information in common, no necessary connection, between *words and objects.* Although language is an excellent tool for human communication, its arbitrary and ambiguous nature makes it ill-suited to represent the world directly. Language does not picture reality. Is is not the best tool for solving philosophical problems.

5) *The experience recorder and reproducer.* The extraordinarily sophisticated connection between words and objects is made in human minds, mediated by the brain's experience recorder and reproducer (ERR). Words stimulate neurons to start firing and to play back relevant experiences that include the objects. The neuroscientist Donald Hebb famously said that "neurons that fire together get wired together." Our ERR model says neurons that were wired together by old experiences will fire together again when a new experience resembles the old in any way, instantly providing guidance to deal with the new.

6) *Dynamic models.* The elements of information philosophy, *dynamical models of information structures*, go far beyond logic and language as a *representation* of the fundamental, metaphysical, nature of reality. They "write" directly into our mental experience recorders. By contrast, words must be *interpreted* in terms of earlier experiences. Without words and related experiences previously recorded in your mental experience recorder, you could not comprehend spoken or written words. They would be mere noise, with no meaning. Compare these two representations of a cat.

CAT

Figure 1-1. Linguistic and picture/model representations compared.

Chapter 1

Compared to a spoken or printed word, a photograph or a moving picture with sound can be seen and mostly understood by human beings, independent of their native tongue.

Computer animated dynamical models can incorporate all the laws of nature, from the differential equations of quantum physics to the myriad processes of biology. At their best, such simulations are not only our most accurate knowledge of the physical world, they are the best teaching tools ever devised. We can transfer knowledge non-verbally to coming generations and most of the world's population via the Internet and ubiquitous smartphones.

A dynamic information model of an information structure in the world is presented immediately to the mind as a look-alike and act-alike simulation, which is experienced for itself, not mediated through ambiguous words.

7) *Laws of nature are statistical.* Because microscopic atomic processes are governed by quantum physics, which is a *statistical* theory, all laws of nature are in fact statistical laws. They give us probabilities, not certainties. When material objects contain large numbers of atomic particles, the statistical uncertainty approaches zero and the laws are *adequately but only statistically deterministic.*

Quantum mechanical *probabilities* (Erwin Schrödinger's wave functions) evolve deterministically and continuously according to the Schrödinger equation, but the *actual* outcomes occur discontinuously and *statistically.* While this may seem like a logical contradiction, it is not.

The average value of *possible* particle positions moves according to classical mechanical laws, but the *actual* positions where particles are found are indeterminate (random), following quantum mechanical laws. The "determinism" we have is only an "adequate" *statistical determinism.*

8) *Entropy and the Second Law.* Abstract immaterial information is mathematically, phenomenologically, and experimentally related to a physical quantity in thermodynamics and statistical mechanics called the entropy. The second law of thermodynamics

says that, left to itself, a closed system approaches a state of maximum entropy, or disorder. This change is "irreversible," without an input of free energy and information (negative entropy) from outside the system.

A *closed system* cannot spontaneously increase its information structure, rearranging its material to contain more information. It can of course spontaneously decay, and will do so according to the second law. The approach to equilibrium destroys information. The lost information equals the amount of entropy (disorder) that is gained. Information is sometimes called *negative entropy*, the amount by which a system is below the maximum entropy possible.

9) *The universe is open.* It began in a state of total disorder, with the maximum entropy possible for the initial conditions, some 13.75 billion years ago. How then can the universe today contain such rich information structures as galaxies, stars, and planets like Earth, with its rich biological information-processing systems? This is the fundamental question of information philosophy.

The answer is that the maximum entropy of the early universe was tiny compared to the maximum possible entropy today, as a result of the expansion of the universe. And because the universe has not had time to reach its potential maximum of disorder, new information (negative entropy) has been and is now being created.

The expansion of the universe is the fundamental *arrow of time.*

10) *Negative entropy has value.* The source for all potential information can be a basis for objective value.

11) *The cosmic creation process.* Information philosophy explains the creation, the *emergence* of new information in the universe as a two-step process beginning with a quantum event (in which possibilities become actualized) and ending with some positive entropy carried away from the resulting low-entropy information structure, to satisfy the second law. [2]

This process explains the creation of every single bit of information, whether the formation of a hydrogen atom from a proton

---

2   See appendix F for more details.

and electron, a complex physical measurement like discovering the Higgs boson, or the creation of a new idea in a human mind.

12) *The two-stage model of free will.* Since every free act creates information, free will is intimately related to cosmic creation, beginning with the generation of *alternative possibilities* for action.

13) *Information is history.* The material particles of physics and chemistry carry no history. Their paths do not tell us where they have been in the past, though some deterministic physicists think so. Cosmological objects do have an evolutionary history. And so does biology. Matter and energy (with low entropy) flows through living things, maintaining their dynamical information structures.

To discover the origin of life, it will be easier to work backwards in time through the history of biological evolution than to start from physics and chemistry that knows nothing of information.

The Three Worlds of Information Philosophy

There is an over arching idea that provides a high-level view of the role of information. It is the notion that the "world" can be divided into "worlds" based on the ancient dualist view, a material world in the here and now and an ideal world above and beyond it, "outside space and time," some think.

Beyond the dualism, many philosophers have argued for a "third world" between these two. Information philosophy strongly defends this notion of a third world, which is distinguished by the interaction of abstract information processing and concrete information structures in the world of living things.

The great logician Gottlob Frege distinguished three "realms;" an external realm of public physical things and events, an internal subjective realm of private thoughts, and an "objective" Platonic realm of ideal "senses" (to which sentences refer, providing their meaning).

Karl Popper (very likely influenced by Frege) made the case for a World I - the realm of physical things and processes, a World II - the realm of subjective human experience, and a World III - the realm of culture and objective knowledge.

Charles Sanders Peirce proposed a triad of Objects, Percepts, and Concepts, which maps well onto the realms and worlds of Frege and Popper.

Information philosophy agrees with these fundamental divisions, but defines them based on the different roles played by information in each world. The three "worlds" of information philosophy are symbolized in our tricolor logo (the colors are visible on the book cover and on our website). The material world is the lower green ball. The biological world is the middle red ball, and the ideal or mental world is the upper blue ball.

We see the biological world as mixing matter from the material world and form from the ideal world. It is much larger than Popper's world of subjective human experience. All living things have experiences and the experience recorder and reproducer (ERR) model of information philosophy lets us understand better "what it's like to be" a conscious living thing by analyzing its experiences.

The biological world is unique in that it not only creates but also processes and communicates information.

The mental world is an *immaterial* world, a world of pure information, the stuff of thought and of philosophy.

We can identify three different roles for information in these three worlds - the purely material, the biological, and the mental.

But we shall see in appendix F that information creation in all three worlds involves the same fundamental process of physical information creation that is common to all creation processes, from the largest galaxies down to the composite matter of nucleons, atoms, and molecules built up from the fundamental particles of physics - quarks, gluons, photons and electrons,

We will show that this cosmic creation process is also present in all biological information creation, including the creation of new ideas in human minds. Understanding this process is vital to the solutions of several of our problems in philosophy and the philosophy of physics.

Information Creation in the Material World

The physical world of material objects, often described by philosophers as the "external world," could not be perceived or distinguished as individual objects if it did not have observable shapes or forms. If the matter were in a state of thermal equilibrium, maximum disorder or entropy, it might resemble the interior of a cloud, uniform in appearance in all directions. The early universe was just such a haze for the first few hundred thousand years. There was no permanent information structure larger than atomic and sub-atomic particles (electrons, protons, neutrons, helium nuclei).

The physical shapes that we do see - the sun, moon, and stars, the mountains and rivers - are the result of physical processes that created the quantifiable information in those shapes and forms. Cosmologists, astrophysicists, and geophysicists have specific models of how visible material objects like galaxies, stars, and planets came into existence and evolved over time.

But, and this is new and philosophically significant, the early universe did not contain the information of later times, just as early primates do not contain the information structures for intelligence and verbal communication that humans do, and infants do not contain the knowledge and remembered experience they will have as adults.

Creation of information in the material world can be described as the "order out of chaos" when matter and radiation first appeared and the expansion of the early universe led to the gravitational attraction of randomly distributed matter into highly organized galaxies, stars, and planets. The expansion - the increasing space between material objects - drove the universe away from thermodynamic equilibrium, increasing the positive entropy and, somewhat paradoxically, at the same time creating negative entropy, a quantitative measure of the order that is the basis for all information. Material information structures were *emergent*.

Information Creation in the Biological World

A qualitatively different second kind of information creation was when the first molecule on earth replicated itself and went on to duplicate its information exponentially. Accidental errors in the duplication provided variations in reproductive success, the basis for evolution. But most important, besides being information creators, biological systems are also *information processors*. Living things use information to guide their actions. All biological systems are built from communicating "cognitive" elements.

Biology is physics and chemistry plus information.

Many biologists have explored the role of information in biological processes. We want to emphasize that all living things are biological information processors, precursors of our man-made information-processing machines. Whereas computers are assembled by humans, even in the case of computers that we design to assemble other computers, biological information processors assemble themselves from atoms and molecules.

Biological evolution can be viewed as a story of information-processing systems becoming steadily more powerful and sophisticated. With the appearance of life in the universe came *teleonomic* purpose. This biological purpose is not a *telos*, an essence preceding the existence of life, but life, once existing, striving to maintain and improve itself. The earliest philosophers, especially Aristotle, recognized this as a unique characteristic, perhaps the defining characteristic, of living things. He called it "*entelechy*," meaning "to have a purpose within."

Matter and energy are conserved. There is the same amount of $E + mc^2$ today as there was at the universe origin. But information is not conserved. It has been increasing since the beginning of time. Everything emergent[3] is new information.

Living things are dynamic and growing information structures, *forms* through which matter and energy continuously flow.

And it is information processing that controls those flows, usually putting each atom or molecule in an appropriate place!

---

3   See chapter 27 on emergence

Information Creation in the World of Ideas

The third process of information creation, and the most important to philosophy, is human creativity. Almost every philosopher since philosophy began has considered the mind as something distinct from the body. Information philosophy provides a new explanation for that critical distinction.

We see the concrete physical information structures of the universe evolving to create abstract information creation and processing systems. Human beings are the current pinnacle of that evolutionary process, especially as we are conscious, indeed self-conscious, of our role externalizing information, sharing knowledge with our fellow human beings and guarding it as our most important gift to future generations.

For better or worse, it is knowledge, pure information, that provides humanity with the Baconian power we have to dominate our planet. Subverting traditional notions of economic scarcity and of fundamental limits to material resources, information creation has continuously provided new and different ways to use the existing material of our planet as new resources.

We identify the mind with the *immaterial* information in the material brain, the knowledge acquired through a combination of heredity and experience. The brain, part of the material body, we see as a biological information processor. As many philosophers and cognitive scientists have speculated in recent decades, the mind is indeed software in the brain hardware.

What Does Creation of Information Mean?

Creation means the coming into existence, the "emergence," of recognizable information structures, from a prior chaotic state in which there was little recognizable order or information.

This fact of increasing information describes very well an undetermined universe with an open future that is still creating itself. Stars are still forming, biological systems are creating new species, and intelligent human beings are co-creators of the world we live in. We are the authors of our lives.

Chapter 2

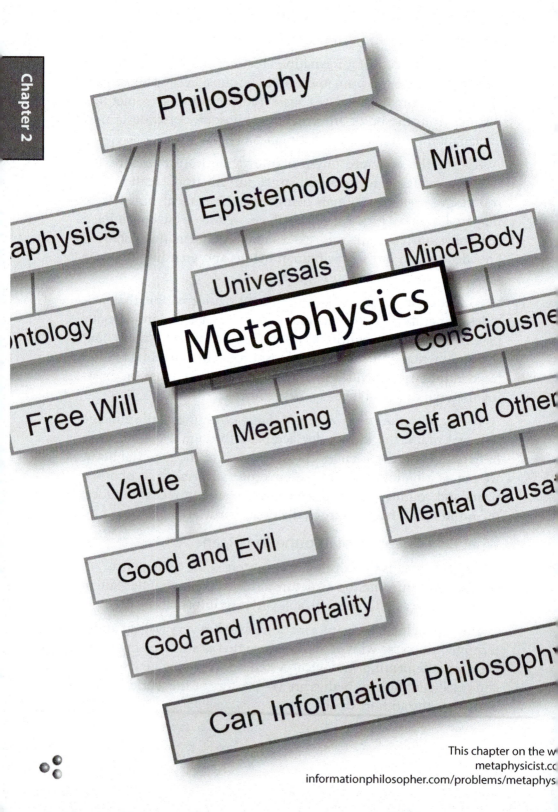

Philosophy

Mind

Epistemology

aphysics

Universals

Mind-Body

Metaphysics

ntology

Consciousne

Free Will

Meaning

Self and Other

Value

Mental Causa

Good and Evil

God and Immortality

Can Information Philosoph

This chapter on the w
metaphysicist.c
informationphilosopher.com/problems/metaphys

Metaphysics

We apply methods of information philosophy to metaphysics and find solutions to several classic problems, puzzles and paradoxes. You can find them all on our new website **metaphysicist. com** and in our forthcoming book *Metaphysics*. In this chapter, we discuss just a few of them, absolute and relative identity, the problem of composition (parts/wholes), coinciding objects (colocation), Aristotelian essentialism, the need for metaphysical possibility, and the semantics and modal logic of "possible worlds."

Many ancient puzzles are variations on the problem of coinciding objects, including Dion and Theon, the Growing Argument, and the Statue and the Clay. We solve these puzzles.

A central problem in information philosophy is the existential or ontological status of ideas. The *creation* of new ideas requires the existence of ontological chance. Metaphysical *possibility* must therefore be a fundamental aspect of metaphysical reality.

Information provides a unique explanation of self-identity and the *relative* identity of numerically distinct objects. It also explains the existential status of abstract entities.

Metaphysics is an abstract human invention about the nature of concrete reality – *immaterial* thoughts about material things. Information philosophy explains the metaphysics of chance and possibilities, which always underlie the creation of new information. Without metaphysical possibilities, there can be no human creativity and no new knowledge.

A materialist metaphysics asks questions about the underlying substrate presumed to *constitute* all the objects in the universe. Unfortunately, most modern philosophers are eliminative materialists and determinists who think there is "nothing but" the substrate of matter. As JAEGWON KIM puts it,

> "bits of matter and their aggregates in space-time exhaust the contents of the world. This means that one would be embracing an ontology that posits entities other than material substances — that is, immaterial minds, or souls, outside physical space, with immaterial, non-physical properties."[1]

---

1   *Physicalism, or Something Near Enough. p.71*

A formalist or idealist metaphysics asks about the *arrangement* and *organization* of matter that shapes material objects, what brings their forms into existence, and what causes their changes in space and time. Information philosophy defends a Platonic realm of *immaterial* ideas in a property dualism with the realm of matter. The information realm is physical and natural. It is not supernatural and "outside space and time." Ideas are embodied in matter and use energy for their communication. But they are neither matter nor energy. They are forms that inform.

The total amount of matter (and energy) in the universe is a conserved quantity. Because of the universe expansion, there is ever more room in space for each material particle, ever more ways to arrange the material, ever more possibilities. The total information in the universe is constantly increasing. This is the *first* contribution of information philosophy to metaphysics.

The *second* contribution is to restore a *dualist* idealism, based on the essential importance of information communication in all living things. Since the earliest forms of proto-life, information stored in each organism has been used to create the following generations, including the variations that have evolved to become thinking human beings who have invented the world of ideas that contains metaphysics. Abstract information is an essential, if *immaterial*, part of reality. Plato was right that his "ideas" (ἰδέας) are real. Plato's forms inform.

A *third* contribution from information philosophy adds biology to the analysis of metaphysical problems which began in puzzles over change and growth. The parts of living things – we call them biomers – are communicating with one another, which integrates them into their "wholes" in a way impossible for mere material parts – we find a *biomereological essentialism*.

The arrangement of individual material particles and their interaction is abstract immaterial information. The metaphysics of information can explain the cosmic creation process underlying the origin of all information structures in the universe and the communication of information between all living things, which we will show use a meaningful biological language, consisting of arbitrary symbols. Biological communications have evolved to become human language.

Ontology asks the question "what is there?"

Eliminative materialism claims that nothing exists but material particles, which makes many problems in ancient and modern metaphysics difficult if not insoluble. To be sure, we are made of the same material as the ancient metaphysicians. With every breath we take, we inspire 10 or 20 of the fixed number of molecules of air that sustained Aristotle. We can calculate this because the material in the universe is a constant.

But information is not a fixed quantity. The stuff of thought and creativity, information has been increasing since the beginning of the universe. There is ever more knowledge (but relatively little increase in wisdom?) With hundreds if not thousands of times as many philosophers as ancient Greece, can we still be debating the same ancient puzzles and paradoxes?

Information philosophy restores so-called "non-existent objects" to our ontology. Abstract entities consist of the same kind of information that provides the structure and process information of a concrete object. What we call a "concept" about an object is some subset of the immaterial information in the object, accurate to the extent that the concept is isomorphic to that subset.

Epistemology asks, "how do we know what there is?"

Immaterial information provides a new ground for epistemology, the theory of knowledge. We know something about the "things themselves" when we discover an isomorphism between our abstract ideas and concrete objects in the material world. But words and names are not enough. Information philosophy goes beyond the logical puzzles and language games of analytic philosophy. It identifies knowledge as information in human minds and in the external artifacts of human culture.

Abstract information is the foundation – the metaphysical ground – of both logic and language as means of communication. It is a dual parallel to the material substrate that the Greeks called ὑποκείμενον - the "underlying." It gives matter its form and shape. Form informs.

Much of formal metaphysics is about necessary relationships between universal ideas, certain knowledge that we can believe independent of any experience, knowledge that is "a priori" and "analytic" (true by logic and reason alone, or by definition). Some of these ideas appear to be unchanging, eternal truths in any possible world.

Information philosophy now shows that there is no necessity in the natural world. Apodeictic certainty is just an idea. There is no *a priori* knowledge that was not first discovered empirically (*a posteriori*). Only after a fact is discovered do we see how to demonstrate it logically as *a priori*. And everything analytic is part of a humanly constructed language, and thus synthetic. All such "truths" are philosophical inventions, mere concepts, albeit some of the most powerful ideas ever to enter the universe.

> There is no necessity in the natural world

Most important, a formal and idealistic metaphysics is about abstract entities, in logic and mathematics, some of which seem to be true independent of time and space. Aristotle, the first metaphysician, called them "first principles" (*archai, axioma*). GOTTFRIED LEIBNIZ said they are true in all possible worlds, which is to say their truth is independent of the world.

But if these abstract metaphysical truths are not material, where are these ideas in our world? Before their discovery, they subsisted as unknown properties. Once invented and discovered to be empirical facts, they are embedded in material objects, artifacts, and minds – the software in our hardware. Those ideas that are invented but not found empirically "real" (imagined fictions, flawed hypotheses, round squares) are also added to the sum of human knowledge, even if never embodied.

Many unchanging abstract entities share a property that the early philosophers Parmenides, Plato, and Aristotle called "Being," to distinguish its nature from "Becoming," the property of all material objects that change with time. Certain truths cannot possibly change. They are eternal, "outside space and time."

It is unfortunate that information philosophy undermines the logical concepts of metaphysical necessity, certainty, the *a priori* and analytic, even truth itself, by limiting their analyticity to the unchanging abstract entities in the realm of Being. But, on the positive side, information philosophy now establishes the metaphysical possibility of ontological possibilities.

Possibilities depend on the existence of irreducible ontological chance, the antithesis of *necessity*. Without metaphysical possibilities, no new information can be created.

Information philosophy and metaphysics restore an *immaterial* mind to the impoverished and deflated metaphysics that we have had since empiricism and naturalism rejected the dualism of RENÉ DESCARTES and its troublesome mind-body problem.

Naturalism is a materialism. Just as existentialism is a humanism. Even stronger, naturalism is an eliminative materialism. It denies the immaterial and particularly the mental.

While information philosophy is a form of the great dualism of idealism versus materialism, it is not a substance dualism. Information is a physical, though immaterial, property of matter. Information philosophy is a property dualism.

Abstract information is neither matter nor energy, although it needs matter for its embodiment and energy for its communication.

Information is *immaterial*. It is the modern spirit, the ghost in the machine. It is the mind in the body. It is the soul. And when we die, our personal information and its communication perish. The matter remains.

Information is the underlying currency of all communication and language. Passive material objects in the universe contain information, which metaphysicians and scientists analyze to understand everything material. But passive material objects do not create, actively communicate, and process information, as do all living things.

Realism is the ontological commitment to the existence of material things. Information realism is equally committed to the existence or subsistence of *immaterial*, but physical, ideas.

Human language is the most highly evolved form of information communication in biology. But even the simplest organisms signal their condition and their needs, both internally among their smallest parts and externally as they compete with other living things in their environment.

Biosemioticians convincingly argue that all the messages in biology, from the intracellular genetic codes sent to the ribosomes to produce more of a specific protein, to the words in sentences like this one, are a meaningful part of one continuously evolving semantic system. All messaging is as purposeful as a human request for food, so biology is called *teleonomic*, though not teleological. This "telos" or purpose in life did not pre-exist life.[2]

Like human language, the signs used in biological messages can be symbolic and arbitrary, having no iconic or indexical or any other intrinsic relation between a signifier and the signified concept or object. Like human signs, the meaning of a biological sign is highly dependent on the context. Only four neurotransmitters act as primary messengers sent to a cell, inside of which one of dozens of secondary messengers may be activated to determine the use inside the particular cell - the ultimate Wittgensteinian "meaning as use" in the message.

Modern Anglo-American metaphysicians think problems in metaphysics can be treated as problems in language, potentially solved by conceptual analysis. They are analytical language philosophers. But language is too flexible, too ambiguous and full of metaphor, to be a diagnostic tool for metaphysics. We must go beyond language games and logical puzzles to the underlying information contained in a concept or object.

---

2   See Appendix G on Biosemiotics.

Information philosophy restores the metaphysical existence of a realm that is "beyond the natural" in the sense since at least DAVID HUME and IMMANUEL KANT that the "laws of nature" completely determine everything that exists, everything that happens, in the phenomenal and material world.

Although the immaterial realm of information is not "supernatural" in any way, the creation of information throws considerable light on why so many humans, though few scientists, believe – correctly as it turns out – that there is a *providential* force in the universe.[3]

MARTIN HEIDEGGER, the philosopher of "Being," called FRIEDRICH NIETZSCHE the "last metaphysician." Nietzsche thought that everything in his *"lebensphilosophie"* was the creation of human beings. Indeed, when we are creative, what we create is new information.

Did we humans "discover" the abstract ideas, or did we "invent" them and then find them to be true of the world, including those true in any possible world?

As opposed to an analytic language metaphysician, a metaphysicist searches for answers in the analysis of immaterial (but physical) information that can be *seen* when it is embodied in external material information structures. Otherwise it can only be *known* – in minds.

Metaphysical truths are pure abstract information, subsisting in the realm of ideas.

Metaphysical facts about the world are discovered when there are isomorphisms between abstract ideas and the concrete structures in the external world that embody those ideas.

Information philosophy bridges the ideal and material worlds of Plato and Aristotle and the noumenal and phenomenal worlds of Kant. It demonstrates how *immaterial* minds are a *causal* force in the material world, connecting the psychological and phenomenological with the "things themselves," which are seen as embodiments of our ideas.

---

3   See chapter 7.

The causal force of ideas, combined with the existence of alternative possibilities, is the information philosophy basis for human free will.

What are we to say about a field of human inquiry whose major problems have hardly changed over two millennia? Information philosophy looks at a wide range of problems in metaphysics, situating each problem in its historical framework and providing accounts of the best work by today's metaphysicians. Metaphysicians today are analytic language philosophers, some of whom work on a surprisingly small number of metaphysical problems that began as puzzles and paradoxes over two thousand years ago.

The *metaphysicist* adds biological knowledge and quantum physics to help investigate the fundamental nature of reality. DAVID WIGGINS called for the former and E. JONATHAN LOWE called for the latter. DAVID CHALMERS thinks information may help solve the "hard problem" of consciousness.

An information-based metaphysics provides a single explanation for the origin and evolution of the universe as well as life on Earth. Since the beginning, it is the creation of material information structures that underlies all possibilities. From the first living thing, biological communication of information has played a causal role in evolution.

Metaphysics must include both the study of matter and its *immaterial* form. A quantum particle is pure matter. The quantum wave function is pure abstract information about possibilities.

The metaphysics of possibility grounds the possibility of metaphysics.

Possibility and Possible Worlds

In the "semantics of possible worlds," necessity and possibility in modal logic are variations of the universal and existential quantifiers of non-modal logic. Necessary truth is defined as "truth in all possible worlds." Possible truth is defined as "truth in some possible worlds." These abstract notions about "worlds" – sets of propositions in *universes of discourse* – have nothing to do with physical possibility, which depends on the existence of real *contingency*. Propositions in modal logic are required to be true or false. Contingent statements that are neither true or false are not allowed. So much for real possibilities in modal logic!

Historically, the opposition to metaphysical possibility has come from those who claim that the only possible things that can happen are the actual things that do happen. To say that things could have been *otherwise* is a mistake, say the eliminative materialists and determinists. Those other possibilities simply never existed in the past. The only possible past is the past we have actually had.

Similarly, there is only one possible future. Whatever will happen, will happen. The idea that many different things can happen, the reality of modality and words like "may" or "might" used in everyday conversation, have no place in metaphysical reality. The only "actual" events or things are what exists. For "presentists," even the past does not exist. Everything we remember about past events is just a set of "Ideas." And philosophers have always been troubled about the ontological status of Plato's abstract "Forms," entities like the numbers, geometric figures, mythical beasts, and other fictions.

Traditionally, those who deny alternative possibilities in this way have been called "Actualists."

Reading the last half-century with the development of modal logic, one might think that metaphysical possibilities have been restored. So-called modal operators like "necessarily" and "possibly" have been added to the structurally similar quantification operators "for all" and "for some." The metaphysical literature is full of talk about "possible worlds."

The most popular theory of possible worlds is DAVID LEWIS's "modal realism," an infinite number of worlds, each of which is just as actual (eliminative materialist and determinist) for its inhabitants as our world is for us.

There are no genuine possibilities in Lewis's "possible worlds"! It comes as a shock to learn that every "possible world" is just as *actual*, for its inhabitants, as our world is for us. There are no alternative possibilities, no contingency, no things that might have been otherwise, in any of these possible worlds. Every world is as physically deterministic as our own.

There are no possibilities in David Lewis's possible worlds   Modal logicians now speak of a "rule of necessitation" at work in possible world semantics. The necessarily operator and the possibly operator are said to be "duals" - either one can be defined in terms of the other, so either can be primitive. But most axiomatic systems of modal logic appear to privilege necessity and de-emphasize possibility. They rarely mention *contingency*, except to say that the necessity of identity appears to rule out contingent identity statements.

The rule of necessitation is that "if p, then necessarily p." It gives rise to the idea that if anything exists, it exists necessarily. This is called "necessitism." The idea that if two things are identical, they are necessarily identical. The "necessity of identity" was "proved" by RUTH BARCAN MARCUS in 1947, by her thesis adviser F. B. FITCH in 1952, and by WILLARD VAN ORMAN QUINE in 1953. DAVID WIGGINS in 1965 and SAUL KRIPKE in 1971 repeated the arguments, with little or no reference to the earlier work.

Naming and Necessity

Perhaps Kripke's most famous work is his idea that proper names are "rigid designators" that are necessarily true in all possible worlds. That is to say, the same individual in other possible worlds must have exactly the same name. This raises the question of "trans-world identity." Must every possible property of any individual be exactly the same? According to Leibniz's Law, which Kripke uses, two entities are only identical if every property they have is identical. So far, so good. But what about the property of being in two different worlds, two different places? If that one property differs, why shouldn't many other propeties, including their names?

Kripke and HILARY PUTNAM famously asked whether the word "water" and the molecular formula H_2O are necessarily the same in all possible worlds, because water is a "natural kind?"

There is simply no necessity in the physical world, neither the actual world nor "possible" other worlds. Necessitism exists only in the ideal worlds of logic and mathenatics.

The emphasis on necessitation in possible-world semantics leads to a flawed definition of possibility, one that has no connection with the ordinary and scientific meanings of possibility.

Modal logicians know little if anything about real possibilities and nothing at all about possible physical worlds. Their possible worlds are abstract universes of discourse, sets of propositions that are true or false. Contingent statements, that may be either true or false, like statements about the future, are simply not allowed in systems of formal logic.

Modal logicians define necessary propositions as those that are "true in all possible worlds." Possible propositions are those that are only "true in some possible worlds." This is the result of forcing the modal operators 'necessarily' and 'possibly' to correspond to the universal and existential quantification operators 'for all' and 'for some.' But the essential nature of possibility is the conjunction of contingency and necessity. Contingency is defined as the not impossible and the not necessary.

We propose the existence of a metaphysical *possibilism* alongside the notion of *necessitism*.

"Actual possibilities" exist in minds and in quantum-mechanical "possibility functions" It is what we might call "actual possibilism," the existence in our actual world of possibilities that may never become actualized, but that have a presence as abstract entities that have been embodied as ideas in minds. In addition, we include the many possibilities that occur at the microscopic level when the quantum-mechanical probability-amplitude wave function collapses, making one of its many possibilities actual.

Actual Possibles

Although there are no genuine possibilities in Lewis's "possible worlds," we can explain the existence of "actual possibles" in metaphysical terms using the possible world semantics of Saul Kripke, who maintained that his semantics could be used to describe various ways our actual world might have been. Unlike many other "possible world" interpretations, Kripke accepts that empirical facts in the physical world are contingent, that many things might have been otherwise. Kripke's *counterfactuals* are genuinely different ways the actual world might have been or might become.

> I will say something briefly about 'possible worlds'. (I hope to elaborate elsewhere.) In the present monograph I argued against those misuses of the concept that regard possible worlds as something like distant planets, like our own surroundings but somehow existing in a different dimension, or that lead to spurious problems of 'transworld identification'. Further, if one wishes to avoid the Weltangst and philosophical confusions that many philosophers have associated with the 'worlds' terminology, I recommended that 'possible state (or history) of the world', or 'counterfactual situation' might be better. One should even remind oneself that the 'worlds' terminology can often be replaced by modal talk—'It is possible that . . .'
>
> 'Possible worlds' are total 'ways the world might have been', or states or histories of the entire world.[4]

Following Kripke, we build a model structure **M** as an ordered triple <**G, K, R**>. **K** is the set of all "possible worlds," **G** is the "actual world," **R** is a reflexive relation on **K**, and **G** ε **K**.

If **H1, H2**, and **H3** are three possible worlds in **K**, **H1RH2** says that **H2** is "possible relative to" or "accessible from" **H1**, that every proposition true in **H2** is possible in **H1**.

Indeed, the **H** worlds and the actual world **G** are all mutually accessible and each of these is possible relative to itself, since **R** is reflexive.

Now the model system **M** assigns to each atomic formula (propositional variable) P a truth-value of T or F in each world **H** ε **K**.

Let us define the worlds **H1, H2**, and **H3** as identical to the real world **G** in all respects except the following statements describing actions of a graduating college student Alice deciding on her next step.

---

4   *Naming and Necessity*, p. 15, 18

In **H1**, the proposition "Alice accepts admission to Harvard Medical School" is true, but false in other worlds, so "possible."

In **H2**, the proposition "Alice accepts admission to MIT" is true.

In **H3**, the proposition "Alice postpones her decision and takes a 'gap year'" is true.

At about the same time, in the actual world **K**, the statement "Alice considers graduate school" is true.

Note that the abstract information that corresponds to the three possible worlds **H** is embodied physically in the matter (the neurons of Alice's brain) in the actual world and in the three possible worlds. There is no issue with the "transworld identity" of Alice as there would be with Lewis's "modal realism," because all these possible worlds are in the same spatio-temporal domain.

The metaphysical question is which of the three possible worlds becomes the new actual world, say at time *t*. What is the fundamental structure of reality that supports the simultaneous existence of alternative possibilities?

Just before time *t*, we can interpret the semantics of the model structure **M** as saying that the above statements were "merely possible" thoughts about future action in Alice's mind.

Note also that just after the decision at time *t*, the three possible alternatives remain in Alice's experience recorder and reproducer as memories.

Some consequences of Alice's alternative possible decisions.

In the future of world **H1**, Alice's research discovers the genetic signals used in messaging by cancer cells and cancer is eliminated. Several hundred million lives are saved (extended) in Alice's lifetime.

In the future of world **H2**, Alice engineers the miniaturization of nuclear weapons so they are small enough to be delivered by tiny drones. One is stolen from an air force base by a terrorist and flown to an enemy country where millions of lives are lost. Alice kills herself the next day.

In the future of world **H3**, a mature Alice returns to school, completes her Ph.D. in Philosophy at Princeton and writes a book titled *Free Will and Moral Responsibility.*

Actualism

Actualism appeals to philosophers who want the world to be determined by physical laws and by theologians who want the world to be in the hands of an omnipotent, omniscient, and benevolent god.

Some physicists think the future is causally closed under deterministic laws of nature and the "fixed past." If the knowledge that a Laplacian "super-intelligence" could gather about all the motions of material particles at a single instant is fixed for all time, then everything today might have been pre-determined from the earliest moments of the physical universe.

The special theory of relativity, for example, describes a four-dimensional "block universe" in which all the possible events of the future already exist alongside those of the past. It makes "foreknowledge" of the future conceivable.

Diodorus Cronus dazzled his contemporaries in the fourth century BCE with sophisticated logical arguments, especially paradoxes, that "proved" there could be only one possible future.

Diodorus' Master Argument is a set of propositions designed to show that the actual is the only possible and that some true statements about the future imply that the future is already determined. This follows logically from his observation that if something in the future is not going to happen, it must have been that statements in the past that it would not happen must have been true.

Modern day "actualists" include Daniel Dennett, for whom determinism guarantees that the actual outcome is and always was the only possible outcome. The notion that we can change the future is absurd, says Dennett, change it from what to what?

The ancient philosophers debated the distinction between necessity and contingency (between the *a priori* and the *a posteriori*). For them, necessity included events or concepts that are logically necessary and physically necessary, contingency those that are logically or physically possible. In the middle ages and the enlightenment, necessity was often contrasted with freedom. In modern times it is often contrasted with mere chance.

Causality is often confused with necessity, as if a causal chain requires a deterministic necessity. But we can imagine chains where the linked causes are statistical, and modern quantum physics tells us that all events are only statistically caused, even if for large macroscopic objects the statistical likelihood approaches certainty for all practical purposes. The apparent deterministic nature of physical laws is only an "adequate" determinism.

In modern philosophy, modal theorists like DAVID LEWIS discuss counterfactuals that might be true in other "possible worlds." Lewis' work at Princeton may have been inspired by the work of Princeton scientist HUGH EVERETT III. Everett's interpretation of quantum mechanics replaces the "collapse" of the wave function with a "splitting" of this world into multiple worlds.

According to the Schrödinger equation of motion, the time evolution of the wave function describes a "superposition" of possible quantum states. Standard quantum mechanics says that interaction of the quantum system with other objects causes the system to collapse into one of these possible states, with probability given by the square of the "probability amplitude."

One very important kind of interaction is a measurement by a "conscious observer."[5]

In standard quantum theory, when a measurement is made, the quantum system is "projected" or "collapsed" or "reduced" randomly into a single one of the system's allowed states. But if the system was "prepared" in one of these "eigenstates," then the measurement will find it in that state with probability one (that is, with certainty).

So modern physics does not deny the possibility of a *certain* measurement outcome, with probability equal to one, or even an *impossible* one, with probability equal to zero. But these are very special physical circumstances.

---

5   See chapter 18

Identity

In information philosophy, identity depends on the total information in an object or concept.

We distinguish the *intrinsic* information inside the object (or concept) from any relational information with respect to other objects that we call *extrinsic* or external. We can "pick out" the *intrinsic* information as that which is "self-identical" in an object. The Greeks called this the πρὸς ἑαυτο - self-relation. or ἰδίος ποιὸν, "peculiar qualifications" of the individual.

Self-identity, then, is the fact that the intrinsic information as well as the extrinsic relational or dispositional information are unique to this single object. No other object can have the same disposition relative to other objects. This is an absolute kind of identity. Some metaphysicians say that such identity is logically necessary. Some say self-identity is the only identity, but we can now support philosophers who argue for a *relative identity*.

To visualize our concept of information identity, imagine putting yourself in the position of an object. Look out at the world from its vantage point. No other object has that same view, that same relation with the objects around you, especially its relation with you. Now another object could have *intrinsic information identicality*. We will in fact identify a very large number of objects and concepts in the world that are intrinsically identical, including natural and artifactual kinds, which we may call digital kinds, since they are identical, bit for bit.

We can now offer three fundamental facts about identity:

Id1. Everything is identical to everything else in some respects.

Id2. Everything is different from everything else in some other respects.

Id3. Everything is identical to itself in all respects at each instant of time, but different in some respects from itself at any other time.

We can rewrite these observations in terms of information philosophy

I1. Any two things have some information in common.

I2. Any two things have some different information.

I3.The identity of anything over time is changing because the information in it (and about it) is changing with time.

These three observations might be called information axioms. Armed with them, we are in a position to "dis-solve" or deconstruct some of the most famous metaphysical puzzles and paradoxes.

A Criterion for Identity

After accepting the fundamental fact that nothing is perfectly identical to anything but itself, the criterion for *relative identity*, for identical "in some respect," or *qua* that respect, is that some subset of the information in two different things must be the same information, bit for bit.

Relative identity means that *a* can be the same *I* as *b*, but not the same *E* as *b*, where *I* is the sum of all the intrinsic properties and relations - internal self-relations between an object's different parts. For physical objects, these could be within some physical boundary, subject to conditions of vagueness. In a biological entity, it also includes the vast communications going on inside and between the cells, which makes it much more than a mereological sum of its parts.

The *E* for an object is the sum of extrinsic relations an object has with things outside, including its disposition in space and time.

Mathematically, $\int_i F(x) = \int_i G(x)$, but $\int_e F(x) \neq \int_e G(x)$, which says that F(x) and G(x) are identical over their intrinsic domains (i) but differ over their extrinsic domains (e) .

Set theoretically, in classical propositional calculus, we can say that I_a is the set of intrinsic properties and internal relations that can be predicated in propositions about an object a. E_a is the set of extrinsic relations. We can now describe why absolute identity is limited to self-identity.

If $I_a + E_a = I_b + E_b$, then a and b are one and the same object.

And, if $I_a = I_b$, then a and b are *relatively* identical, *qua* their information content.

Note that while self-identity is reflexive, symmetric, and an equivalence self-relation, relative identity is often none of these. This is because, unlike MAX BLACK's identical spheres, SAUL KRIPKE's natural kinds, and our many digital clones, some part of the information in a and b may be identical, but the information that is not identical may also differ in quantity. We can say that if aRb is 60% identical, bRa may be only 10% identical.

Extensional quantification over things in analytic language philosophy is about their set membership, which is dependent on language references to the properties of objects.

By contrast, quantification in information philosophy is a calculation of the total information content in the entities, in principle, free of language ambiguities, in practice, very difficult.

A Criterion for Essence

Information identity suggests a possible definition of the "essence" of an object, what is "essential" about it. Furthermore, if two objects are considered "essentially" the same, we can pick out the subset of information that corresponds to that "essence."

A subset of the intrinsic information may be essential with respect to (*qua*) some concept of the object. As EDMUND HUSSERL emphasized, our concepts about objects depend on our intentions, our intended uses of the object, which give it different (pragmatic) meanings. We can say that an essence is the subset of an object's information that is isomorphic to the information in the concept.

What we call a "concept" about a material object is usually some subset of the information in the object, accurate to the extent that the concept is isomorphic to that subset. By "picking out" different subsets, we can sort objects. We can compare objects, finding them similar *qua* one concept and different *qua* another concept. We can say that "$a = b$" *qua* color but not *qua* size.

But there are concepts that may have little to do with the intrinsic peculiar information about an object. They are concepts imposed on the object by our *intended* uses of it.

We must distinguish these extrinsic essences – our external ideas and concepts about what the object is – from the intrinsic essences that depend only on the object itself and its own purposes, if any. The essences we see in an object are subjective, but we may define an objective essence as the total intrinsic information, including internal messaging, in the object.

Husserl and GOTTLOB FREGE both pointed out that our ideas are dependent on our personal experience. Experience constrains and amplifies our possible concepts. Two persons may get the general "sense" or "meaning" of something referred to, but Frege said the "idea" or representation (*Vorstellung*) in each mind can be very different, based on that individual's experience. Information philosophy locates the creation of meaning in the responses of the experience recorder and reproducer (ERR) to different stimuli.

The relation "identical to," between two numerically distinct concrete or abstract entities, is the source of logical puzzles and language games through the ages that are little more than verbal disputes. Most such disputes are easily resolved or "dis-solved" by paying careful attention to all the information, all the particular properties, intrinsic and extrinsic, of the two entities that may be identical *qua* some particular properties.

Coinciding Objects

The problem of coinciding objects (sometimes called colocation) is whether two things can be in the same place at the same time. Common sense says that they cannot.

JOHN LOCKE described the impossibility that two things of the same kind should exist in the same place at the same time.

ANOTHER occasion the mind often takes of comparing, is the very being of things, when, considering anything as existing at any determined time and place, we compare it with itself existing at another time, and thereon form the ideas of wherein identity and diversity. When we see anything to be in any identity place in any instant of time, we are sure (be it what it will) that it is that very thing, and not another which at that same time exists in another place, how like and undistinguishable soever it may be in all other respects: and in this consists identity, when the ideas it is attributed to vary not at all from what they were that moment wherein we consider their former existence, and to which we compare the present. For we never finding, nor conceiving it possible, that two things of the same kind should exist in the same place at the same time, we rightly conclude, that, whatever exists anywhere at any time, excludes all of the same kind, and is there itself alone. [6]

In modern metaphysics, the problem of coinciding objects should be the question of whether one mass of material – what the Greeks called substrate or ὑποκείμενον ("the underlying") – could contain the whole of two (or more) separate objects containing that same mass.

It is now common for many identity theorists to claim that the whole of one object and the whole of another can occupy just the same place at just the same time. Among them, according to MICHAEL BURKE, are RODERICK CHISHOLM, E. JONATHAN LOWE, SAUL KRIPKE, and DAVID WIGGINS.

But it is not clear that this was the ancient problem in debates between the Academic Skeptics and the Stoics. In modern times, multiple ancient puzzles are used to pose the problem of coinciding objects. One is the Statue and the Clay from which it is sculpted. Another is Dion and Theon, known as the "body-minus" problem. Another is Tibbles, the Cat and a similar cat missing his tail. A third is the Stoic CHRYSIPPUS's so-called "Growing Argument."

All these modern claims that there can be two "coinciding objects" can be shown to be distinguishing between different aspects, in particular, the matter and form, of a single object,

---

6   *Essay Concerning Human Understanding*, Of Identity and Diversity, Book II, ch xxvii

giving them different names, and then arguing that they have different *persistence* conditions.

Aristotle's Metaphysics makes perhaps the earliest and clearest such distinction, using the example of a statue and its matter.

> The term "substance" (οὐσία) is used, if not in more, at least in four principal cases; for both the essence and the universal and the genus are held to be the substance of the particular (ἑκάστου), and fourthly the substrate (ὑποκείμενον). The substrate is that of which the rest are predicated, while it is not itself predicated of anything else. Hence we must first determine its nature, for the primary substrate (ὑποκείμενον) is considered to be in the truest sense substance.

> Now in one sense we call the matter (ὕλη) the substrate; in another, the shape (μορφή); and in a third, the combination Both matter and form and their combination are said to be substrate of the two. By matter I mean, for instance, bronze; by shape, the arrangement of the form (τὸ σχῆμα τῆς ἰδέας); and by the combination of the two, the concrete thing: the statue (ἀνδριάς). Thus if the form is prior to the matter and more truly existent, by the same argument it will also be prior to the combination.[7]

Aristotle clearly sees the statue as a combination of its form/shape and its matter/clay.

Of course Aristotle sees no problem with the body and soul of a person being combined in one substance (οὐσία), but a hundred or so years after Aristotle, the Academic Skeptics attacked the Stoics, saying Stoics were making single things into dual beings, two objects in the same place at the same time, but indistinguishable. And this may have been the beginning of the modern problem.

The "two things" that bothered the Skeptics appeared first in the "growing argument" described by the later second century BCE Stoics, Posidonius and Mnesarchus, as reported by Stobaeus in the fifth century CE. What is it that grows, they asked, the material substance or the peculiar qualities of the individual? But note that this is still matter versus form. The substance (matter) does not grow. It is the individual that grows.

> The substance neither grows nor diminishes through addition or subtraction, but simply alters, just as in the case of numbers and measures. And it follows that it is in the case of peculiarly qualified indi-

---

7   *Metaphysics*, Book VII, § iii, 1-2

viduals, such as Dion and Theon, that processes of both growth and diminution arise.

Therefore each individual's quality actually remains from its generation to its destruction, in the case of destructible animals, plants and the like. In the case of peculiarly qualified individuals they say that there are two receptive parts, the one pertaining to the presence of the substance, the other to that of the qualified individual...

The peculiarly qualified thing is not the same as its constituent substance. Nor on the other hand is it different from it, but is all but the same, in that the substance both is a part of it and occupies the same place as it, whereas whatever is called different from something must be separated from it and not be thought of as even part of it...[8]

Like Aristotle, the Stoics were distinguishing the individual's "constituent substance" from the "peculiar qualifications" of the individual.

The Stoic term for "constituent substance" or substrate, following Aristotle, was ὑποκείμενον. Their term for the unique person, possibly separate from the material body, was ἰδίος ποιὸν - a particular individual "who," for example, Socrates, as opposed to κοινός ποιὸν, a general "whoness," for example, a human being.

But in the vehement debates of the third century BCE the Academic skeptics laughed at the Stoics for seeing a dual nature in man. Their most famous puzzle was the coinciding objects of Dion and Theon (reframed by PETER GEACH as the puzzle of Tibbles, the Cat and a similar cat lacking a tail).

Plutarch, writing in the first century CE, accused the Stoics of "crazy arithmetic" and absurdity, that "each of us is a pair of twins, two-natured and double, joined in some parts but separate in others, two bodies sharing the same color, the same shape, the same weight, the same place,"

Yet this difference and distinction in us no one has marked off or discriminated, nor have we perceived that we are born double, always in flux with one part of ourselves, while remaining the same people from birth to death with the other...

---

8   Stobaeus (I,177,21 - 179,17, in *The Hellenistic Philosophers*, A.A.Long and D.N.Sedley, v.1, p.168

If when we hear Pentheus in the tragedy say that he sees two suns and a double Thebes we say he is not seeing but mis-seeing, going crazy in his arithmetic, then when these people propose that, not one city, but all men, animals, trees, furniture, implements and clothes are double and two-natured, shall we not reject them as forcing us to misthink rather than to think?[9]

Another early statement is in the first century BCE.

That what concerns the peculiarly qualified is not the same as what concerns the substance, Mnesarchus says is clear. For things which are the same should have the same properties. For if, for the sake of argument, someone were to mould a horse, squash it, then make a dog, it would be reasonable for us on seeing this to say that this previously did not exist but now does exist. So what is said when it comes to the qualified thing is different.

So too in general when it comes to substance, to hold that we are the same as our substances seems unconvincing. For it often comes about that the substance exists before something's generation, before Socrates' generation, say, when Socrates does not yet exist, and that after Socrates' destruction the substance remains although he no longer exists.[10]

An Information Analysis of "Coinciding Objects"

Most of these metaphysical puzzles start with a single object, then separate it into its matter and its form, giving each of them names and declaring them to be two coinciding objects. Next we postulate a change in either the matter or the form, or both. It is of course impossible to make a change in one without the other changing, since we in fact have only one object.

But our puzzle maker asks us to focus on one and insist that the change has affected the status of only that one, usually claiming that the change has caused that one to cease to exist. This follows an ancient view that any change in material constitutes a change in identity. But the modern metaphysicist knows that all objects are always changing and that a change in identity may always preserve some information of an entity. The puzzle claims that an

---

9   "Against the Stoics on Common Conceptions" 1083, *The Hellenistic Philosophers*, A.A.Long and D.N.Sedley, v.1, p.166-7

10   *ibid*, p.168

aspect of the object persists if the relative identity, or identity "in some respect" has not changed.

To create a paradox, we use two of our axioms about identity,

Id1. Everything is identical to everything else in some respects.

Id2. Everything is different from everything else in some other respects.

We (in our minds) "pick out" one respect whose identity persists over time because of Id1 and a second respect which changes in time because of Id2.

We now have one object that both persists and does not persist (in different respects, of course), the very essence of a paradox. We call them different objects to create the puzzle.

For example, in the case of the statue and the clay, Mnesarchus's original version assumed that someone moulds a horse, then squashes it. We are asked to pick out the horse's shape or form. The act of squashing changes that shape into another relatively amorphous shape. The object changes its identity with respect to its shape. Mnesarchus said it would be reasonable to see this sequence of events as something coming into existence and then ceasing to exist. The most obvious thing changing is the horse shape that we name "statue."

By design of the puzzle, there is no change in the amount of clay, so the matter is considered identical over time with respect to the amount of clay. The clay persists.

We now claim to have seen a difference in persistence conditions. The object *qua* clay persists. The object *qua* statue goes in and out of existence.

But this is just a *way of talking* about what has happened because a human observer has "picked out" two different aspects of the one object. As the statue is being smashed beyond recognition, every part of the clay must move to a new position that accommodates the change in shape of the statue. There are changes in the clay with identical information to the change in the shape of the statue. These we ignore to set up the puzzle.

In more modern versions of the statue and clay puzzle, we can make a change in the matter, for example by breaking off an arm and replacing it with a new arm made of different material but restoring the shape. We ignore the change in form, although it was obviously a drastic change until the restoration, and we focus on the clay, making the claim that the original clay has ceased to exist and new clay come into existence.

In either case, the claim to see different persistence conditions is the result of focusing on different subsets of the total information.

When identity theorists say that the whole of one object and the whole of another can occupy just the same place at just the same time, they are never talking about two objects of the same type, kind, or sort. They are always "picking out" different aspects of a single object and giving them differing existential status.

Composition (Parts and Wholes)

Debates about the relation of parts to wholes is a major part of modern metaphysics. Many puzzles have to do with different persistence conditions of the "parts" of a composited whole, as we saw with the idea of coinciding objects.

"Mereological universalism" or extensional mereology is an abstract idea, defined in 1937 by Stanislaw Leśniewski and later by Henry Leonard and Nelson Goodman (1940). It claims that any collection of things, for example the members of a set in symbolic logic, can be considered as the parts of a whole, a "fusion" or "mereological sum," and thus can *compose* an object. Critics of this idea says that such arbitrary collections are just "scattered objects." A mind-independent connection between things is needed for them to be considered *integral* "parts."

That connection is to be found in the *information* that led to the whole in the first place and/or is now maintaining that integrity.

Chapter 2

"Mereological essentialism" is RODERICK CHISHOLM's radical idea that every whole has its parts necessarily and in every possible world. This goes too far. No physical object can maintain its parts indefinitely and freeze its identity over time. Recall our third axiom of identity:

Id3. Everything is identical to itself in all respects at each instant of time, but different in some respects from itself at any other time.

"Mereological nihilism" is the opposite extreme. PETER VAN INWAGEN and the early PETER UNGER denied the existence of composites, seeing them as simples (partless entities) arranged to look like a composite object. For van Inwagen, a table is "simples arranged table-wise."

It is the *information* in the process that is doing the arranging is responsible for the composite whole.

Van Inwagen made a surprising exception for living objects. He bases the composite nature of biological entities on the Cartesian dualist view that humans are thinking beings!

Van Inwagen's says that his argument for living beings as composite objects is based on the Cartesian "Cogito," I think, therefore I am.

> My "reasons for believing in organisms," therefore, are reasons for stopping where I do and not going on to maintain that there are no organisms but are only simples arranged organically. My argument for the existence of organisms, it will be remembered, involved in an essential way the proposition that I exist.[11]

With van Inwagen's exception of living things, and now that Unger has abandoned his own form of nihilism in recent years, both philosophers now accept that they themselves exist (*sic*).

Van Inwagen could see no obvious demarcation level at which even the simplest living things should not be treated as composite objects. We shall see that it is *biological information* that makes a whole being out of just matter and energy.

Information philosophy and metaphysics ask who or what is doing the arranging? Information provides a more fundamental

---

11   *Material Beings*, p.213

reason than van Inwagen's for treating living things as integrated composites and not simply mereological sums of scattered objects. Furthermore, it extends a true composite nature to artifacts and to groupings of living things because they share a *teleonomic* property – a purpose. And it shows how some "proper parts" of these composites can have a holistic relation with their own parts, enforcing transitivity of part/whole relations.

A process that makes a composite object an integrated whole we call *teleonomic* (following COLIN PITTENDRIGH, JACQUES MONOD, and ERNST MAYR) to distinguish it from a teleological cause with a "telos" pre-existing all life. Teleonomy is the explanatory force behind van Inwagen's "arrangement" of simple parts.

Biological parts, which we can call *biomers*, are communicating systems that share information via biological messaging with other parts of their wholes, and in many cases communicate with other living and non-living parts of their environments. These communications function to maintain the biological integrity (or identity) of the organism and they control its growth. Artifacts have their teleonomy imposed by their creators. For example, when a carpenter cuts the wood for a table, it is the "telos," the end or purpose for the table, that "arranges it table-wise."

Biocommunications are messages transferring information, inside the simplest single-cell organisms. For the first few billion years of life these were the only living things, and they still dominate our planet. Their messages are the direct ancestors of messages between cells in multicellular organisms. They evolved to become all human communications, including the puzzles and problems of metaphysics. A straight line of evolution goes from the first biological message to this book of *Great Problems*.

Like many metaphysical problems, composition arose in the quarrels between Stoics and Academic skeptics that generated several ancient puzzles still debated today. But it has roots in Aristotle's definition of the essence (ουσία), the unchanging "Being" of an object. We will show that Aristotle's essentialism has a biological basis that is best understood today as a biomereological essentialism. It goes beyond mereological sums of scattered objects because of the teleonomy shared between the parts, whether living or dead, of a biomeric whole.

The *essence* of an object, the "kind" or "sort" of object that it "is", its "constitution," its "identity," includes those "proper" parts of the object without which it would cease to be that sort or kind. Without a single essential part, it loses its absolute identity.

While this is strictly "true," for all practical purposes most objects retain the overwhelming fraction of the information that describes them from moment to moment, so that information philosophy offers a new and quantitative measure of "sameness" to traditional philosophy, a measure that is difficult or impossible to describe in ordinary language.

Nevertheless, since even the smallest change in time does make an entity at $t + \Delta t$ different from what it was at t, this has given rise to the idea of "temporal parts."

Temporal Parts

Philosophers and theologians, e.g., ALFRED NORTH WHITEHEAD and JONATHAN EDWARDS, have argued for distinct temporal parts, with the idea that each new part is a completely new creation *ex nihilo*. The world is newly created at every instant! Even modern physicists (e.g., HUGH EVERETT III) talk as if parallel universes are brought into existence at an instant by quantum experiments that collapse the wave function.

DAVID LEWIS, who claims there are many possible worlds, is a proponent of many temporal parts. His theory of "perdurance" asserts that the persistence through time of an object is as a series of completely distinct entities, one for every instant of time. Lewis's work implies that the entire infinite number of his possible worlds (as "real" and actual as our world, he claims), must also be entirely created anew at every instant.

While this makes for great science fiction and helps to popularize metaphysics, at some point attempts to understand the fundamental nature of reality must employ Occam's Razor and recognize the fundamental conservation laws of physics. If a new temporal part is created *ab initio*, why should it bear any resemblance at all to its earlier version?

It is extravagant in the extreme to suggest that all matter disappears and reappears at every instant of time. It is astonishing enough that matter can spontaneously be converted into energy and back again at a later time.

Most simple things (the elementary particles, the atoms and molecules of ordinary matter, etc.) are in stable states that exist continuously for long periods of time, and these compose larger objects that persist through "endurance," as Lewis describes the alternative to his "perdurance." Large objects are not absolutely identical to themselves at earlier instants of time, but the differences are infinitesimal in terms of information content.

The doctrine of temporal parts ignores the physical connections between all the "simples" at one instant and at the following moment. It is as if this is an enormous version of the Zeno paradox of the arrow. The arrow cannot possibly be moving when examined at an instant. The basic laws of physics describe the continuous motions of every particle. They generally show very slow changes in configuration – the organizational arrangement of the particles that constitutes abstract information about an object.

One might charitably interpret Lewis as admitting the endurance of the elementary particles (or whatever partless simples he might accept) and that perdurance is only describing the constant change in configuration, the arrangement of the simples, the *information*, that *constitute* or *compose* the whole.

Then Lewis's temporal parts would be a series of self-identical objects that are not absolutely identical to their predecessors and successors, just a temporal series of highly theoretical abstract ideas, perhaps at the same level of (absurd) abstraction as his possible worlds?.

Is a temporal part a reasonable concept? What exactly is a part? And what constitutes a whole? For each concept, there is a strict philosophical sense, an ordinary sense, and a functional or *teleonomic* sense.

In the strict sense, a part is just some subset of the whole. The whole itself is sometimes called an "improper part."

In the ordinary sense, a part is distinguishable, in principle separable, from other neighboring parts of some whole. The smallest possible parts are those that have no smaller parts. In physics, these are the atoms, or today the elementary particles, of matter.

In the functional sense, we can say that a part serves some purpose in the whole. This means that it has may be considered a whole in its own right, subordinate to any purpose of the whole entity. Teleonomic examples are the pedals or wheel of a bicycle, the organs of an animal body, or the organelles in a cell.

The *teleonomic* sense of an object is that it seems to have a *purpose*, the Greeks called it a *telos*, either intrinsic as in all living things, or extrinsic as in all artifacts, where the purpose was invented by the object's creator.

The most important example of a teleonomic process is of course biology. Every biological organism starts with a first cell that contains all the information needed to accomplish its "purpose," to grow into a fully developed individual, and, for some, to procreate others of its kind.

By contrast, when a philosopher picks out an arbitrary part of something, declaring it to be a whole something for philosophical purposes, perhaps naming it, the purpose is simply the philosopher's intention of analyzing it further.

For example, something that has no natural or artifactual basis, that does not "carve nature at the joints," as Plato described it, that arbitrarily and violently divides the otherwise indivisible, may be a perfectly valid philosophical "idea," an abstract entity.

But temporal parts do not "carve nature at the joints." They do not capture the fundamental nature of reality.

Temporal parts are bad metaphysics.

Aristotelian Essentialism

Aristotle knew that most living things can survive the loss of various parts (limbs, for example), but not others (the head). By analogy, he thought that other objects (and even concepts) could have parts (or properties) that are essential to its definition and other properties or qualities that are merely accidental.

Aristotelian essentialism is the study of those essential parts.

For Aristotle, and in ordinary use, not every part of a whole is a *necessary* part (let alone in all possible worlds). Much of the verbal quibbling in metaphysical disputes is about objects that are defined by language conventions as opposed to "natural kinds" that we can recognize by their information contents.

When we can identify the origin and current processing of that information, we have the deep metaphysical sense of essence. Aristotle called the arrangement "the scheme of the ideas."

> By matter I mean, for instance, bronze; by shape, the arrangement of the form (τὸ σχῆμα τῆς ἰδέας); and by the combination of the two, the concrete thing: the statue (ἀνδριάς)[12]

Information philosophy provides the deep reason behind Aristotle's essentialism for living things and artifacts.

The "parts" of biological organisms are created and maintained (arranged) by anti-entropic processes that distribute matter and energy to all the vital parts. There is a purpose or "telos." Aristotle called it a built-in telos or "entelechy" (loosely translated as "having the final cause within"). The telos is implemented by messaging between all the vital parts or "proper parts." A bio-mereological essentialism notes that every biomer (a biological part) is normally in direct or indirect communication with vast numbers of other biomers in the living organism and with the extra-cellular environment. Communication is information that

---

12   *Metaphysics*, Book VII, § vii

is neither matter nor energy. It is the ideal content of the message that implements the organism's "telos." Some examples...

• Human artifacts. Here the "telos" comes from the creator. The leg of a table is an essential part of the original design. Such proper parts often have recognizable functions, so when they are missing the whole is no longer functional.

• Physical combinations of elementary particles into nuclei and chemically emergent combinations of atoms – water from hydrogen and oxygen and salt from sodium and chlorine.

• Cosmological and other material objects formed with an anti-entropic process that created their information. Astronomical bodies were pulled together by gravity into information structures. Crystals grow information rich structures (e.g., snowflakes).

Many of these "wholes" can survive the loss of some parts. But we are back quibbling. When their efficient/material causes and their formal and final causes are "teleonomic" and not simply arbitrary human conventions, we can say these are "natural kinds."

The problem of composition becomes more severe when some metaphysicians consider matter to be infinitely divisible, just as the real number line contains an infinite number of numbers between any two numbers (and a higher order of infinity of irrational numbers!).

By contrast, the metaphysicist's view is that matter is discrete, not infinitely divisible like the continuous spatial and temporal dimensions. The Greek materialists argued for simple atoms separated by a void. LUDWIG BOLTZMANN and ALBERT EINSTEIN showed that the atoms of nineteenth-century chemistry really exist. In modern physics the simplest elementary particles are quarks, leptons, and bosons. So let's suppose that we have a region of space with two oxygen atoms in it. It seems reasonable to say that it contains two simple things (the atoms).

PETER VAN INWAGEN denies the mereological sum. DAVID LEWIS defends it. Recent mereological debates in metaphysics have taken this form:

Mereological nihilist: There are two things in this region.

Mereological universalist: There are three things in this region (the two simples and the mereological sum).

Now a metaphysicist can still argue cleverly and cogently about the proper number of parts and the choice of the proper whole. The oxygen atoms each contain eight protons, eight neutrons, and eight electrons. So one possible count is the 48 sub-atomic particles that are visible. We can go deeper by noting that the nuclear particles are each made up of three quarks, which are not observable. We then can count 112 parts to the whole?

And the metaphysicist has a strong argument for the two simple atoms to be considered a whole. If the two atoms are very close, they can form an oxygen *molecule*. Even when disassociated, quantum mechanics that treats them as a quasi-molecule is more accurate than a description as two independent atoms.

Why Modal Logic Is *Not* Metaphysics

Modal logicians from RUTH BARCAN MARCUS to SAUL KRIPKE, DAVID LEWIS, and the necessicist TIMOTHY WILLIAMSON are right to claim metaphysical necessity as the case in the purely abstract informational world of logic and mathematics. But when information is embodied in concrete matter, which is subject to the laws of quantum physics and ontological chance, the fundamental nature of material reality is possibilist.

There are two reasons for the failure of modal logic to represent metaphysical reality. The first is that information is vastly superior to language as a *representation* of reality. The second is that truths and *necessity* cannot be the basis for metaphysical *possibility*.

Possible world semantics is a *way of talking* about universes of discourse - sets of true propositions - that considers them "worlds." It may be the last gasp of the attempt by logical positivism and analytic language philosophy to *represent* all knowledge of objects in terms of words.

LUDWIG WITTGENSTEIN's core idea from the *Tractatus* had the same goal as GOTTFRIED LEIBNIZ's ambiguity-free universal language,

"The totality of true propositions is the whole of natural science (or the whole corpus of the natural sciences)"[13]

Information philosophy has shown that the meaning of words depends on the experiences recalled in minds by the experience recorder and reproducer (ERR).[14] Since every human being has a different set of experiences, there will always be variations in meaning about words between different persons.

The goal of intersubjective agreement in an open community of inquirers hopes to eliminate those differences, but representation of knowledge in words will always remain a barrier and source of philosophical confusion. The physical sciences use analytic differential equations to describe the deterministic and *continuous* time evolution of simple material objects, which is a great advance over ambiguous words. But these equations fail at the quantum level and where *discrete* digital messages are being exchanged between biological interactors. Moreover, while mathematical methods are precise, their significance is not easily grasped.

The very best *representation* of knowledge is with a dynamic and interactive model of an information structure, what LUDWIG WITTGENSTEIN may have seen as a model and "picture of reality." Today that is a three-dimensional model implemented in a digital computer with a high-resolution display, even a virtual reality display, some day visible on the Internet. While computer models are only "simulations" of reality, they incorporate the best "laws" of physics, chemistry, and biology.

Sadly, modal logicians have never proposed more than a handful of specific propositions for their possible worlds, and many of these generated controversies, even paradoxes, about substitutivity of presumed identicals in modal contexts. Word and object have degenerated to words and objections. By comparison, molecular models of the extraordinary biological machines that

---

13   *Tractatus Logico-Philosophicus*, 4.11
14   See Appendix E.

have evolved to keep us alive and let us think can be "shown," not said, just as Wittgenstein imagined.

His later work can be summed up as the failure of language to be a picture of reality. Information philosophy gives us that picture, not just a two-dimensional snapshot, but a lifelike animation and *visualization* of the fundamental nature of metaphysical reality.

Our information model incorporates the irreducible ontological chance and future contingency of quantum physics. The claimed "necessity of identity," and the "necessary *a posteriori*" of natural and artificial digital "kinds" with identical *intrinsic* information content are just more "ways of talking." There is no necessity in the physical world.

Truths and necessity are ideal concepts "true in all possible worlds," because they are *independent* of the physical world. They have great appeal as eternal ideas "outside space and time."

Possible worlds semantics defines *necessity* as "propositions true in all possible worlds" and *possibility* as "propositions true in some possible worlds." There is no *contingency* here, as the only allowed propositions are either true or false. Modal logicians have little knowledge of our actual physical world and zero factual knowledge, by definition, of other possible worlds. The possible worlds of "modal realism" are all *actual* worlds, deterministic and eliminatively materialist. There are no possibilities in possible worlds, even the equally deterministic "many worlds" of physics.

A necessicist metaphysics is only a half-truth. Without metaphysical possibility, we cannot account for the information in the universe today, nor can we explain the cosmic, biological, and human creation of new information in our free and open future.

Necessitism and possibilism are another variation of the great duals of idealism and materialism.[15] See **possibilist.com**.

History of Metaphysics

Metaphysics has signified many things in the history of philosophy, but it has not strayed far from a literal reading of "beyond

---

15   See the table of dualisms in chapter 9.

the physical." The term was invented by the first-century BCE head of ARISTOTLE's Peripatetic school, Andronicus of Rhodes, who edited and arranged Aristotle's works, giving the name Metaphysics (τα μετα τα φυσικα βιβλια), literally "the books beyond the physics," perhaps the books to be read after reading Aristotle's books on nature, which he called the Physics.

Aristotle never used the term metaphysics. For Plato, Aristotle's master, the realm of abstract ideas was more "real" than that of physical objects, because ideas could be more permanent (the Being of PARMENIDES), whereas material objects are constantly changing (the Becoming of HERACLITUS). Neoplatonists like PORPHYRY worried about the existential status of the Platonic ideas. Does Being exist? What does it mean to say "Being Is"?

Aristotle's original concerns in his "First Philosophy" were ontology (the science of being), cosmology (the fundamental processes and original causes of physical things), and theology (is a god required as a "first mover" or "first cause?").

Aristotle's Physics describes four "causes" or "explanations" (*aitia*) of change and movement of objects already existing in the universe (the ideal formal and final causes, vs. the efficient and material causes). Aristotle's metaphysics can then be seen as explanations for existence itself. What exists? What is it to be? What processes can bring things into (or out of) existence? Is there a cause or explanation for the universe as a whole?

In critical philosophical discourse, metaphysics has perhaps been tarnished by its Latinate translation as "supernatural," with its strong theological implications. But from the beginning, Aristotle's books on "First Philosophy" considered God among the possible causes of the fundamental things in the universe. Tracing the regress of causes back in time as an infinite chain, Aristotle postulated a first cause or "uncaused cause." Where every motion needs a prior mover to explain it, he postulated an "unmoved first mover." These postulates became a major element of theology down to modern times.

Metaphysics is the division of philosophy which includes ontology, or the science of being, and cosmology, or the science of the fundamental causes and processes of things. The primary meaning of metaphysics is derived from those discussions by Aristotle which later commentators suggested should be read before Aristotle's great works on Physics and other subjects.

For medieval philosophers, metaphysics was understood as the science of the supersensible. ALBERTUS MAGNUS called it science beyond the physical. THOMAS AQUINAS narrowed it to the cognition of God. Aquinas argued that 1) God had given man the power of reason, 2) God had used reason to create the universe, so that 3) man can use reason alone to understand the world.

JOHN DUNS SCOTUS disagreed with Aquinas, arguing that God's omnipotence is not constrained by reason. God has freedom of the will, so only study of the world as it has been created can yield knowledge of the world and thus God. Scotus was arguably the origin of British empiricism, just as Aquinas was the source of Continental rationalism.

RENÉ DESCARTES began a turn from what exists to knowledge of what exists. He changed the emphasis from a study of being to a study of the conditions of knowledge or epistemology. For empiricists in England like JOHN LOCKE and DAVID HUME, metaphysics includes the "primary" things beyond psychology and "secondary" sensory experiences. They denied that any knowledge was possible apart from experimental and mathematical reasoning. Hume thought metaphysics is sophistry and illusion.

> If we take in our hand any volume; of divinity or school metaphysics, for instance; let us ask, Does it contain any abstract reasoning concerning quantity or number? No. Does it contain any experimental reasoning concerning matter of fact and existence? No. Commit it then to the flames: for it can contain nothing but sophistry and illusion.[16]

---

16   (Enquiry Concerning Human Understanding, section XII)

In Germany, IMMANUEL KANT's *Critiques of Reason* claimed a transcendental and noumenal realm for pure, or *a priori*, reason beyond the merely phenomenal. The phenomenal realm is deterministic, matter governed by Newton's laws of motion. The noumenal is the metaphysical realm of the "things themselves" along with freedom, God, and immortality. Kant also identified ontology not with the inaccessible things themselves but what we can think - and reason - about the things themselves. In either case, he thought metaphysical knowledge might be impossible for "finite" minds.

The notion that metaphysics transcends experience and the material world led to nineteenth-century positivists like AUGUST COMTE and ERNST MACH, and twentieth-century empiricists like RUDOLF CARNAP and MORITZ SCHLICK, also denying the possibility of metaphysical knowledge.

Naturalism is the anti-metaphysical claim that there is nothing in the world beyond the material (including energy), that everything follows "laws of nature," and that these laws are both causal and deterministic. So "supernatural" appears to imply the freedom to break the laws of nature. Information philosophy denies the supernatural. But it defends *immaterial* information as that which constitutes the human spirit, or soul, the "ghost in the machine." And it defends ontological chance as the generator of novel possibilities that are not determined by the "fixed past."

Positivism is the claim that the only valid source of knowledge is sensory experience, reinforced by logic and mathematics. Together these provide the empirical evidence for science. Comtean positivism rejected metaphysics and theology as obsolete earlier phases in the development of knowledge.

Mach's positivism claimed that science consists entirely of "economic summaries" of the facts (the results of experiments). He rejected theories about unobservable things like LUDWIG BOLTZMANN's atoms, just a few years before ALBERT EINSTEIN used Boltzmann's work to prove that atoms exist.

The logical positivism of BERTRAND RUSSELL and LUDWIG WITTGENSTEIN claims that all valid knowledge is scientific knowledge, though science is often criticized for "reducing" all phenomena to physical or chemical events. The logical positivists may have identified ontology not with the things themselves but what we can say - using concepts and language - *about* the things themselves. Logical positivists and the logical empiricists of the Vienna Circle asserted that all knowledge is scientific knowledge, that it is derived from experience, i.e., from verifiable observations. They added the logical analysis of language as a tool for solving philosophical problems. They divided statements into those reducible to simpler statements about experience and those with no empirical basis, which they called "metaphysical" and "meaningless."

Most analytic language philosophers of the mid-twentieth century continued to deny traditional metaphysics, which P. F. STRAWSON famously called "obscure and panicky." But starting in the 1970's a new group of analytic-language metaphysicians defended a new materialist and determinist metaphysics grounded in modal thinking about possible worlds.

See **metaphysicist.com** for discussions of the work of David Armstrong, Michael Burke, David Chalmers, Rod Chisholm, Peter Geach, David Lewis, E. Jonathan Lowe, Trenton Merricks, Huw Price, Willard van Orman Quine, Michael Rea, Nicholas Rescher, Alan Sidelle, Ted Sider, Richard Taylor, Peter Unger, Peter van Inwagen, David Wiggins, and Timothy Williamson.

Philosophy

Mind

Epistemology

Metaphysics

Mind-Body

Universals

Ontology

Ontology

ciousne

Free Will

Meaning

Self and Othe

Value

Mental Caus

Good and Evil

God and Immortality

Can Information Philosoph

Ontology

Ontology asks the question "what is there?"

Eliminative materialism claims that nothing exists but material particles, which makes many problems in ancient and modern philosophy difficult if not insoluble. To be sure, we are made of the same material as the ancients. With every breath we take, we inspire 10 to 20 of the same molecules of air that sustained ARISTOTLE. The total matter and energy of the universe is a fixed or "conserved" quantity

But information is not a fixed quantity. The stuff of thought and creativity, information has been increasing since the beginning of the universe. Information is an abstract entity. Digital information is just bits of data, yet it is capable of representing any physical object or process and arguably can also represent abstract concepts.

The ontological status of abstract concepts is a completely different question from the ontology of concrete physical objects, though these questions have often been confounded in the history of philosophy.

Information philosophy provides distinct answers to these two ontological questions. Physical objects are pure material or particles of energy that exist in the world of space and time. Abstract concepts (like redness) are pure information, neither matter nor energy, although they need matter for their embodiment and energy for their communication. For example, the abstract idea of "two" is embodied in any two objects. The idea of a circle is embodied in a round object. Redness is embodied in the red photons being emitted or reflected from an object. The arrangement of material objects, whether continuous matter like the wood in a table top, or the momentary position of billiard balls, is pure *information.*

The ancients sometimes said that these abstract concepts do not "exist," but rather are said to "subsist." Information philosophy claims that the "form" of an object can not be separated from the matter and so deserves to be ontological, even metaphysical?

The contrast between physical objects and abstract concepts can be illustrated by the difference between invention and discovery.

We *discover* physical objects through our perceptions of them. To be sure, we *invent* our ideas about these objects, their descriptions, their names, theories of how they are structured and how they interact energetically - with one another and with us. But we cannot arbitrarily invent the natural world. We must test our theories with experiment. The experimental results select those theories that best fit the data, the information coming to us from the world. This makes our knowledge of an independent external world scientific knowledge.

By contrast, we humans invent many abstract concepts such as the names we give to objects. We know that these cultural constructs do not exist somewhere in nature as physical structures before we create them. Cultural knowledge is conventional, relative to and dependent on the society that creates it.

However, some of our invented abstract concepts seem to clearly have an existence that is independent of us, like the numbers and the force of gravity.

Consider the shape of a given object. The abstract representation of the shape in the mind, or in a computer model, is (quantitatively) much less information than the total information in the shape of the physical object.

But when the *representation* is accurate, it is isomorphic with a proper subset of the information in the object itself. We can assert that at least this similar information is in the world and should be included in our physical ontology.

The Metaphysicist's Approach

Rather than simply ask "Do abstract entities like numbers and properties exist," a metaphysicist prefers to ask in what way they might exist that is different from the way in which "concrete" objects exist.

Concrete objects can be seen and touched by our senses. They are material, with causal relations that obey the physical laws of nature.

Abstract entities are *immaterial*, but some of them can still play a *causal* role, for example when agents use them to decide on their actions, or when chance events (particularly at the quantum level) go this way instead of that.

Just as the mind is like software in the brain hardware, the abstract information in a material object is the same kind of immaterial stuff as the information in an abstract entity, a concept or a "non-existent object." Some philosophers say that such immaterial things "subsist," rather than exist.

Broadly speaking, the distinction between concrete and abstract objects corresponds to the distinction between the material and the ideal. Ideas in minds are *immaterial*. They need the matter of the brain to be embodied and some kind of energy to be communicated to other minds. But they are not themselves matter or energy. Those "eliminativists" who believe the natural world contains only material things deny the "existence" of ideas and immaterial information.

Some ideas may be wholly fictitious and nonsensical, whether mere possibles or even impossibles, like the round square, but most ideas correspond to actual objects or processes going on in the world. In either case, we can usually specify the informational content of the idea. Some anti-metaphysicians like to say that names of non-existent objects are "meaningless." But this is wrong. There is a wealth of meaningful information in our knowledge base about unicorns, for example.

Metaphysicists identify abstract entities with the information contained in them. They may be concepts that did not exist in the world until they were invented. Or the information may have existed in material structures and so we say they were discovered. For example, the idea of the moon includes the concepts of a distinct shape, color, and even the appearance of a face.

Many such ideas are mind-independent. Consider properties of the moon. Most observers agree the shape is round and the color is white. (Actually, the moon is blacker than most any terrestrial black object. It only appears white compared to the blackness of space.) Some metaphysicians deny the existence of a universal property such as roundness or whiteness. But metaphysicists see the information needed to specify circularity and the wavelengths of radiation that correspond to whiteness. And that information is embodied in the moon, just as a software program is embodied in computer hardware, and a mental idea is embodied in a brain.

Many ideas or concepts are created by human minds by "picking out" some of the information in physical objects. Whether such concepts "carve nature at the joints" (Plato, *Phaedrus*, 265e) depends on their usefulness in understanding the world.

Plato's Theory of the Forms held that an Idea like the circle pre-exists material beings, where Aristotle argued that the Ideas are abstractions from the most general properties, for example, in all the actual circles.

Information philosophy restores so-called "non-existent objects" to our ontology. They consist of the same kind of information that provides the structure and process information of a concrete object. What we call a "concept" about an object is some subset of the information in the object, accurate to the extent that the concept is isomorphic to that subset. By "picking out" different subsets, we can sort objects, e.g., into sets or "*natural kinds.*"

Information philosophy settles deep philosophical issues about absolute and *relative identity*. All material objects are self-identical, despite concerns about vague boundaries. All objects have relations with other objects that can be interpreted as relative identities. All objects are identical to other objects in some respects and different qua other respects.

Continuous or Discrete?

Is the fundamental nature of reality continuous fields or discrete particles? What about space and time? Are they perhaps also digital and discrete and only appear to be continuous? The Academic Skeptic argument about growth said that even the smallest material change destroys an entity and another entity appears. A change in the instant of time also destroys every material object, followed instantaneously by the creation of an almost "identical" object.

The Skeptics argued that an individual cannot survive material change. When any material is subtracted or added, the entity ceases to exist and a new numerically distinct individual comes into existence. By contrast, the Stoics saw the identity of an individual as its *immaterial* bundle of properties or qualities that they called the "peculiarly qualified individual" or ἴδιος ποιὸν.

The Stoics were following Aristotle. Like him, they called the material substance or substrate ὑποκείμενον (or "the underlying"). They believed the material substrate is "transformed" when matter is lost or gained. The Stoics suggested these changes should be called "generation (γενέσεις) and destruction (φθορὰς)." They said it is wrong to call material changes "growth (αὐξήσεις) and decay (φθίσεις)." These terms were already present in Aristotle, who said that the form, as essence, is not generated. He said that generation and destruction are material changes that do not persist. The Stoics argued that the peculiarly qualified individual does persist. Aristotle commented on his use of words about persistence:

> It is therefore obvious that the form (or whatever we should call the shape in the sensible thing) is not generated—generation does not apply to it—nor is the essence generated; for this is that which is induced in something else either by art or by nature or by potency. But we do cause a bronze sphere to be, for we produce it from bronze and a sphere; we induce the form into this particular matter, and the result is a bronze sphere...
>
> For if we consider the matter carefully, we should not even say without qualification that a statue is generated from wood, or a house from bricks; because that from which a thing is generated should not persist, but be changed. This, then, is why we speak in this way.[1]

The basic definition of persistence is to show that an object is the same object at different times. Although this may seem trivially obvious for ordinary objects, information philosophy shows that there is strictly no such thing as identity over time. The "same" object at two different times contains different information (minimally, its time coordinate in four-dimensional space-time has changed). Metaphysicians say it is better considered as two objects that are not absolutely identical.

---

1   Aristotle, *Metaphysics*, Book VII, § vii & viii.

Chapter 3

WILLARD VAN ORMAN QUINE's ontology proposed that we consider an object as existing in "stages." Quine's student, DAVID LEWIS argues that at every instant of time, every object disappears, ceases to exist, to be replaced by a very similar new entity.

As we saw in chapter 2, Lewis proposes *temporal parts* as a solution to the problem of persistence. He calls his solution "*perdurance*," which he distinguishes from "*endurance*," in which the whole entity exists at all times. Lewis says:

> Our question of overlap of worlds parallels the this-worldly problem of identity through time; and our problem of accidental intrinsics parallels a problem of temporary intrinsics, which is the traditional problem of change. Let us say that something persists iff, somehow or other, it exists at various times; this is the neutral word... Something perdures iff it persists by having different temporal parts, or stages, at different times, though no one part of it is wholly present at more than one time; whereas it endures iff it persists by being wholly present at more than one time. Perdurance corresponds to the way a road persists through space; part of it is here and part of it is there, and no part is wholly present at two different places. Endurance corresponds to the way a universal, if there are such things, would be wholly present wherever and whenever it is instantiated. Endurance involves overlap: the content of two different times has the enduring thing as a common part. Perdurance does not.[2]

Lewis's perduring road parts do not exactly persist. They are intrinsically different parts. The enduring entity does persist *simpliciter*.

In their thinking about persistence, many science-minded metaphysicians have been inspired by Einstein's theory of special relativity. The idea of a four-dimensional manifold of space and time supports the idea that the "temporal parts" of an object are as distinct from one another as its spatial parts. This raises questions about its continued identity as it moves in space and time. But what if space and time are not themselves continuous?

As to the more common sense view of endurance, it is metaphysically necessary, both logically and in terms of an information analysis, the case that everything is identical to itself. Self-identity is a necessary truth. If you exist, you do not exist necessarily, but you are necessarily self-identical at each instant of time.

---

2   *On the Plurality of Worlds*, p. 202

And if you exist, you are very *nearly* identical to yourself a moment ago. But because your information content is a strong function of time, you at time *t + 1* is not exactly equal to you at time *t*. This will make the perdurantists happy, but the change in information is such a tiny fraction of your total that endurance theorists are closer to the truth in the problem of persistence.

But will this continuity of the preponderance of the intrinsic information in an entity be continuous if there is a "gap" in the time itself? Can we fall back to the pre-Socratic insight of Parmenides, who said that if there is nothing between two objects, they must be in contact? This felt like nonsense in the case of space, is it the same with the time?

Meta-Ontology

The deepest of all ontological questions for information philosophy is the meta-ontological question, does information exist? Does it help if we change the question and look for another way information might exist, different from the way matter exists?

Some say form - information *subsists*. But this feels like a verbal quibble. We can say that whatever it *consists* of, it is not matter. But this only says what it is not. More wordplay, ways of talking.

Information *consists* of numbers, ideas, thoughts, composites of simples, arrangements of matter, its organization, order out of chaos, software in the hardware, above all, it is communications between entities. But is it "nothing but," nothing *over and above* the matter itself?

Quantificationally, information is increasing in the universe while matter (with energy) is a conserved and constant quantity.

Quintessentially, information is the metaphysical and ontological locus of possibility and chance.

Quantum mechanically, the one irreducible mystery is how a purely abstract probability wave can acausally move information, if not matter, from one place to another at speeds faster than light.

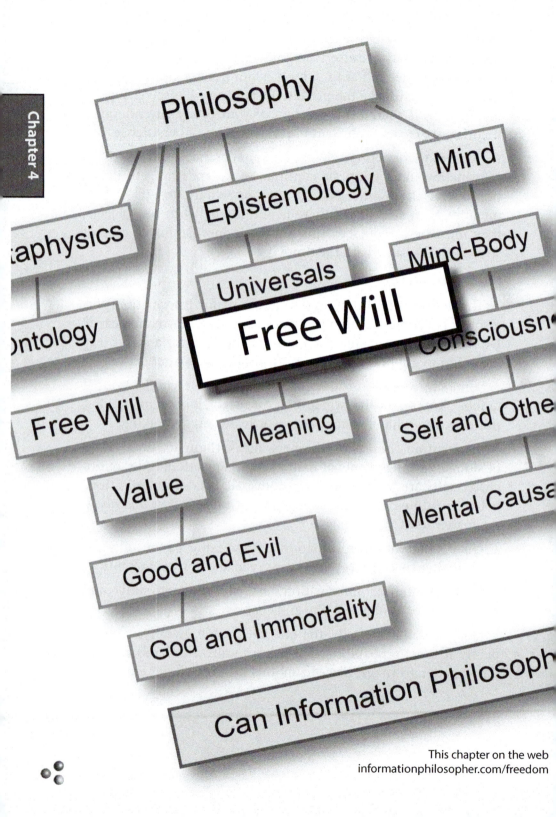

Philosophy

Mind

Epistemology

Metaphysics

Mind-Body

Universals

Free Will

Ontology

Consciousness

Free Will

Meaning

Self and Other

Value

Mental Causation

Good and Evil

God and Immortality

Can Information Philosophy

This chapter on the web
informationphilosopher.com/freedom

Free Will

In our 2011 book *Free Will: The Scandal in Philosophy*, our mind model was a combination of a rudimentary *experience recorder and reproducer (ERR)*[1] and our *two-stage model of free will*. Recent information analysis of the mind and the mind-body problem has greatly strengthened our mind model. We now see the mind as *immaterial* information, the "software in the hardware" of the material brain, which we view as a *biological information processor*.

Five years ago, we saw the quantum randomness in the first stage as adding "uncaused" events to fit a picture of *"event causality"* and to attack the "causal closure" of the eliminative materialists.

Now that our mind model is unapologetically *immaterial*, it is in fact an example of the kind of *metaphysical* entities that the famous philosopher P. F. Strawson rejected as "panicky metaphysics - uncaused causes, immaterial minds, non-empirical noumenal selves, non-event agent causes, and prime movers unmoved." We now endorse the idea of *agent causality*,[2] in which the mind has causal powers over the material world.

We argue that freedom of the will begins in the pre-deliberative *thoughts* of the agent. Although ALBERT EINSTEIN was a strong believer in determinism, he saw our thoughts and theories as "free creations of the human mind." These creative thoughts bring *new information* into the universe. New information *emerges*[3] from the material and biological worlds to become part of the mental or ideal world, even as it is embodied in the material world.

Without alternative possibilities for an open future, there can be no new information in the universe, in biology, or in human minds. But there continues to be new information, in stars still forming, in the evolution of new species, and in creative minds.

---

1   See Appendix E.
2   See informationphilosopher.com/freedom/agent-causality.html
3   See chapter 27 on emergence and appendix F on cosmic creation..

The Two-Stage Model of Free Will

Our two-stage model is now the most plausible explanation, not only for human free will, but also for *creativity*, cited in the American Psychological Association's *Review of General Psychology* as supporting the Campbell-Simonton BVSR model of creative thought.[4]

Given the "laws of nature" and the "fixed past" just before a decision, many philosophers wonder how a free agent can have any possible alternatives. This is partly because they imagine a timeline for the decision that shrinks the decision process to a single moment.

Decision

Fixed Past | Future

Collapsing the decision to a single moment between the closed fixed past and the open ambiguous future makes it difficult to see the role of free thoughts of the mind - which bring new information into the universe - followed by the willed and adequately determined action in a temporal sequence, as shown here.

Decision

| Fixed Past | Generate Possibilities | Evaluate Alternatives | Future |

But the two-stage model is not limited to a single step of generating alternative possibilities followed by a single step of determination by the will. It is better understood as a continuous process of possibilities generation by what we call the micro mind (parts of the brain that leave themselves open to noise) and adequately determined choices made from time to time by the macro mind (the same brain parts, perhaps, but now averaging over and filtering out the noisiness that might otherwise make the determination random).

---

4   Review of General Psychology, APA, 2013, Vol 17, No 4, 374

In particular, note that a special kind of decision might occur when the macro mind finds that none of the current options are good enough for the agent's character and values to approve. The macro mind then might figuratively say to the micro mind, "Think again!" Thus we can say that the agent has control over the generation of alternative possibilities, without controlling the specific new idea that may come to mind

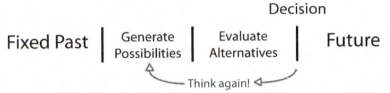

Many philosophers have puzzled how an agent could do otherwise in exactly the same prior circumstances. Since humans are intelligent organisms, and given the myriad of possible circumstances, it is impossible that an agent is ever in exactly the same circumstances. The agent's memory (stored in the *experience recorder and reproducer*) of earlier similar circumstances guarantees that.

The two-stage model may make an artificial temporal separation between micro-mind creative randomness and macro-mind deliberative evaluation. These two capabilities of the mind can clearly be going on at the same time. That can be visualized by the occasional decision to go back and think again, when the available alternatives are not good enough to satisfy the demands of the agent's character and values, or by noticing that the subconscious micro mind might be still generating possibilities while the macro mind is in the middle of evaluations.

Finally, not all decisions in the two-stage model end with an adequately determined "de-liberation" or perhaps better we can call it simply self-determination. Many times the evaluation of the possibilities produces two or more alternatives that seem more or less of equal value.

In this case, the agent may choose randomly among those alternatives, yet have very good reasons to take responsibility for whichever one is chosen. This is related to the ancient liberty of indifference.

I like to call such a decision an "undetermined liberty," because it remains undetermined at the moment of the decision. Though not determined by the deliberations, we can say that the agent "deliberately" chooses at random between equal options.

Undetermined liberties include ROBERT KANE's Self-Forming Actions, although Kane limits his SFAs to "torn" decisions between moral and self-interested alternatives.

Neuroscientific Evidence for the Two-Stage Model

BENJAMIN LIBET's famous experiments are widely cited by compatibilists and determinists as showing that the decision has been made a long time before the conscious will can act. We shall interpret them as supporting the temporal sequence in the two-stage model of free will, creating new information in the first stage.

The original discovery that an electrical potential (of just a few microvolts - μV) is visible in the brain long before the appearance of conscious will was made by Kornhuber and Deecke (1964). They called it a *"Bereitschaftspotential"* or readiness potential.

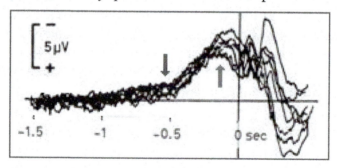

Figure 4-1. Kornhuber and Deecke "readiness potential"

The neurobiologist John Eccles had speculated that the subject must become conscious of the intention to act before the onset of this readiness potential. Benjamin Libet decided to test Eccles's idea.

Libet's 1983 experiments measured the time when the subject became consciously aware of the decision to move the finger. Libet created a dot on the screen of an oscilloscope circulating like the hand of a clock. The subject was asked to note the position of the moving dot when he/she was aware of the conscious decision to move a finger or wrist..

As shown on the RP diagram, Libet found that although conscious awareness of the decision preceded the subject's finger motion by only 200 milliseconds (the up arrow), the rise in the readiness potential was clearly visible at about 550 milliseconds before the flex of the wrist (down arrow). The subject showed unconscious activity to flex about 350 milliseconds before reporting conscious awareness of the decision to flex. Indeed an earlier very slight rise in the readiness potential can be seen as early as 1.5 seconds before the action.

Of course the kinds of deliberative and evaluative processes that are essential for free will involve much longer time periods than those studied by Libet. Nevertheless, we can correlate the beginnings of the readiness potential (350ms before Libet's "conscious will" time "W" appears) with the early stage of the two-stage model, when alternative possibilities are being generated, in part at random.

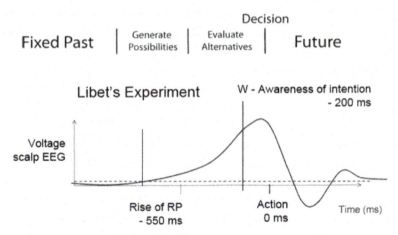

Figure 4-2. Readiness potential and the two-stage model

The early stage may be attributed to the subconscious, which is capable of considering multiple alternatives (William James'

Chapter 4

"blooming, buzzing confusion") that would congest the low-data-rate single stream of consciousness.

ALFRED MELE criticized the interpretation of the Libet results on two grounds. First, the appearance of the RP a half-second or more before the action in no way makes the RP the cause of the action. It may simply mark the beginning of forming an intention to act. In our two-stage model, it corresponds to the agent's thoughts that generate possible options, which may create new information.

Libet himself argued that even if a decison has been made, there is enough time after the W moment (a window of opportunity perhaps 50 ms) to veto the action, but Mele's second criticism points out that such examples of "free won't" would not be captured in Libet experiments, because the recording device is triggered by the action (typically flicking the wrist) itself.

Thus, although all Libet experiments ended with the wrist flicking, we are not justified in assuming that the rise of the RP (well before the moment of conscious will) is a *cause* of the wrist flicking.

Libet knew that there were very likely other times when the RP rose, but which did not lead to a flick of the wrist. All such events could create *immaterial* information about new possibilities, but might not be acted upon immediately. Libet noted that in normal decisions we might deliberate all day.

> We should also distinguish between deliberations about what choice of action to adopt (including preplanning of when to act on such a choice), and the final intention to actually "act now." One may, after all, deliberate all day about a choice but never act... However, conscious will definitely can control whether the act takes place. We may view the unconscious initiatives for voluntary actions as "burbling up" unconsciously in the brain. The conscious will then selects which of these initiatives may go forward to an action, or which ones to veto and abort so no act occurs.[5]

We conclude that Libet's neuroscientific experiments may be interpreted as supporting the two-stage model. We know little about what goes on in the early rise of the readiness potential. But only a dogmatic determinist would claim that it already contains and directly causes any later decision.

---

5   B. Libet, *Mind Time*, pp.148-149

History of the Free Will Problem[6]

In our research on the history of the free will problem, we have identified several thinkers who developed two-stage solutions to the classical problem of free will, first WILLIAM JAMES, then HENRI POINCARÉ, JACQUES HADAMARD, ARTHUR HOLLY COMPTON, KARL POPPER, DANIEL DENNETT, HENRY MARGENAU, ROBERT KANE, DAVID SEDLEY and ANTHONY LONG, ROGER PENROSE, DAVID LAYZER, JULIA ANNAS, ALFRED MELE, JOHN MARTIN FISCHER, STEPHEN KOSSLYN, STORRS MCCALL and E. J. LOWE, JOHN SEARLE, and MARTIN HEISENBERG.[7]

Some of course were more clear and comprehensive about the two stagesthan others, but our goal is to give them all credit.[8]

Recently we discovered a possible two-stage argument many centuries before WILLIAM JAMES.

TITUS LUCRETIUS CARUS is our main source for the work of EPICURUS, who provided the first argument for chance with his "swerve" of the atoms. Lucretius eloquently made Epicurus' case. Shortly after describing the swerve, he says:

> "If all motion is always one long chain, and new motion arises out of the old in order invariable, and if first-beginnings do not make by swerving a beginning of motion so as to break the decrees of fate, whence comes this free will?"[9]

But now we have found evidence that Lucretius made the case for *alternative* thoughts *coming to mind* before a willed decision, and the possible new ideas sound very much like Epicurus' random swervings.

> Now listen, and hear what things stir the mind, and learn in a few words whence these things come into the mind. In the first place I tell you that many images of things are moving about in many ways and in all directions.[10]

---

6   Doyle, 2011, chapter 7 is a 60-page history of the problem
7   See Doyle, 2011, chapter 12, for these two-stage solutions.
8   Also see informationphilosopher.com/freedom/two-stage_models.html
9   *De Rerum Natura*, Book 2, 251
10   *De Rerum Natura*, Book 4, 722

This also sounds a great deal like William James' "blooming, buzzing, confusion" of the subconscious and Libet's "burbling up."

> even in things plainly visible you can observe that, it is just as if the thing were all the while withdrawn and far removed from you. Then what wonder is it, if the mind misses everything except what it is itself intent on?[11]

Lucretius again sounds like James, who explains choice as the focusing of attention. Next comes the will (*voluntas*).

> Next I will say how it comes about that we can carry onwards our steps when we please...I say in the first place images of movement come in contact with our mind, and strike the mind, as I said before, After this comes will; for no one ever begins anything until the intelligence has first foreseen what it wills to do.[12]

So Lucretius may have long ago captured the essence of the *temporal sequence* in our two-stage model.

The classic problem of free will is to reconcile an element of freedom with the apparent determinism in a world of causes and effects, a world of events in a great causal chain.

Determinists deny any such freedom.

Compatibilists redefine freedom. Although they say that our will is determined by prior events in the causal chain (including our reasons, motives, etc.), our will is in turn causing and determining our actions. Compatibilists say that determinism of our actions by our will allows us to take moral responsibility for our actions. This is correct. The second stage of our model makes us responsible.

Libertarians think the will is free when a choice can be made that is not *pre-determined* or *necessitated* by prior *events*. The will is free when *alternative* choices could have been made with the same pre-existing conditions.

Freedom of the will allows us to say, "I could have chosen (and done) *otherwise*."

In a deterministic world, everything that happens follows ineluctably from natural or divine laws. There is but one possible future. We cannot have chosen *otherwise*,

In the more common sense view, we are free to shape our future, to be creative, to be unpredictable.

---

11   *De Rerum Natura*, Book 4, 815
12   *De Rerum Natura*, Book 4, 881

From the ancient Epicureans to modern quantum mechanical indeterminists, some thinkers have suggested that chance or randomness is an explanation for freedom, an explanation for the unpredictability of a free and creative act. A truly random event would break the causal chain and nullify determinism, providing room for human freedom.

Freedom of human action does require the randomness of absolute unpredictability, but if our actions are the direct consequence of a random event, we cannot feel responsible. That would be mere indeterminism, as unsatisfactory as determinism.

Moreover, indeterminism appears to threaten reason itself, which seems to require certainty and causality to establish truth, knowledge, and the laws of nature.

Most philosophers in all ages have been committed to one or more of the dogmas of determinism,[13] refusing to admit any indeterminism or chance. ARISTOTLE said chance was "obscure to human reason." CHRYSSIPUS described the case of "indeterminism is true" as a disaster for reason. DAVID HUME found "no medium betwixt chance and necessity." Many theologians thought chance *atheistic*, doubting God's omniscience,

Many scientists agree that science is predicated on strict causality and predictability, without which science itself, considered as the search for causal laws, would be impossible.

For those scientists, laws of nature would not be "laws" if they were only statistical and probabilistic. Sadly for them, all laws of nature turn out to be thoroughly statistical and our predictions merely probable, though with probabilities approaching certainty. Science is irreducibly statistical.

But fortunately, for large objects the departure from deterministic laws is unobservable. Probabilities become indistinguishable from certainties, and we can show there is an "adequate (or statistical) determinism"[14]

Important elements of the model have been proposed by many philosophers since Aristotle, the first indeterminist. A number of modern philosophers and scientists, have proposed models of free

---

13   See Doyle, 2011, chapter 9, for a review of many determinisms.
14   See informationphilosopher.com/freedom/adequate_determinism.html

will. But none of them has been able to locate the randomness so as to make free will "intelligible," as libertarian Robert Kane puts it.

The insoluble problem for previous free-will models has been to explain how a random event in the brain can be timed and located - perfectly synchronized! - so as to be relevant to a specific decision. The answer is it cannot be, for the simple reason that quantum events are totally unpredictable.

The two-stage model is not a single random event, one per decision, but many random events in the brain as a result of ever-present noise, both quantum and thermal noise, inherent in any information storage and communication system.

The mind, like all biological systems, has evolved in the presence of constant noise and is able to ignore that noise, unless the noise provides a significant competitive advantage, which it clearly does as the basis for freedom and for creativity that brings new information into the universe.

Let's see how randomness in the two-stage model is never the direct cause of our decisions. Decisions are always adequately, i.e., statistically, but near certainly, determined by reasons and motives.

We assume that there are always many contributing causes for any event, and in particular for a mental decision. In both the Newell-Simon "Blackboard" model[15] and BERNARD BAARS' "Theater of Consciousness" and "Global Workspace" models,[16] there are many competing possibilities for our next thought or action. Where do they come from? And, most importantly, does the agent have any control over their generation?

Each of these possibilities is the result of a sequence of events that goes back in an assumed causal chain until its beginning in an uncaused event. Aristotle called this original event an *arche* (ἀρχῆ), one whose major contributing cause (or causes) was itself uncaused.

What this means is that tracing any particular sequence of events back in time will come to one event - a "starting point" or "fresh start" - Aristotle's origin or *arche* - the dreaded "*causa sui.*" Today we say it must involve quantum indeterminacy.

---

15   Newell and Simon, 1972
16   Baars, 1997

Whether a particular thing happens, says Aristotle, may depend on a series of causes that

> "goes back to some starting-point, which does not go back to something else. This, therefore, will be the starting-point of the fortuitous, and nothing else is the cause of its generation."[17]

We can thus in principle assign times, or ages, to the starting points of the contributing causes of a decision. Some of these may in fact go back before the birth of an agent, hereditary causes for example. To the extent that such random causes adequately determine an action, we can understand why hard determinists think that the agent has no control over such actions. Of course if we can always opt out of an action at the last moment, so we retain control, even if the origin of the option was inherited.

Other contributing causes may be traceable back to environmental and developmental events, perhaps education, perhaps simply life experiences, that were "character-forming" events. These and genetic or hereditary causes would now be present in the mind of the agent as fixed habits, with a very high probability of "adequately determining" the agent's actions in many situations.

But other contributing causes of a specific option may have been undetermined up to the very near past, even fractions of a second before an important decision. The causal chains for these contributing causes may originate in the noisy brain. They include the free generation of new *alternative possibilities* for thought or action during the agent's deliberations. They fit Aristotle's criteria for causes that "depend on us" (ἐφ' ἡμῖν) and originate "within us" (ἐν ἡμῖν).

Causes with these most recent starting points are the fundamental reason why an agent can do *otherwise* in what are essentially (up to that starting point) the same circumstances.

These alternatives are likely generated from our internal knowledge of practical possibilities based on our past experience. They are stored in our experience recorder and reproducer. Those that are handed up by the ERR for consideration to Baars' "executive function" in his "Theater of Consciousness" may be filtered to some extent by unconscious processes to be "within reason." They likely consist of random variations of similar actions willed many times in the past.

---

17   Metaphysics Book VI 1027b12-14

Note that the evaluation and selection of one of these possibilities by the will is as deterministic and causal a process as anything that a determinist or compatibilist could ask for, consistent with our current knowledge of the physical world.

Remember also that instead of strict causal determinism, the world offers only adequate (or statistical) determinism, and it is the random origins of possibilities that provides libertarian freedom of thought and adequately determined but not pre-determined action.

Why have philosophers been unable for millennia to accept the common sense view that humans are free? Partly because their logic and language preoccupation makes them say that either determinism or indeterminism is "true," and the other must be "false." This is the standard (but flawed) argument against free will.

But there is a deeper concern. If the origin of possibilities is truly random, have we lost the control needed to assert moral responsibility? Can the two-stage model provide a measure of control over the creative generation of alternative possibilities that does not make them pre-determined? Let us see.

The Standard Argument *Against* Free Will

Simple variations of this standard argument are found throughout the somewhat unsophisticated philosophical literature on free will,[18] and even in some of the most extensively cited work, for example, GALEN STRAWSON's "Basic Argument on the Impossibility of Moral Responsibility."[19]

The standard argument has two parts.

If determinism is the case, the will is not free.

If indeterminism and real chance exist, our will would not be in our control, we could not be responsible for randomly caused actions.

The two-stage model provides the two essential requirements needed to defeat this standard argument

The first requirement is some indeterminism (objective chance) to break the causal chain of determinism and to generate creative thoughts and alternative possibilities for action. But this indeterminism must somehow not destroy our moral responsibility. It must not be the *direct cause* of action.

---

18   See Doyle, 2011, chapter 4, for dozens of examples.
19   Philosophical Studies: Vol. 75, No. 1/2, (Aug., 1994), pp. 5-24

Thus the second requirement is that our deliberations and evaluations are "adequately" (or statistically) determined, so that we can be responsible for our choices, so that they are "up to us."

"Adequate" (i.e., statistical) determinism means that the indeterministic alternative possibilities themselves are not the direct cause of our actions. The cause is the agent's decision.

Objective chance in the generation of alternatives means that at least some of the possibilities are not causally determined by immediately preceding events, so they are unpredictable by any agency, including us. They can then be the source of the creativity that adds new information to the universe.

Chance gives us the "free" in free will.

Adequate determinism gives us the "will" in free will.

Thoughts come to us freely. Actions go from us willfully.

We must admit indeterminism, but not permit it to produce random actions as some Determinists mistakenly fear.

We must also limit the determinism, but not eliminate it as some Libertarians mistakenly think is necessary.

The evaluation and careful deliberation of all the available possibilities, both ingrained habits and creative new ideas, can be recognized as "self-determination." This makes us the responsible "agent cause" of our actions.

But we must not thing that our "self-determination" was in any way pre-determined before we began to consider our possibilities. Self-determination is only "adequately and statistically" determined. It is not completely immune from random noise.

Compatibilists should be comfortable that the reasons, motives, feelings and desires of the agent are causal factors that were evaluated by the agent during the second-stage deliberations and the ultimate choice of an action.

This is all that is needed for the agent to accept what ROBERT KANE calls "ultimate responsibility" for the action.

But some event *acausality* is a prerequisite for any kind of *agent causality* that is not pre-determined by the moments before deliberations begin. This *acausality* is the quantum indeterminism, the

Chapter 4

ontological chance, that accompanies the new information creation in the first stage of the two-stage model, where the agent freely generates alternative possibilities for action.

The two-stage model of free will proves that our actions are not predetermined, even from moments just before we begin thinking about freely generating new options for action.

We can summarize our criticism of the standard argument against free will in a few simple lines.

"Free Will" is really two independent stages that combine a limited indeterminism with a limited determinism.

First comes the "free" generation of alternative possibilities, then our adequately determined "willed" actions.

Our thoughts are free. Our actions are willed.

First "free," then "will."

Possible Worlds and Alternative Possibilities

In the twentieth century the study of modal logic (the truth conditions for statements about necessity and possibility) led to a model theory involving possible worlds. The philosopher DAVID LEWIS maintained there are an infinite number of possible worlds, all just as real for their inhabitants as our actual world. The physicist HUGH EVERETT III said that the world splits in two whenever a quantum experiment is performed.

Lewis and Everett were materialists and determinists. In their worlds everything is determined by the laws of nature and the fixed past. Each world has but one future. Free will is an illusion.

But SAUL KRIPKE, who formulated the theory of possible world semantics for modal logic, described the use of possible worlds as representations of how our actual world might be. "'Possible worlds' are total 'ways the world might have been,'" he said, which means they can describe the *alternative possibilities* of our two-stage model for free will.

They are "counterfactual situations" in Kripke's sense, involving a single individual. Suppose the agent is considering five different courses of action. During the second stage of evaluation and deliberation only one of the five options (each a "possible world") will become *actualized*.

Note that Kripke's possible worlds are extremely close to one another, "nearby" in the sense of their total information content, the difference between them is very small amount of information compared to the typical examples given in possible worlds cases.

For typical cases of a free decision, the possible worlds require only small differences in the mind of a single person. Kripke argued against the thesis that mind and body (or brain) are identical. In this example, it would only be the thoughts in the mind of the agent that pick out the possible world that will be actualized.

Free Will and Creativity

Creativity requires that *new information* come into the world. It must be information that was not implicit in earlier states of the world. Information is only fixed in a deterministic universe.[20]

It is new information creation that explains *agent causality*.

When we create new information, we do it freely. Our thoughts are "free creations of the human mind," as Einstein said.

Humans are conspicuous creators and consumers of new information structures, altering the face of planet Earth. And we create the constructed ideal world of thought, of intellect, of spirit, including the invention of the laws of nature, followed by the discoveries that confirm them experimentally.

We are authors of our lives and co-creators of our natural world.

---

20   See appendix A.

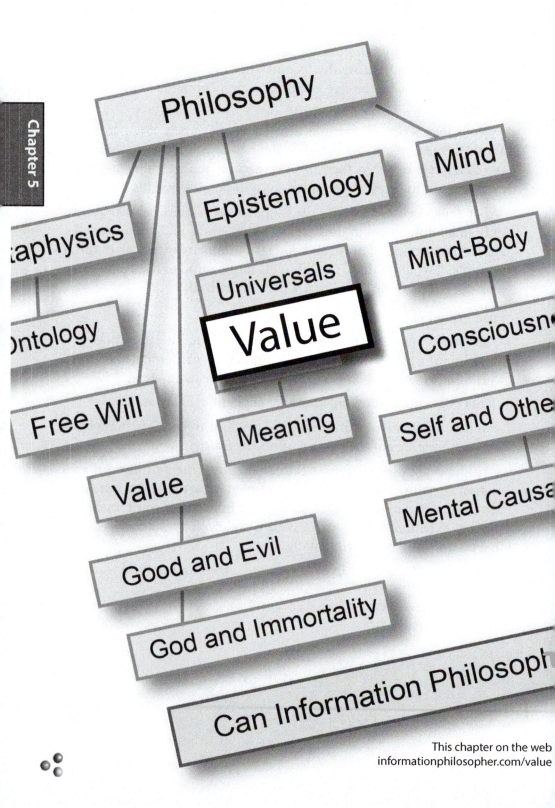

Philosophy

Mind

Epistemology

Metaphysics

Mind-Body

Universals

Value

Consciousne

Ontology

Free Will

Meaning

Self and Othe

Value

Mental Causa

Good and Evil

God and Immortality

Can Information Philosoph

This chapter on the web
informationphilosopher.com/value

Value

Is the Good something that exists in the world? Existentialists thought not. They thought we have freedom, but saw freedom as *absurd*, because there are no values to help choose. Without values, no evaluations. Most religions place the origin of good in a supernatural Being. Existentialists denied that Being. "God is dead," they said, and thus denied any essential objective Good.

The traditional source of normative values, of morality, of ethics, of what one "ought to do," has been religion. It is often said that science, the empirical study of the natural world, cannot possibly help us to define the good. DAVID HUME is often cited as saying we cannot derive "Ought" from "Is." This is sometimes called the "fact/value" dichotomy. Science, it is said, can help us to do what we decide to do. It can help with prudential or instrumental decisions about "means," but not with moral decisions that depend on the intrinsic value of "ends."

It is difficult to generalize about the thousands of religions invented over the ages by their prophets and founders, but most include a code of moral behavior. Some founders told their followers that they had simply discovered the correct moral codes. Some prophets claim to have been explicitly told the "truth" about good and evil in a conversation with God, or by a mystical vision. With founders and prophets mostly long gone today, moral codes are typically handed down by various traditions.

The power of the institutions that has grown up around world religions lies entirely in their ability to limit the knowledge of their members to their beliefs about the "truth." Where these traditions vary in their beliefs, and they do disagree in fundamental ways, they cannot possibly all be right, unless all cultural beliefs are relative, which they may well be at the present time.

Humanists think that good and evil are human inventions, that value systems are relative to a local community or society. "Man is the measure of all things." Comparative ethics is the study of disparate value systems in the hope of finding come commonly held rules, for which one can claim some universal or objective significance, for example, the golden rule, "Do unto others" or commandments like "Thou shall not kill." Some philosophers make human life an objective good. Some make one own's life the ultimate good. Some think the good is the maximization of pleasure, or happiness, or well-being, for all humans (or maybe just one own's family, tribe, community, or nation?),

Modern bioethicists hope to avoid all this relativism by situating value in all life, seeing humanism as short-sighted, if generalized, self-interest. A variety of ancient religions looked to the Sun as the sustainer of all life and thus found an objective good outside of human life. They anthropomorphized the sun or the "bright sky" as God. Dark and night were stigmatized as evil and "fallen." Echoes of these ancient views persist in our metaphors of light, of enlightenment, as good.

Philosophers have ever longed to discover a cosmic good. The ideal source of a cosmic good is perhaps as remote as possible from the Earth in space and as distant in time. Many theologians and philosophers think it must be "outside space and time." For PLATO, it was a timeless Good to be found in Being itself. For his student ARISTOTLE, it was a property of the first principles that set the world in motion. For KANT, it was a transcendental and "noumenal" God outside the everyday "phenomenal" world of experience.

Information philosophy has found that the story of human evolution does not start with DARWIN and DNA. It starts much, much earlier, at the very beginning of the universe. For those of you thinking that your origins and place in the universe might be found outside of animal evolution, beyond a mere material explanation, you might be happy to learn that your most distant beginning was in the primeval formation of *immaterial*, abstract information, a kind of metaphysical spirituality you can tie directly to the information content of your innermost thoughts.

Has information philosophy discovered the cosmic good? Does it at least identify the prerequisite source of anything resembling the Good? Yes, it does. Does it resemble the Good anthropo-morphized as a God personally concerned about our individual goods? No, it does not. But it has one outstanding characteristic of such a God. It is *Providence*. Information philosophy has discovered the fundamental process in the universe that provides for our well-being. It provides the light, it provides life, it provides intelligence. For all of these things, should we not be thankful and reverent toward such a creative process, attitudes humans normally feel towards a providential god?

Information philosophy replaces the difficult problem of "Does God exist?" with the more tractable problem "Does Goodness exist?" Humanists situate values in reason or human nature. Bioethicists seek to move the source of goodness to the biosphere. Life becomes the *summum bonum*. Information philosophers look out to the universe as a whole, beyond the obviously beneficent Sun to find a cosmos that grew from a chaos. The growth of that cosmos continues today, in a cosmic creative process that formed the galaxies, stars, and planets, that led to life and then to the evolution of the information-processing minds that created language and logic. It is this process that we propose creates objective value.

Exactly how that is possible requires a subtle understanding of the second law of thermodynamics in an expanding and open universe. The second law is the tendency of isolated systems to become more disorderly, to increase the "entropy," a quantitative measure of disorder. When entropy increases in a closed system, information is destroyed irreversibly.[1]

A very small number of processes that we call *ergodic* can reduce the entropy locally to create macroscopic information structures like stars and planets as well as microscopic ones like atoms and molecules. And most important to human beings, this creative process is not only responsible for our existence, it has made us creative individuals in its own image! In what sense? It is that we are creative beings. We are co-creators of the world we live in, wielding a power to create, for better or for worse, that is unparalleled in the history of the world.

---

1   See appendix B for entropy flows in the universe.

Every living thing is an information processor and communicator. But the handling of information suggests four different levels of processing among the animals - instinctive, learning, predictive, and normative (reflective).

• The lowest organisms are created with a fixed amount of information that is essentially constant their entire lives. Their behavioral repertoire is almost completely instinctive. They have little or no learning capability. Their automatic reactions to environmental conditions are "built in," transmitted genetically. Information about past experiences (by prior generations of the organism) is only present implicitly in those inherited reactions.

• Animals with a learning capability can acquire new information during their lifetimes. Their past experiences condition their current choices. Mostly habitual reactions are developed through experience, including instruction by parents and peers.

• The ability to predict the future evolved in animals with an *experience recorder and reproducer* (ERR) that can play back beyond the current situation. These animals have foresight and imagination that help them evaluate the future consequences of their choices. They can generate *alternative possibilities* for future actions, based on the playback of multiple past experiences in similar situations.

• Normative information appears in human societies that have externalized and codified their past social experiences. Future actions are evaluated based in part on ideas about the past, in addition to the individual's actual experiences. Conscious deliberation about community and universal values influences the choice of behaviors.

All four levels are *emergent*,[2] in the sense that they did not exist in the lower, earlier levels of biological evolution. The emergence of human beings also marks the emergence of information and information processing that is going on outside of biological organisms. The storage and retrieval of information in the form of writing, then printing, and now the world-wide web, has enabled the transmission of knowledge to leap over vast distances in space and time.

---

2   See chapter 27 on emergence.

FRANCIS BACON saw clearly that knowledge is power. Information philosophy defines knowledge as information that has meaning[3] for humans, in the sense that it expands the possible alternative actions to let us choose the best means to achieve our ends. The power of this knowledge is shown in the exponential growth of humanity on the planet. A mere ten thousand years ago the biomass of humans and their domesticated animals was less than one percent of the biomass of terrestrial vertebrates. Today it is near ninety percent. Humans have taken over the planet.

The *Sum* of human knowledge will soon be accessible to anyone in the world with a tablet computer or smartphone. We estimate this will be nearly the entire human population by the year 2020. If this comes to be the case, there is an opportunity to expose young children to the most universal of human values, perhaps before they have been indoctrinated by their local cultural values.

This will be vehemently opposed by conservative governments and fundamentalist religious forces whose hold on power depends on keeping young minds closed to "outside" ideas.

A battle rages between cosmic ergodic processes and chaotic entropic processes that destroy structure and information. Anthropomorphizing these processes as good and evil gives us a dualist image that nicely solves the monotheistic problem of evil." If God is the Good, God is not responsible for the Evil. Instead, we can clearly see an impersonal *Ergod* behind *Providence* – the cosmic source without which we would not exist and so a proper object of our reverence. And Entropy is the "devil incarnate," as NORBERT WIENER described it.

The fundamental moral guide to action found in information philosophy is then very simple – when faced with a moral dilemma, we ought to choose to preserve information structures against the entropy. Beyond moral standards, the discovery of a cosmic source of value suggests a basis for societal and legal norms.

Celebrating the first modern philosopher, RENÉ DESCARTES, we call our model for value the *Ergo*. For those who might want to anthropomorphize on the slender thread of discovering a natural

---

3   See chapter 11 on meaning.

Providence, call it *Ergod*. No God can be God without being Ergo-dic, standing in opposition to forces of darkness and destruction.

Ergodic processes are those that resist the terrible and universal Second Law of Thermodynamics, which commands the increase of chaos and entropy (disorder). Without violating the inviolable second law overall, ergodic processes reduce the entropy locally, producing pockets of cosmos and negative entropy (order and information-rich structures). *Ergo* is the ultimate *sine qua non*.

The idea of a moral science has a long history. JOHN STUART MILL's Logic of the Moral Sciences was a major influence. Translated into German as *Geisteswissenschaft*, or science of the spirit, Mill's "moral science" was then back-translated into English as the Human Sciences or what has become the humanities in today's universities. Of course, DAVID HUME and his great English colleague, ADAM SMITH, a hundred years before Mill, had given us great insights into what they saw as "natural" moral sentiments or feelings. Hume thought he could make a science of human nature based on laws as definite as ISAAC NEWTON's laws of motion. But this was to be a failure.

Maybe so, but we believe a moral society should be and can be informed by the best scientific knowledge about human origins, human capacities, and our current status in the universe.

An Information-based Moral Code?

The first rule of an information-based morality is that all choices should be made so as to minimize the destruction of abstract information and concrete information structures. All natural processes increase the entropy. A very few (life, gravitation) decrease the entropy locally. These we call *ergodic*. In principle, one should calculate the entropy increase and the negative entropy gain for each choice and maximize production and preservation of information.

Because abstract information can be duplicated and disseminated at near-zero cost in the information age ("information wants to be free"), our second rule is that we should share all information (our knowledge *Sum*) to the maximum possible extent. Practically, this means nourishing and educating all the world's children, especially the females, who are more likely to assist in this project of nourishing and education than are the males.

By contrast, a concrete "information structure," or "wealth" in the form of low-entropy information-rich matter and energy, is subject to the laws of economic scarcity. The natural distribution of wealth and income among individuals follows statistics like Pareto's "80/20" rule, where the largest percentage of wealth is "normally" concentrated in a minority of the population.

Some inequality is the unavoidable consequence of the "normal" distribution of human intelligence and capability due to chance. It is also the avoidable consequence of the historically random distribution of opportunity, including the inheritance of material property. Redistribution of wealth through a progressive taxation system is the means to regulate income and wealth inequality to a societally acceptable norm that allows even the least capable humans to exercise their creative freedom to their limits.

A Minimum Moral/Political Message?

Information philosophy has established that every human being is uniquely capable of creating new information. This includes the abstract ideas of our ancestors that have become the Sum of human knowledge. It also includes the creation of concrete information structures which add to the stock of material wealth, although material objects are subject to the laws of economic scarcity. From this, we can formulate our basic insight into human freedom and creativity,

Thoughts Are Free, Actions Are Willed, Self-Determined, Limited Only by Creative Control Over Matter and Energy.

Everything we know and much of the material value that we enjoy today is the product of past and present creative human beings. It is therefore of vital interest, a core value, for human society to protect that free creative power for everyone.

We can say it is in the interest of future society that every human being should have the right to exercise their ergodic freedom to create new ideas to the maximum of their individual potential.

This right requires a minimum standard of well-being and education, and a minimum of constraints on self-expression so society can hear those new ideas.

The right to exercise this creative freedom comes with a responsibility, an obligation to protect that freedom and opportunity for others, and to see that the fruits of that creativity are distributed as fairly as possible to all humanity, while preserving adequate property rights for the creator.

This is a kind of freedom that some philosophers have only dreamed of. Sadly, many more have denied this creative freedom as logically or physically impossible. We are finite beings, they say, compared to the infinite powers that they mistakenly imagine are in charge. It is their own limited imaginations that have sadly embraced the idea of such infinite powers.

The fact is that human beings are the universe's highest form of pure information creator, a natural outgrowth of the universe's cosmic creative process. Humans are inferior to the cosmic process in its power over useful matter and energy. That is the providential gift of the negative entropy or *Ergo* in the form of incoming solar radiation. But humans are superior to the cosmic process as the creators of ideas. Ideas are *immaterial*, potentially *immortal* if added to the *Sum* of human knowledge.

Additions to human knowledge mean that the lives of our descendants will almost always be richer and fuller than those of our ancestors, both materially and spiritually. As ALBERT EINSTEIN knew, it is our ideas that let us comprehend the almost incomprehensible nature of the universe.

Unfortunately, as the material wealth and overall well-being of humanity has greatly increased, and world poverty is nearing elimination, there is also an increase in *anomie*. As agricultural and industrial productivity has soared, without the need to struggle every day to provide our livelihood, we may face the danger of a life of leisure that lacks a sense of meaningful purpose.

Beyond individual, family, tribe, and nation, can we develop the sense of a universal *telos,* understanding why we live, love, and die?[4]

---

4   See the end of chapter 28 on the origins of information and life.

An Information-based Social Contract?

With reference to past declarations of human rights, the discovery of a universal and objective standard of value by information philosophy suggests the following elements of a universal social contract, to be accepted by individuals reaching the age of consent, in order to have full participation in society.

As a person coming of age in human society, I freely consent to the following limits on my natural free agency, in order to preserve a more perfect society.

As I seek maximum freedom and opportunity for myself, I will protect equal freedom and opportunity for all other human beings.

As I am free to think whatever thoughts come to my mind, my self-determined actions will be responsible, limited only by the equal rights of others.

As I seek to gain my maximum allowable share of economic wealth and personal well-being, I will do my best to help others earn their own maximal shares.

As I seek to acquire the knowledge that will ensure my own future well-being, I will help disseminate that knowledge to the world, insofar as knowledge is our common human creation and inheritance from our ancestors, and since the cosmic creation process provides more than enough negative entropy for everyone.

I will do nothing to others, nor advocate such things, that I do not expect would be done to me in similar circumstances, according to the laws of society. Liberty consists of doing anything which does not harm others.

I respect the limited protection of an individual's right to their created intellectual and material property, but eventually some ideas become common property. These include the laws that govern our social behaviors. Laws should forbid only actions harmful to society. Anything which is not forbidden by law should not be prevented.

All persons can contribute personally or through their representatives to the formation of the laws. Laws must be the same for all, either as they protect, or as they punish.

All persons, being equal in the eyes of the law, are equally admissible to all public places and employments, according to their capacity and without distinction other than that of their virtues and of their talents.

Since the laws are our common property, I will not use my financial or political power to change those laws in order to advance my own personal cause, or that of my family, my business, my community, not even my nation. My power to change the laws I will limit to my powers of persuasion and my power through the ballot box to approve legislation.

I will respect the right of others to hold and to express conflicting beliefs. But I will not impose my beliefs on others, for example, by insisting they be encoded as laws of society. I will not allow others to impose their own beliefs on me, other than by their powers of public persuasion.

My right to think freely and to determine my own actions means that I take responsibility for them, and will accept punishment for my illegal acts which harm others.

No one can be punished except under a law approved by the legislature, with information about the law published before the fact of any particular offending action.

Punishment may include incarceration to prevent further physical harm to others. Government has a monopoly on the use of force to prevent illegal behavior, because it is necessary for the common good. But that force must be only that necessary and must minimize harm to the offending person.

A person is presumed innocent until proven guilty, but if arrested for cause, does not have the right to resist arrest by authorities. Resistance is itself illegal. However, if the arrest is found to have been unjustifiable, a person is deserving of appropriate compensation for the harm, the loss of abstract freedom, and possibly loss of material value such as wages.

No one should face arrest for an act that does no physical harm or dangerously threaten such harm to others. No law should prevent behavior simply because others find that behavior objectionable.

No form of speech expressing unpopular opinions, however harmful to the feelings of others, shall be cause for arrest.

Information and Negative Entropy as Objective Values

Perhaps the most radical suggestion of information philosophy is the idea that the negative entropy flows in the universe - which make possible the creation of all passive information structures as well as dynamic, interactive, purposeful living things - should be considered as an objective basis for the concept of value.

The Nobel-prize-winning economist Nicolas Georgescu-Roegen once proposed negative entropy as the ultimate source of all economic value.[5] Information philosophy agrees.

Critics may complain that there can be no single criterion for the good, that any tool can be both harmful and helpful, we ask them to look deeper.

A knife in the hands of a surgeon can save a life, in the hands of a killer take one. But just look at the information implications to judge the moral value of this example. Consider the evil in a single thermonuclear weapon, which can destroy information structures faster and more thoroughly than any other human invention. How can we have built and maintain thousands of these devices, each one capable of destroying all the lives in one of the world's largest cities?

Imagine a panel of ethicists choosing the better alternative in cases of moral dilemmas. Then imagine a panel of scientists calculating the increase in entropy (destructive disorder) versus the preservation of information (negative entropy) in each case. We suggest there would be a high correlation between moralists and scientists on the better alternative.

For centuries, values were considered a theological question, something given to humanity. Then humanists began to make human life the ultimate basis. Some philosophers assign infinite worth to each life, to block any comparative worth analysis.

In recent decades, bioethics has shifted the locus of values to the earth's biosphere and beyond to the overall environment.

Information philosophy hopes to enlarge the sphere of ethics to the cosmos itself, where the process of information creation appears as a sort of divine *providence*.

---

5   *The Entropy Law and the Economic Process*, Harvard, 1971.

Chapter 6

Philosophy

Mind

Epistemology

Metaphysics

Mind-Body

Universals

Good and Evil

Ontology

Consciousn

Free Will

Meaning

Self and Othe

Value

Mental Caus

Good and Evil

God and Immortality

Can Information Philosoph

This chapter on the web
informationphilosopher.com/value/good

Good and Evil

The abstract philosophical Idea of the Good began with PLATO, who first defined the notion of abstract Ideas in his Theory of Forms. At the end of Book VI of the *Republic* (509D-513E), Plato describes what he called a "divided line," at the top of which is the "Form of the Good, followed by theories (*noesis*), hypotheses (*dianoia*), techniques (*pistis*), and stories (*eikasia*)

Plato describes the visible world of perceived physical objects and the images we make of them (in our minds and in our drawings, for example). The Sun, he said, not only provides the visibility of the objects, but also generates them and is the source of their growth and nurture. Many primitive religions identify the Sun with God, for good reason.

Beyond this visible world, which later philosophers (especially IMMANUEL KANT) would call the *phenomenal* world, lies an intelligible world (that Kant calls *noumenal*). The intelligible world is (metaphorically) illuminated by "the Good" (τον ἀγαθὸν), just as the visible world is illuminated by the Sun.

Plato's Line is also a division between Mind and Body. The upper half of the divided line is usually called Intelligible as opposed to Visible, meaning that it is "seen" by the mind (510E). Illuminated by "the Good," it is seen by the mind, in Greek, the *nous* (voῦς), rather than by the eye.

The division of Plato's Line between Visible and Intelligible is then a divide between the Ideal and the Material, the foundation of most Dualisms.[1] Plato may have coined the word "idea" (ἰδέα), using it somewhat interchangeably with the Greek word for shape or form (εἶδος). The word idea derives from the past participle in Greek for "to have seen." The word "wisdom" comes from the same source.

In many ways, Plato's theory of immaterial forms existing outside space and time and providing the shape of material things is consonant with information philosophy's focus on immaterial information as the basis for thought, for mind, for knowledge, and

---

1   See chapter 3 for the many names of this fundamental dualism.

Chapter 6

for the abstractable elements of information structures in the real world. Plato's distinction between Form and Matter stands at the beginning of the great dualism between Idealism and Materialism.

Information philosophy is a return to a kind of Idealism. It situates the Idea of the Good in the Platonic realm of Ideas, which we now recognize as *immaterial* information. And it shows how immaterial ideas can have causal force in the world of matter and energy, solving the mind/body problem, among others.

Now the Good embodied in an information structure such as a material thing, a living thing, or a complex situation including many things, can in principle be calculated as the quantitative amount of negative entropy that it contains. Perhaps it is equally easy to see the Bad in something by measuring its destructive force. Think of the evil in a thermonuclear weapon, whose only use is to destroy a city and its population.

But it is plain that no single monotonic value can decide between the goodness of two things, since values are deeply context dependent. Indeed, Kenneth Arrow's theorem in economics shows that values are not strictly transitive. A can be preferred to B, B preferred to C, and yet C can be preferred to A.

Information (Negative Entropy) as Objective Good?

Nevertheless, however imperfect it may be, information, or more generally negative entropy, provides an objective, human-independent, starting point for value comparisons, without which all preferences are hopelessly subjective and relative to the individual or to the society. This is as it should be. Facts of the matter are questions for science. What should be or ought to be are cultural question for society or individual persons.

Free will, for example, is a scientific question. But moral responsibility is a cultural and conventional question for society. Nevertheless, those answering the conventional questions of right and wrong can consult the informational and entropic implications of different choices.

Consider utilitarianism, which hopes to achieve the "greatest good for the greatest number." The measure of utility in something correlates strongly with the amount of free or available energy (negative entropy) in that thing.

Evil

It is a sad but necessary observation to note that our definition of Evil as the creation of Entropy or Disorder - that is, the destruction of Information or Negative Entropy - means that the greater of the dualistic forces at work in the universe, at least in quantitative terms, is not the Cosmos but the Chaos.

The unavoidable Second Law of Thermodynamics, the Entropy Law, has been confirmed in the kinetic theory of gases by LUDWIG BOLTZMANN with his H-Theorem, and in statistical mechanics and quantum mechanics by ALBERT EINSTEIN with his analysis of fluctuations in the entropy.

As the universe evolves, the increase in the total entropy, the disorder and chaos, is unstoppable. Fortunately, there are important places where the entropy is reduced locally, leaving behind information structures, pockets of negative entropy or cosmos.

The established fact of increasing entropy led many scientists and philosophers to assume that the universe we have is "running down" to a "heat death." They think that means the universe began in a very high state of information, since the second law requires that any organization or order is susceptible to decay. The information that remains today, in their view, has always been here. There is "nothing new under the sun."

But the universe is not a closed system. It is in a dynamic state of expansion that is moving away from thermodynamic equilibrium faster than entropic processes can approach it. The maximum possible entropy is increasing much faster than the actual increase in entropy. The difference between the maximum possible entropy and the actual entropy is potential information.

Creation of information structures means that in parts of the universe the local entropy is actually going down. Our Sun-Earth system is one such place. All life depends on the flow of negative entropy from Sun to Earth, as ERNST SCHRÖDINGER told us.

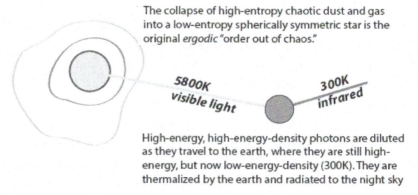

The collapse of high-entropy chaotic dust and gas into a low-entropy spherically symmetric star is the original *ergodic* "order out of chaos."

5800K visible light

300K infrared

High-energy, high-energy-density photons are diluted as they travel to the earth, where they are still high-energy, but now low-energy-density (300K). They are thermalized by the earth and radiated to the night sky

Figure 6-1. Photons from the sun are our major source of negative entropy.

It is a necessary evil that creation of negative entropy (the Good) is always accompanied by radiation of an even larger amount of positive entropy (the Bad) away from the local structures to distant parts of the universe. Ultimately, it goes to the night sky and away through our transparent universe to the most distant cosmic microwave background.

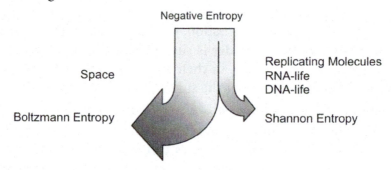

Negative Entropy

Space

Boltzmann Entropy

Replicating Molecules
RNA-life
DNA-life

Shannon Entropy

Figure 6-2. Positive and negative entropy flows to the earth.

As the universe expands, both positive and negative entropy are generated. The normal thermodynamic entropy, known as the Boltzmann Entropy, is the larger darker arrow. The negative entropy, often called the Shannon Entropy, is a measure of the information content in the evolving universe.

A Statistical Comparison with Societal Norms

The pre-Socratic philosopher PROTAGORAS famously said that "man is the measure of all things." The relativism of good and evil, of right and wrong, is a great problem in post-modern society. Any particular action may be judged good in some circumstances, evil in others. No single monotonic criterion of value can possibly serve in all cases. So what does the information theory of value amount to?

It is a claim about how an independent panel of ethicists, including a full range of traditional sources from humanists to theists who cite ancient religious doctrines, would judge a large number of moral choices.

An information-based ethics claims that if a second panel of judges consisted of scientists with expertise in chemical thermodynamics were asked to consider the same list of choices, there would be a significant statistical correlation between those deemed good by the traditional panel and those found by the second panel to preserve the most information, or to produce the least destruction of information, the least increase in entropy and disorder.

So the moral advice from information philosophy is very simple. When confronted with a moral desicion, take the alternative that minimizes the increase in disorder, that minimizes the destruction of information.

Since living things are rich in information, this coincides with a morality that regards life as an ultimate good, but it does not go the extreme of regarding each life as of *infinite* worth, which is designed to make value comparisons impossible when lives are involved..

Chapter 7

Philosophy

Mind

Epistemology

Metaphysics

Mind-Body

Universals

Ontology

God and Immortality

Consciousn

Free Will

Self and Othe

Meaning

Value

Mental Caus

Good and Evil

God and Immortality

Can Information Philosoph

This chapter on the web
informationphilosopher.com/value/ergod

God and Immortality

Most of the world's religions have some concept of gods or a God, with some notable exceptions such as Buddhism.

Theologians claim to have discerned the essential attributes of a monotheistic God, such as omniscience (perfect foreknowledge), omnipotence (unlimited power), omnipresence (present everywhere), omnibenevolence (perfect goodness), and a necessary and eternal existence.

Information philosophy offers a simple test of the "revealed truth" of these attributes, specifically the visions by inspired thinkers that have no empirical evidence. Although these visions are in the realm of "pure ideas," we can say that if every world religion agreed completely on the attributes of God, it would increase their believability. As it is, the comparative study of religions with the incredible diversity of their claims, renders the idea of God as implausible as Santa Claus.

At the present time, arguments like these will carry little weight with the believers in a religion, most of whom have little exchange of knowledge with those of other faiths. This can be expected to change with the reach of the Internet via smartphones to most of the world's population by 2020.

In theism, God is the creator and sustainer of the universe. In deism, God is the creator, but not the sustainer of the universe, which is now assumed to be running itself following deterministic laws of motion. Open theism denies that God's foreknowledge has already determined the future. Monotheism is the belief in the existence of one God or in the oneness of God. In pantheism, God is the universe itself. Polytheists hold that there are many gods. For atheists, no gods exist.

God is sometimes conceived as an immaterial being (without a body), which information philosophy accepts, since God is quintessentially an idea, pure information. Some religions think an avatar of God has come to earth in the past. Some religions see God as a personal being, answering human supplications and prayers. A God intervening in human affairs is thought to be the source of all moral norms. Logical "proofs" of God's existence are based on various of these assumed attributes.

Now that information philosophy and physics has identified the essential attributes and properties of the cosmic creation process,[1] the problem for theologians is to reconcile their views of their gods with these new discoveries.

No Creator, But There Was/Is A Creation

Modern cosmology confirms that the universe came into existence at a definite time in the past, some 13.8 billion years ago. Although this does not need the Creator some religions want, it does confirm a *creation process*. Because this process continues today (indeed human beings are co-creators of the world), deists are wrong about a creative act at the beginning followed by a mechanical clockwork universe tending to itself ever since.

So "creationism" is wrong. What about "intelligent design?" This is the ancient notion that the "essence" or idea of some things was there before the thing itself came into existence. Since all information structures, first cosmological and then biological, were "emergent,"[2] at least some of their peculiar specific information did not pre-exist them. The "existentialists," from Nietzsche to Sartre, were correct in this respect, but their idea that "God is dead" was absurd.

Now a metaphysicist might argue that the laws of nature, how things behave, might pre-exist, or come into existence simultansously with, the first matter and energy. But laws, beginning with the Heraclitean *logos*, contain nothing specific about future *arrangements* of matter and energy that is information.

Theodicy (The Problem of Evil)

The problem of evil is only a problem for monotheists who see their God as omnipotent. "If God is Good, He is not God. If God

---

1   See appendix F.
2   See chapter 27..

is God, He is not Good."[3] The information philosophy solution to the problem is a dualist world with both entropic destruction and ergodic creation. If ergodic information is an objective good, then entropic destruction of information is "the devil incarnate," as NORBERT WIENER put it.

Omniscience and Omnipotence Contradictory?

The idea of God as an omniscient and omnipotent being has an internal logical contradiction that is rarely discussed by the theologians. If such a being had perfect knowledge of the future, like Laplace's demon, who knows the positions, velocities, and forces for all the particles, such a God would be perfectly impotent, because the future is already determined. That is, if God had the power to change even one thing about the future, his presumed perfect knowledge would have been imperfect. Omniscience entails impotence. Omnipotence entails some ignorance. Prayer is useless.

The discovery by ALBERT EINSTEIN of ontological chance poses an even greater threat to the omniscience of God and the idea of foreknowledge. The great mathematicians who invented probability always regarded chance as atheistic. The use of statistics was simply to make estimates of outcomes of many independent events when detailed knowledge of those events was not possible because of human ignorance. Ontological chance means that even God cannot know some things.

For example, in quantum physics, if knowledge exists of which slot a particle will go through in a two-slit experiment, the outcome of the experiment would be different. The characteristic interference caused by the wave function passing through both slits disappears.

The Ergod

There is absolutely nothing supernatural about the cosmic creation process. But it is the source of support for human life. And many theologically-minded thinkers have long assumed that life and mind were a gift to humanity from a divine providence.

---

3   from J.B., a play by Archibald MacLeish

The physical product of the cosmic creation process is all the negative entropy in the universe. While thermodynamics calls it "negative," information philosophy sees it as the ultimate positive and deserving of a better name. So we call it the Ergo, which etymologically suggests a fundamental kind of energy ("erg" zero), e.g., the "Gibbs free energy," G_0, energy that is available to do work because it has low entropy.

We co-opted the technical term "*ergodic*" from statistical mechanics as a replacement for anti-entropic, and because it contains the highly suggestive "ergod.

An anthropomorphization (or theomorphization) of the process that creates all the energy with low entropy that we call Ergo has a number of beneficial consequences. Most all human cultures look for the source of their existence in something "higher" than their mundane existence. This intuition of a cosmic force, a providence that deserves reverence, is validated in part by the discovery of what we can provocatively call "Ergod," as the ultimate source of life.

Such an Ergod has the power to resist the terrible and universal Second Law of Thermodynamics, which commands the increase of chaos and entropy (disorder).

Without violating that inviolable Second Law overall, the Ergod reduces the entropy locally, creating pockets of cosmos and negative entropy (order and information-rich structures). All human life, and any possible extraterrestrial life, lives in one of these pockets.

Note that the opposition of Ergod and Entropy, of Ergodic processes and Entropic processes, coincides with the ancient Zarathustrian image of a battle between the forces of light (*Ahura Mazda*) and darkness (*Angra Manyu*), of good and evil, of heaven and hell. Many religions have variations on this dualist theme, and the three major Western religions all share the same Biblical source, probably incorporated into Judaism during the Babylonian exile.

The Ergod is "present" and we can say enthusiastically is "in us." The Ergod's work is to create new information, so when we create and share information we are doing the Ergod's work.

The Problem of Immortality

The two basic kinds of immortality available today may not satisfy those looking for an "afterlife," but they are both very real and important, and there is a third, medical technology solution visible on the horizon that should satisfy many persons.

The first is least satisfying - partial immortality of your genes through children. This is of no significance to the childless.

The second is the ancient notion of fame or *kleos* (κλέος) among the Greeks. When Homer sang of Achilles and Odysseus, it was to give them undying fame, which they have today among many literate persons.

A third kind of immortality will result from a solution to the problem of aging, almost certainly from stem cell research, which should allow vital organ replacement, and from a cure for runaway cancer cells, a devastating entropic force.

This should satisfy even WOODY ALLEN, who famously said,

I don't want to achieve immortality through my work.

I want to achieve it through not dying.

The second kind we call "information immortality." It is more realizable than ever with the development of world-wide literacy through print and now through the world-wide web, which makes the Information Philosopher available anywhere. In five years time, a majority of the world's population will be carrying a smartphone and thus able to read this work.

The great online Wikipedia will be capable of having something about everyone who has made a contribution to human knowledge.

If we don't remember the past, we don't deserve to be remembered by the future.

ST. JOHN THE BAPTIST PARISH LIBRARY
2920 NEW HIGHWAY 51
LAPLACE, LOUISIANA 70068

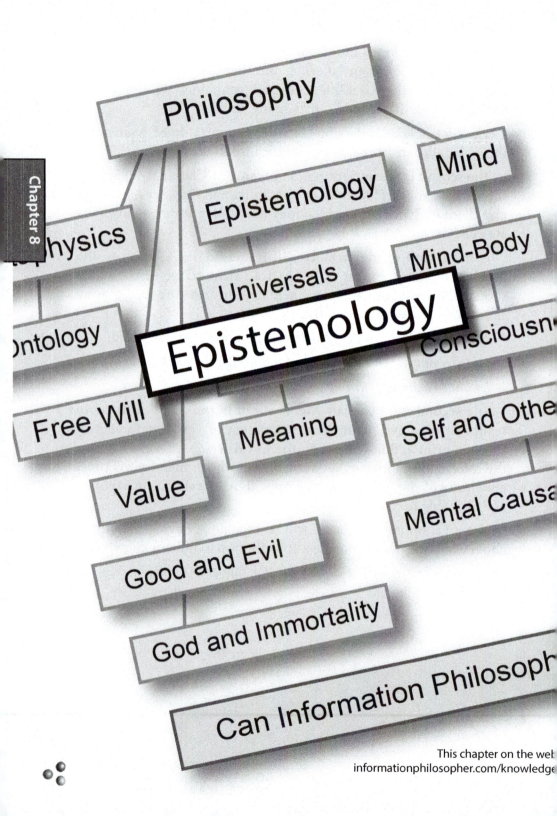

Philosophy

Mind

Epistemology

hysics

Mind-Body

Universals

Ontology

Epistemology

Consciousn

Free Will

Meaning

Self and Othe

Value

Mental Causa

Good and Evil

God and Immortality

Can Information Philosoph

This chapter on the web
informationphilosopher.com/knowledge

Epistemology

Epistemology asks, "how do we know what there is?"

Immaterial information provides a new ground for epistemology, the theory of knowledge. We know something about the "things themselves" when we discover an *isomorphism* between our abstract ideas and concrete objects in the material world. Information philosophy goes beyond the logical puzzles and language games of analytic philosophy. It identifies knowledge as information in human minds and in the external artifacts of human culture.

Abstract information is the foundation – the metaphysical ground – of both logic and language as means of communication. It is the part of a dualism parallel to the material substrate that the Greeks called ὑποκείμενον - the "underlying." It gives matter its form and shape. Form informs.

Knowing how we know is a fundamentally circular problem when it is described in human language, as a set of logical propositions. And knowing something about what exists adds another complex circle, if the knowing being must itself be one of those things that exists.

These circular definitions and inferences need not be vicious circles. They may simply be a coherent set of ideas that we use to describe ourselves and the external world. If the descriptions are logically valid and/or verifiable empirically, we think we are approaching the "truth" about things and acquiring knowledge.

How then do we describe the knowledge itself - an existing thing in our existent minds and in the existing external world? An information epistemology does it by basing everything on the abstract but quantitative notion of information.

Information is stored or encoded in physical and biological structures. Structures in the world build themselves, following natural laws, including physical and biological laws. Structures in the mind are partly built by biological processes and partly built by human intelligence, which is free, creative, and unpredictable.

Chapter 8

Knowledge is the Sum of information created and stored in minds and in human artifacts like stories, books, and internet-worked computers.

The History of Epistemology

Although the English word "epistemology" is relatively new (coined in the 19th century), it has been known for centuries as the problem of knowledge (*Erkenntnisproblem* in German), and appears in the earliest philosophical works - by the Presocratics, Plato and Aristotle, and especially by the Skeptics, who doubted that it could be proved that knowledge is possible.

Sophists

The great sophist GORGIAS challenged the many physicists (φυσικοι) who lectured and wrote on "what there is" in treatises called "Peri Physis" (Περι Φύσις) - roughly, About Nature, or the Nature of the Physical World.

The content of a typical physicist/philosopher lecture in Gorgias' time was usually in three parts:

Things exist

You can know what things exist

You can tell others about what exists

Gorgias is reported to have dazzled and delighted his audiences by proving the opposites, by using nearly identical arguments:

Nothing exists

If by chance something did exist, you could not know anything about it

If you did accidentally learn something about it, you could not communicate your knowledge to others

The lesson we can take away from Gorgias is that arguments, especially verbal reasoning alone, can be used to prove anything by clever rhetoricians. Logical and linguistic arguments can tell us nothing "true" about the physical world.

This is the problem of knowledge. How can we know - how can we be certain about - what we know? It is related closely to the question of what abstract concepts and physical objects (ontology and cosmology) exist in the universe - what are "the things themselves" - for us to know.[1] How is what we perceive through our senses related to the physical things and the abstract concepts that our reason tells us lies behind the laws of nature (metaphysics).

Plato/Socrates

In his *Theaetetus*, PLATO tells us that SOCRATES considered, but ultimately rejected, three possibilities for what knowledge (ἐπιστήμη) is and how we come to have it.

• The first is perception (αἴσθησις). Our perceptions are "true" (ἀληθῆ), at least to us, a kind of private knowledge. But they may be dreams or illusions. (160D)

• The second is true (ἀληθῆ) opinion or belief (δόξαν). Socrates asserts that PROTAGORAS's relativistic argument that "man is the measure of all things," means "what is true is what is true for me." But "myriad" others may properly judge your opinion false (ψευδῆ).(170D)

• The third is true belief that had some reasons (λόγος) or justification (συλλογισμῷ), a rational explanation for the belief. True (or right) opinion accompanied by reason is knowledge. (δόξαν ἀληθῆ μετὰ λόγου ἐπιστήμην εἶναι) (202C)

This third possibility that knowledge is "justified true belief" has come down to modern times as the three-part "traditional" theory of knowledge. Although Socrates' "negative" dialectic never established any certain knowledge, Plato believed that Socrates' method of inquiry (ἔλεγχος) is a way to achieve knowledge.

Nevertheless, the *Theaetetus* ends with Socrates' utter rejection of perception, true belief, or even true belief combined with reasons or explanations as justification. Socrates says:

> "And it is utterly silly, when we are looking for a definition of knowledge, to say that it is right opinion with knowledge, whether of difference or of anything else whatsoever. So neither perception, Theaetetus, nor true opinion, nor reason or explanation combined with true opinion could be knowledge (epistéme)."[2]

---

1   See chapter 3 on ontology.
2   Plato's Theaetetus, (210A-B)

Chapter 8

Aristotle

Aristotle revised his master Plato's theory of Forms and Ideas. Although he too sought the fundamental essences of things and ideas (their Being - τὸ ὄν), for Aristotle all things were a combination of form (εἴδος) and matter (ὑλῆ), and understanding how real physical things change (their Becoming) was as important as knowing their essences (their Being).

In his *Metaphysics*, Aristotle dealt with the problem of knowledge (epistemology) and with the question of Being (ontology of both physical and abstract things). The opening line of Book I of the *Metaphysics* is "All men desire knowledge by nature." (πάντες ἄνθρωποι τοῦ εἰδέναι ὀρέγονται φύσει.) He uses the word to know (εἰδέναι) based on "to have seen (the form)."

Aristotle sharpened the use of language (dialectic) and logic as our means of knowing to a level still in use today. He analyzed subject-predicate sentences and puzzled over the relationship between being or essence and the copula "is." He elucidated the simplest rules of logic - needed for the reasoning (συλλόγος) behind justification of knowledge - the Law of Identity (A is A), the Law of Non-Contradiction, and the Law of the Excluded Middle. And he developed the rules for logical inference, identifying many types of syllogism. Socrates had already identified the simplest syllogism - S is M, M is P, therefore S is P.

But Aristotle went beyond pure reason and the Platonic dialectic. He added the need for demonstration (ἀπόδειξις) to discover the cause (ἀιτια) and find an explanation of a phenomenon. This was the beginning of empirical knowledge, the observations and experiments that form the basis of modern science, as opposed to the kind of personal and subjective knowledge available directly to our perception, intuition, or reflective introspection.

Aristotle identified four basic causes (material, formal, efficient, and final) and said that chance might be a fifth cause. Not everything happens of causal necessity, but some things are just as chance will have it, he said.

He distinguished certain *a priori* knowledge, for example logic and mathematics, which was true by necessity, from the merely probable and contingent *a posteriori* knowledge of ethics and politics. He denied that the truth of a proposition about the future entailed the necessity of a future event (as claimed by the actualist DIODORUS CRONUS). The future is open and contingent.

For Aristotle, there were different methods of inquiry and different kinds of knowledge depending on the subject matter, for example knowledge of the things themselves in the external world (ontology and metaphysics) that we would call today the physical sciences, and knowledge about people (ethics and politics) that today we would call the social sciences. We might add psychology, especially the subjective and reflective knowledge of self by introspection. And although he wanted to be more empirical than Plato, he held onto some necessary truths or first principles that were self-evident. He also recognized "theses" (θέσισ) and "axioms" (ἄξιος).

And Aristotle distinguished many kinds of logical argument. When the premises are true and certain (he does not explain how this can be the case except for those that are self-evident "first principles" - ἀρχὴ or πρῶτων), and when the deductive syllogism is correct, the conclusions must follow. Aristotle calls this a demonstration, the truth of it is apodeictic (ἀπόδειξις), a logical proof. The resulting knowledge is demonstrative knowledge (ἀποδεικτικὲω ἐπιστήμην).

Aristotle realized that not all reasons given to justify beliefs could themselves have reasons without an infinite regress or circular argument, so he proposed that some reasons could be "self-evident" axioms, worth believing on their own merits or because they are popular opinion.

Returning to Plato here, Aristotle says that all parts of this demonstration - premises, deductions, and conclusions - are necessary. When the premises are popular opinion, their truth merely probable, the argument is dialectical. When the premises are false, the argument is sophistical, and can prove anything. Much of modern epistemology feels disturbingly *sophistical*.

Skeptics

Shortly after Aristotle, PYHRRO OF ELLIS reacted to the many methods of inquiry (σκέπσις) and their knowledge claims by denying all of them. His skeptical followers argued that happiness and serenity can be had by avoiding unjustified dogmatic knowledge claims and simply follow traditional customs as a guide to life.

Plato's Academy itself came to adopt skepticism under ARCESILAUS in the third century. Arcesilaus doubted that the senses could discover truths about the physical world. Skeptics, especially CARNEADES, who followed Arcesilaus as leader of the Academy, denied the claims of their opponent Stoics as mere dogmatism.

PHILO OF LARISSA, the last leader of Academic Skepticism in Athens, escaped the Mithradatic wars and went in 88 BCE to Rome where he mentored MARCUS TULLIUS CICERO. Cicero gave us perhaps the best ancient comparison of the Stoic, Epicurean, and Skeptical schools of philosophy in his dialogue *De Natura Deorum* (On the Nature of the Gods), which was DAVID HUME's model for his *Dialogues Concerning Natural Religion.* and a source for his own mitigated skepticism.

AENESIDEMUS, the first-century leader of Academic skepticism in Alexandria, qualified the obvious self-referential error in the skeptical claim that nothing could be known. He encouraged a return to Pyrrho's suspension (εποχή) of any judgment. Aenesidemus identified ten tropes or modes of knowing by perception through different senses, which he showed can be mutually inconsistent. Epistemological justification of any absolute objective knowledge is therefore impossible.

According to SEXTUS EMPIRICUS,[3] these ten tropes were reduced by Agrippa to five

- Disagreement among the philosophers
- An infinite regress of justification
- Relativity - concepts are meaningful only in some context
- Hypotheses cannot be self-evident
- Circular reasoning

---

3   *Outlines of Pyrrhonism*, 1.164-77

And finally, Sextus Empiricus says (1.178-79) the reasons to suspend judgment can be reduced to only the first two. He says that nothing can be apprehended through itself (immediate knowledge) or through another thing (mediate knowledge) is shown by the controversies among the philosophers. And the infinite regress of reasons is caused by the lack of a criterion for truth (κριτεριόν τῆσ ἀληθείας). These two problems are still very much with us today,

An infinite regress arises when we ask what are the justifications for the reasons themselves.

For the reasons to count as knowledge, they must themselves be justified with reasons for the reasons, etc., *ad infinitum*.

Stoics

CHRYSIPPUS, the greatest and most prolific of the Stoic leaders, separated the idea of *necessity* in certain knowledge from necessity in human actions, without denying the Stoic belief in physical determinism and fate. He helped to develop propositional logic, a language advance on Aristotle's predicate logic that GOTTLOB FREGE revived in the nineteenth century as the propositional calculus.

Chrysippus saw logic as the core of a divine reason that rules the universe. He saw Laws of Nature are synonymous with the Laws of God, since Stoics identified God with Nature. In his time, Chrysippus' logic was considered superior to Aristotle's.

The Search for Knowledge Turns Inward

"What can I know with certainty?" asked RENÉ DESCARTES. What is it that cannot logically be doubted? Starting with his famous "*Cogito, ergo sum,*" Descartes said he could not doubt his own existence, then - since "God is no deceiver" - he could not be wrong about his perceptions. This is despite Plato, who knew perceptions can be illusions, such as the stick appearing bent in the water.

Descartes shifted the emphasis of knowledge from the external world to his internal thoughts, and began an effort to find indubitable truths as foundations for all knowledge. Descartes' introspective "quest for certainty" changed the focus of problem of knowledge to what twentieth-century philosophy would come to call "foundationalism and "internalism.""

Even if Descartes could have arrived at subjective knowledge that he personally could not doubt, such knowledge would be inaccessible to others. And others would be properly skeptical of his egocentric knowledge claims.

GOTTFRIED LEIBNIZ argued that certainty could be had for necessary truths that are "true in all possible worlds." Leibniz's *Principle of Sufficient Reason* was a claim that knowledge of the physical future was implicit in the fact that every event has a sufficient cause. This is despite Aristotle, who knew that future events might or might not happen, for example, the famous "sea battle."

DAVID HUME, skeptical that anything could be proved true by induction, declared causality to be simply a matter of repeated conjunctions of apparent cause and effect. With his empirical colleagues, JOHN LOCKE and GEORGE BERKELEY, he denied any knowledge of the "things themselves" behind our perceptions. We have only the sense impressions of Locke's "secondary qualities."

Hume, following Leibniz, admitted as knowledge only two things, analytical mathematical logical reasoning, and empirical facts. This is essentially the *analytic-synthetic* knowledge distinction.

> "If we take into our hand any volume; of divinity or school metaphysics, for instance; let us ask, Does it contain any abstract reasoning concerning quantity or number? No. Does it contain any experimental reasoning concerning matter of fact and existence? No. Consign it then to the flames: For it can contain nothing but sophistry and illusion."[4]

Despite his skepticism about causality, Hume's "naturalism" convinced him of the practical truth of strict causal determinism.

"What can I know?" asked IMMANUEL KANT. Faced with the skepticism of Hume which put into doubt all phenomenal knowledge gained by perception alone, Kant postulated a noumenal world accessible to the mind by introspection. There the "things themselves" exist along with God, human freedom, and immortality. But since they are outside the phenomenal world - the physical world governed by strict causal deterministic laws of motion - Kant's claim to knowledge was as weak as Hume's skeptical claim was strong.

---

4   *Enquiry Concerning Human Understanding*, section XII

Kant accepted Hume's (and Aristotle's) distinction between abstract analytic *a priori* knowledge and experimental or empirical synthetic *a posteriori* knowledge. But he claimed that the human mind imposed certain categories of understanding on the world, leading to some necessary empirical truths, or what he called *synthetic a priori* knowledge. Among these are that space must necessarily be Euclidean, that "7 + 5 = 12" is mathematically necessary, and that the deterministic laws of Newton must be strictly true.

Although all these "truths" have been found empirically to be false, modern developmental psychology finds that some ideas are indeed "built-in" to the mind, as Kant held. Infants are born able to recognize continuity, contiguity, causality, and form. These conceptual abilities are transmitted genetically and are immediately available. They do not need a set of prior experiences from which to abstract. KONRAD LORENZ described them as the experiences of our ancestors. What is *a priori* for ontogeny in the phenotype was *a posteriori* for the phylogeny of the genotype. Thus Locke's *tabula rasa* dictum that everything that is known comes first through the senses is wrong.

The nineteenth-century hermeneuticists Schleirmacher and Dilthey argued for some knowledge accessible in non-scientific ways. They claimed that cultural knowledge can only be appreciated and understood by someone immersed in the culture.

CHARLES SANDERS PEIRCE defined knowledge - truths about the real world - as that knowledge that would eventually be agreed upon "intersubjectively" by a community of inquirers who follow an open scientific method of hypothesis, deduction, and experimental testing of predictions by means of observations.

As to Descartes' search for indubitable certain knowledge, Peirce agreed that any knowledge should be doubted. But, explaining Descartes' two errors, Peirce says first that everything cannot be doubted at the same time. And second, that nothing is ever certain because the method of science always leaves open the possibility for improvements in our knowledge. Peirce's pragmatic "truth" is something that is only asymptotically approached over time by the *intersubjective agreement* of an open community of inquirers.

Chapter 8

Peirce's "pragmatic" philosophy identified truth with beliefs that informed action and had valuable consequences. This led to JOHN DEWEY's idea of truth as "warranted assertability," with the warrants to be found in the empirical consequences.

BERTRAND RUSSELL declared that science is the only source of knowledge, "What science cannot discover, mankind cannot know." This came to be called "scientism."

Logical empiricists, following Russell's student and colleague LUDWIG WITTGENSTEIN, could never agree on the method of justification. The Vienna Circle philosophers, RUDOLF CARNAP and MORITZ SCHLICK, never could get general agreement on what constitutes the "verification" of a proposition about the world.

A. J. AYER, who sat in on some Vienna Circle meetings, put their ideas forward in his book *Language, Truth, and Logic.* He said (again following Hume and Aristotle) that two kinds of propositions are meaningful - analytic sentences (tautologies and definitions of language terms) or statements that can be empirically verified.

KARL POPPER denied that "verification" could ever lead to certain knowledge, but argued that even one negative experimental result can "falsify" a proposition.

In the early 1950's, WILLARD VAN ORMAN QUINE challenged the ancient analytic-synthetic distinction, arguing that in the end the "truth" of analytic statements, the proofs of mathematical theorems, and the use of logic, also depend on some empirical verification.

The key idea of Quine's empiricism is to deny the existence of any *a priori* knowledge of the world (or of words - statements, propositions), whether analytic or synthetic. As Peirce had said, nothing is logically and necessarily true of the physical world. Logical truths like the Principles of Non-Contradiction and Bivalence (Excluded Middle) might be true in all possible worlds, but they tell us nothing about our physical world, unless they are applicable and empirically verified.

Gettier Problems

In 1963, EDMUND GETTIER published two logical counterexamples to knowledge defined as justified true belief. His counterexamples were true, but not for the reasons cited as the evidence for justification. So the result is a justified false belief, or perhaps simply not knowledge.

The conditions postulated in Gettier-type examples are extraordinarily unlikely to occur, but the mere possibility demonstrates the difficulty of making logical arguments about contingent real world situations. The most sophisticated linguistic analysis is problematic as a source of "truth" or justification.

There is a technical similarity between Gettier cases and Frankfurt-type examples of an agent who apparently acts "freely" but a counterfactual demon ensures that there is only one possibility for action. In 1969 HARRY FRANKFURT developed logical counterexamples to the traditional idea that *alternative possibilities* are a prerequisite for free agency, because compatibilism had no alternatives.

Gettier cases artificially construct a "true" situation which is not true for the apparent reasons. Frankfurt cases artificially construct a "free" action in which the agent actually is not free to choose the apparent alternative possibilities. Gettier and Frankfurt cases have spawned a vast philosophical literature in the past few decades. But they have produced little advance in understanding either knowledge or freedom. They are little more than clever examples of the sophistry in today's analytic language philosophy.

Skepticism alone should have indicated that logical proofs of knowledge, or logical analyses of any justification scheme for knowledge, were bound to fail. Gettier and Frankfurt cases are applied skepticism or sophistry that cast doubt on the likely validity of common sense justifications and knowledge, by developing extremely unlikely if not implausible cases. They depreciate the value of the central project of epistemology, which is to help us to know (if only in a virtuous circle) when our arguments for knowledge are as strong as we can make them.

Chapter 8

Epistemology Returns to "Externalist" Justification

Until the 1960's, debates in epistemology were primarily divided between Cartesian foundationalist and coherentist theories of justification, both of which focused on egocentric subjective "internalist" theories.

Until Descartes's turn inward, theories of knowledge had assumed that justification included the relation of beliefs to objects and events in the world. Descarte's "internalist" turn continued well into the twentieth century, with most epistemologists endorsing his "foundationalist" theory of knowledge. They included C.I. Lewis (1946), Roderick Chisholm, John Pollock (1986), Richard Foley (1987), Paul Moser (1989), William P. Alston (1989), and Robert Audi (1993).

But several philosophers moved toward an "external" view of epistemology. As early as the 1920's, Frank Ramsey had proposed the idea of *reliability*, which depends on some kind of external causal process. He said that a belief was knowledge if it was (i) true, (ii) certain, and (iii) obtained by a *reliable* process.

In 1967, Alvin Goldman amplified the Ramsey view, endorsing both a "causalist" theory of knowledge and what he called "reliabilism." He claimed that justification for a belief is to be found in the natural cause of the belief.

In 1971, Fred Dretske offered what he called "Conclusive Reasons" as a form of justification. They included evidence, grounds, and reasons.

In 1973, David Armstrong called for a return to what he called "externalism," defined as "a certain relation holding between the believer and the world." For example, one can not only believe, but know, that the room is hot because the excessive heat one feels is the cause of one's belief. Armstrong further divided externalist theories into "causal" (like Goldman) and "reliability" (like Dretske and Ramsey) theories.

There are other externalist theories, including naturalism, evidentialism, and evolutionary epistemology.

Epistemology Naturalized

In the late 1960's, WILLARD VAN ORMAN QUINE argued that epistemology, the justification of knowledge claims, should be "naturalized." All knowledge claims should be reduced to verification by the methods of natural science. "For suppose we hold," he says, "with the old empiricist Peirce, that the very meaning of a statement consists in the difference its truth would make to possible experience." Quine wrote:

> "The Vienna Circle espoused a verification theory of meaning but did not take it seriously enough. If we recognize with Peirce that the meaning of a sentence turns purely on what would count as evidence for its truth, and if we recognize with Duhem that theoretical sentences have their evidence not as single sentences but only as larger blocks of theory, then the indeterminacy of translation of theoretical sentences is the natural conclusion.

> "Philosophers have rightly despaired of translating everything into observational and logico-mathematical terms. They have despaired of this even when they have not recognized, as the reason for this irreducibility, that the statements largely do not have their private bundles of empirical consequences. And some philosophers have seen in this irreducibility the bankruptcy of epistemology. Carnap and the other logical positivists of the Vienna Circle had already pressed the term "metaphysics" into pejorative use, as connoting meaninglessness; and the term "epistemology" was next. Wittgenstein and his followers, mainly at Oxford, found a residual philosophical vocation in therapy: curing philosophers of the delusion that there were epistemological problems.

> "Epistemology, or something like it, simply falls into place as a chapter of psychology and hence of natural science. It studies a natural phenomenon, viz., a physical human subject...

> "The old epistemology aspired to contain, in a sense, natural science; it would construct it somehow from sense data. Epistemology in its new setting, conversely, is contained in natural science, as a chapter of psychology. But the old containment remains valid too, in its way... There is thus reciprocal containment, though containment in different senses: epistemology in natural science and natural science in epistemology."[5]

Although Quine's reciprocal containment suggested that epistemology might still play a foundational role in scientific understanding, his work appeared to many to reduce epistemology to psychology. Quine seemed to deny the normative role of traditional epistemology to justify all knowledge, including scientific knowledge. An information epistemology can restore that role.

---

5   *Ontological Relativity and Other Essays* 1969, pp.80-3

An Information Epistemology?

Second only to Kant's "scandal" that philosophers cannot logically prove the existence of the external world, it is scandalous that professional philosophers are in such profound disagreement about what it means to know something. They may not all be wrong, but few of them are likely to be right.

This is especially dismaying for those epistemologists who still see a normative role for philosophy that could provide a foundation, perhaps even *a priori*, for scientific or empirical, *a posteriori* knowledge.

Information epistemology avoids the traditional identification of knowledge with "belief." Belief is a psychological state that may be, and often is, disjoint from knowledge. We may empirically verify that a person knows something by analyzing her behavior, without her consciously articulating or holding a belief in that knowledge. A famous example is the difference between linguistic competence and mere performance, knowing the grammatical rules for one's language without being able to state those rules. Those rules have been learned tacitly, by multiple trials and errors, and stored in a person's mind, in our experience recorder and reproducer (ERR).[6]

Human knowledge is not only information stored in the mind. It is also recorded in human artifacts like stories, books, buildings, and internetworked computers. Knowledge is information that forms the basis for human thoughts and actions. In information philosophy, knowledge is information that is "actionable," meaning that if we act on the basis of the information, our actions will have fruitful consequences. The validity or pragmatic "truth" of knowledge is to be found in those consequences.

Since information is also stored in animal minds, we can reject the exceptionalist fiction that only humans can have knowledge. Where humans are indeed exceptional is their ability to communicate their knowledge - and their reasons for their knowledge - symbolically by means of language.

Information is stored or encoded in information structures. Although structures in the material world build themselves,

---

6   See Appendix E for details.

following natural laws, they do not *assemble* themselves. This is the material *first world* of information philosophy.

In our second world, biological systems are cognitive systems in the sense that they also *process* and *communicate* knowledge (information). They bring *purpose* into the universe. They are "*teleonomic*." They cannot be reduced to the laws of physics and chemistry. They are not machines, which must be assembled. Biological systems assemble themselves, using their internal knowledge. This is the biological *second world* of information philosophy.

Structures in the mind are partly built by biological processes and partly built by human intelligence, which is free, creative, and unpredictable. The information in mental structures is uniquely mobile. It is not confined to its structure. As knowledge, it is the *immaterial* stuff of thought - our ideal *third world*."

A majority of the *Sum* of unique human knowledge may now be stored external to our minds. Even collectively, we don't know (in the sense of having it in mind) all that we know. But we (including almost anyone in the world) can look it up extremely quickly.

Among the sources of knowledge are the theories and experiments of natural scientists, who collaborate to establish our knowledge of the external world, social scientists who study our cultures, and psychologists, cognitive scientists, and neuroscientists, who investigate our personal subjective worlds.

To the extent of the correspondence, the isomorphism, the one-to-one mapping, between structures (and processes) in the world and representative information structures in our minds, we can claim to have knowledge of the world, and of other minds.

Such knowledge claims are not based on logical arguments about justification, but on the pragmatic truth that the knowledge has consequences that can be empirically or "naturally" confirmed.

Information epistemology is a *naturalized* epistemology.

Chapter 8

Philosophy

Mind

Epistemology

hysics

Mind-Body

Universals

Ontology

Universals

ciousn

Free Will

Meaning

Self and Othe

Value

Mental Causa

Good and Evil

God and Immortality

Can Information Philosoph

Universals

A "universal" in metaphysics is a property or attribute that is shared by many particular objects (or concepts). It has a subtle relationship to the problem of the one and the many.

It is also the question of ontology.[1] What exists in the world? Ontology is intimately connected with epistemology - how can we know what exists in the world?

Knowledge about objects consists in describing the objects with properties and attributes, including their relations to other objects. Rarely are individual properties unique to an individual object. Although a "bundle of properties" may uniquely characterize a particular individual, most properties are shared with many individuals.

The "problem of universals" is the existential status of a given shared property. Does the one universal property exist apart from the many instances in particular objects? PLATO thought it does. ARISTOTLE thought it does not.

Consider the property having the color red. Is there an abstract concept of redness or "being red?" Granted the idea of a concept of redness, in what way and where in particular does it exist? Nominalists (sometimes called anti-realists) say that it exists only in the particular instances, and that redness is the name of this property. Conceptualists say that the concept of redness exists only in the minds of those persons who have grasped the concept of redness. They might exclude color-blind persons who cannot perceive red.

Realism is the view that a "reality" of physical objects, and possibly of abstract concepts like redness, exists in an external world independently of our minds and perceptions.

Platonic Realism is the view that abstract things like numbers, perfect geometric figures, and other things that Plato called the Forms or the Ideas, have a real and independent existence, though they are not material objects.

---

1   See chapter 3.

But for his student, Aristotle, these "universals" exist only in the concrete objects which share some property. For him, the universal idea of a perfect circle is a shared property of the many actual circles in nature.

Naive realists think that we can access concrete physical objects directly and fully with our perceptual sense data. This is sometimes called the "copy theory." Our perceptions are fully apprehending the physical objects, so that the content of a perception is the same as the object of perception. In information philosophy terms, naive realism mistakenly assumes that the information in the perceived sense data (or the representation in the mind) is (quantitatively) equal to (a copy of) the information in the physical object. In the case of the abstract concept of redness, it may be that the copy-theory is most tenable. The perception of a red object may in a strong sense bring the concept of redness into existence (at least in the observer's mind).

Historically, realism is a metaphysical claim about this independently existing world where redness might be found. Since Aristotle's Metaphysics, two kinds of metaphysical questions (ontological and epistemological) are raised - what exists, and how can we know what exists.

The ontological status of abstract concepts is a completely different question from the ontology of concrete material objects, though these questions have often been confounded in the history of philosophy.

Information philosophy provides distinct answers to these two ontological questions. Material objects exist in the world of space and time. They are information structures embodied in matter and interacting with energy. Abstract concepts (like redness) are pure information, neither matter nor energy, although they need matter for their embodiment and energy for their communication.

The contrast between physical objects and abstract concepts can be illustrated by the difference between invention and discovery.

We discover physical objects through our perceptions of them. To be sure, we invent our ideas about these objects, their descriptions, their names, theories of how they are structured and how they interact energetically - with one another and with us. But we cannot arbitrarily invent the natural world. We must test our theories with experiment. The experimental results select those theories that best fit the data, the information coming to us from the world. This makes our knowledge of an independent external world scientific knowledge.

By contrast, we humans invent abstract concepts like redness. We know that these cultural constructs exist nowhere in nature as physical structures. We create them. Cultural knowledge is relative to and dependent on the society that creates it.

However, some of our invented abstract concepts seem to clearly have an existence that is independent of us, like the numbers and the force of gravity.

Critical realists, like scientists, start with observations and sense data, but they add hypotheses and experiments to develop theories about the physical objects and the abstract concepts in the external world. Nevertheless, the abstract representation in the mind is (quantitatively) much less information than the information in the physical object represented.

The idea of an independent reality claims that the reality known exists independently of the knowledge of it.

The British empiricists JOHN LOCKE and DAVID HUME argued that what we were "given" in our perceptions of sense data is limited to so-called "secondary qualities." These are properties that produce the sensations in the observer's senses - color, taste, smell, sound, and touch. Knowledge that comes from secondary qualities does not provide objective facts about things "in themselves."

IMMANUEL KANT described these secondary qualities as "phenomena" that could tell us nothing about the "noumena," which the empiricists called the "primary qualities." These are properties the objects have that are independent of any observer, such as solidity, extension, motion, number and figure. These qualities exist in the thing itself (Kant's *"Ding an sich"*). Kant thought that some of these qualities can be determined with certainty, as *"synthetic a priori"* truths. Some of these qualities are analytic truths, defined by the logical meanings of linguistic terms. For example, a round circle cannot be a square.

The One and the Many

Some philosophers are monists, arguing that the world must be a unity, one unchanging thing, and that all the multiplicity and change that we see is mere illusion.

Some are dualists, puzzled how the immaterial One (usually Mind or the Ideal) can possibly interact with the material Many (the Body or the World). There are other kinds of dualists, but the idealism/ materialism divide has a long history in philosophy under dozens of different names through the ages.

Some philosophers prefer triads, triplicities, or trinities as their fundamental structures, and in these we may find the most sensible way to divide the world as we know it into "worlds," realms, or orders.

Those who divide their philosophy into four usually arrange it two by two (Schopenhauer, Heidegger, Derrida - who did it in jest, and against Christian trinities). There are a few who think a pentad has explanatory power. Another handful look to the mystical seven (the number of planets and thus days of the week) for understanding.

Since the Pythagoreans drew their triangular diagram of the tetractus, ten has been a divine number for some. Aristotle found ten categories. The neo-Platonist Kabalists have ten sephiroth. In string theory, there are ten dimensions reflecting the components of Einstein's general relativity equations.

The most important philosopher since Aristotle, Kant, structured his architectonic into twelve categories, arranged four by three.

We will scrutinize these architectures to see if the thinkers divide their worlds the same way, whatever names they call their divisions. There is a surprising amount of agreement among them, considering their disagreements on terminology.

Over the centuries many philosophers have seen a fundamental dualism. Most have invented their own names for this dualism. Not all have meant the very same things, but the great similarities allow us to collect all these dualisms into a quasi-chronological table, where similarities and slight differences become more clear.

Of course many have claimed to be monists. "All is One," they said, as they generally reduce the physical world to the ideal world, or vice versa. "Neutral monists" argue that the ideal and physical worlds are somehow both something else. But the underlying dualism remains in these monistic claims.

Many philosophers saw the need for the two sides to work together.

IMMANUEL KANT wrote,

> *Gedanken ohne Inhalt sind leer.*
> *Anschauungen ohne Begriffe sind blind.*

CHARLES SANDERS PEIRCE rewrote this as,

> *If Materialism without Idealism is blind,*
> *Idealism without Materialism is void.*

With a nod to Kant and Peirce, we can say,

> *Concepts without Percepts are empty.*
> *Percepts without Concepts are blind.*

And although freedom and values are not a dualism, they too require one another and we can observe

> *Freedom without Values is Absurd (as Continental Existentialists like Jean-Paul Sartre thought).*
> *Values without Freedom are Worthless (as British Utilitarians and later Positivists may have thought).*

The founder of quantum mechanics. NIELS BOHR, saw the wave-particle dual nature of quantum mechanics as connected to many other "complementary" philosophical dualisms.

Chapter 9

We have compiled a semi-chronological list of various philosophical terms used through the ages that seem highly correlated with the fundamental ideal-material duality.

The ONE	The MANY
Monism	Pluralism
IDEALISM	MATERIALISM
Being	Becoming
Necessity	Contingency
Plato's Divided Line	
Theories (*noesis*) Hypotheses (*dianoia*)	Techniques (*pistis*) Stories (*eikasia*)
Eternal	Ephemeral
ESSENCE	EXISTENCE
Universals	Accidentals / Particulars
Aristotle's Four Causes	
Final Cause Formal Cause	Efficient Cause Material Cause
Realism	Nominalism
Intelligible	Sensible
Form	Content
Universal	Particular
Absolute	Relative
RATIONALISM	EMPIRICISM
MIND	BODY
a priori	*a posteriori*
Certainty	Probability
Intellect - Innate	Tabula Rasa - Learned
Nature	Nurture
Analytic	Synthetic

Kant's Transcendental Critique	
Noumena	Phenomena
Concepts/Thoughts	Percepts/Senses
Freedom	Determinism
Subject	Object
Dialectical IDEALISM	Dialectical MATERIALISM
Superstructure	Base
Romanticism	Positivism
Transcendentalism	Pragmatism
Supernaturalism	Naturalism
Phenomenology	Behaviorism/Existentialism
Linguistic Analysis	
Ideal Language	Ordinary Language
Intension	Extension
Sense/Semantic	Meaning/Pragmatic
Autonomy	Mimesis
Deduction	Induction
Theory	Experiment
Consistency	Correspondence
Quantum Complementarity	
WAVE	PARTICLE
Possible	Actual
Thought	Action

Intension and Extension describe two ways of indicating the meaning of a word or name. Intension assumes the word has an intrinsic, essential meaning, perhaps simply by definition and thus "analytic."

Extension is the set of existing objects in the world to which the word corresponds. There is a special kind of definition called "ostensive" which defines a word by pointing to those objects. Because extension involves things in the world it is called "synthetic."

The mathematician GOTTLOB FREGE distinguished intension and extension by the German words *Sinn und Bedeutung* (which usually translate as Sense and Reference, though Denotation is better).

Vienna Circle philosophers, notably RUDOLF CARNAP, described intension and extension as *semantisch* and *pragmatisch* (semantic and pragmatic).

WILLARD VAN ORMAN QUINE used the terms Meaning and Reference for intension and extension, conflicting with Frege's terms. But note that Frege conflicts with the ancient intelligible/sensible distinction. Words are ambiguous tools to describe objects. And language should therefore not be the primary tool for philosophical analysis.

Philosophical Triads

After dualisms, the next most popular philosophical architectonic structures are triads, triplicities, or trinities.

Some philosophers describe their triads as three "worlds," just as dualism is often described in terms of an Ideal World and a Material World. The deep philosophical (and scientific) question is - do these divisions "carve nature at the joints," as Plato put it in the *Phaedrus*, (265e)?

We analyze examples, and find that the three worlds are most often simply the canonical Ideal/Material dualism with an interpolated third world corresponding to a human world (or more broadly, the biological world), with its obvious connection to the world of "subjective?" ideas above and the "objective" material world below.

GOTTLOB FREGE's Three Realms

An External Realm of Public Physical Things and Events

An Internal Subjective Realm of Private Thoughts

An "Objective" Platonic Realm of Ideal "Senses" (to which sentences refer, providing their meaning)

KARL POPPER's Three Worlds (clearly influenced by Frege)

World I - "the realm of physical things and processes"

World II - "the realm of subjective human experience"

World III - "the realm of culture and objective knowledge" - of human artifacts (our Sum)

CHARLES SANDERS PEIRCE's triad of Objects - Percepts - Concepts is in the same order as Frege and Popper.

In information philosophy, we divide the world into three fundamental parts, the material, the ideal (ideas are the same kind of abstraction as pure information), and the biological/human, a middle world that combines ideality and materiality. In these three worlds, information emerges in different ways. They are symbolized in our tri-color I-Phi logo.

•The Physical/Material World (lower/green) - ILYA PRIGOGINE's "order out of chaos," when the matter in the universe spontaneously forms information structures.

•The Biological/Material World (middle/red) - ERWIN SCHRÖDINGER's "order out of order," when the biological information structures form purposeful ("teleonomic") self-replicating organisms that depend on or "feed on" a negative entropy stream from the sun.

•The Mental/Immaterial/Ideal World (upper/blue) - BOB DOYLE's abstract "information out of order," when organisms with minds process and externalize information, communicating it to other minds and storing it in the environment.

MERLIN DONALD's three levels of Culture Emergence.

•Mimetic: the "copycat" or "monkey see, monkey do" ability of primates facilitated transfer of learning, ritual

•Mythic: language in humans, mental/brain development is influenced by social network of speakers generating symbols for ideas

•Informatic: External storage of knowledge - writing, printing, computers, Internet

Three Sources for Authoritative Knowledge

•The Tradition - Knowledge is inherited, handed down, from the great thinkers of the past (compare Frege's "Objective" Platonic Realm of Ideal "Senses" to which sentences "refer," providing their meaning)

•The Modern - Knowledge is created by Reason, by providing a rational account (logos) of how things are, augmented by modern empirical science since the Enlightenment

•The Post-Modern - all knowledge is "relative" to the culture that invented it. For conservative post-moderns, science can establish knowledge about an objective external world. For radical post-moderns, "anything goes", even science "invents or creates reality." There are no grounds/foundations for cultural knowledge that can "justify true beliefs."

Types of Triads

Levels: Material - Biological/Human - Ideal

(physis - bios/nomos - logos)

Inner Levels: Body - Brain - Mind/Spirit

Plato: Truth - Goodness - Beauty

Aristotle/Kant: Epistemology - Ethics - Aesthetics

Number: One - Two/Many - All (unity - duality/plurality - totality)

Person: I - You - We (self - other - society/community)

Truth: Correspondence - Coherence - Consistency

(empirical - conventional/pragmatic - logical)

Time: Past - Present - Future

Family: Father - Mother (chauvinists changed to Spirit) - Son

Dialectic: Thesis - Antithesis - Synthesis (Aufhebung new Thesis)

Hume's Relations: Similarity - Contiguity - Causality

(form - space - time)

Medieval Trivium: Grammar - Rhetoric - Logic

Rhetoric: Simile - Metonym - Metaphor

Language - Syntax - Semantics - Pragmatics

Peirce: Objects - Percepts - Concepts

Peirce's Semiotics: Icon - Index - Symbol

Peirce's Symbol: Ground - Object - Interpretant

Peirce's Science: Abduction (hypothesis) - Induction - Deduction

Grounds: Tradition - Modern - Postmodern

Beliefs: Naturalism - Humanism - Spiritualism

Matter: Solid - Liquid - Gas (earth - water - air)

Time: Beginning - Middle - End (archos - physis/nomos - telos)

Journey: Eden - Fall - Atonement (home - travels - homecoming)

Life: Birth - Life - Death

A Few Tetrads

Classical kinds of matter: Earth - Water - Air - Fire

(anticipating today's solid - liquid - gas - plasma)

Plato's Divided Line: Stories - Techniques - Hypotheses - Theories (eikasia - pistis - dianoia - noesis)

Aristotle's Causes: Material cause - Efficient cause - Formal cause - Final cause   (He considered chance to be a possible fifth cause.)

Graeco-Roman Four Temperaments (or humors): Choleric (yellow bile), Melancholic (black bile), Sanguine (blood), and Phlegmatic (phlegm)

Medieval cosmology: Earth (below us) - Water (with us) - Air (above us) - Stars (beyond us)

The medieval scholastic Quadrivium: Math - Geometry - Music - Astronomy (number - space - time - motion)

Schopenhauer's Fourfold Root of Sufficient Reason

Heidegger's Geviert (2x2): Earth - Mortals - Heavens - Gods

Derrida's *Jeu des Cartes*

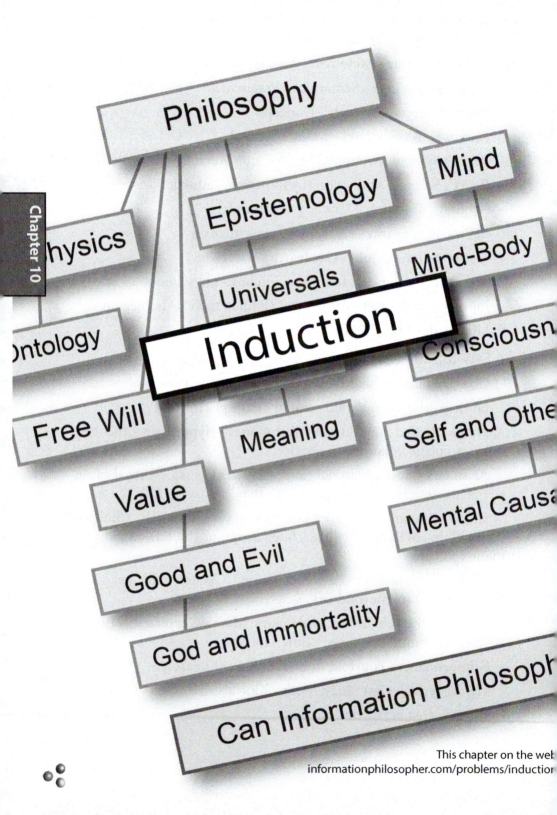

Philosophy

Mind

Epistemology

hysics

Mind-Body

Universals

Induction

Consciousn

Ontology

Free Will

Self and Othe

Meaning

Value

Mental Causa

Good and Evil

God and Immortality

Can Information Philosoph

The Problem of Induction

FRANCIS BACON described "genuine Induction" as the new method of science. Opposing his new idea to what he thought ARISTOTLE's approach had been in his *Organon* (as misinterpreted by the medieval Scholastics), Bacon proposed that science builds up knowledge by the accumulation of data (information), which is of course correct. This is simply the empirical method of collecting piece by piece the (statistical) evidence to support a theory.

The "problem of induction" arises when we ask whether this form of reasoning can lead to apodeictic or "metaphysical" certainty about knowledge, as the Scholastics thought. THOMAS AQUINAS especially thought that certain knowledge can be built upon first principles, axioms, and deductive or logical reasoning. This certain knowledge does indeed exist, within a system of thought such as logic or mathematics. But it can prove nothing about the natural material world.

Bacon understood logical deduction, but like some proto-empiricists among the Scholastics (notably JOHN DUNS SCOTUS and WILLIAM OF OCCAM), Bacon argued in his *Novum Organum* that knowledge of nature comes from studying nature, not from reasoning in the ivory tower.

Bacon likely did not believe certainty can result from inductive reasoning, but his great contribution was to see that (empirical) knowledge gives us power over nature, by discovering what he called the form of nature, the real causes underlying events.

It was of course DAVID HUME who pointed out the lack of certainty or logical necessity in the method of inferring causality from observations of the regular succession of "causes and effects." His great model of scientific thinking, ISAAC NEWTON had championed induction as the source of his ideas. This is as if his laws of motion were simply there in the data from TYCHO BRAHE's extensive observations and JOHANNES KEPLER's elliptical orbits.

"*Hypotheses non fingo,*" Newton famously said, denying the laws were his own ideas. Although since Newton it is a commonplace that the gravitational influence ("action at a distance") of the Sun causes the Earth and other planets to move around their orbits, Hume's skepticism led him to question whether we could really know, with certainty, anything about causality, when all we ever see in our inductive study is the regular succession of events.

Thus it was Hume who gave us the "problem of induction" that has bothered philosophers for centuries, spilling a great deal of philosophical ink. Hume's skepticism told him induction could never yield a logical proof. But Hume's mitigated skepticism saw a great deal of practical value gained by inferring a general rule from multiple occurrences, on the basis of what he saw as the uniformity of nature. It is reasonable to assume that what we have seen repeatedly in the past is likely to continue in the future.

While Hume was interested in causal sequences in time, his justification of induction also applies to modern statistical thinking. We infer the frequency of some property of an entire population in the future from the statistics of an adequately large sample of that population in the present.

The information philosopher's solution to this problem (more properly a "pseudo-problem," to use the terminology of twentieth-century logical positivists, logical empiricists, and linguistic analysts) is easily seen by examining the information involved in the three (or four) methods of reasoning - logical deduction, empirical induction, mathematical induction (actually a form of deduction), and what CHARLES SANDERS PEIRCE called "abduction," to complete one of his many philosophical triads.

Mathematical induction is a method of proving some property of all the natural numbers by proving it for one number, then showing that if it is true for the number n, it must also be true for $n + 1$. In both deduction and mathematical induction, the information content of the conclusion is often no more than that already in the premises. To be sure, the growth of our systems of thought such as logic, mathematics, and perhaps especially geometry, has generated vast amounts of new knowledge, new information, when surprising new theorems are proved within the system.

And much of this information has turned out to be isomorphic with information structures in the universe. But the existence of an isomorphism is an empirical, not a logical, finding.

The principal role of deduction in science is to derive, logically or mathematically, predictable consequences of the new theory that might be tested by suitable experiments. This step simply draws out information already present in the hypothesis. Theory, including deductions and predictions, is all done in the realm of ideas, pure information.

Abduction is the creative formation of new hypotheses, one step (rarely the first) in what some philosophers of science in the twentieth century described as the scientific method - the hypothetico-deductive-observational method. It can be described more simply as the combination of theories and experiments. Observations are very often the spur to theory formation, as the old inductive method emphasized. A scientist forms a hypothesis about possible causes for what is observed.

Although the hypothesis is an immaterial idea, pure information, the abduction of a hypothesis creates new information in the universe, albeit in the minds of the scientists.

By contrast, an experiment is a material and energetic interaction with the world that produces new information structures to be compared with theoretical predictions. Experiments are Baconian accumulations of data that can never logically "prove" a theory (or hypothesis). But confirmation of any theory consists entirely of finding that the statistical outcomes of experiments match the theory's predictions, within reasonable experimental "error bars." The best confirmation of any scientific theory is when it predicts a phenomenon never before seen, such that when an experiment looks, that phenomenon is found to exist.

These "surprising" results of great theories shows the extent to which science is not a mere "economic summary of the facts," as claimed by ERNST MACH, the primary exponent of logical positivism in science.

Mach had a great influence on the young ALBERT EINSTEIN, who employed Mach's idea in discovering his special theory of relativity. The positivists insisted on limiting science to "observable" facts. Atoms were not (yet) observable, so despite the great chemical theories of JOHN DALTON explaining molecules, the great statistical mechanical work of JAMES CLERK MAXWELL and LUDWIG BOLTZMANN explaining thermodynamics, it remained for Einstein to predict the observable effects of atomic and molecular motions on the motions of visible particles like pollen seeds in a liquid.

The experimental measurements of those visible motions, with exactly the extent of motion predicted by Einstein, confirmed the physical reality of atoms. The motions had been observed, almost eighty years earlier, by ROBERT BROWN. Einstein's 1905 work was a paradigmatic example of the scientific method - first a "free creation of the human mind," as he called it and his other extraordinary theories - next the deduction of mathematically exact predictions from the theory, and finally the 1908 confirming experiments by JEAN PERRIN.

In information philosophy terms, the abstract immaterial information in the Einstein theory of Brownian motion, was found to be isomorphic to material and energetic information structures in the universe.

In his early years, Einstein thought himself a disciple of Mach, a positivist. He limited his theories to observable facts. Special relativity grew from the fact that absolute motions are not observable.

But later when he realized the source of his greatest works were his own mental inventions, he changed his views. Here is Einstein in 1936,

> "We now realize, with special clarity, how much in error are those theorists who believe that theory comes inductively from experience. Even the great Newton could not free himself from this error ("*Hypotheses non fingo*")...
>
> "There is no inductive method which could lead to the fundamental concepts of physics. Failure to understand this fact constituted the basic philosophical error of so many investigators of the nineteenth century. It was probably the reason why the molecular theory and Maxwell's theory were able to establish themselves only at a relatively late date. Logical thinking is necessarily deductive; it is based upon hypothetical concepts

and axioms. How can we expect to choose the latter so that we might hope for a confirmation of the consequences derived from them?

"The most satisfactory situation is evidently to be found in cases where the new fundamental hypotheses are suggested by the world of experience itself. The hypothesis of the non-existence of perpetual motion as a basis for thermodynamics affords such an example of a fundamental hypothesis suggested by experience; the same holds for Galileo's principle of inertia. In the same category, moreover, we find the fundamental hypotheses of the theory of relativity, which theory has led to an unexpected expansion and broadening of the field theory, and to the superseding of the foundations of classical mechanics."[1]

And here, Einstein wrote in his 1949 autobiography,

"I have learned something else from the theory of gravitation: No ever so inclusive collection of empirical facts can ever lead to the setting up of such complicated equations. A theory can be tested by experience, but there is no way from experience to the setting up of a theory. Equations of such complexity as are the equations of the gravitational field can be found only through the discovery of a logically simple mathematical condition which determines the equations completely or [at least] almost completely."[2]

WERNER HEISENBERG told Einstein in 1926 that his new quantum mechanics was based only on "observables," following the example of Einstein's relativity theory that was based on the fact that absolute motion is not observable. For Heisenberg, the orbital path of an electron in an atom is not an observable. Heisenberg said of his first meeting with Einstein,

"Einstein himself discovered the transition probabilities between states in the Bohr atom, ten years before this conversation with Heisenberg. I defended myself to begin with by justifying in detail the necessity for abandoning the path concept within the interior of the atom. I pointed out that we cannot, in fact, observe such a path; what we actually record are frequencies of the light radiated by the atom, intensities and transition-probabilities, but no actual path. And since it is but rational to introduce into a theory only such quantities as can be directly observed, the concept of electron paths ought not, in fact, to figure in the theory.

"To my astonishment, Einstein was not at all satisfied with this argument. He thought that every theory in fact contains unobservable quantities. The principle of employing only observable quantities simply cannot be consistently carried out. And when I objected that in this I had merely been applying the type of philosophy that he, too, had made the basis

---

1   "Physics and Reality," *Journal of the Franklin Institute*, Vol.221, No.3, March, 1936. pp. 301, 307

2   "Autobiographical Notes," in *Albert Einstein: Philosopher-Scientist*, Ed. Paul Arthur Schilpp, 1949, p.89

of his special theory of relativity, he answered simply "Perhaps I did use such philosophy earlier, and also wrote it, but it is nonsense all the same." Thus Einstein had meanwhile revised his philosophical position on this point. He pointed out to me that the very concept of observation was itself already problematic. Every observation, so he argued, presupposes that there is an unambiguous connection known to us, between the phenomenon to be observed and the sensation which eventually penetrates into our consciousness. But we can only be sure of this connection, if we know the natural laws by which it is determined. If however, as is obviously the case in modern atomic physics, these laws have to be called in question, then even the concept of "observation" loses its clear meaning. In that case it is theory which first determines what can be observed. These considerations were quite new to me, and made a deep impression on me at the time; they also played an important part later in my own work, and have proved extraordinarily fruitful in the development of the new physics."[3]

Since philosophy has made the "linguistic turn" to abstract propositions, the problem of induction for today's philosophers is subtly different from the one faced by David Hume. It has become an epistemological problem of "justifying true beliefs" about propositions and thus lost the connection to "natural philosophy" it had in Hume's day. Information philosophy hopes to restore at least the "metaphysical" elements of natural philosophy to the domain of philosophy proper.

In contemporary logic, epistemology, and the philosophy of science, there is now the problem of "enumerative induction" or universal inference, an inference from particular statements to general statements. For example, the inference from the propositions p_1, p_2,... p_n, which are all F's that are G's, to the general inference that all F's are G's.

This is clearly a purely linguistic version of the original problem. Divorcing the problem of induction from nature empties it of the great underlying principle in Hume, Mill, and other philosophers, namely the assumption of the uniformity of nature, which alone can justify our "true?" belief that the sun will come up tomorrow.

In information terms, the problem of induction has been reduced, even impoverished, to become only relations between ideas. Perhaps

---

3   *Encounters with Einstein*, 1983, pp.113-4

"ideas" is too strong, much of philosophy has become merely logical relations between statements or propositions. Because of the inherent ambiguity of language, sometimes philosophy appears to have become merely a game played using our ability to make arbitrary meaningless statements, then critically analyze the resulting conceptual paradoxes.

KARL POPPER famously reprimanded LUDWIG WITTGENSTEIN's claim that there are no real philosophical problems, only puzzles and language games.

Induction and the Scientific Method

We can conclude that induction corresponds roughly to the gathering of large numbers of observations or experiments, which today are seen as the statistical basis for accepting a scientific theory. Induction is supplemented today with abduction, which is the free creation of theories or hypotheses to be tested against the results of experiments. Deduction is a third tool that allows predictions to be derived logically and mathematically from the theory.

Freely developed *theories* are then seen to generate predictions about alternative possibilities and probabilities.

Experimental facts provide the statistical evidence that either confirms or denies those predictions.

Theories are probabilities. Experiments are statistics.

This chapter on the we
informationphilosopher.com/knowledge/meanin

The Problem of Meaning

The "meaning" of any word, concept, or object is different for different individuals, depending on the information (knowledge) about the word, concept, or object currently available to them. All meaning is "contextual" and the most important context is what is currently in the individual's mind. This obviously includes the immediate external context, for example, a puzzling word being heard or read is surrounded by text, both explicitly and implicitly. *Explicit* text includes the words preceding the word whose meaning is not yet clear. Structural linguists call this the diachronic dimension. *Implicit* words are synonyms and other words that might come to mind as substitutes for the questionable word. This is the synchronic dimension - those alternative words that could *substitute* with little change in meaning.

How exactly does our information-based model of the mind generate meaning? It is the past experiences that are reproduced (played back) from the *experience recorder and reproducer* (ERR) that provide most of the meaningful context for a word or object. For example, if the agent has had no past experiences that resemble the current experience in some way, the agent may not find any meaning at all. The simplest case would be a new word, seen for the very first time. Worst case would be listening to an unknown foreign language.

If the word is not isolated, the meanings of familiar surrounding text may bring back their own past uses clearly enough to allow the agent to guess the meaning of the new word, in that context. In any case this fresh experience with the word will be stored away along with that context for future reference.

The problem of the "Meaning of Meaning" has a rich history in the past century or two of analytic language philosophy. Three centuries ago, GOTTFRIED LEIBNIZ hoped for an ambiguity-free ideal language with exactly one term for each concept. It would reduce language to a kind of mathematics where the meaning of complex combinations of terms could be "calculated" precisely. In the middle of the nineteenth century, JOHN STUART MILL tried to simplify proper nouns by insisting that they are just names for the things we are talking about in sentences or propositions. Nouns are subjects, predicates are the attributes of the subject.

Leibniz and Mill were inspirations for BERTRAND RUSSELL, whose logical positivism imagined "logical atoms" of meaning that could be combined following strict rules to form complex concepts - "logical molecules." But Russell and the great logician GOTTLOB FREGE tangled over exactly how words describe, denote, or refer to concepts and objects. How do words mean?

Is the absolute meaning to be found in the dictionary definitions of how a word refers to an object, independent of the intentions of a speaker or inferences of the hearer? Frege distinguished between the straight reference of a word and what he called the "sense." Why does the statement "Aristotle is the author of *De Anima*" carry more information than the identity statement "Aristotle is Aristotle." Our information theory of meaning finds the answer in the reader's past experience (or none) of *De Anima.*

Russell's young collaborator in early logical positivism, LUDWIG WITTGENSTEIN, eventually broke with Russell and insisted that meaning depends on the *use* to which a word is being put. There is no objective independent meaning for a word as the object it "stands for." Wittgenstein's relativism became more extreme when JACQUES DERRIDA showed how the meaning of a word can be deferred and "disseminated," shifting according to words following it in time - in the diachronic dimension.

CHARLES SANDERS PEIRCE, and the great linguist and inventor of structuralism, FERDINAND DE SAUSSURE, had accepted straightforward connections between words and objects, like Peirce's triad "concept-percept-object" and Saussure's dual "signifier/signified" (s/S) for an arbitrary symbol and its object. These were captured in the C. K. OGDEN and I. A. RICHARDS book, "*The Meaning of Meaning,*" as their "semantic triangle," symbol (word), reference (thought/concept), and object.

WILLARD VAN ORMAN QUINE thought he could escape ambiguities in meaning. In his book *Word and Object,* he urged the "naturalizing" of epistemology by focusing on the empirical connections made by speakers when they say what they mean. Favoring extensionality over intentionality, he said to look at how a speaker of another language shows what a word means, or how a baby learns the meaning of new words, by a process of behavioral conditioning and ostension (pointing at things). Quine said one may not be a behaviorist in psychology, but cannot avoid being a behaviorist in linguistics. But behaviorists are determinist and materialist.

Post-moderns like Derrida and ROLAND BARTHES showed that fundamental ambiguities of language cannot be removed, that the dictionary definitions summarizing the past uses in a community of discourse only trap meaning in a "circle of signifiers" without a referent object (s/Z). New uses are always being created, a consequence of our theory of humans as "co-creators" of our universe.

Are we then living in a Humpty Dumpty world of "When I use a word, it means just what I choose it to mean - neither more nor less." H. P. GRICE insisted that the *intentions* of the "utterer" are carrying the meaning. Or do we need to consider the "reader response" to any text, where meaning is generated by the reader and any supposed author intentions are deliberately ignored.

In CLAUDE SHANNON's theory of the communication of information, the emphasis is on the new information arriving at the receiver carried in the message from the sender. But Shannon never claimed the meaning was carried in the message itself. So it is with our information theory of meaning.

The information theory of meaning starts with the information model of the mind, which asserts that the *immaterial* mind *is* the abstract information being processed by the brain. The brain is a material information structure, which works as a biological information processor and experience recorder.[1]

The meaning in a message incoming to the mind (which could be just a perception of sensations from the environment and not

---

1   See appendix E on the experience recorder and reproducer.

necessarily words from another human being with intentions) is completely dependent on the past experiences of the agent that are brought to mind by the content of the message. This nicely captures the subjectivism or relativism of meaning, since it so greatly depends on the content of the individual's mind.

Our model for the mind also gets close to answering THOMAS NAGEL's provocative question *"What Is It Like To Be a Bat?"*[2] The past experiences reproduced by the ERR, complete with their feelings, depends on what has been recorded and what can be reproduced (played back). A frog cannot play back the experience of concave objects flying by, because the frog's eye has filtered them out, preventing them from reaching the frog's brain and its experience recorder.

The bat's current experiences are beyond human comprehension just because we lack the past experiences of what life has been like for a bat.

Meaning in the Theory of Information

Although Shannon's 1948 theory of the communication of information explicitly denied that it had anything to do with the meaning of the information communicated, other information theorists made efforts to connect abstract information with real objects, with their structural content, and even with concepts that humans use to "represent" objects and concepts.

DONALD MACKAY, R.A. FISHER, and DENNIS GABOR had independently made efforts before Shannon, just at the end of World War II, to define an "amount of information."[3]

Gabor suggested that a signal occupying an elementary area of $\Delta f\, \Delta t = 1$ could be regarded as a 'unit of information', which he termed a 'logon'. Multiplied by Planck's constant h, this corresponds to Heisenberg's minimum uncertainty in a physical measurement.

Fisher had proposed a measure of 'information' in a statistical sample, which in the simplest case amounted to the reciprocal of the variance. MacKay interpreted Fisher's measure as the "weight of evidence," proposing that for a probability of 1/2, it should be termed a "metron."

---

2   Mortal Questions, p.165
3   *Information, Mechanism, and Meaning*, pp. 4-5

Chapter 11

MacKay defined his "amount of information" as the number of yes/no questions that need to be answered to extract the information in a "representation," which he defined as a structure which has some abstract features in common with something else it purports to represent. This is very close to our definition of *intrinsic* information[4] and somewhat similar to the idea of "logical atomism" that knowledge is the total of true statements, if each provides one bit.

Of course, all these attempts to quantify *intrinsic* information scientifically do not get close to the meaning or *significance* that a Peircean *interpretant* may find in a perception or in a message, given the surrounding *context*, as ROMAN JAKOBSON said would be needed to add meaning to Shannon's theory.

We can use Shannon's famous diagram on the communication of information to integrate the thinking about meaning by many great philosophers, linguists, and literary critics.

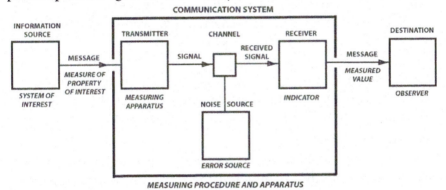

Figure 11-3. Claude Shannon's communication of informtion diagram.

To begin with, we must think of the above flow of information as another flow of negative entropy, the ultimate source of all value in the universe.[5] See appendix B on cosmic, solar, biological, and human entropy flows and the second law of thermodynamics.

We need to see Shannon's "information source" as a speaker or writer creating a new message that has more than just the generic meaning or "sense" that anyone familiar with the language would interpret in the message. It also carries the intentions of the message sender, which may or may not be clear to the receiver.

We must also interpret Shannon's destination and observer as something more than a communications device. It is an intelligent

---

4   See chapter 2 on identity as intrinsic information.
5   See chapter 5 on negative entropy as value.

agent who will find meaning in the message by *interpreting* it, drawing *inferences* from the message content and context, which includes knowing the sender and thus the sender's possible implications.

Edmund Husserl, perhaps following Franz Brentano, said meaning depends on the *intentions*, the implications, of a speaker. Among twentieth-century logicians, C.I. Lewis insisted that the meaning in logical implication must be more than the "material implication" that Russell, Wittgenstein, Carnap, and Quine saw in any "if p, then q" statement. In the *Principia Mathematica*, q is true even if the antecedent p is false and totally unrelated to the consequent q. This turns out to work well for mathematics and computer logic, but is bizarre and non-intuitive for human communications. Lewis insisted that "strict implication" would be intensional, not extensional. Quine fought Lewis and historically won the argument.

It was the greatest American logician, Charles Sanders Peirce, who stressed the role of the message receiver, whom Peirce called the *interpretant*. Post-modern literary critics have come to say all meaning in a text depends only on the receiver, the "reader-response" theory, but this clearly goes too far. Jacques Derrida's idea that the meaning of any word is diachronically deferred, his "*differance*," is actually quite insightful. We cannot discern the meaning until a message is complete.

Most logicians follow Gottlob Frege's distinction between the reference (denotation, name) and the sense (meaning) of a word. But few know that Frege limited the "sense" to the everyday meaning attached to a word by the users of the language. Frege also described the "idea" or "representation" (*Vorstellung*) that would form in the mind of the message receiver. This, he said, would be *different* in every mind, since it is dependent on the peculiar experiences of each person. This fits perfectly with our experience recorder and reproducer (ERR) as a model of mind, memory, and knowledge.

We revise Shannon's diagram to center the "message" between sender and receiver and also center it vertically between the context below (e.g, an object) and the concept (the idea) above.

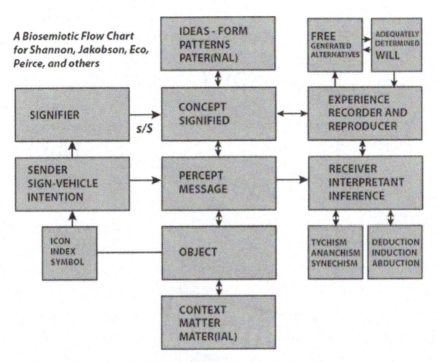

Figure 11-4.   Shannon's diagram enhanced with semiotic information flows.

This reflects our triad of worlds, material, biological, and ideal as well as Peirce's object, percept, and concept. The various flow arrows represent *recursive* paths in the complicated process of extracting meaning

Our information theory of meaning combines all three of Wittgenstein's theories - meaning as a *picture (Peirce's icon)*, meaning as *verification* (Peirce's *abduction*), and meaning as *use* (Peirce's *interpretant*). It is only weakly related to the logical empiricists (e.g., Carnap, Quine) who viewed the meaning of a word as the *extension* of things in the world of which the term is "true" (independent of any users) and to the modern logicians (e.g, Kripke and Putnam) who think meaning is found in the *necessity* of naming.[6]

They could at most get Frege's "sense," not ideas in minds,[7] which, as materialists, they dismissed as "psychological."

---

6   See chapter 2 on the metaphysics of necessity.
7   See chapter 12 on our information model of the mind.

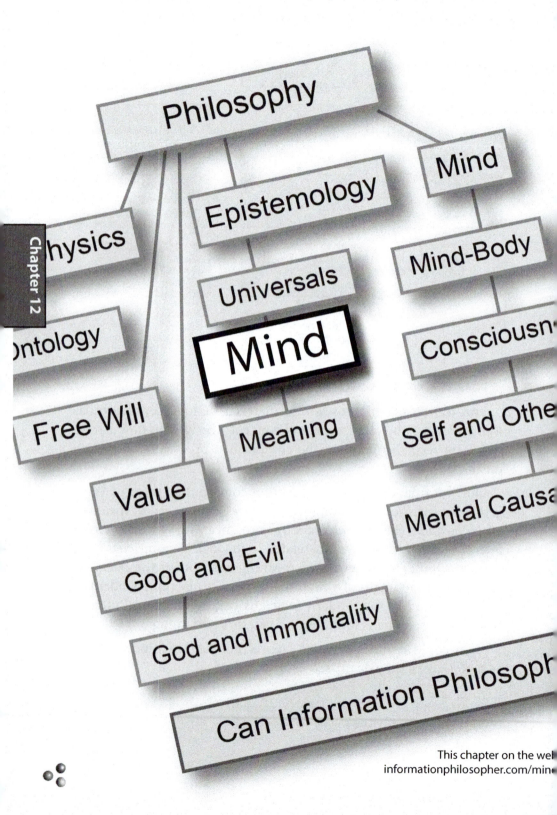

Mind

Of all the problems that information philosophy may help to solve, few are more important than the question of Mind. There is little in philosophy and science that is more dehumanizing than the logic chopping and sophistical word juggling that denies the existence of both mind and consciousness.

Some of the earliest philosophers saw an *immaterial* mind as the source of eternal truths about reality that could not be based on mere phenomena - unreliable sensations emanating from material bodies.

RENÉ DESCARTES' dualism left room for a non-mechanistic, *immaterial*, and *indeterministic* human mind above and beyond the deterministic limits set by the laws of nature, when the bodies of all animals are reduced to living machines.

IMMANUEL KANT renamed the ancient division of sensible and intelligible worlds. The sensible he called phenomena. He located God, freedom, and immortality in a noumenal world.

Information philosophy hopes to show that information is itself that immaterial "substance" above and beyond matter and energy that the ancients, Descartes, and Kant were all looking for. Mind is metaphysical, but not supernatural.

The Scandal in Psychology

It's a scandal that psychology today is a science without a subject - it has lost its mind! In the 19th century, positivism and materialism left the new science of psychology dis-spirited. In the 1920's psychology surrendered its soul to behaviorism. In the 1950's it gave up consciousness, when cognitive science found no "ghost in the machine." Since the 1970's it has been replaced by cognitive science and neuroscience.

Can there be a psychology without a psyche?

A survey of today's four leading textbooks on psychology finds only one that defines psychology as "the science of mind." Another has for its main index entry, "mind, theory of, see theory of mind. A third, has "mind, see brain," and the last has no entry at all under "mind." Today mind is a psychologist's taboo.

The assault on the mind and the study of mind by introspection was led by JOHN B. WATSON, who in the early twentieth century applied positivist ideas to psychology, reducing it to objectively possible observations and measurements of the motor behavior of animals and humans.

Like the positivists, Watson and later B. F. SKINNER, were materialists and determinists who not only ruled out the mind and consciousness, but also free will. Although behaviorism faded with the retirement of Skinner, the basic position of denying free will, consciousness, and mind continues as the fundamental stance of cognitive science and neuroscience.

The most popular representational theory of mind today is the computational mind model. Leading philosophers of mind claim to prove that the "causal closure" of the physical world reduces mental events to physical events. Eliminative materialism does not bother to say the mind is an epiphenomenon. Mental states simply do not exist. Consciousness cannot be explained. It is explained away.

It is a scandal today that some academic psychologists are convincing students that they are machines, their brains are computers, and their actions are completely determined.

Mind as *Immaterial* Information

Information philosophy views the mind as the immaterial information in a brain. The material brain is seen as a biological information processor. Mind is software in the brain's hardware, although it is altogether different from the logic gates, bit storage, algorithms, computations, and input/output systems of the type of digital computer that is used as a "computational model of mind" by today's cognitive scientists.

The "stuff" of thought is pure information, neither matter nor energy, though it needs matter for its embodiment and energy for its communication. Information is the modern spirit, the soul in the body, the ghost in the machine.

The Evolution of Information to Become Mind

How did material substances come to be able to think? Ancient philosophers assumed that mind and thought must be primordial, perhaps prior to the creation of matter. In recent centuries philosophers argued that mind must be an inherent "panpsychist" property of all matter, because they could not identify a time when material things acquired a mental property.

But we can now outline the creation and evolution of information from an initial state of the universe (with minimal, essentially zero information and the most elementary of particles and radiation) to the "information age" of today.

The first proto-minds appear not long after the beginnings of life. We identify the origin of life with the ability of some large molecules to replicate and communicate information so as to harness a cosmic flow of information-rich energy that we describe as negative entropy.

Information philosophy makes the straightforward claim that human beings, especially their minds, are the most highly evolved form of information generating, processing, and communicating system in the known universe. Recognizing this simple fact provides a radically new perspective on the central problems of psychology and philosophy of mind.

In a very deep sense, *we are information.*

The story of evolution, from a minimal information universe origin, through 4 billion years of biology, to the information-processing brain/mind, now contemplating the universe, can be told in three major emergences:

Chapter 12

- the self-organization of elementary matter, quarks to protons and neutrons etc., then atoms, then galaxies, stars, and planets, all material information structures,

- the first appearance of life, information structures that create, process, and communicate information inside an organism and between generations by variation, natural selection, and heredity,

- the appearance of human minds, which create, process, and store information external to their bodies.

With the appearance of life, purpose entered the universe. The fundamental purpose of all life is to survive, at least long enough to replicate. For most species, all of the information needed to survive is transmitted in the genes and the supporting biological machinery of the cell. To benefit from the experiences of an ancestor, those experiences must somehow be encoded genetically, so they show up as *a priori,* built-in capabilities of the offspring. KONRAD LORENZ said that what is *a priori* for an individual (ontogeny) was *a posteriori* for its ancestors (phylogeny).[1]

The appearance of human minds marks the beginning of significant amounts of knowledge stored extra-biologically. Externally stored information needed for human survival is transmitted culturally between the generations - parents teaching children. The development of the highest forms of philosophical and scientific thought would have been impossible without the externally stored information we call the *Sum.* Arguably, even language itself could not have developed. A child deprived of its senses for access to human culture would never speak. According to MERLIN DONALD, human culture did not develop because humans had acquired language to communicate. We developed language to improve on the primitive communication capabilities (grunting, miming, pointing, signing) of pre-linguistic humans.[2]

An Information Mind Model

Our model of mind as pure information coincides with Plato's "Ideas" or "Forms" as pure form, with an ontology different from that of matter. The *immaterial* Forms, seen by the intellect (nous), illuminated by the Good, allow us to understand the world. If this

---

1   *Evolution and Modification of Behavior.*
2   *A Mind So Rare.*

theory of mind seems *metaphysical*, that is appropriate, but we do not view the mind as non-physical. The mind is physical but it is not material.

After all, the information stored in our *experience recorder and reproducer* is embodied. Like the information embodied in matter, it corresponds simply to a reorganization of the matter. So we can also accept Aristotle's more practical view. For him, Plato's Ideas were mere abstractions generalized from many existent particulars. Form without matter is empty, matter without form is inconceivable, unimaginable. Kant rewrote this pre-Socratic observation somewhat obscurely as "Thoughts without content are empty, intuitions without concepts are blind."[3]

In our model of the mind, the great difference between the mental and the material is that the information in a material object is generally passive. The information in the mind is active, with real causal power.[4]

But there are other characteristic differences between the mental and the material world that modern science, even neuroscience, may never fully explain. The most important is the internal and private first-person point of view, the essential subjectivity, the "I" and the "eye" of the mind, its capability of introspection and reflection, its intentionality, its purposiveness, its consciousness. The mind records an individual's experiences as internal information structures in the ERR and then can play back these recordings to compare them to new perceptions, new external events. The recordings include an individual's emotional reactions to past experiences, our feelings. The reproduction of recorded personal experiences, stimulated by similarities in current experience, provide the core of "what it's like to be" an individual.

The external and public physical world, by contrast, is studied from the third-person point of view. Although putatively "objective," science in fact is the composite "intersubjective" view of the "community of inquirers," as Charles Sanders Peirce put it. Although this shared subjectivity can never directly experience what goes on in the mind of an individual member of the community, science is in some sense the collective mind of the physical world. It is a pale record of the world's experiences, because it lacks the emo-

---

3   *Critique of Pure Reason*, 2nd ed. Second Part, I, Transcendental Logic,
4   See the discussion of agent causality in chapter 4.

tional aspect of personal experience. The physical world itself has no sense of its history. It does not introspect or reflect. It lacks consciousness, that problem in philosophy of mind second only to the basic mind-body problem itself. We see consciousness as based on a highly evolved experience recorder and reproducer (ERR) that even the lowest organisms may have.

Aristotle, in his Book III, Parts IV and V, of *De Anima* (On the Soul), perhaps the most controversial and confusing part of his entire corpus, says that the soul (psyche) or mind is *immaterial*. He was right. For Aristotle, Intellect (*nous*) is that part of the soul whose active thinking gives it a causal (*aition*) power (*dynamis*) over the material (*hyle*) body (*soma*). This claim anticipates the mind-body problem of RENÉ DESCARTES. How exactly does an immaterial thing (substance) or property exert a causal force on the material body?

It is sometimes forgotten that Descartes made the mind the locus of undetermined freedom. For him, the body is a deterministic mechanical system of tiny fibres causing movements in the brain (the afferent sensations), which then can pull on other fibres to activate the muscles (the efferent nerve impulses). This is the basis of stimulus and response theory in modern physiology (reflexology). It is also the basis behind connectionist mind models. An appropriate network need only connect the afferent to the efferent signals. Descartes said no thinking mind is needed for animals (or computers where inputs completely determine outputs).

The popular idea of animals as machines included the notion that man too is in part a machine - the human body is thought to obey strictly deterministic causal laws. But for Descartes man also has a soul or spirit that is exempt from determinism and thus from what is known today as "causal closure." But how, we must ask, can the mind both cause something physical to happen and yet itself be *acausal*, exempt from causal chains? This is the problem of mental causation.[5]

Since IMMANUEL KANT, this problem has become even more severe. The freedom in Kant's noumenal world - outside space and time - has no apparent connection with his deterministic phenomenal world. For Kant, causality is a category of understanding applicable only to the phenomenal world. In a similar vein, the twenti-

---

5   See chapter 16.

eth-century philosopher GILBERT RYLE called the concept of mind a "category mistake."[6]

Information philosophy hopes to solve the mind/body problem, the "hard problem" of consciousness, the problem of other minds, and the problem of mental causation, not by postulating a non-physical world, but instead a world that answers to the ancient description of "*metaphysical*," because it is non-material. This metaphysical world is the locus of everything Aristotle included in his first philosophy, the laws of thought and today the laws of physics.

The *metaphysical* world of information is abstract, not concrete, intangible, yet with causal power as Aristotle thought. The material world is made up in part of information structures. (We shall see that most of the matter in the universe is chaotic and contains little or no information.) But material information structures, from the galaxies, stars, and planets, to all of life on the planet, can be perceived because of their information content. What we see is their abstract information which we then re-present as information structures in the mind/brain. To the extent that the information in the mind is isomorphic with the information in the object, we can say that a subject has knowledge of the external world. To the extent that information in other minds is isomorphic, we have intersubjective shared knowledge, something very difficult to show with words or logic alone.

Information philosophy goes "beyond logic and language."

---

6   *The Concept of Mind.*

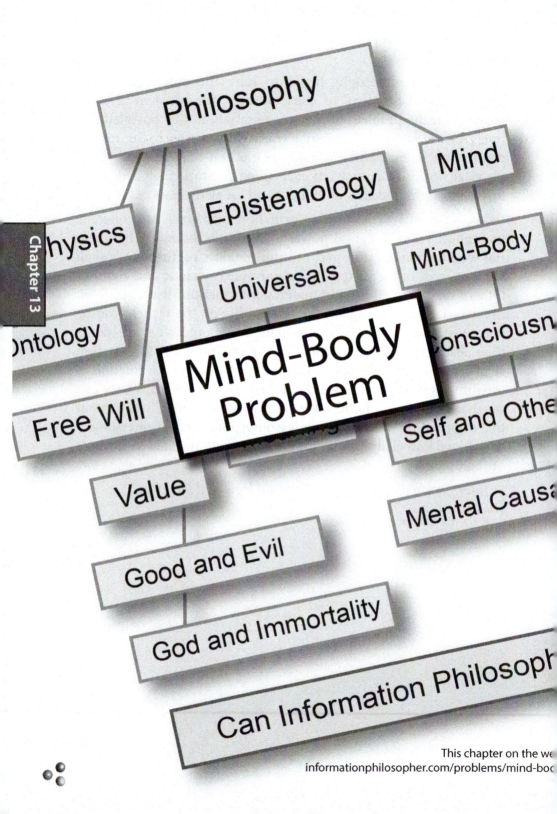

This chapter on the we
informationphilosopher.com/problems/mind-bod

The Mind-Body Problem

Information philosophy views the mind as the *immaterial* information in the brain, which is seen as a biological information processor. Mind is software in the brain's hardware.

The "stuff" of thought is pure information. Information is neither matter nor energy, though it needs matter for its embodiment and energy for its communication.

In ancient philosophy, mind and body formed one of the classic dualisms,[1] like idealism versus materialism, the problem of the one (monism) or the many (pluralism), the distinction between essence and existence, between universals and particulars, between the eternal and the ephemeral.

When mind and body are viewed today as a dualism, it is because the mind is considered to be fundamentally different from the material brain, though perhaps not another "substance." We propose an easily understandable and critically important physical difference between matter and *immaterial* information. Whereas the total amount of matter is conserved, the universe is continuously creating new information - by rearranging existing matter into new information structures. The total amount of information (a kind of order) in the universe is increasing, despite the second law of thermodynamics, which requires that the total amount of disorder (entropy) is also increasing.[2]

Matter, along with energy (mc^2), cannot increase. It is conserved, a constant of the universe. Information is not conserved. As information grows, it is the source of genuine novelty in the universe. The future is not determined by the past and present, because the future contains unpredictable new information. New information is continuously created.

If mind and matter then are to be considered part of a dualism, it will not be a "material substance" dualism, but it can still be a "physical substance" dualism, since mind and matter are both physical and are "substantial," in the sense of having real causal

---

1   See chapter 3 for more on dualisms.
2   See appendices A and B for how this is possible.

power. We recognize that something *immaterial* with causal power also fits the description of *metaphysical*. See chapter 2 on metaphysics.

A mind-body dualism coincides with Plato's "ideas" as pure form, distinct from matter. The ontology and the nature of an idea is different from that of matter. The ancients asked about the existential status of Platonic Ideas. On the other hand, monists may see both mind and body as pure physicalism, since information embodied in matter corresponds to a mere reorganization of the matter. This was Aristotle's more practical view. For him, Plato's Ideas were mere abstractions generalized from many existent particulars.

Mind-body as a "problem" is generally traced to RENÉ DESCARTES, who asked how the *immaterial* mind (or soul) could influence the material body. Would not the interaction between the two have to partake somehow of the character of both? Descartes famously identified the tiny pineal gland as the point of contact between mind and body.

Importantly, Descartes also made the mind the locus of *freedom*. He saw the body as a mechanical system of tiny fibres causing movements in the brain (the afferent sensations), which then can pull on other fibres to activate the muscles (the efferent nerve impulses). This is the basis of stimulus and response theory in modern physiology(reflexology).

The popular idea of animals as machines included the notion that man too is a machine - the body obeys strictly deterministic causal laws - but that man has a soul or spirit that is exempt from determinism and thus from what is known today as "causal closure." But how can the mind both cause something physical to happen and yet itself be exempt from causal chains?

Interactionists

In modern times some philosophers and scientists have proposed interactionist models and have also attempted to locate specific parts of the brain (beyond Descartes' pineal gland), for example at the synapses between neurons, where quantum effects might be important. The neuroscientist JOHN ECCLES and philosopher KARL POPPER considered such models in their articles and books over many years.

Attempts to use the mysterious properties of quantum mechanics to explain the mysterious problems of consciousness and psycho-physical relations between mind and body have resolved little, since they explain one mystery with another mystery.

Information philosophy identifies the (immaterial) mind with the incredible biological information processing going on in the brain. This processing operates on two levels.

At the macro level, the mind/brain is adequately determined to make its decisions and resulting actions in ways that are causally connected with the agent's character and values. It is everything that determinist and compatibilist philosophers expect it to be.

At the micro level, the mind/brain leaves itself open to significant thermal and quantal noise in its retrieval of past experiences. This generates creative and unpredictable alternative possibilities for thought and action. This is our best hope for a measure of libertarianism.

Our mind/brain model emphasizes the abstract information content of the mind. Information is neither matter nor energy, yet it needs matter for its concrete embodiment and energy for its communication. Information is the modern spirit, the ghost in the machine.

Because it is *embodied* in the brain, this mind can control the actions of a body that is macroscopic and is normally unaffected by its own quantum level uncertainty (excepting when we want to be creative and unpredictable.

Thus our mind-body model explains how an *immaterial*, "free," unpredictable, and creative mind can control the adequately determined material body through the self-determinate and responsible actions selected by the will from an agenda of alternative possibilities.

Moreover, since some "mental events" are large enough informa-tion structures to be adequately determined, these mental events can act causally on lower biological and physical levels in the hierar-chy, in particular, the mind can move the body and all its contained physical particles, thus solving the mind-body problem.

A specific example of the mind causing an action, while not itself being caused by antecedent events is the following. Faced with a decision of what to do next, the mind considers several possible alternatives, at least some of which are creatively invented based on random ideas that just "come to mind." Other possible alternatives might be familiar options, even habits, that have frequently been done in earlier similar situations.

Some of these mental alternatives are *new information* that show up as "neural correlates" - brain neurons firing. When the alterna-tives are evaluated and one is selected, the selected action results in still other neurons firing, some of which connect to the motor cortex that signals muscles to move the body.

Apart from the occasional indeterministic generation of new information in the creative new alternative ideas, this whole causal process is adequately determined and it is downwardly causal. Mental events are causing physical body events.

The Mind-Brain Identity Theory

In the mid-twentieth century a number of philosophers proposed a monistic and physicalistic solution to the mind-body problem by simply identifying the mind and brain as one physical thing, subject to the normal laws of physics.

Holistic critics attacked this view as reducing the mind to the brain, leaving the mind merely an epiphenomenon or illusion. This fit well into the reductionist program of the logical empiricists of the Vienna Circle, who promoted the idea of the Unity of Science. All events should be reducible to physical events, and in particular, all explanations should be traceable to causes originating in the physi-cal material components of the universe.

The first philosophers to argue for an identity of mind (or consciousness) and brain include ULLIN T. PLACE, HERBERT FEIGL, and J.J.C.SMART (1959).

Place explicitly describes "consciousness as a brain process," specifically as "patterns" of brain activity. He does not trivialize this identity as a succession of individual "mental events and physical events" in some kind of causal chain. He compares this identity to the idea that "lightning is a motion of electrical charges."[3]

Feigl's work was independent of Place's, but he said that the fundamental idea had been held by many earlier materialist (monist) thinkers. He thought it was stated clearly by Vienna Circle philosopher RUDOLF CARNAP in 1925. Feigl describes his own thesis:

> The identity thesis which I wish to clarify and to defend asserts that the states of direct experience which conscious beings "live through" and those which we confidently ascribe to some of the higher animals, are identical with certain (presumably configurational) aspects of the neural processes in these organisms.[4]

Smart clarified and extended the identity theory of Place.

> When I say that a sensation is a brain process or that lightning is an electric discharge, I am using "is" in the sense of strict identity. (Just as in the — in this case necessary — proposition "7 is identical with the smallest prime number greater than 5.") When I say that a sensation is a brain process or that lightning is an electric discharge I do not mean just that the sensation is somehow spatially or temporally continuous with the brain process or that the lightning is just spatially or temporally continuous with the discharge.[5]

Smart is a strong materialist. He says "A man is a vast arrangement of physical particles, but there are not, over and above this, sensations or states of consciousness." (*ibid.*) Compare ANTHONY CASHMORE, who says in the *Proceedings of the National Academy of Sciences* that we are "just a bag of chemicals."[6]

Eliminative Materialism

Philosophers who accept the idea that all laws of nature are deterministic and that the world is causally closed still cannot under-

---

3   *British Journal of Psychology,* 47, pp.44-50 1956
4   *Concepts, Theories, and the Mind-Body Problem* , Feigl, 1958, p.150
5   *Philosophical Review,* 68 pp.141-156 (1959)
6   *PNAS,* vol. 107, no. 10, p. 4500

stand how an immaterial mind can be the cause of an action. On this view, every physical event is reducible to the microscopic motions of physical particles. The laws of biology are reducible to those of physics and chemistry. The mind is reducible to the brain, with no remainder.

These philosophers of mind are content to simply eliminate the mind. *Psychology without a psyche!*

For these philosophers of mind, essentially no progress has been made on the mind-body problem since Descartes. "Reductionists" who accept "causal closure" think that every brain event must have been determined by causes coming "bottom-up" from the brain's atoms and molecules. Any additional mental cause should be excluded, according to JAEGWON KIM.

Since the early twentieth century, quantum mechanics adds the possibility that some processes are indeterministic, but random quantum-mechanical events have generally been thought to be unhelpful by philosophers of mind. Adding indeterminism to mental events apparently would only make our actions random and our desires the product of pure chance. If our willed actions are not determined by anything, they say, we are neither morally responsible nor truly free. Whether mental events are reducible to physical events, or whether mental events can be physical events without such a reduction, the interposition of indeterministic quantum processes apparently adds no explanatory power. And of course if mental events are epiphenomenal, they are not causally related to bodily actions. Epiphenomenal access to quantum physics would not help.

Mental causation is a special case of the more general problem of downward causation, for example the downward control of the motions of a cell's atoms and molecules by supervening biological macromolecules. Is the molecular biology of a cell reducible to the laws governing the motions of its component molecules, or are there emergent laws governing motions at the cellular level, still different laws at the organ level, at the organism level up to the mental level?

Emergent properties or laws at the higher levels of a physical-chemical-based biological system would have to prevent those higher levels from being reduced to the properties and laws of the base physical level? These emergent properties are not a new kind of "stuff," but they are nevertheless often described as an emergent dualism, specifically a property dualism.

Is it illogical to deny reductionist ideas of bottom-up causation (because of indeterministic quantum noise) and yet to defend adequately determined downward causation (because quantum effects are averaged out by macroscopic objects)? The arguments are subtle and depend on the complementary roles of determinism (Schrödinger evolution of the wave function) and indeterminism (wave-function collapse) in quantum physics.

Perhaps the most critically important emergent law of all is the abstract idea of determinism itself. Determinism in the macroscopic world emerges from the indeterministic microscopic quantum world by averaging over vast numbers of atoms and molecules. Even before quantum mechanics, LUDWIG BOLTZMANN knew that the macroscopic gas laws were only adequately or statistically determined by the average motions of extremely large numbers of molecules.

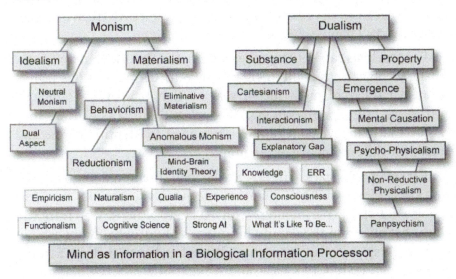

Figure 13-5. A taxonomy of philosophy of mind positions.

Idealism claims that all is mind, perhaps a Western panpsychism or Eastern philosopical ideas like Advaita Vedanta or Mahayana Buddhism? The neutral monism of WILLIAM JAMES, ERNST MACH, and BERTRAND RUSSELL is closely related to CARL JUNG's "dual-aspect" monism. They are looking for a basic underlying substance.

BARUCH SPINOZA claimed mind and body are one ontological substance. The mind-brain identity theory of HERBERT FEIGL, J. J. C. SMART, and U. T. PLACE is a materialism and an epiphenomenalism. DANIEL DENNETT, the CHURCHLANDS (Paul and Patricia), FRANCIS CRICK, CHRISTOF KOCH, and JAEGWON KIM are eliminative materialists.

DONALD DAVIDSON's anomalous monism may be a non-reductive physicalism? Property dualisms assume just one substance, so are in a sense monistic. KARL POPPER and JOHN ECCLES' interactionism and JOSEPH LEVINE's "explanatory gap" are modern forms of Cartesianism.

GOTTLIEB LEIBNIZ's pre-established harmony is psycho-physicalism or psycho-physical parallelism. It denies interactionism, which remains unexplained. In later years, Leibniz' monadology leaned toward a monism. Occasionalists are parallelists who say God creates an interaction when needed. GALEN STRAWSON's realistic physicalism or "realistic monism" resembles ARTHUR STANLEY EDDINGTON's panpsychism.

Panpsychists can hold that there is a material world, but that every material object has some mentality. DAVID CHALMERS has leaned toward panpsychism in recent years. Other panpsychists include MICHAEL LOCKWOOD, WILLIAM LYCAN, and THOMAS NAGEL. They argue that panpsychism removes the need to identify a time and place for the emergence of the mind.

For over 20 years, HENRY STAPP has attempted to reconcile WERNER HEISENBERG's quantum mechanics, especially the "free choice" of the experimenter, with ALFRED NORTH WHITEHEAD's idea that quantum theory and his process philosophy might explain panpsychism. Today "Quantum Whiteheadians" include STUART HAMEROFF, ROGER PENROSE, and ABNER SHIMONY.

Non-reductive physicalism is an emergent dualism in which mental events are physical and have causal powers over brain events and the material body.

The information philosophy mind model is a dualist non-reductive physicalism. The mind is physical, but immaterial. Thoughts have causal powers because they are considered as freely generated alternative possibilities for actions by a will that is adequately determined by the agent's reasons, motives, desires, feelings, etc. - in short, by the agent's character.

Mind/Body and the ERR

As opposed to the philosophers above who *identify* the mind with the brain, we look to those philosophers and scientists such as Popper and Eccles who have proposed interactionist models and have also attempted to locate specific parts of the brain, for example at the synapses between neurons, where quantum effects might be important.

But all the attempts to use the mysterious properties of quantum mechanics to explain the mysterious problems of consciousness and psycho-physical relations between mind and body have been just that, explaining one mystery with another mystery.

Information philosophy identifies the *immaterial* mind with the incredible biological information processing going on in the brain. What we might call pre-processing is happening in the experience *recorder*, which is growing new synapses in the brain where neurons have fired in response to current experiences.

Abstract information, the stuff of the mind, is being *embodied* in those newly wired neurons.

What we might call post-processing is when the experience *reproducer* is stimulated to generate those older patterns of information that most resemble current experience, because they lie in nearby neurons of the brain.

Reproducing information is likely to be very noisy and thus the source of genuinely new *alternative possibilities*.

The experience recorder and reproducer (ERR) is both mind and body, both information and its embodiment. Although the ERR implements both levels, it does not make them *identical*.

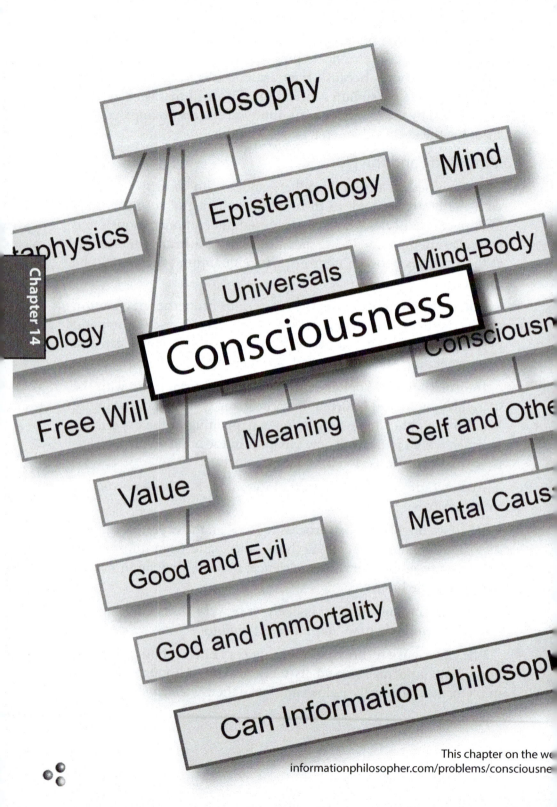

Consciousness

Consciousness can be defined in information terms as a property of an entity (usually a living thing but we can also include artificially conscious machines or computers) that interacts with the information (especially reacting to any changes in the information) in its environment and in itself.

We can define this as *information consciousness*.

Thus an animal in a deep sleep is not conscious because it ignores changes in its environment. And robots may be conscious in our sense. Artificial intelligence normally has artificial consciousness in our sense. Even the lowliest control system using negative feedback (a thermostat, for example) is in a minimal sense conscious of (aware of, exchanging information about) changes in its environment.

This definition of consciousness fits with our model of the mind as an experience recorder and reproducer (ERR).[1] The ERR model stands in contrast to the popular cognitive science or "computational" model of a mind as a digital computer or connectionist neural network modeled with logic gates. No algorithms or stored programs are needed for the ERR model, although we do see mind as software in the brain hardware.

Our consciousness model assumes that neurons that get wired together during an organism's experiences, in multiple sensory and limbic systems, are such that later firing of even a part of those wired neurons (caused by a new experience that resembles an original experience in one or more ways) can stimulate firing of all or part of the original complex.

If the neural correlate of consciousness is neurons firing, firing them again can *reproduce* consciousness of the past.

Whereas DONALD HEBB famously argued that "neurons that fire together wire together," our experience recorder and reproducer (ERR) model assumes that "neurons that *have been wired together* will fire together."

---

1   See appendix E for details.

Chapter 14

The Binding Problem

Neuroscientists are investigating how diverse signals from multiple pathways can be unified in the brain. The ERR offers a very simple and specific insight into this "binding" problem. We also hope to shed some light on the question of philosophical "meaning"[2] of any given information structure, beyond the obvious relevance (survival value) for the organism of remembering past experiences.

There is a great deal of controversy about whether most living things have some form of consciousness. Defining consciousness as interactions, with exchanges of meaningful information, especially exchanges that involve coding and decoding and translations between symbolic systems, may allow applications to biological subsystems like organs and organelles.

A higher-level conscious being is constantly recording information about its perceptions of the external world, and most importantly for ERR, it is simultaneously recording its feelings. Sensory data such as sights, sounds, smells, tastes, and tactile sensations are recorded in a sequence along with pleasure and pain states, fear and comfort levels, etc.

All these experiential and emotional data are recorded in association with one another. This means that when the experiences are reproduced (played back in a temporal sequence), the accompanying emotions are once again felt, in synchronization.

The capability of reproducing experiences is critical to learning from past experiences, so as to make them guides for action in future experiences. We see the ERR model as the *minimal mind model* that provides for such learning by living organisms.

The ERR model does not need a single "central processor unit" (CPU) or even several "parallel processors." It does not use computer-like "data retrieval," based on the "address" of the data, to reproduce past experiences. All that is required is that past experiences "play back" (are reproduced) whenever they are stimulated by present experiences that resemble the past experiences in one or more ways. When the organism repeats past experiences by acting them out, they can become "habitual" behaviors, "subconscious" information structures.

---

2   See chapter 11.

It is critical that the original emotions also play back, along with any variations in current emotions that are experienced on playback. ERR might then become an explanatory basis for conditioning experiments, classical Pavlovian and operant conditioning, and in general a model for associative learning.

Bernard Baars's Global Workspace Theory uses the metaphor of a "Theater of Consciousness," in which there is an audience of purposeful agents calling for the attention of the executive on stage.[3]

In the ERR model, vast numbers of past experiences clamor for the attention of the central executive at all times, whenever anything in current experience has some resemblance.

If we define "current experience" as all afferent perceptions plus the current contents of consciousness itself, we get a dynamic self-referential system with plenty of opportunities for negative and positive feedback.

William James's description of a "stream of consciousness" together with a "blooming, buzzing confusion" of the unconscious appear to describe the ERR model very well.

In the "blackboard" model of Allan Newell and Herbert Simon, concepts written on the blackboard call up similar concepts by association from deep memory structures. The ERR model supports this view, and explains the mechanism by which concepts (past experiences) are retrieved and come to the blackboard.

In Daniel Dennett's consciousness model, the mind is made up of innumerable functional homunculi, each with its own goals and purposes. His mind architecture is an amalgam of ideas like Marvin Minsky's *Society of Mind*, Baars' Global Workspace, and the Simon-Newell "Blackboard."

Dennett says

> "There is no single, definitive "stream of consciousness," because there is no central Headquarters, no Cartesian Theater where 'it all comes together' for the perusal of a Central Meaner. Instead of such a single stream (however wide) there are multiple channels in which specialist circuits try, in parallel pandemoniums, to do their various things, creating Multiple Drafts as they go." [4]

---

3   In the Theater of Consciousness.
4   *Consciousness Explained*, p.253.

Dennett describes the "binding problem" as a "single representational space in the brain" where the various results come together.[5] In our consciousness model, the playback of all the combined sensations of a past experience fire exactly the same neurons wherever they were originally recorded, anywhere in the entire cortex, including the association areas, for example.

Dennett says the idea has been around for several years that human consciousness might be the activity of some sort of serial virtual machine implemented on the parallel hardware of the brain.[6]

But our consciousness model is not a machine at all. It is simply the idea that whatever we are aware of at any moment is stimulating the firing of the complex network of neurons that were wired together in many similar past moments, giving the current moment a vast collection of contextual references that supply the information needed for interpretation.

Like Dennett's model, there is no Cartesian Theater for a "Central Meaner." In the ERR as mind model, we expect the mind would interpret the new firing of multiply connected neurons coming from visual, auditory, olfactory, tactile areas, as reproducing the original experience (much more than a simple memory). These are likely pale shadows, mere "gists" of the original conscious experience, and likely very noise-susceptible, but they provide context, meaning, and emotional reactions to past actions.

David Chalmers is a philosopher of mind whose characterization of consciousness as "the hard problem" has set a very high bar for understanding the mind. Chalmers describes his position as a naturalistic dualism. Chalmers says that the failure of supervenience implies that materialism - as a monistic theory of the complete contents of the world, that there is "nothing but" matter, and that the world is "causally closed," for example - is "false." We agree with this and believe that the reductionist arguments of Jaegwon Kim can be shown wrong. Chalmers says:

Chapter 14

---

5   *ibid,,* p.254.
6   *ibid,* p.258.

In our world, there are conscious experiences.

There is a logically possible world physically identical to ours, in which the positive facts about consciousness in our world do not hold.

Therefore, facts about consciousness are further facts about our world, over and above the physical facts.

So materialism is false.[7]

Chalmers suggests that the dualistic (non-physical) element might be information. Indeed it might. With this idea, information philosophy completely agrees. Mind/body is a property dualism

Chalmers says that "physical realization is the most common way to think about information embedded in the world, but it is not the only way information can be found. We can also find information realized in our phenomenology."[8]

He is quite correct. Information is neither matter nor energy. It needs matter to be embedded temporarily in the brain. And it needs energy to be communicated. But information is *immaterial.*

Four "Levels" of Consciousness

• *Instinctive Consciousness* - by animals with little or no learning capability. Automatic reactions to environmental conditions are transmitted genetically. Information about past experiences (by prior generations of the organism) is only present implicitly in the inherited reactions

• *Learned Consciousness* - for animals whose past experiences guide current choices. Conscious, but mostly habitual, reactions are developed through experience, including instruction by parents and peers.

• *Predictive Consciousness* - The Sequencer in the ERR system can play back beyond the current situation, allowing the organism to use imagination and foresight to evaluate the future consequences of its choices.

• *Reflective (Normative) Consciousness*– in which conscious deliberation about values influences the choice of behaviors.

All four levels are emergent, in the sense that they did not exist in the lower, earlier levels of biological evolution.

---

7 *The Conscious Mind*, p.123

8 *ibid.* p.284

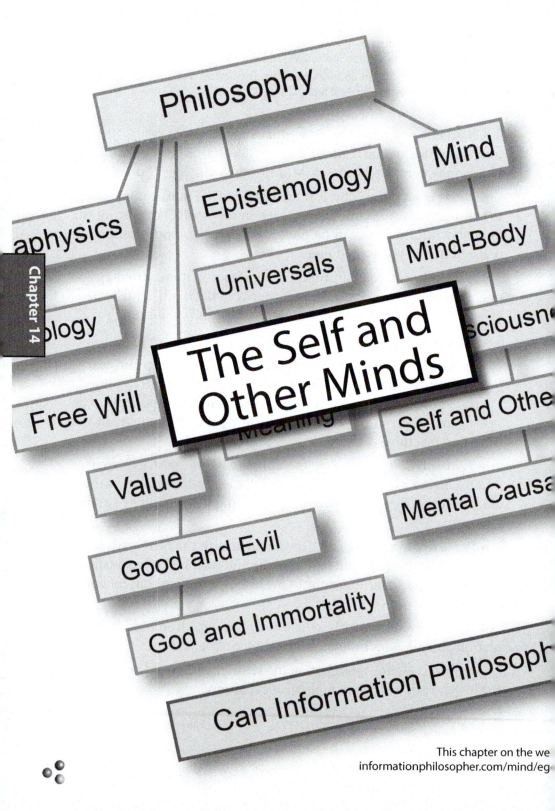

Philosophy

Mind

Epistemology

Chapter 14

aphysics

Mind-Body

Universals

ology

sciousn

The Self and
Other Minds

Free Will

Self and Othe

Meaning

Value

Mental Causa

Good and Evil

God and Immortality

Can Information Philosoph

The Self and Other Minds

Celebrating René Descartes, the first modern philosopher, and his famous phrase *Ego cogito, ergo sum*, we call our model for mind the *Ego*. It is implemented with our *experience recorder and reproducer* (ERR).

Our two-stage model for free will we call the *Cogito*. Our model for an objective value, independent of humanity and earthly bio-ethics, we call *Ergo*. And our model for knowledge we call the *Sum*.

The *Ego* is more or less synonymous with the Self, the Soul, or the Spirit - Gilbert Ryle's "ghost in the machine." We see it as *immaterial* information. An immaterial self with causal power is almost universally denied by modern philosophers as *metaphysical*, along with related problematic ideas such as consciousness and libertarian or indeterministic free will.

Descartes illustrated a mechanical reflex path, from a foot feeling pain from a fire, up a nerve to the pineal gland in the *mind*, and back down to pull away the foot.

It is important to note that Descartes made that gland the locus of *undetermined* freedom in humans. For him, the *body* was a deterministic mechanical system of tiny fibres causing movements in the brain (the afferent sensations), which then can pull on other fibres to activate the muscles (the efferent nerve impulses). This is the basis of stimulus and response theory in modern physiology (reflexology). It is also the basis behind simple connectionist theories of mind. An appropriate neural

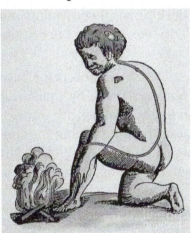

Figure 15-6. Descartes' reflex arc.

network (with all the necessary logical connections) need only connect afferent to efferent signals. No thinking mind is needed for animals. This "reflex arc" model is still common in biology.

Descartes' suggestion that animals are machines included the notion that man too is in part a machine - the human body obeys deterministic causal laws. Although for Descartes man also has a soul or spirit that is exempt from determinism and thus from what is known today as "causal closure," Cartesian dualism was the first step to eliminative materialism.

Mind Over Matter?

But as all critics of Descartes do, we must ask, how can the mind both cause something physical to happen and yet itself be *acausal*,? How is it exempt from causal chains coming up from the body?

Descartes' vision of undetermined freedom for the mind is realized since our *immaterial* thoughts are free, whereas our actions are adequately determined by our will. This combination of ideas is the basis for our *two-stage model* of free will.[1] It is a model of *agent causation*. New causal chains originate as ideas in our minds. Once evaluated and chosen they are adequately determined to lead to willed actions. This is a model for *self-determination*.

The "self" or ego, the psyche or soul, is the self of this self-determination. Self-determination is of course limited by our control over matter and energy, but within those physical constraints our selves can consider ideas, decide to act on one and take full responsibility for our actions.

The Self is often identified with one's "character." This is the basis for saying that our choices and decisions are made by evaluating freely generated *alternative possibilities* in accordance with our reasons, motives, feelings, desires, etc. These are in turn often the consequence of our past experiences, along with inherited (biologically built-in) preferences. And this bundle of motivating factors is essentially what is known as our character. Someone familiar with all of those preferences would be able to predict our actions with some certainty, though not perfectly, when faced with particular options and the circumstances. The self is the agent that is responsible for those actions.

---

1   See chapter 4.

The self is also often described as the seat of *consciousness*. Information philosophy defines consciousness as attention to information coming in to the mind and the resulting actions that are responsive to the external stimuli (or bodily proprioceptions). Consciousness thus depends in part on past experiences which are recalled by the experience recorder and reproducer as responses to external stimuli. In this way, what it's like to be a conscious agent depends on the kinds of experiences that the agent can notice.

DAVID HUME's so-called "bundle theory" of the self is quite consistent with the information philosophy view. His fundamental ideas of causality, contiguity, and resemblance as the basis for the association of ideas are essential aspects of the experience recorder and reproducer. He said,

> It is plain, that in the course of our thinking, and in the constant revolution of our ideas, our imagination runs easily from one idea to any other that resembles it, and that this quality alone is to the fancy a sufficient bond and association. It is likewise evident that as the senses, in changing their objects, are necessitated to change them regularly, and take them as they lie contiguous to each other, the imagination must by long custom acquire the same method of thinking, and run along the parts of space and time in conceiving its objects.[2]

The frog's eye famously filters out some visual events (moving concave images) while triggering strong reactions to others, like sticking out a tongue to capture moving convex objects. What it's like to be a frog depends then on some experiences that are never recorded and thus not meaningful to the frog. Hume might say such perceptions have no resemblance to anything in the mind of the frog. The frog's self is simply not conscious of any sensations that are filtered out of its perceptions.

The Problem of Other Minds

The problem of other minds is often posed as just one more problem in epistemology, that is, how can we be certain about the existence of other minds, since we can't be certain about anything in the external world. But it can also be seen as a problem about meaningful communications and agreement about shared concepts in two minds. This makes information philosophy an excellent tool for approaching the problem.

---

2   *A Treatise of Human Nature.* 4.1, 2

For some philosophers, the problem of other minds is dis-solved by denying the existence of the mind in general - as merely an epiphenomenon with no causal powers. Other philosophers identify the problem with Hume's claim that when he looked inside he saw no self. Our positing the self as the immaterial information about stored past experiences clearly helps here.

Still others admit that they have perceptions and sensations, but how could they possibly know what another person is experiencing. For example, I know when I feel pain, but I don't know what is really happening in another person who looks to be feeling pain.

The standard answer here is that other persons seem in most respect to be similar to ourselves, and so by analogy their experiences must be similar to ours. This analogical inference is weak because of its literal superficiality, because we don't get an inside view of the other mind.

For information philosophy, the problem of knowledge can solved by identifying partial isomorphisms in external information structures with the pure information in a mind. This suggests the solution of other minds. Looked at this way, the problem of other minds is easier to solve than the general epistemological problem. The general problem must compare different things, the pure information of mental ideas with the information abstracted from concrete external information structures. The problem of other minds compares concepts in minds about similar things.

When, by interpersonal communications, we compare the pure information content in two different minds, we are reaching directly into the other mind in its innermost immaterial nature. To be sure, we have not felt the same sensations nor had identical experiences. We have not "felt the other's pain." But we can plant ideas in the other mind, and then watch those ideas alter the other person's actions in a way totally identical to what that information, that knowledge, has been used for in our own actions.

This establishes the existence, behind the external bodily (material) behaviors of the other person, of the same *immaterial*, metaphysical mind model in the other mind, as the one in our own.

CHARLES SANDERS PEIRCE offered us a vision of an open "community of inquirers," seeking "intersubjective agreement" to find common ground, common ideas, and common information structures that are processing information in similar if not identical ways.

The very first item of intersubjective agreement in that community should be to accept the existence of minds in all the members of the community.

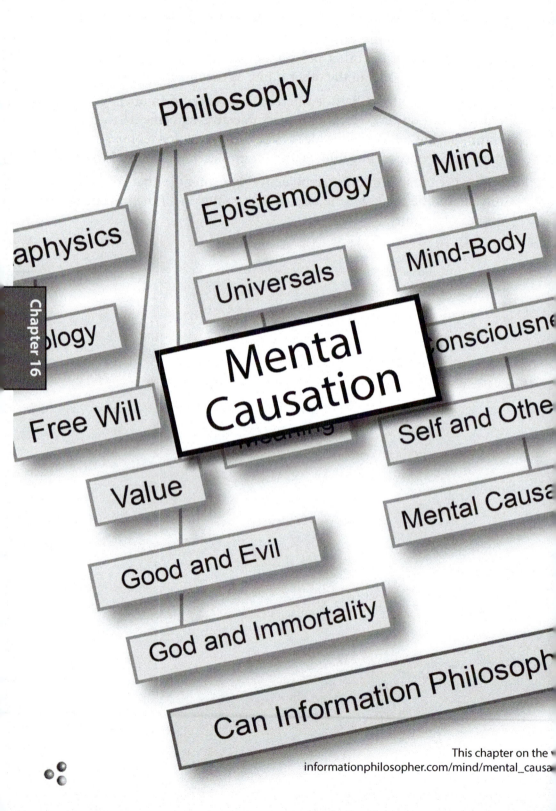

Chapter 16

Philosophy

Mind

Epistemology

...aphysics

Mind-Body

Universals

...logy

Mental
Causation

...consciousne...

Free Will

Self and Othe...

Value

Mental Causa...

Good and Evil

God and Immortality

Can Information Philosoph...

This chapter on the ...
informationphilosopher.com/mind/mental_causa...

Mental Causation

The Problem of Mental Causation is a major problem in the Philosophy of Mind. It has been with us at least since RENÉ DESCARTES claimed that mind and body are separate substances. If the body is material, how can an immaterial mind possibly act on the body. More importantly, how can a "mental" action or event in the mind be the cause of a physical action by the body?

Mental causation is a specific case of the more general problem of *downward causation*, for example the downward control of the motions of a cell's atoms and molecules by supervening biological macromolecules. Is the molecular biology of a cell reducible to the laws governing the motions of its component molecules, or are there *emergent* laws governing motions at the cellular level, the organ level, the organism level, and so on up to the mental level?

Can emergent properties or laws at the higher levels of a physical-chemical-based biological system prevent those higher levels from being reduced to the properties and laws of the base physical level?[1]

In the 1960's the neuroscientist ROGER SPERRY claimed that higher levels in a hierarchy could act causally on the base level. He cited a wheel rolling downhill as an example of what he called "downward causal control." The atoms and molecules are caught up and overpowered by the higher properties of the whole. Sperry compared the rolling wheel to an ongoing brain process or a progressing train of thought in which the overall properties of the brain process, as a coherent organizational entity, determine the timing and spacing of the firing patterns within its neural infrastructure. A few years later (1974), DONALD CAMPBELL coined the phrase "downward causation."

The locus classicus of recent discussions of mental causation is DONALD DAVIDSON's 1970 essay "Mental Events," which was revisited in his 1993 essay, "Thinking Causes," published together with 15 critical essays on Davidson's work in the 1993 book *Mental Causation*, edited by JOHN HEIL and ALFRED MELE.

---

1   See chapter 26 for more on emergence.

Davidson claimed three things:

• That mental events are causally related to physical events

• That causal relations are normally governed by strict (deterministic) laws

• But that there are no such strict laws for mental events acting on physical events

Davidson's goal is to deny the reducibility of mental events to physical events in the lower levels, especially to deny the physicist's reductionist claim that the motions of the atoms and molecules at the lowest level are causally determinative of everything that happens at all higher levels.

Information is neither matter nor energy. It is sometimes embodied in matter and sometimes communicated as pure energy. It is the scientific basis for an *immaterial*, yet causally efficacious, mind that can control the body and affect the physical world. Information is the modern spirit.

But prominent philosopher of mind JAEGWON KIM says that Davidson's goal of "non-reductive physicalism" is simply not possible. The physical world is "causally closed," says Kim:

> "what options are there if we set aside the physicalist picture? Leaving physicalism behind is to abandon ontological physicalism, the view that bits of matter and their aggregates in space-time exhaust the contents of the world. This means that one would be embracing an ontology that posits entities other than material substances — that is, immaterial minds, or souls, outside physical space, with immaterial, nonphysical properties."[2]

Kim diagrams Davidson's view of mental events M_1 and M_2 supervening on physical events P_1 and P_2, to illustrate his claim that having both mental and physical causes would be "overdetermination." Mental causes are redundant and must be excluded.

M_1		M_2
supervenes on		supervenes on
P_1	- causes -	P_2

---

2   *Physicalism, or Something Near Enough*, p. 71

By causal closure of the physical world, Kim says it is the mental events that are superfluous and must go.[3]

This view of the physical and biological world as made up of isolatable and discrete events is much too simplistic. A physical "event" is subjectively singled out by a human observer from a practically infinite number of biological processes and material events at the atomic and molecular level. The idea of a single "cause" is arbitrarily abstracted from complex processes with enormous numbers of possible causes. A mental event is embedded in a biological system beyond "astronomical" in complexity.

The Problem of Mental Causation according to Kim

While the Cartesian mind-body problem was simply the puzzle of how an *immaterial* mind could cause a material body to move, lately the problem of mental causation has been recast as the *logical* resolution of one basic premise and a conclusion, which we might call the standard argument against mental causation:

• The only causes are physical causes. (These causes need not be deterministic. An indeterministic quantum statistical event gives us the probabilities for subsequent events, "causing" them in a way that is not pre-determined.)

• Therefore, mental events cannot cause physical events.

But information philosophy sees mental activity just as physical as bodily actions. The proper distinction between mind and body is between the immaterial and the material.

The Emergence of Life from Matter and Mind from Life

According to British Emergentism, there is a hierarchy of levels of organizational complexity of material particles that includes, in ascending order, the strictly physical, the chemical, the biological, and the psychological level. As we have seen, upper hierarchical levels have the power to influence motion in ways unanticipated by laws governing less complex kinds and conditions concerning the arrangements of particles. Emergentism is committed to the nomological possibility of what has been called "downward causation," control by an upper level of the component particles

---

3   *Physicalism, or Something Near Enough.*, pp. 44-45

Chapter 16

of the lower levels. We can now demonstrate that the emergentists' hypothesis is actually realized in biological systems.[4]

An informational analysis of non-reductive physicalism must show exactly how *information does not move in the upward direction* between hierarchical levels (fundamentally because noise in the lower level makes motions incoherent), but that *information does move down* as the higher-level information-processing system manipulates individual physical particles (maintaining a high signal-to-noise ratio in the upper level), as the British empiricists imagined.

Some critics think the emergentists' claim is illogical or maybe physically impossible. How can causality be only "one way?" If there are "top-down" causes, there must be "bottom-up" causes by symmetry, must there not? If the contents of the world were only the material particles of physics and chemistry, would not this be so? The short answer is no. The hierarchical organization of material systems, from the galaxies, stars, and planets, to everyday objects like Sperry's wheel, means that atoms and molecules are often controlled by causes from above.

The reduction of biology to molecular biology sharpens the question. How is it that some "living" molecules can have power, downward causal control, over others?

We shall see that quantum and thermal noise breaks any upwardly causal deterministic chains between the physics of the atomic and molecular level and the biophysics of the organic world. It also breaks any upward deterministic chains between the neurobiological brain and the mind, replacing them with a statistical causality that provides us with what WILLIAM JAMES called "some looseness in the joints."

We present two biological processes that exhibit randomness in the component atoms and molecules, thus blocking any organized upward influences. The first is present in every biological cell. The other is critically important in the operation of neurons. The first separates the living from the simply material. The latter is at the mind/brain boundary.

---

4   See chapter 25 for details on emergence.

Ribosomes Select Randomly Moving Amino Acids

Twenty amino acids move about randomly in all cells at surprisingly high speeds, the consequence of thermal and quantum noise. Attached to some of them are lumps of transfer RNA, each with three letters of the genetic code that identify a specific amino acid. They bump randomly into the ribosome, a huge macromolecular information processor built from a few strands of RNA and a complex of protein enzymes. The ribosome has just received a message from the DNA in the cell nucleus and is busy decoding its meaning.

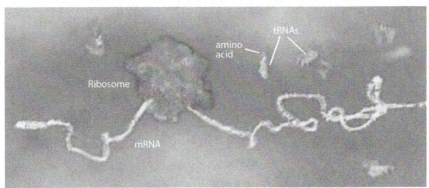

Figure 16-7. A messenger RNA strand passes through the ribosome.

The nucleus had received a signal that a certain protein or enzyme was now in short supply. The signal activated a transcription process that locates the section in the DNA gene with the sequence of three-letter codes that describes the needed protein. Another enzyme called a synthetase moves along the DNA, reads the nucleotide code, and builds a strand of messenger RNA encoded with the sequence that tells the ribosome which protein is needed.

The long strand of messenger RNA moving through the ribosome above is a script, a text, sent from the cell nucleus, with the intended purpose that the ribosome will replenish a protein. As the thread of mRNA moves through the ribosome, each transfer RNA adds one amino acid to the growing protein. The random motions of the tRNAs shows us that no organized or coherent information is present in the tRNAs that could cause something from the bottom up to emerge at a higher level. The tRNAs do not know which protein they will soon be part of.[5]

_____

5   See informationphilosopher.com/knowledge/mental_caustion.html/#ribo

Notice the absurdity of the idea that the random motions of the transfer RNA molecules, each holding a single amino acid, are carrying pre-determined information of where they belong in the protein.

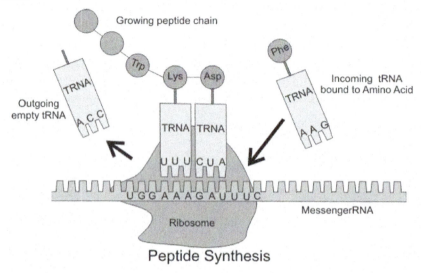

Peptide Synthesis

Figure 16-8. A transfer RNA carries an amino acid for the growing protein.

Of course the DNA, the RNA enzymes encoding the message, and the ribosome translating it, do not have the information-processing power to reflect on or become conscious of what they are doing. But their activities are at least proto-mental, because they are very similar to the more symbolic communications of human beings.

It is the information processing of the higher-level ribosome that is in control. As the ribosome moves along the string of mRNA, it reads the next three-letter codon and waits for a tRNA with the matching anti-codon to collide randomly. With over 60 codons for the 20 amino acids, it might be some time before the desired amino acid shows up. It is the high speed of random motions that allows this process to proceed rapidly. Consider the case of hemoglobin.

When a ribosome assembles 330 amino acids in four symmetric polypeptide chains (globins), each globin traps an iron atom in a heme group at the center to form the hemoglobin protein. This is downward causal control of the amino acids, the heme groups, and the iron atoms by the ribosome. The ribosome is an example of

ERWIN SCHRÖDINGER's emergent "order out of order," life "feeding on the negative entropy" of digested food.

When 200 million of the 25 trillion red blood cells in the human body die each second, 300 million new hemoglobins must be assembled in each of 200 million new blood cells. With the order of a few thousand bytes of information in each hemoglobin, this is 10 thousand x 300 million x 200 million = 6 x 10^{20} bits of information per second, millions of times more information processing than today's fastest computer CPU.

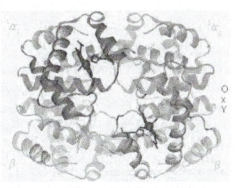

Figure 16-9. Hemoglobin's protein chains.

The ribosome is an information-processing biological system that has emerged from the lower level of chemistry and physics to exert downward causation on the molecular components (amino acids) needed to manufacture hemoglobin.

Ion Pumps in Neurons Select Individual Atoms

When a single neuron fires, the active potential rapidly changes the concentration of sodium (Na+) ions inside the cell and potassium (K+) ions outside the cell. Within milliseconds, thousands of sodium-potassium ion transporters in the thin lipid bilayer of the cell wall must move billions of those ions, two or three at a time between inside and outside the cell wall, to get the neuron ready to fire again.[6]

All the individual ions, atoms, and molecules in the cell are moving rapidly in random directions. The indeterministic motions of the ions randomly move some near a pump opening, where quantum collaborative forces can capture them in a lock-and-key structure. The idea that the physical/chemical base level contains enough information in the motion of its atoms and molecules to cause and thus explain the operations of the higher levels of life and mind is simply absurd.

---

6   See informationphilosopher.com/knowledge/mental_caustion.html/#ion

Chapter 16

The sodium-potassium ion pump is energized by a single ATP (adenosine triphosphate) molecule to execute four steps. The first is to capture three sodium (Na^+) ions into lock-and-key matched positions (a quantum cooperative phenomenon shown as spherical shapes for sodium). The complex of surrounding proteins then changes its configuration, closing at the bottom and opening at the top to release the sodium ions outside the cell membrane.

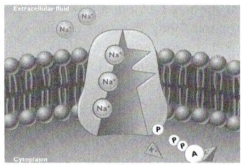

Figure 16-10. The Na^+/K^+ ion pump

The pump then attracts two potassium ions (K^+) from the extracellular fluid, capturing them in the quantum cooperative bonding shapes shown scematically as triangular pyramids. When two potassiums are captured, the surrounding protein complex again changes its configuration, closing at the top and opening at the bottom to release the potassiums into the cytosol.

In each four-step cycle, the available free energy (energy with low entropy) of a single ATP molecule has moved three sodiums and two potassiums across the lipid bilayer of the cell membrane. The ATP has lost a single phosphate group and the depleted ADP (adenosine diphosphate) must travel to an ATP synthase complex in the cell wall of nearby mitochondria to be re-energized with a new phosphate group attached.[7]

This emergent biological machinery of the sodium-potassium pump has clearly exerted *downward causation* on the ions, powered by ATP energy carriers feeding on negative entropy.

The sodium-potassium pump in our neurons is as close to a Maxwell's Demon evading the second law of thermodynamics as anything we are ever likely to see.[8]

And when many motor neurons fire, innnervating excitatory post-synaptic potentials (EPSPs) that travel down through the thal-

---

7   See chapter 28 for the working of ATP synthase.
8   See informationphilosopher.com/solutions/scientists/maxwell/#demon

amus and the spinal cord where they cause muscles to contract, that is as literal as *downward causation* gets between the mind and the body. When the emergent *immaterial* mind decides to move the material body, *mental causation* is realized as *downward causation*.

Information Solves the Problem of Mental Causation.

Information philosophy understands mental events as immaterial thoughts, which are normally only unrealized possibilities for action. Thoughts are embodied in the neural information structures of the brain, where they are stored along with memories of past experiences in the experience recorder and reproducer (ERR). As such, they are physical and are temporarily embodied and material, in some sense.

But when thoughts are transferred (communicated) to other parts of the brain, out to other minds, or for storage in the external environment, thoughts are converted from a material substrate to various forms of energy. Temporarily, they are quite non-material, as philosophers for centuries have imagined thoughts in an *immaterial* mind might be. Once stored, they are again embodied in matter.

Of course, thoughts or ideas can be unpredictably altered before storage, by noise in the communication. They can also be altered randomly by irreducibly indeterministic errors in the retrieval of the information. Here lies the basis for creative mistakes, to be evaluated by a process of intelligent selection. (As Augustine noted, the Latin *intelligere* means "to select.")

The information solution to the mind-body problem can be interpreted as providing a non-reductive physical interpretation of mind. This model of mind supervenes on the neural brain structures that embody the information (while it is being stored). But the intellectual content of the information is not the resultant of whatever physical processes are coming from lower layers in a hierarchical structure. The physical brain is a plastic storage medium adequately determined to store the information content of these immaterial thoughts, and normally to store it accurately.

With reference to popular (if flawed) computational theories of mind, we note that the "software" contents of a computer program, as well as the execution of the program, is in no way determined or

Chapter 16

"caused" by the computer "hardware." Similarly, ideas are not determined by the ink on a printed page or the pixels on a computer screen, but by the human minds that put them there.

"Bottom-up" Physical Processes Are Not Deterministic

When small numbers of atoms and molecules interact, their motions and behaviors are indeterministic, governed by the rules of quantum mechanics.

However, when large numbers of microscopic particle get together in aggregates, the indeterminacy of the individual particles gets averaged over and macroscopic adequately deterministic laws "emerge."

Determinism is an emergent property that shows up in the macroscopic world.

The "laws of nature," such as Newton's laws of motion, are all statistical laws, however close they appear to being certain. They "emerge" when large numbers of atoms or molecules get together. For large enough numbers, the probabilistic laws of nature approach practical certainty. But the fundamental indeterminism of component atoms never completely disappears.

It therefore follows that physical brain events are not pre-determined by the events in lower hierarchical levels, not events in the base physical level, nor in the biological level.

And the world is not "causally closed" by deterministic physical laws of nature, as assumed by so many philosophers (e.g., Feigl, Smart, Kim).

Moreover, since some "mental events" are large enough information structures to be adequately determined, these mental events can act causally on lower biological and physical levels in the hierarchy, in particular, the mind can move the body and all its contained physical particles, thus solving the mind-body problem.

A specific example of the mind causing an action, while not itself being caused by antecedent events is the following. Faced with a decision of what to do next, the mind considers several possible alternatives, at least some of which are creatively invented based on random ideas that just "come to mind." Other possible alternatives might be familiar options, even habits, that have frequently been chosen in many earlier similar situations.

All these alternatives show up as "neural correlates" - brain neurons firing as the experience recorder and reproducer (ERR) plays back past experiences that in some way resemble the current situation. When the alternatives are evaluated and one is selected, the selected action results in still other neurons firing, some of which connect to the motor cortex that signals muscles to move the body.

Apart from the occasional indeterministic generation of creative new alternative ideas, this whole causal process is adequately determined and it is downwardly causal. Mental events are causing physical body events.

Mind can move matter. Ideas can move mountains.

Molecular Machines

The ribosomes in every cell, the ion pumps in the neuron, and ATP synthase in the mitochondria are examples of dozens of incredibly tiny molecular machines that microbiologists have been discovering over the past few decades.

Ribosomes produce quadrillions (10^{21}) of bits of information per second. Ion pumps move trillions of sodium and potassium ions per second. And our mitochondria produce hundreds of trillions of the ATP molecules. Each ATP synthase produces a few thousand ATP molecules per minute, spinning at 10,000 RPM (faster than most of our motors) to do so.

Mental causation depends on these incredible machines to control the motions of physical and chemical particles that philosophers of mind have imagined might be exerting "bottom-up" causation on the biological and psychological levels.

There simply is no such "causal closure of the physical world" that is controlling our minds.

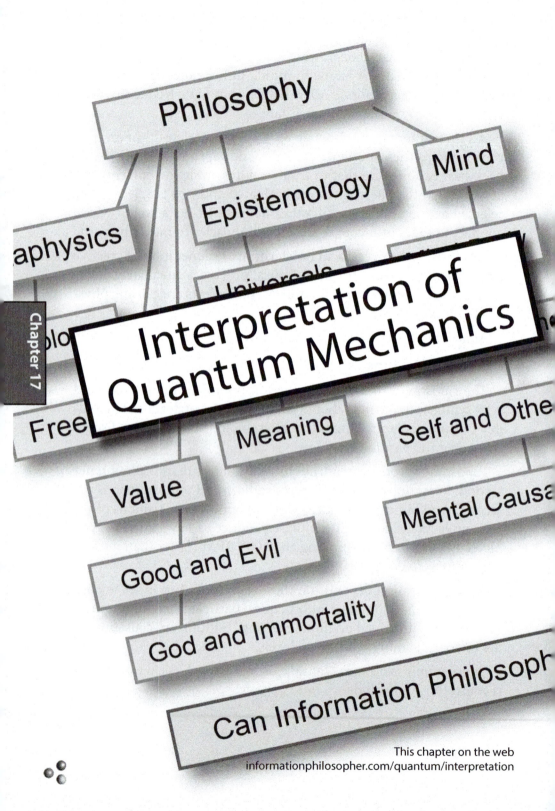

Philosophy

Mind

Epistemology

aphysics

Chapter 17

Interpretation of
Quantum Mechanics

Free

Meaning

Self and Othe

Value

Mental Causa

Good and Evil

God and Immortality

Can Information Philosoph

This chapter on the web
informationphilosopher.com/quantum/interpretation

Information Interpretation of Quantum Mechanics

Our information interpretation is simply "standard quantum physics" plus information being recorded irreversibly. Unlike the Copenhagen Interpretation, we offer a *visualization* of what is going on in quantum reality, with animations (on-line) of the wave function evolution and the appearance of the particle, when the wave function shrinks to its minimum possible size h^3.

The information interpretation of quantum mechanics is based on three simple premises:

1) Quantum systems evolve in two ways:

• The first is the wave function deterministically exploring all the possibilities for interaction,

• The second is the particle randomly choosing one of those possibilities to become actual.

2) No knowledge can be gained by a "conscious observer" unless new information has already been irreversibly recorded in the universe. New information can be created and recorded in three places:

• In the target quantum system,

• In the combined target system and measuring apparatus,

• It can then become knowledge in the observer's mind.

3) The measuring apparatus is quantal, not deterministic or "classical." It need only be statistically determined and capable of recording the irreversible information about an interaction. The human mind is also only statistically or adequately determined.

• There is only one world.

• It is a quantum world, which only *appears* to be classical.

• The world only *appears* to be determined.

Ontologically, the quantum world is indeterministic, but in our everyday common experience it appears be causal and deterministic, the so-called "classical" world. Information physics claims there is only one world, the quantum world, and the so-called "quantum to classical transition" occurs for any macroscopic object of mass m that contains a large enough number of atoms. For large enough systems, independent quantum events are "averaged over." The uncertainty in position x and velocity v of the large object becomes less than the quantum indeterminacy

$\Delta v \, \Delta x \geq h / m$ goes to zero as h / m goes to zero.

The classical laws of motion, with their apparent determinism and strict causality, *emerge* when objects are large enough so that microscopic events can be ignored, but this determinism is fundamentally *statistical* and physical causes are only probabilistic, however near they seem to certainty.

Information philosophy interprets the wave function ψ as a "possibilities" function. With this simple change in terminology, the mysterious process of a wave function "collapsing" becomes a much more intuitive discussion of ψ evolving to explore all the possibilities (with mathematically calculable probabilities), followed by a single actualization, at which time the probabilities for all non-actualized possibilities go to zero (they "collapse") instantaneously.

Information physics is standard quantum physics. It accepts the Schrödinger equation of motion, the *principle of superposition*, the *axiom of measurement* (now including the actual information "bits" measured), and - most important - the *projection postulate* of standard quantum mechanics (the "collapse" that so many unorthodox interpretations deny).

But unlike some interpretations, the conscious observer of the Copenhagen Interpretation is not required for a projection, for the wave-function to "collapse", for one of the possibilities to become an actuality. What the collapse does require is an interaction between systems that creates irreversible and observable, but not necessarily observed, information.

Among the founders of quantum mechanics, almost everyone agreed that irreversibility was a key requirement for a measurement. Irreversibility introduces thermodynamics into a proper formulation of quantum mechanics, and this is what the information interpretation requires.

Information is not a conserved quantity like energy and mass, despite the view of many mathematical physicists, who generally accept determinism and think information is a constant.. The universe began in a state of equilibrium with minimal information, and information is being created every day, despite the second law of thermodynamics. Classical interactions between large macroscopic bodies do not generate new information. Newton's laws of motion imply that the information in any configuration of bodies, motions, and the force laws, is enough to know all past and future configurations. Classical mechanics conserves information.

In the absence of interactions, an isolated quantum system evolves according to the unitary Schrödinger equation of motion. Just like classical systems, the deterministic Schrödinger equation conserves information.

Unlike classical systems however, when there is an interaction between quantum systems, the two systems become entangled and there may be a change of state in either or both systems. This change of state may create new information.

If that information is instantly destroyed, as in most interactions, it may never be observed macroscopically. If, on the other hand, the information is stabilized for some length of time, it may be seen by an observer and considered to be a "measurement." But it need not be seen by anyone to become new information in the universe. The universe is its own observer!

Compare Schrödinger's Cat (chapter 23) as its own observer.

For the information (negative entropy) to be stabilized, the second law of thermodynamics requires that an amount of positive entropy greater than the negative entropy must be transferred away from the new information structure.

Exactly how the universe allows pockets of negative entropy to form as "information structures" we describe as the "cosmic

Chapter 17

creation process." This core two-step process has been going on since the origin of the universe. It continues today as we add information to the *Sum* of human knowledge.

Note that despite the Heisenberg principle, quantum mechanical measurements are not always uncertain. When a system is measured (prepared) in an eigenstate, a subsequent measurement (Pauli's measurement of the first kind) will find it in the same state with perfect certainty.

What are the normal possibilities for new quantum states? The transformation theory of PAUL DIRAC and PASCUAL JORDAN lets us represent ψ in a set of basis functions for which the combination of quantum systems (one may be a measurement apparatus) has eigenvalues (the *axiom of measurement*). We represent ψ as in a linear combination (the *principle of superposition*) of those "possible" eigenfunctions. Quantum mechanics lets us calculate the probabilities of each of those "possibilities."

Interaction with the measurement apparatus (or indeed interaction with any other system) may select out (the *axiom of measurement*) one of those possibilities as an actuality. But for this event to be an "observable" (a JOHN BELL "beable"), information must be created and positive entropy must be transferred away from the new information structure, in accordance with our two-step information creation process.

All interpretations of quantum mechanics predict the same experimental results. The information interpretation is no exception, because the experimental data from quantum experiments is the most accurate in the history of science.

Where interpretations differ is in the picture (the *visualization*) they provide of what is "really" going on in the microscopic world - so-called "quantum reality." Schrödinger called it *Anschaulichkeit*. He and Einstein were right that we should be able to picture quantum reality.

However, the Copenhagen interpretation of Niels Bohr and Werner Heisenberg discourages attempts to visualize the nature of the "quantum world," because they say that all our experience is derived from the "classical world" and should be described in ordinary language. This is why Bohr and Heisenberg insisted on some kind of "cut" between the quantum event and the mind of an observer.

The information interpretation encourages visualization. (See our on-line animation of the two-slit experiment[1], our EPR experiment visualizations[2], and Dirac's three polarizers[3] to visualize the superposition of states and the projection or "collapse" of a wave function.)

Bohr was of course right that classical physics plays an essential role. His Correspondence Principle allowed him to recover some important physical constants by assuming that the discontinuous quantum jumps for low quantum numbers (low "orbits" in his old quantum theory model) converged in the limit of large quantum numbers to the continuous radiation emission and absorption of classical electromagnetic theory.

In addition, we know that in macroscopic bodies with enormous numbers of quantum particles, quantum effects are averaged over, so that the uncertainty in position and momentum of a large body still obeys Heisenberg's indeterminacy principle, but the uncertainty is for all practical purposes unmeasurable and the body can be treated classically.

We can say that the quantum description of matter also converges to a classical description in the limit of large numbers of quantum particles. We call this "adequate" or statistical determinism. It is the apparent determinism we find behind Newton's laws of motion for macroscopic objects. The statistics of averaging over many independent quantum events then produces the "quantum to classical transition" for the same reason as the "law of large numbers" in probability theory.

Both Bohr and Heisenberg suggested that just as relativistic effects can be ignored when the velocity is small compared to the velocity of light ($v / c \rightarrow 0$), so quantum effects might be ignorable

---

1   .informationphilosopher.com/solutions/experiments/two-slit_experiment/
2   informationphilosopher.com/solutions/experiments/EPR/
3   www.informationphilosopher.com/solutions/experiments/dirac_3-polarizers/

when Planck's quantum of action $h \to 0$. But this is quite wrong, because h is a constant that never goes to zero. In the information interpretation, it is always a quantum world. As we saw, the conditions needed for ignoring quantum indeterminacy are when the mass of the macroscopic "classical" object is large.

Note that the macromolecules of biology are large enough to stabilize their information structures. DNA has been replicating its essential information for billions of years, resisting equilibrium despite the second law of thermodynamics The creation of irreversible new information also marks the transition between the quantum world and the "adequately deterministic" classical world, because the information structure itself must be large enough (and stable enough) to be seen. The typical measurement apparatus is macroscopic, so the quantum of action h becomes small compared to the mass m and h / m approaches zero.

Decoherence theorists say that the measurement problem is our failure to see quantum superpositions in the macroscopic world. The information interpretation thus explains why quantum superpositions like Schrödinger's Cat are not seen in the macroscopic world. Stable new information structures in the dying cat reduce the quantum possibilities (and their potential interference effects) to a classical actuality. Upon opening the box and finding a dead cat, an autopsy will reveal that the time of death was observed/recorded. The cat is its own observer.

The "Possibilities Function"

The central element in quantum physics is the "wave function" ψ, with its mysterious wave-particle dual nature (sometimes a wave, sometimes a particle, etc.). We believe that teaching and understanding quantum mechanics would be much simpler if we called ψ the "possibilities function." It only looks like a wave in simple cases of low-dimensional coordinate space. But it always tells us the possibilities - the possible values of any observable, for example.

Given the "possibilities function" ψ, quantum mechanics allows us to calculate the "probabilities" for each of the "possibilities." The calculation depends on the free choice of the experimenter as to which "observables" to look for. If the measurement apparatus can register n discrete values, ψ can be expanded in terms of a set of basis functions (eigenfunctions) appropriate for the chosen observable, say φ_n. The expansion is

$$\psi = \Sigma \, c_n \, \varphi_n$$

When the absolute squares of the coefficients c_n are appropriately normalized to add up to *1*, the probability P_n of observing an eigenvalue n is

$$P_n = \mid c_n \mid^2 = \mid <\psi \mid \varphi_n> \mid^2$$

These probabilities are confirmed statistically by repeated identical experiments that collect large numbers of results. Quantum mechanics is the most accurate physical theory in science, with measurements accurate to fifteen decimal places.

In each individual experiment, generally just one of the possibilities becomes an actuality (although some experiments leave the quantum system in a new superposition of multiple possibilities).

In our information interpretation, a possibility is realized or actualized at the moment when information is created about the new state of the system. This new information requires that positive entropy be carried away from the local increase in negative entropy.

Note that an "observer" will not be able to make a "measurement" unless new information exists to be "observed." Information must be (and is in all modern experimental systems) created and recorded *before any observer looks at the results*. Measurements do not depend directly on the mind of the observer, only indirectly when the observer sets up the experimental apparatus and decides what it will measure.

This is called the "free choice" of the experimenter.[4]

An information approach can help philosophers to think more clearly about quantum physics. Instead of getting trapped in talk about mysterious "collapse of the wave function," "reduction of the wave packet," or the "projection postulate" (all important issues),

Chapter 17

---

4   informationphilosopher.com/freedom/free_choice.html

the information interpretation proposes we simply say that one of the "possibilities" has become "actual."

It is intuitively obvious that when one possibility becomes actual, all the others are annihilated, consigned to "nothingness," as JEAN-PAUL SARTRE put it. And because the other possibilities may have been extremely "distant" from the point of actualization, their instantaneous disappearances looked to Einstein to violate his principle of relativity, but they do not.

Quantum theory lets us put quantitative values on the "probabilities" for each of the "possibilities." But this means that quantum theory is fundamentally statistical, meaning indeterministic and "random." It is not a question of our being ignorant about what is going on (an epistemological problem). What's happening is ontological chance, as Einstein first showed, but as he forever disliked.

We can describe the "possibilities function" ψ as moving through space (at the speed of light, or even faster, as Einstein feared?), exploring all the possibilities for wherever the particle might be found. This too may be seen as a special kind of information. In the famous "two-slit experiment[5]," the "possibilities function" travels everywhere, meaning that ψ passes through both slits, interfering with itself and thus changing the possibilities where the particle might be found. Metaphorically, ψ "knows" when both slits are open, even if our intuitive classical view imagines that the particle must go through only one. The slits being open changes the probabilities associated with each of the possibilities.

Possibilities and Information Theory

It is of the deepest philosophical significance that information theory is based on the mathematics of probability. If all outcomes were certain, there would be no "surprises" in the universe. Information would be conserved and a universal constant, as some mathematicians mistakenly believe. Information philosophy requires the ontological uncertainty and probabilistic outcomes of modern quantum physics to produce new information.

---

5   informationphilosopher.com/solutions/experiments/two-slit_experiment/

In CLAUDE SHANNON's theory of the communication of information, there must be multiple possible messages in order for information to be communicated. If there is only one possible message, there is no uncertainty, and no information can be communicated.

In a universe describable by the classical Newtonian laws of motion, all the information needed to produce the next moment is contained in the positions, motions, and forces on the material particles.

In a quantum world describable by the unitary evolution of the deterministic Schrödinger equation, nothing new ever happens, there is no new "outcome." Outcomes are added to standard quantum mechanics by the addition of the "projection postulate" or "collapse of the wave function," when the quantum system interacts with another system.

Information is constant in a deterministic universe. There is "nothing new under the sun." The creation of new information is not possible without the random chance and uncertainty of quantum mechanics, plus the extraordinary temporal stability of quantum mechanical structures needed to store information once it is created.

Without the extraordinary stability of quantized information structures over cosmological time scales, life and the universe we know would not be possible. That stability is the consequence of an underlying digital nature. Quantum mechanics reveals the architecture of the universe to be discrete rather than continuous, to be digital rather than analog. Digital information transfers are essentially perfect, whereas analog transfers are "lossy."

It is Bohr's "correspondence principle" of quantum mechanics for large quantum numbers and the "law of large numbers" of statistics which ensure that macroscopic objects can normally average out microscopic uncertainties and probabilities to provide the statistical or "adequate" determinism that shows up in all our classical "laws of nature."

There is no separate classical world and no need for a quantum-to-classical transition. The quantum world becomes statistically deterministic when the mass of an object is such that h / m approaches zero. We conclude, contrary to the views of Bohr and Heisenberg, that there is no need for a separate classical world. The classical laws of nature emerge statistically from quantum laws. Quantum laws, which are therefore universally applicable, converge in these two limits of large numbers to classical laws. There is no "transition" from the quantum world to a separate classical world. There is just one world, where quantum physics applies universally, but its mysterious properties, like interference, entanglement, and nonlocality, are normally invisible, averaged over, in the macroscopic world.

The problem for an informational interpretation of quantum mechanics is to explain exactly how these two convergences (large numbers of particles and large quantum numbers) allow continuous and apparently deterministic macroscopic information structures to emerge from the indeterministic and discontinuous microscopic quantum world.

We show how the determinism in the macroscopic world is only a *statistical* or adequate determinism, the result of "averaging over" the large number of independent quantum events happening in a macroscopic object. And even more important, we must show how the occasional magnification or amplification of microscopic quantum events leads to new macroscopic information that makes human beings the "authors of their lives", that makes them "co-creators of our universe," and that guarantees a genuinely open future with alternative possibilities, not in inaccessible "parallel universes" but in the one universe that we have.

Other Interpretations of Quantum Mechanics

Standard "orthodox" interpretations of quantum mechanics include the *projection postulate*, the "collapse of the wave function."

Today there appear to be about as many unorthodox interpretations that deny the collapse, as there are more standard views. We characterize each interpretation as deterministic or not, local or non-local reality, if they assume hidden variables, need a conscious observer, and accept particles. Their proponents are in parentheses.

No-Collapse Interpretations

Statistical Ensemble - indeterministic, non-local, no observer - (Einstein-Born- Ballentine)

Pilot-Wave Theory - deterministic, non-local, hidden variables, no observer, particles - (de Broglie-Bohm, 1952)

Many-Worlds - deterministic, local, hidden variables, no observer - (Everett-De Witt, 1957)

Time-Symmetric Theory - (Aharanov, 1964)

Decoherence - deterministic, local, no particles - (Zeh-Zurek, 1970)

Modal Interpretation - (van Frassen, 1972)
Consistent Histories - local - (Griffith-Omnès-Gell-Mann-Har-tle, 1984)

Collapse Interpretations

Copenhagen Interpretation - indeterministic, non-local, observer - (Bohr-Heisenberg-Born-Jordan, 1927)

Conscious Observer - indeterministic, non-local, observer - (Von Neumann-Wigner)

Objective Collapse - indeterministic, non-local, no observer - (Ghirardi-Rimini-Weber, 1986; Penrose, 1989)

Transactional Interpretation - indeterministic, non-local, no observer, no particles - (Cramer, 1986)

Relational Interpretation - local, observer - (Rovelli, 1994)
Pondicherry Interpretation - indeterministic, non-local, no observer - (Mohrhoff, 2005)Probabilities

Information Interpretation - Our interpretation is statistical, indeterministic, non-local, and no observer is needed. It interprets the "collapse" of the "possibilities" function according to Dirac's *"projection postulate."* New is the requirement for the physical recording of information before any "observation" can be made.

Chapter 18

The Measurement Problem

The "problem of measurement" in quantum mechanics has been defined in various ways, originally by scientists, and more recently by philosophers of science who question the "foundations" of quantum mechanics.

Measurements are described with diverse concepts in quantum physics such as:

• wave functions (probability amplitudes) evolving unitarily and deterministically (preserving information) according to the linear Schrödinger equation,

• superposition of states, i.e., linear combinations of wave functions with complex coefficients that carry phase information and produce interference effects (the *principle of superposition*),

• quantum jumps between states accompanied by the "collapse of the wave function" that can destroy or create information (PAUL DIRAC's *projection postulate*, JOHN VON NEUMANN's Process 1),

• probabilities of collapses and jumps given by the square of the absolute value of the wave function for a given state,

• values for possible measurements given by the eigenvalues associated with the eigenstates of the combined measuring apparatus and measured system (the *axiom of measurement*),

• the indeterminacy or uncertainty principle.

The original measurement problem, said to be a consequence of NIELS BOHR's "Copenhagen Interpretation" of quantum mechanics, was to explain how our measuring instruments, which are usually macroscopic objects and treatable with classical physics, can give us information about the microscopic world of atoms and subatomic particles like electrons and photons.

Bohr's idea of "complementarity" insisted that a specific experiment could reveal only partial information - for example, a particle's position or its momentum. "Exhaustive" or "complete" information requires two complementary experiments. Measurement of both a particle's momentum and its position can only be within the limits of WERNER HEISENBERG's uncertainty principle. This demands that the product of the indeterminacy in the position Δx multiplied by the indeterminacy in the momentum Δp be equal to or greater than Planck's quantum of action h.

Some define the problem of measurement simply as the logical contradiction between two laws describing the motion of quantum systems; the unitary, information preserving, continuous, and deterministic time evolution of the Schrödinger equation versus the non-unitary, discontinuous, and indeterministic collapse of the wave function. JOHN von Neumann saw a problem with these two distinct (indeed, logically opposing) processes.

The mathematical formalism of quantum mechanics provides no way to predict when the wave function stops evolving in a unitary fashion and collapses. Experimentally and practically, however, we can say that this occurs when the microscopic system interacts with a measurement apparatus. or indeed just with another quantum system.

Others define the measurement problem as the failure to observe macroscopic superpositions.

Decoherence theorists[1] (e.g., H. DIETER ZEH and WOJCIECH ZUREK, who use various non-standard interpretations of quantum mechanics, denying the projection postulate, quantum jumps, and even the existence of particles), define the measurement problem as the failure to observe superpositions such as Schrödinger's Cat. Unitary time evolution of the wave function according to the Schrödinger wave equation should produce such macroscopic superpositions, they claim.

Information physics treats a measuring apparatus quantum mechanically by describing parts of it as in a metastable state like the excited states of an atom, the critically poised electrical potential energy in the discharge tube of a Geiger counter, or the supersaturated water and alcohol molecules of a Wilson cloud chamber. (The pi-bond orbital rotation from cis- to trans- in the light-sensitive retinal molecule is an example of a critically poised apparatus).

---

1   See chapter 22.

Excited (metastable) states are poised to collapse when an electron (or photon) collides with the sensitive detector elements in the apparatus. This collapse is macroscopic and *irreversible*[2], generally a cascade of quantum events that release large amounts of energy, increasing the (Boltzmann) entropy. But in a "measurement" there is also a local decrease in the entropy. This negative entropy corresponds to the information gained in the measurement. The global entropy increase is normally orders of magnitude more than the small local decrease in entropy (an increase in stable information or Shannon entropy) that constitutes the "measured" experimental data available to human observers.

The creation of new information in a measurement thus follows the same two core processes of all information creation - quantum cooperative phenomena and thermodynamics. These two are involved in the formation of microscopic objects like atoms and molecules, as well as macroscopic objects like galaxies, stars, and planets.

According to the correspondence principle, all the laws of quantum physics asymptotically approach the laws of classical physics in the limit of large quantum numbers and large numbers of particles. Quantum mechanics can be used to describe even the largest macroscopic systems.

Does this mean that the positions and momenta of macroscopic objects are uncertain? Yes, it does. Although the uncertainty becomes vanishingly small for large objects, it is not zero.

Noting that the momentum p is the product of mass and velocity mv, Heisenberg's indeterminacy principle, $\Delta p\, \Delta x > h$, can be rewritten as $\Delta v\, \Delta x > h\,/\,m$. It is thus not when h is small, but when the mass m is large enough and $h\,/\,m$ is small enough, that errors in the position and momentum of macroscopic objects become smaller that can be measured.

Niels Bohr used the uncertainty of macroscopic objects to defeat Albert Einstein's several objections to quantum mechanics at the 1927 Solvay conference.

---

2   See chapter 25.

But Bohr and Heisenberg also insisted that a measuring apparatus must be a regarded as a purely classical system. They can't have it both ways. Can the macroscopic apparatus also be treated by quantum physics or not? Can it be described by the Schrödinger equation? Can it be regarded as in a superposition of states?

The most famous example of macroscopic superposition is no doubt Schrödinger's Cat[3], which is claimed to be in a superposition of live and dead cats, and the Einstein-Podolsky-Rosen experiment, in which entangled electrons or photons are in a superposition of two-particle states that collapse over macroscopic distances to exhibit properties "nonlocally" at speeds faster than the speed of light.

The radical treatments of macroscopic systems, by Schrödinger and Einstein and his colleagues, were intended to expose inconsistencies and incompleteness in quantum theory. The critics hoped to restore determinism and "local reality" to physics. They resulted in some strange and extremely popular "mysteries" about "quantum reality," such as the "many-worlds" interpretation, "hidden variables," and signaling faster than the speed of light.

We develop a quantum-mechanical treatment of macroscopic systems, especially a measuring apparatus, to show how it can create new information. If the apparatus were describable only by classical deterministic laws, no new information could come into existence. The apparatus need only be adequately determined, that is to say, "classical" to a sufficient degree of accuracy.

As Landau and Lifshitz described it in their 1958 textbook,

> "The possibility of a quantitative description of the motion of an electron requires the presence also of physical objects which obey classical mechanics to a sufficient degree of accuracy. If an electron interacts with such a "classical object", the state of the latter is, generally speaking, altered. The nature and magnitude of this change depend on the state of the electron, and therefore may serve to characterise it quantitatively...

> "We have defined "apparatus" as a physical object which is governed, with sufficient accuracy, by classical mechanics. Such, for instance, is a body of large enough mass. However, it must not be supposed that

---

apparatus is necessarily macroscopic. Under certain conditions, the part of apparatus may also be taken by an object which is microscopic, since the idea of "with sufficient accuracy" depends on the actual problem proposed.

"Thus quantum mechanics occupies a very unusual place among physical theories: it contains classical mechanics as a limiting case [correspondence principle], yet at the same time it requires this limiting case for its own formulation."[4]

Von Neumann's Two Processes

The measurement problem was analyzed mathematically in 1932 by John von Neumann. Following the work of Bohr and Heisenberg, he divided the world into a microscopic (atomic-level) quantum system and a macroscopic (classical) measuring apparatus.

Von Neumann explained that two fundamentally different processes are going on in quantum mechanics.

First, a non-causal **Process 1**, in which the measured electron winds up randomly in one of the possible physical states (eigenstates) of the measuring apparatus plus electron.

This process came to be called the "collapse of the wave function" or the "reduction of the wave packet."

The probability for finding the electron in a specific eigenstate is given by the square of the coefficients c_n of the expansion of the original system state (wave function ψ) in an infinite set of wave functions φ_n that represent the eigenfunctions of the measuring apparatus plus electron.

This is as close as we get to a description of the motion of the particle aspect of a quantum system. According to von Neumann, the particle simply shows up somewhere as a result of a measurement.

Information physics says that the particle "shows up" only when a new stable information structure is created, information that subsequently can be observed.

So we can also add a **Process 1b**. The information created in von Neumann's **Process 1** will only be stable if an amount of positive entropy greater than the negative entropy in the new information

4   *Quantum Mechanics, non-relativistic theory*, pp.1-2

structure is transported away, in order to satisfy the second law of thermodynamics.

Next, von Neumann's causal **Process 2**, in which the electron wave function ψ evolves deterministically according to Schrödinger's equation of motion for the wavelike aspect.

(ih/2π) ∂ψ/∂t = Hψ.

This evolution describes the motion of the probability amplitude wave ψ between measurements. The wave function exhibits interference effects. But the particle path itself can not be observed. Interference is destroyed if the particle has a definite position or momentum. *The particle does not have a definite position between measurements.*

Von Neumann claimed there is another major difference between his two processes. **Process 1** is thermodynamically irreversible. **Process 2** is reversible. This confirms the fundamental connection between quantum mechanics and thermodynamics that information physics finds at the heart of all information creation.

Information physics can show quantum mechanically how **Process 1** creates information. Something like **Process 1** is always involved when any information is created, whether or not the new information is ever "observed" by a human being.

Process 2 is deterministic and information conserving.

Just as the new information recorded in the measurement apparatus cannot subsist unless a compensating amount of entropy is transferred away from the new information, something similar to **Process 1b** must happen in the mind of an observer if the new information is to constitute an "observation."

It is only in cases where information persists long enough for a human being to observe it that we can properly describe the observation as a "measurement" and the human being as an "observer." So, following von Neumann's "process" terminology, we can complete his theory of the measuring process by adding an anthropomorphic third process.

Process 3 is a conscious observer recording new information in a mind. For this we need two local reductions in the entropy (new information in the measurement apparatus, new information in the mind), both balanced by even greater increases in positive entropy that must be transported away from the apparatus and the mind, so the overall increase in entropy can satisfy the second law of thermodynamics.

Designing a Quantum Measurement Apparatus

The first step is to build an apparatus that allows different components of the wave function to evolve along distinguishable paths into different regions of space, where the different regions correspond to (are correlated with) the physical properties we want to measure. We then can locate a detector in these different regions of space to catch particles travelling a particular path.

We do not say that the system is on a particular path in this first step. Knowing the position would cause the probability amplitude wave function to collapse. This first step is reversible, at least in principle. It is deterministic and an example of von Neumann **Process 2**.

Let's consider a birefringent crystal separating a beam of photons into horizontally and vertically polarized photons.[5]

We need a beam of photons (and the ability to reduce the intensity to a single photon at a time). Vertically polarized photons pass straight through the crystal. They are called the ordinary ray. Horizontally polarized photons, however, are deflected at an angle though the crystal, then exit the crystal back at the original angle. This is the extraordinary ray.

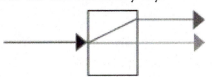

Figure 18-11. Separating horizontal and vertical polarized photons

Note that this first part of our apparatus accomplishes the *separation* of our two states into distinct physical regions.

---

5   See http://www.informationphilosopher.com/problems/measurement/#design for an animation of the birefringent crystal experiment

We have not actually measured yet, so a single photon passing through our measurement apparatus is described as in a linear combination (a superposition) of horizontal and vertical polarization states,

$$| \psi > = (1/\sqrt{2})\,| h > + (1/\sqrt{2})\,| v > \qquad (1)$$

A Reversible Example of Process 2

To show that process 2 is reversible, we can add a second birefringent crystal upside down from the first, but inline with the superposition of physically separated states,

Figure 18-12. If we don't measure, we can recombine the beams

Since we have not made a measurement and do not know the path of the photon, the phase information in the (generally complex) coefficients of equation (1) has been preserved, so when they combine in the second crystal, they emerge in a state identical to the state they had before entering the first crystal.

An Irreversible Example of Process 1

But now suppose we insert something between the two crystals that is capable of a measurement to produce observable information. We need detectors that may locate the photon in one of the two rays.

Let's consider an ideal photographic plate capable of precipitating visible silver grains upon the receipt of a single photon (and subsequent development). Today photography cannot detect single photons, but detectors using charge coupled devices (CCDs) are approaching this sensitivity.

We can write a quantum description of the plate as containing two sensitive collection areas, the part of the apparatus measuring horizontally polarized photons, $| A_h >$ (shown as the upper spot), and the part of the apparatus measuring vertically polarized photons, $| A_v >$ (shown as the lower spot).

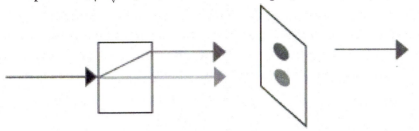

Figure 18-13. Two possible paths become one actual when detected.

We treat the detection systems quantum mechanically, and say that each detector has two eigenstates, e.g., $| A_{h0} >$, corresponding to

- the jump of the probability amplitude wave function $| \psi >$ of the photon in equation (1) into the horizontally polarized state $| h >$.

- the quantum jump of the horizontal detector from $| A_{h0} >$ to $| A_{h1} >$.

These two happen together, as the initial states of the detectors are correlated with no photons, and the final state $| A_{h1} >$, in which the upper detector has registered a horizontal photon.

When we actually detect the photon, say in a horizontal polarization state with statistical probability 1/2, two "collapses" or "jumps" occur. They are correlated with the states of the sensitive detectors in the classical apparatus.

One can say that the photon has become *entangled* with the sensitive horizontal detector area, so that the wave function describing their interaction is a superposition of photon and apparatus states that cannot be observed independently.

$$| \psi > + | A_{h0} > \quad => \quad | \psi, A_{h0} > \quad => \quad | h, A_{h1} >$$

These jumps destroy (unobservable) phase information, raise the (Boltzmann) entropy of the apparatus, and increase visible information (Shannon entropy) in the form of the visible spot. The entropy increase takes the form of a large chemical energy release when the photographic spot is developed (or a cascade of electrons in a CCD).

Note that the birefringent crystal and the parts of the macroscopic apparatus other than the sensitive detectors are treated classically.

We animate these irreversible and reversible processes on our website.[6]

We see that our example agrees with Von Neumann **Process 1**. A measurement which finds the photon in a specific state n is thermodynamically irreversible, whereas the deterministic evolution described by Schrödinger's equation is reversible.

We thus establish a clear connection between a measurement, which increases the information by some number of bits (Shannon entropy), and the necessary compensating increase in the (Boltzmann) entropy of the macroscopic apparatus, and the cosmic creation process, where new particles form, reducing the entropy locally, and the energy of formation is radiated or conducted away as Boltzmann entropy.[7]

Note that the Boltzmann entropy can only be radiated away (ultimately into the night sky to the cosmic microwave background) because the expansion of the universe provides a sink for the entropy, as pointed out by DAVID LAYZER. Note also that this cosmic information-creating process requires no conscious observer. The universe is its own observer.

The Boundary between the Classical and Quantum Worlds

Some scientists, von Neumann and Heisenberg for example, have argued that in the absence of a conscious observer, or some "cut" between the microscopic and macroscopic world, the evolution of the quantum system and the macroscopic measuring apparatus would be described deterministically by Schrödinger's equation of motion for the wave function $| \psi + A >$ with the Hamiltonian H energy operator,

$(ih/2\pi) \, \partial/\partial t \, | \psi + A > = H | \psi + A >.$

Our quantum mechanical analysis of the measurement apparatus in the above case allows us to locate the "cut" precisely at those components of the "adequately classical and deterministic" apparatus that put the apparatus in an *irreversible* stable state providing *new information* to the observer.

---

6   informationphilosopher.com/problems/measurement/#birefringence
7   See appendix B for details

John Bell drew a diagram to show the various possible locations for what he called the "shifty split." Information physics shows us that the correct location for the boundary is the first of Bell's possibilities.

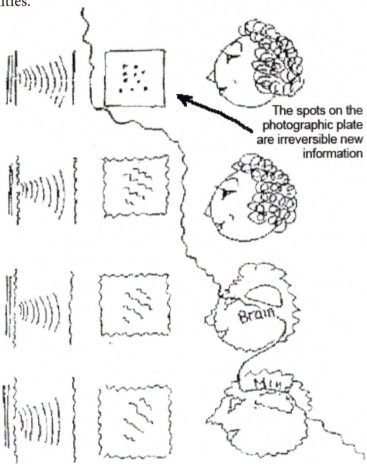

The spots on the photographic plate are irreversible new information

Figure 18-14. John Bell's illustration of the "shifty split."

The Role of the Conscious Observer

In 1941, Carl von Weizsäcker described the measurement problem as an interaction between a Subject and an Object, a view shared by the philosopher of science Ernst Cassirer.

Chapter 18

FRITZ LONDON and EDMOND BAUER made the strongest case for the critical role of a conscious observer in 1939:

"So far we have only coupled one apparatus with one object. But a coupling, even with a measuring device, is not yet a measurement. A measurement is achieved only when the position of the pointer has been observed. It is precisely this increase of knowledge, acquired by observation, that gives the observer the right to choose among the different components of the mixture predicted by theory, to reject those which are not observed, and to attribute thenceforth to the object a new wave function, that of the pure case which he has found.

"We note the essential role played by the consciousness of the observer in this transition from the mixture to the pure case. Without his effective intervention, one would never obtain a new function." [8]

In 1961, EUGENE WIGNER made quantum physics even more subjective, claiming that a quantum measurement requires a conscious observer, without which nothing ever happens in the universe.

"When the province of physical theory was extended to encompass microscopic phenomena, through the creation of quantum mechanics, the concept of consciousness came to the fore again: it was not possible to formulate the laws of quantum mechanics in a fully consistent way without reference to the consciousness All that quantum mechanics purports to provide are probability connections between subsequent impressions (also called "apperceptions") of the consciousness, and even though the dividing line between the observer, whose consciousness is being affected, and the observed physical object can be shifted towards the one or the other to a considerable degree [cf., von Neumann] it cannot be eliminated." [9]

Other physicists were more circumspect. Niels Bohr contrasted Paul Dirac's view, which stressed the randomness of the outcome, with that of Heisenberg, who stresses the observer's "free choice" of what is to be measured:

'The question was whether, as to the occurrence of individual effects, we should adopt a terminology proposed by Dirac, that we were concerned with a choice on the part of "nature," or, as suggested by Heisenberg, we should say that we have to do with a choice on the part of the "observer" constructing the measuring instruments and reading their recording. Any such terminology would, however, appear dubious since, on the one

---

8   Theory of Observation in Quantum Mechanics, in Wheeler and Zurek, p.251
9   Remarks on the Mind-Body Question, in Wheeler and Zurek, p.169

hand, it is hardly reasonable to endow nature with volition in the ordinary sense, while, on the other hand, it is certainly not possible for the observer to influence the events which may appear under the conditions he has arranged. To my mind, there is no other alternative than to admit that, in this field of experience, we are dealing with individual phenomena and that our possibilities of handling the measuring instruments allow us only to make a choice between the different complementary types of phenomena we want to study.' [10]

Landau and Lifshitz said clearly that quantum physics was independent of any observer:

"In this connection the 'classical object' is usually called apparatus, and its interaction with the electron is spoken of as measurement. However, it must be most decidedly emphasised that we are here not discussing a process of measurement in which the physicist-observer takes part. By measurement, in quantum mechanics, we understand any process of interaction between classical and quantum objects, occurring apart from and independently of any observer." [11]

DAVID BOHM agreed that what is observed is distinct from the observer:

"If it were necessary to give all parts of the world a completely quantum-mechanical description, a person trying to apply quantum theory to the process of observation would be faced with an insoluble paradox. This would be so because he would then have to regard himself as something connected inseparably with the rest of the world. On the other hand,the very idea of making an observation implies that what is observed is totally distinct from the person observing it." [12]

And John Bell said:

"It would seem that the [quantum] theory is exclusively concerned about 'results of measurement', and has nothing to say about anything else. What exactly qualifies some physical systems to play the role of 'measurer'? Was the wavefunction of the world waiting to jump for thousands of millions of years until a single-celled living creature appeared? Or did it have to wait a little longer, for some better qualified system... with a Ph.D.? If the theory is to apply to anything but highly idealised laboratory operations, are we not obliged to admit that more or less 'measurement-like' processes are going on more or less all the time, more or less everywhere? Do we not have jumping then all the time?" [13]

10   *Atomic Physics and Human Knowledge*, Niels Bohr, p.51
11   *Quantum Mechanics,* Lev Landau and Evgeny Lifshitz, p.2
12   *Quantum Theory*, David Bohm, p.584
13   "Against Measurement," in *Speakable and Unspeakable in Quantum Mechanics*, p. 216)

Chapter 18

Three Essential Steps in a "Measurement" and "Observation"

We can distinguish three required elements in a measurement that can clarify the ongoing debate about the role of a conscious observer.

1) In standard quantum theory, the first required element is the collapse of the wave-function. This is the Dirac *projection postulate* and von Neumann **Process 1**.

However, the collapse might not leave a determinate record. If nothing in the environment is macroscopically affected so as to leave an indelible record of the collapse, we can say that no information about the collapse is created. The overwhelming fraction of collapses are of this kind. Moreover, information might actually be destroyed. For example, collisions between atoms or molecules in a gas that erase past information about their paths.

2) If the collapse occurs when the quantum system is entangled with a macroscopic measurement apparatus, a well-designed apparatus will also "collapse" into a correlated "pointer" state.

As we showed above for photons, the detector in the upper half of a Stern-Gerlach apparatus will fire, indicating detection of an electron with spin up. As with photons, if the probability amplitude | *up* > in the upper half does not collapse as the electron is detected, it can still be recombined with the probability amplitude | *down* > in the lower half to reconstruct the unseparated beam.

When the apparatus detects a particle, the second required element is that it produce a determinate record of the event. But this is impossible without an irreversible thermodynamic process that involves: *a*) the creation of at least one bit of new information (negative entropy) and *b*) the transfer away from the measuring apparatus of an amount of positive entropy (generally much, much) greater than the information created.

Notice that no conscious observer need be involved. We can generalize this second step to an event in the physical world that was not designed as a measurement apparatus by a physical scientist, but nevertheless leaves an indelible record of the collapse of a quantum state. This might be a highly specific single event, or the macroscopic consequence of billions of atomic-molecular level of events.

3) Finally, the third required element is an indelible determinate record that can be looked at by an observer (presumably conscious, although the consciousness itself has nothing to do with the measurement).

When we have all three of these essential elements, we have what we normally mean by a measurement and an observation, both involving a human being.

When we have only the first two, we can say metaphorically that the "universe is measuring itself," creating an information record of quantum collapse events. For example, every hydrogen atom formed in the early recombination era is a record of the time period when macroscopic bodies could begin to form. A certain pattern of photons records the explosion of a supernova billions of light years away. When recorded by the CCD in a telescope, it becomes a potential observation at a later time when an astronomer looks at the data.

Craters on the back side of the moon have for billions of years recorded collisions with solar system debris. But that could become observations only when the first NASA Apollo mission circled the moon.

Quantum Collapses Can Produce New Information

But they are *not measurements*, or even observations, until the existence of a semi-permanent record has been made first.

And that permanence requires positive entropy to be carried away from the event, whether in a physics lab, on the back of the moon, in a distant supernova, or a photon emitted by an atom in the cosmic microwave background.

If the positive entropy is not carried away, there is no permanent (or semi-permanent) record to be observed.

In that case, the new information is simply destroyed. The vast fraction of all quantum collapses do not produce lasting new information. Just as the vast fraction of negative entropy streams available do not create any new information structures.[14]

---

14   See Appendix B for more details,

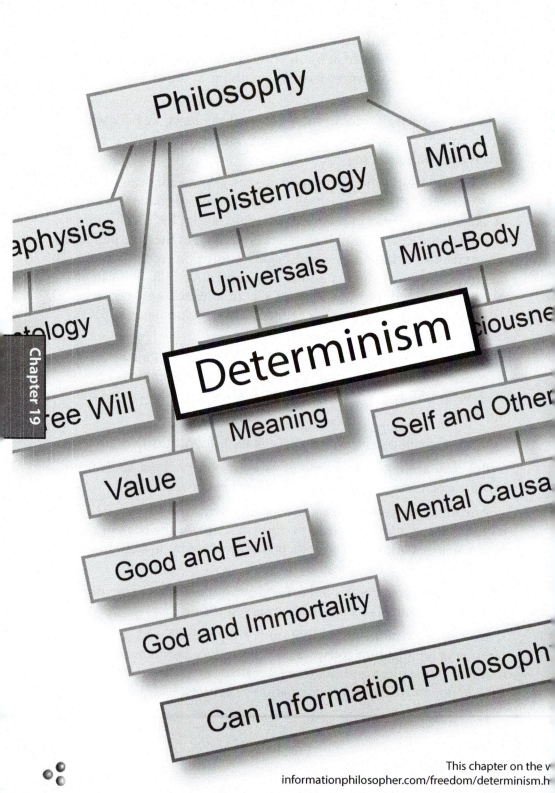

Chapter 19

Determinism

The "problem of determinism" looms large in philosophy, where it appears as the powerful alternative to libertarian freedom in the "problem of free will."[1]

But determinism is equally powerful in physics today. It appears to be the logical, the rational, even the metaphysical foundation of classical Newtonian physics. The alternative of chance is thought to be irrational. Chance cannot be a "reason" or an explanation, which the Greeks called a "logos." Chance is *alogos*, illogical. An uncaused cause has long been considered oxymoronic by analytic language philosophers who, to be sure, placed too much explanatory power in words.

Despite the fact that quantum physics seems to have shown that the microscopic world at least is ontologically indeterministic, the critics of quantum theory, who have developed several alternative "interpretations" of quantum mechanics, are equally divided into those who accept the indeterminism and those, following ALBERT EINSTEIN, ERWIN SCHRÖDINGER, and many others, hope to show that determinism can be restored to quantum theory by discovering "hidden variables," forces coming in "from outside space and time," or that there is only the "appearance" of randomness.

Determinism is the philosophical idea that every event or state of affairs, including every human decision and action, is the inevitable and necessary consequence of antecedent states of affairs. There is but one possible future.

More strictly, determinism should be distinguished from *pre-determinism*, the idea that the entire past (as well as the future) was determined at the origin of the universe.

Nor should determinism be confused with determination, the idea that events (including human actions) can be adequately determined by immediately prior events (such as an agent's reasons, motives, desires), without being *pre-determined* back to before the agent's birth or even back to the origin of the universe.

---

1   See chapter 4

Since modern quantum physics shows that the universe is indeterministic, with profound effects on microscopic processes at the atomic scale, we will find it valuable to distinguish pre-determinism from the adequate or *statistical* determinism that we have in the real world. Adequate determinism, which may be *arbitrarily close to and indistinguishable from certainty,* is the basis for the classical physical laws that apply in the macrocosmos.

Determinism is a modern name (coined in the nineteenth-century) for the ancient idea of DEMOCRITUS that causal deterministic laws control the motion of atoms, and that everything - including human minds - consists merely of atoms in a void.

Democritus' mentor and fellow materialist LEUCIPPUS said absolute necessity leaves no room in the cosmos for chance.

> "Nothing occurs at random, but everything for a reason and by necessity."

Determinism, especially the variation of "soft" determinism (cf. WILLIAM JAMES) or *compatibilism*, is supported as a theory of free will by a majority of philosophers, each with special vested interests in one or more of the many determinisms.

Compatibilists accept determinism but argue that man is free as long as his own will is one of the steps in the causal chain, even if his choices are completely predetermined for physical reasons or preordained by God.

And fatalism is a special form of determinism where every event in the future is fated to happen. Fatalism does not normally require that any causal laws or higher powers are involved. *Que sera, sera.*

The core idea of determinism is closely related to the idea of *causality.* But we can have causality without determinism, especially the "soft" causality that follows an "uncaused" event (a *causa sui*) that is not predictable from prior events.

ARISTOTLE called such events archai (ἀρχαί) - starting points or "fresh starts" in new causal chains which break the bonds of determinism.

Despite DAVID HUME's critical attack on the necessity of causes, many philosophers embrace causality and determinism strongly. Some even connect it to the very possibility of logic and reason. And Hume himself believed strongly, if inconsistently, in necessity. "'tis impossible to admit any medium betwixt chance and necessity,"[2] he said.

BERTRAND RUSSELL said causation may be *a priori*,

> "The law of causation, according to which later events can theoretically be predicted by means of earlier events, has often been held to be *a priori*, a necessity of thought, a category without which science would not be possible." [3]

Indeterminism

The idea of indeterminism appears to threaten causality and the basic idea of causal law. But it does not.

Indeterminism for some is simply an occasional event without a cause. We can have an adequate causality without strict determinism. Strict determinism means complete predictability (in principle, if not in practice) of events and only one possible future. Adequate determinism provides statistical predictability, which in normal situations for physical objects approaches statistical certainty.

An example of an event that is not strictly caused is one that depends on chance, like the flip of a coin. If the outcome is only probable, not certain, then the event can be said to have been caused by the coin flip, but the head or tails result itself was not predictable. So this causality, which recognizes prior events as causes, is undetermined and the result of chance alone.

We call this "soft" causality. Events are caused by prior (uncaused) events, but not determined by events earlier in the causal chain, which has been broken by the uncaused cause.

Determinism is critical for the question of free will. Strict determinism implies just one possible future. Chance means that the future is unpredictable. Chance allows alternative futures and the

2   *Treatise of Human Nature*, Book I, Part I, Section XIV, p.171
3   *Our Knowledge of the External World*, p.179

Chapter 19

question becomes how the one actual present is realized from these alternative possibilities.

The departure required from strict determinism is very slight compared to the miraculous ideas associated with the "*causa sui*" (self-caused cause) of the ancients.

Even in a world that contains quantum uncertainty, macroscopic objects are adequately, statistically determined to an extraordinary degree. The macroscopic "laws of nature" are just statistical laws that "emerge" when large numbers of atoms or molecules get together. For large enough numbers, the probabilistic laws approach practical certainty.

Determinism is an emergent property.[4]

Newton's laws of motion are deterministic enough to send men to the moon and back. Our two-stage model of free will[5] is large enough to ignore quantum uncertainty for the purpose of the reasoning will. The neural system is robust enough to insure that mental decisions are reliably transmitted to our limbs.

We call this determinism, only ineffective for extremely small structures, "adequate determinism." It is adequate enough to predict eclipses for the next thousand years or more with extraordinary precision.

Determination

Unlike his compatibilist predecessors, R.E.HOBART (the pseudonym of Harvard philosopher Dickinson S. Miller, a student of WILLIAM JAMES) explicitly does not endorse strict logical or physical determinism. He uses the word "determination," not determinism. And he explicitly endorses the existence of *alternative possibilities*, which can depend on absolute chance. Hobart is writing about six years after the discovery of quantum indeterminacy.

He says:

> I am not maintaining that determinism is true...it is not here affirmed that there are no small exceptions, no slight undetermined swervings, no ingredient of absolute chance.[6]

---

4   See chapter 26.
5   See chapter 4.
6   *Mind*, Vol XLIII, No. 169, January, 1934, p.2

"We say," I can will this or I can will that, whichever I choose ". Two courses of action present themselves to my mind. I think of their consequences, I look on this picture and on that, one of them commends itself more than the other, and I will an act that brings it about. I knew that I could choose either. That means that I had the power to choose either.[7]

Much later, PHILLIPA FOOT argued that because our actions are determined by our motives, our character and values, our feelings and desires, in no way leads to the conclusion that they are predetermined from the beginning of the universe.

For instance, an action said to be determined by the desires of the man who does it is not necessarily an action for which there is supposed to be a sufficient condition. In saying that it is determined by his desires we may mean merely that he is doing something that he wants to do, or that he is doing it for the sake of something else that he wants. There is nothing in this to suggest determinism.[8]

The presence of quantum uncertainty leads some philosophers to call the world undetermined. But indeterminism is somewhat misleading, with strong negative connotations, when most events are overwhelmingly "adequately determined." Nevertheless, speaking logically, if a single event is undetermined, then indeterminism is true, and determinism false.

There is no problem imagining that the three traditional mental faculties of reason - perception, conception, and comprehension - are all carried on more or less deterministically in a physical brain where quantum events do not interfere with normal operations.

There is also no problem imagining a role for randomness in the brain in the form of quantum level noise. Noise can introduce random errors into stored memories. Noise could create random associations of ideas during memory recall. This randomness may be driven by microscopic fluctuations that are amplified to the macroscopic level.

Our macro mind needs the micro mind for the free action items and thoughts in an *agenda* of alternative possibilities to be de-liberated by the will. The random micro mind is the "free" in free will and the source of human creativity. The adequately determined macro

Chapter 19

---

7   ibid, p.8
8   "Free Will as Involving Determinism," *The Philosophical Review*, vol LXVI, (1957), p.441

mind is the "will" in free will that de-liberates, choosing actions for which we can be morally responsible.

Determinism must be disambiguated from its close relatives causality, certainty, necessity, and predictability.

The Emergence of Determinism

Since the physical world is irreducibly indeterministic at the base level of atoms and molecules, there is actually no strict determinism at any "level" of the physical world.

With random motions at the base level, what emerges at the higher level of the macroscopic physical world and the human mind is adequate determinism. Determinism is an abstract theoretical idea that simplifies physical systems enough to allow the use of logical and mathematical methods on idealized abstract "objects" and "events." The apparent "determinism" of classical physics is the consequence of averaging over extremely large numbers of microscopic particles.

Adequate determinism "emerges" when we have large enough objects to be averaging over vast numbers of atoms and molecules.

Determinism is an emergent property, just as the concept of determinism emerged historically.

The History of Determinism[9]

The term (sic) determination is first attested in the late fourteenth century, "to come to an end," also "to settle, decide," from O.Fr. *determiner* (12c.), from L. *determinare* "set limits to," from *de-* "off" + *terminare* "to mark the end or boundary," from *terminus* "end, limit."

Its sense of "coming to a firm decision" (to do something) is from 1450. Determination as a "quality of being resolute" dates from 1822.

Before the nineteenth century determinists were usually called Necessarians. WILLIAM BELSHAM contrasted them (favorably) with the "incoherent" Libertarians in 1789. This was the first use of Libertarian. Libertarians were thought incoherent because liberty was

---

9   Sources, *OED, Webster's Third International*

thought to be unruly, random, unlawful, and - in a related term of the day - libertine.

The noun "determinism" appears first in 1846 in Sir WILLIAM HAMILTON's edition of THOMAS REID's works as a note on p.87.

> "There are two schemes of Necessity - the Necessitation by efficient - the Necessitation by final causes. The former is brute or blind Fate; the latter rational Determinism."

At about the same time, determinism is used by theologians to describe lack of free will.

In 1855, WILLIAM THOMSON (later LORD KELVIN) wrote,

> "The theory of Determinism, in which the will is determined or swayed to a particular course by external inducements and forced habits, so that the consciousness of freedom rests chiefly upon an oblivion of the antecedents of our choice."

ERNST CASSIRER claimed (mistakenly?) that determinism in the philosophical sense of a "doctrine that everything that happens is determined by a necessary chain of causation" dates from the work of EMIL DU BOIS-REYMOND in 1876.

Note that many ancient philosophers worried about this causal chain (ἄλυσις), but those philosophers who allowed the existence of chance, (ARISTOTLE, EPICURUS, LUCRETIUS, and ALEXANDER OF APHRODISIAS), denied such a causal chain, while maintaining that human decisions were caused by neither chance nor necessity but by a tertium quid - our autonomous human agency.

The adjective "determinist" appeared first in the *Contemporary Review* of October 1874 - "The objections of our modern Determinists." In the *Contemporary Review* of March 1885, R. H. Hutton described "The necessarian or determinist theory of human action."

WILLIAM JAMES's essay on "The Dilemma of Determinism" appeared at about the same time, in 1884. In it he coined the terms "soft determinism" (today's compatibilism), and "hard determinism" (strict determinism, indeed, pre-determinism from the beginning of time).

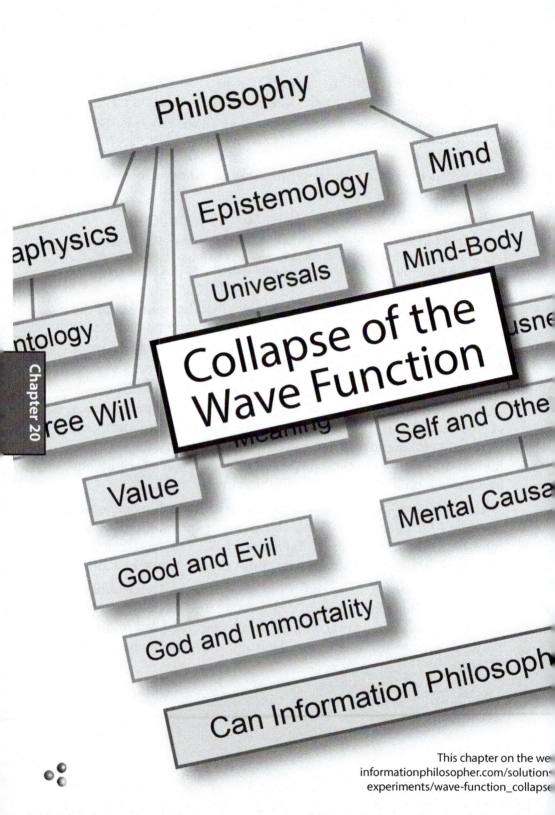

This chapter on the we
informationphilosopher.com/solution
experiments/wave-function_collapse

Collapse of the Wave Function

The probability amplitude wave function in quantum mechanics and its indeterministic collapse during a measurement is without doubt the most controversial problem in physics today. Of the several "interpretations" of quantum mechanics, more than half *deny the collapse* of the wave function[1]. Some of these deny quantum "jumps" and even the existence of particles!

So it is very important to understand the importance of what Paul Dirac called the *projection postulate* in quantum mechanics. The "collapse of the wave function" is also known as the "reduction of the wave packet." This usually describes the change from a system that can be seen as having many possible quantum states (Dirac's *principle of superposition*) to its randomly being found in only one of those possible states.

Although the collapse is historically thought to be *caused* by a measurement, and thus dependent on the role of a conscious observer[2] in preparing the experiment, collapses can occur whenever quantum systems interact (e.g., collisions between particles) or even spontaneously (radioactive decay).

The claim that a conscious observer is needed to collapse the wave function has injected a severely anthropomorphic element into quantum theory, suggesting that nothing happens in the universe except when physicists are making measurements. An extreme example is Hugh Everett III's Many Worlds theory, which says that the universe splits into two nearly identical universes whenever a measurement is made.

What is the Wave Function?

Perhaps the best illustration of the wave function is to show it passing though the famous slits in a two-slit experiment. It has been known for centuries that water waves passing through a small opening creates circular waves radiating outward from that opening. If there are two openings, the waves from each opening

---

1   See Other Interpretations of Quantum Mechanics on p.198
2   See The Role of the Conscious Observer on p.212

interfere with those from the other, producing waves twice as tall at the crests (or deep in the troughs) and cancelling perfectly where a crest from one meets a trough from the other.

When we send light waves through tiny slits, we see the same phenomenon.

Most of the light that reaches light detectors at the back lands right behind the barrier between the slits, which seems non-intuitive. Most amazingly, at some places there are null points, where no light at all appears in the interference pattern.

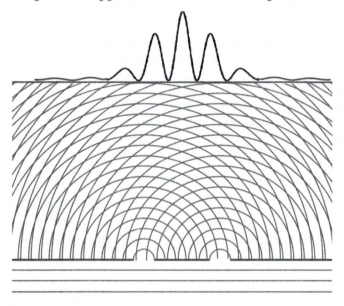

Figure 20-15. Interfering waves show crests and troughs.

Since Einstein's great hypothesis in 1905, we know that light actually consists of large numbers of individual photons, quanta of light. Our experiment can turn down the amount of light so low that we know there is only a single photon, a single particle of light in the experiment at any time. What we see then is the very slow accumulation of photons at the detectors, but with exactly the same overall interference pattern. And this leads to what RICHARD FEYNMAN called not just a "mystery," but actually the "only mystery" in quantum mechanics. How can the particle go through both slits to interfere with itself?

We can show that a single particle does not interfere with itself. It may only go through one slit, but with two slits open, its possible motions are different from the case with only one slit. Look at the possibilities function with the right slit closed. We have a *completely different interference pattern.*

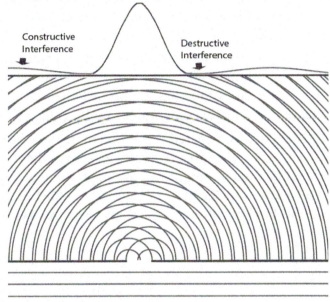

Constructive
Interference

Destructive
Interference

Figure 20-16. Many accounts say the interference fringes are lost, but there is still interference between particles that come from different parts of the slit.

Information Physics Explains the Two-Slit Experiment

Although we cannot say anything about a single particle's whereabouts, information philosophy can help us to see clearly in these two figures that while it may only go through one slit, what goes through the two slits and what it is that interferes with itself is *abstract information*, the mathematical probability of finding the particle at each of the possible places it may go.

Neither matter nor energy, we call this abstract information the "possibilities function." The wave function is exploring all the possible locations where a particle may be found. So the quantum wave going through the slit is an abstract number, neither material nor energy, just a probability. It is *information* about where particles of matter (or particles of light if we shoot photons at the slit) will be found when we record them. Only large numbers of experiments reveal the wave nature and its interference. The location of a single particle is indeterminate, the result of ontological chance.

But the average locations of millions of particles shows the wave-like interference and demonstrates the *causal* power of the *immaterial* and abstract possibilities function. For example, no particle lands at the null points!

Now information philosophy accepts that information needs matter for its embodiment and energy for its communication. So where is the "possibilities function" embodied? Before we explain that, let's first review why this function is said to "collapse."

When Einstein first considered this problem in 1905, he thought of the light wave as *energy* spread out everywhere in the wave. So it was energy that he thought might be traveling faster than light, violating his brand new principle of relativity (published just two months after his light quantum paper). Let's visualize his concern.

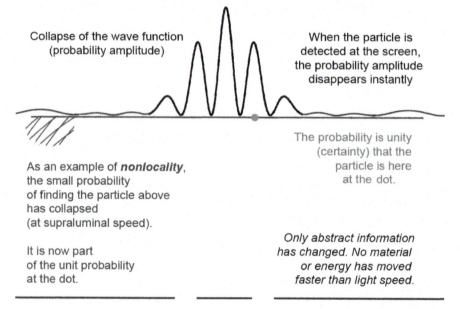

Collapse of the wave function
(probability amplitude)

When the particle is
detected at the screen,
the probability amplitude
disappears instantly

As an example of **nonlocality**,
the small probability
of finding the particle above
has collapsed
(at supraluminal speed).

It is now part
of the unit probability
at the dot.

The probability is unity
(certainty) that the
particle is here
at the dot.

*Only abstract information
has changed. No material
or energy has moved
faster than light speed.*

Figure 20-17. Once the particle appears anywhere, the possibilities of it appearing anywhere else must immediately vanish.

Einstein assumed

> the energy of a beam of light from a point source (according to the Maxwellian theory of light or, more generally, according to any wave theory) is continuously spread over an ever increasing volume... In accordance with the assumption to be considered here, the energy of a light ray spreading out from a point source is not continuously distributed over an increasing space but consists of a finite number of energy quanta which are localized at points in space, which move without dividing, and which can only be produced and absorbed as complete units.[3]

The interfering probability amplitude waves disappear instantly everywhere once the particle is detected, but we left a small fragment of interfering waves on the left side of the figure to ask a question first raised by Einstein in 1905.

What happens to the small but finite probability that the particle might have been found at the left side of the screen? How has that probability instantaneously (with "action-at-a-distance faster than light speed) been collected into the unit probability at the dot?

The answer provided by information philosophy is that nothing collapsed, nothing moved at any speed. The wave function is not energy or matter, it is only abstract information that tells us the probabilities of various possibilities.

The idea of probability - or possibilities - "collapsing" is much easier to understand than something material or energetic gathering itself suddenly in one location. Probability and possibilities are abstract ideas. They are *immaterial*.

It was at the Solvay conference in Brussels in 1927, twenty-two years after Einstein first tried to understand what is happening when the wave collapses, when he noted;

> "If $|\psi|^2$ were simply regarded as the probability that at a certain point a given particle is found at a given time, it could happen that the same elementary process produces an action ... assumes an entirely peculiar mechanism of action at a distance." [4]

Einstein later came to call this *spukhafte Fernwerkungen*, "spooky action at a distance." It is now known as *nonlocality*.

---

3   "A Heuristic Viewpoint on the Production and Transformation of Light," English translation - American Journal of Physics, 33, 5, 367

4   *Quantum Theory at the Crossroads*, Bacciagaluppi and Valentini, 2009. p.442

Chapter 20

Where Is Information About Probabilities Embodied?

Information philosophy can now answer this critical part of the mystery. The information is not embodied in energy, as Einstein finally realized. It is also not embodied in the matter of a particle, such as an electron. Einstein said that quantum mechanics is "incomplete" because the particle has no definite position before a measurement. He was right. But that is not because the particle is distributed in space.

What is distributed in space is seen clearly in the figures above, the waves of probability information. But where is that information embodied? The answer is astonishingly simple. It is embodied in the material of the experimental apparatus. It is in the "boundary conditions" of the wall with its slits and the screen with its detectors.

The waves are simply the mathematical solutions of the Schrödinger wave equation given the boundary conditions and the wavelength of the particles. When one slit is closed, the abstract "possibilities function" looks quite different from the two-slit open case. The mystery of how the particle going through one slit is aware that the other slit is open or closed is completely solved.

We can regard those mathematical possibilities as the values of what Einstein in 1921 called a "ghost field" or "leading field" that predicts the probability of finding his light quanta. A few years later, inspired by Einstein, Louis de Broglie called it a "pilot wave" in his 1924 thesis. Then in 1926, Max Born used Einstein's idea as the basis for a "statistical interpretation" of quantum mechanics. He wrote:

> I shall recall a remark that *Einstein* made about the behavior of the wave field and light quanta. He said that perhaps the waves only have to be wherever one needs to know the path of the corpuscular light quanta, and in that sense, he spoke of a "ghost field." It determines the probability that a light quantum - viz., the carrier of energy and impulse – follows a certain path; however, the field itself is ascribed no energy and no impulse.

> ... from the complete analogy between light quanta and electrons, one might consider formulating the laws of electron motion in a similar manner. This is closely related to regarding the *de Broglie-Schrödinger* waves as "ghost fields," or better yet, "guiding fields."

... The paths of these corpuscles are determined only to the extent that they are constrained by the law of energy and impulse; moreover, only a probability that a certain path will be followed will be determined by the function ψ. One can perhaps summarize this, somewhat paradoxically, as: The motion of the particle follows the laws of probability, but the probability itself propagates in accord with causal laws.[5]

The sudden change in probability also occurs in the Einstein-Podolsky-Rosen experiments, where measurement of one particle transmits neither matter or energy to the other "entangled" particle. Instead, new information has come into the universe instantaneously. That information, together with conservation of angular momentum, makes the state of the coherently entangled second particle *certain*, however far away it might be after the measurement.[6]

The standard "orthodox" interpretation of quantum mechanics includes the *projection postulate*. This is the idea that once one of the possibilities becomes actual at one position, the probabilities for actualization at all other positions becomes instantly zero. New information has appeared, but there is no information transfer that could be used to communicate that information.

The *principle of superposition* tells us that before a measurement, a system may be in one of many possible states. In the two-slit experiment, this includes all the possible positions where $|\psi(x)|^2$ is not zero. Once the quantum system (the photon or electron) interacts with a specific detector at the screen, all other possibilities vanish. It is unfortunate that the word "collapse" was chosen, since it suggests some physical motion, where nothing at all is moving when probabilities change.

When we deny the appropriateness of the word "collapse," we do not deny the underlying indeterministic physics. Just as in philosophy, where it is the language used that is often the source of confusion, we find that thinking about the information involved, rather than the words, clarifies the problem in physics.

Chapter 20

---

5   Quantum mechanics of collision processes (*Quantenmechanik der Stoßvorgänge*), *Zeitschrift für Physik*. 38 (1926), 803-827
6   See the next chapter for the two-particle wave function.

Entanglement

Entanglement is a mysterious quantum phenomenon that is widely, but mistakenly, described as capable of transmitting information over vast distances faster than the speed of light. It has proved very popular with science writers, philosophers of science, and many scientists who hope to use the mystery to deny one or more of the basic concepts underlying quantum physics.

Some commentators say that *nonlocality* and *entanglement* are a "second revolution" in quantum mechanics, "the greatest mystery in physics," or "science's strangest phenomenon," and that quantum physics has been "reborn." They usually quote ERWIN SCHRÖDINGER as saying

> "I would not call that one but rather the characteristic trait of quantum mechanics," the one that enforces its entire departure from classical lines of thought."[1]

SCHRÖDINGER knew that his two-particle wave function could not have the same simple interpretation as the single particle, which can be visualized in ordinary three-dimensional configuration space. And he is right that entanglement exhibits a richer form of the "action-at-a-distance" and nonlocality that ALBERT EINSTEIN had already identified in the collapse of the single particle wave function.

The main difference is that two particles instead of one acquire new properties, and they do it instantaneously (at faster than light speeds), just as in the case of a single-particle measurement, where the finite probability of appearing at various distant locations collapses to zero at the instant the particle is found somewhere. This two-particle instantaneous interaction is *nonseparability*.

We can disagree with Schrödinger, who was enthusiastic about the Einstein-Posolsky-Rosen attack in 1935 on quantum mechanics as "incomplete" and who gave the phenomenon the name "entanglement." In fact, the entanglement of two indistinguishable

Chapter 21

---

1   *Mathematical Proceedings of the Cambridge Philosophical Society*, Volume 31, Issue 04, October 1935, pp 555-563

particles can be completely understood with PAUL DIRAC's *principle of superposition,* his *axiom of measurement,* and his *projection postulate.* These three fundamentals of quantum mechanics already explain the "mysterious" phenomena that are impossible in classical mechanics, notably the one-particle mystery in the two-slit experiment that RICHARD FEYNMAN calls "the only mystery" in quantum mechanics.

Information philosophy analyzes both the single-particle and two-particle wave function "collapses" as a question of who knows what when, that is, what information exists at each moment and where about the particle(s).

Entanglement depends on two quantum properties that are simply impossible in "classical" physics. One is called *nonlocality.* The other is *nonseparability.* Each of these might be considered a mystery in its own right, but fortunately *information physics* (and the information interpretation of quantum mechanics) can explain them both, with no equations, in a way that should be understandable to the lay person.

This may not be good news for the science writers and publishers who turn out so many titles each year claiming that quantum physics implies that there are multiple parallel universes, that the minds of physicists are manipulating "quantum reality," that there is nothing "really" there until we look at it, that we can travel backwards in time, that things can be in two places at the same time, that we can teleport material from one place to another, and of course that we can send signals faster than the speed of light.

A second concern for Einstein was that the wave function ψ for an isolated free particle evolves in time to occupy all space. All positions become equally probable. Yet when we observe the particle, it is always located at some particular place. This does not prove that the particle had a particular place before the observation, but Einstein had a commitment to "elements of reality" that he thought no one could doubt. One of those elements is a particle's position. He asked the question, "Does the particle have a precise position the moment before it is measured?" The Copenhagen answer was sometimes "no," more often it was "we don't know," or "Don't ask?"

Einstein's Discovery of Nonlocality and Nonseparability

ALBERT EINSTEIN was the first to see the nonlocal character of quantum phenomena. He may have seen it as early as 1905, the same year he published his special theory of relativity. But it was perfectly clear to him twenty-two years later (ten years after his general theory of relativity and his explanation of how quanta of light are emitted and absorbed by atoms), when he described non-locality to a conference of physicists from around the world in Belgium in 1927 at the fifth Solvay conference.

Then a few years later, in 1935, Einstein, BORIS PODOLSKY, and NATHAN ROSEN proposed a thought experiment (known by their initials as EPR) to exhibit what they thought were internal contradictions in the new quantum physics. Einstein hoped to show that quantum theory could not describe certain intuitive "elements of reality" and thus was either *incomplete* or, as he hoped, demonstrably incorrect.

Einstein and his colleagues Schrödinger, MAX PLANCK, DAVID BOHM, and others hoped for a return to deterministic physics, and the elimination of mysterious quantum phenomena like *superposition of states* and the "*collapse*" of the wave function. EPR continues to fascinate determinist philosophers of science who hope to prove that quantum indeterminacy does not exist.

Beyond the problem of nonlocality, the EPR "thought experiment" introduced the problem of "*nonseparability*." This mysterious phenomenon appears to transfer something physical faster than the speed of light. Actually there is merely an instantaneous change in the *immaterial* information about probabilities or possibilities for locating the particles.

The 1935 EPR paper was based on a question of Einstein's about two electrons fired in opposite directions from a central source with equal velocities. He imagined them starting at time t_0 some distance apart and approaching one another with high velocities. Then for a short time interval from t_1 to $t_1 + \Delta t$ the particles are in contact with one another.

After the particles are measured at t_1, quantum mechanics describes them with a single two-particle wave function that is not separable into the product of two independent single-particle wave functions. Because electrons are *indistinguishable* particles, it is not proper to say electron *1* goes this way and electron *2* that way. (Nevertheless, it is convenient to label the particles, as we do in the illustrations below.) Until the next measurement, it is misleading to think that specific particles have distinguishable paths. Either particle could be anywhere.

Einstein said correctly that at a later time t₂, measurement of one electron's position would instantly establish the position of the other electron - without measuring it explicitly.

Electrons are prepared with opposite linear momenta and travel apart from the center.

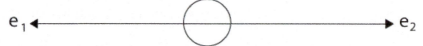

If the position of electron 1 is measured at some time, the position of electron 2 must be exactly opposite by conservation of linear momentum. So measuring one tells you something about the other at a great distance. Apparently information travels faster than light speed.

Figure 21-19. Einstein's first explanation of "action-at-a-distance."

In this first discussion of the problem, Einstein simply used *conservation of linear momentum* to calculate the position of the second electron. Although conservation laws are rarely cited as the explanation, they are the reason that entangled particles always produce correlated results. If the results were not always correlated, the implied violation of a fundamental conservation law would be a much bigger story than entanglement itself, as interesting as that is.

Although Einstein mentioned conservation in the original EPR paper, it is noticeably absent from later work. An exception is EUGENE WIGNER, writing on the problem of measurement in 1963:

> If a measurement of the momentum of one of the particles is carried out — the possibility of this is never questioned — and gives the result p, the state vector of the other particle suddenly becomes a (slightly damped) plane wave with the momentum $-p$. This statement is synonymous with

the statement that a measurement of the momentum of the second particle would give the result -*p*, as follows from the conservation law for linear momentum.[2]

This idea of something measured in one place "influencing" measurements far away challenged what Einstein thought of as "local reality." He famously called nonseparability "*spukhafte Fern-wirkungen*" or "spooky action at a distance."

Einstein had objected to nonlocal phenomena as early as the Solvay Conference of 1927, when he criticized the collapse of the wave function as "instantaneous-action-at-a-distance."

Oddly, Einstein's criticism resembles the criticisms by RENÉ DESCARTES and others about Newton's theory of gravitation. Newton's opponents charged that his theory was "action at a distance" and instantaneous. Einstein's general relativity shows that gravity is not instantaneous. It travels at the speed of light and is mediated by a gravitational field that can be viewed mathematically as curvature in space-time.

But note that when a probability function collapses to unity in one place and zero elsewhere, nothing physical is moving from one place to the other.

In 1964, JOHN BELL showed how the 1935 "thought experiments" of Einstein, Podolsky, and Rosen (EPR) could be made into real physical experiments. Bell put limits on the "hidden variables" that might deny *nonlocality* and possibly restore a deterministic physics. His test was in the form of what he called *inequalities*, the violation of which would confirm standard quantum mechanics.

Since Bell's work, many other physicists have defined other "Bell inequalities" and developed increasingly sophisticated experiments to test them. Every test has confirmed standard quantum mechanics.

The first practical and workable experiments to test the EPR paradox had been suggested by DAVID BOHM in 1952. Instead of only linear momentum conservation, Bohm proposed using two electrons that are prepared in an initial state of known total spin. If one electron spin is 1/2 in the up direction and the other is spin down or -1/2, the total spin is zero. The underlying physical law of impor-

Chapter 21

2   "The Problem of Measurement," in *Quantum Theory and Measurement*, Wheeler and Zurek, p,340

tance is a second conservation law, in this case the conservation of angular momentum. If electron *1* is prepared with spin down and electron *2* with spin up, the total angular momentum is zero.

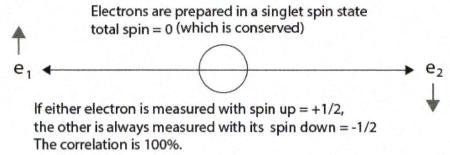

Electrons are prepared in a singlet spin state
total spin = 0 (which is conserved)

If either electron is measured with spin up = +1/2,
the other is always measured with its spin down = -1/2
The correlation is 100%.

Figure 21-20. David Bohm changed EPR to measure electron spins.

Quantum theory says the two electrons are in a *superposition* of combined spin up (+) and spin down (-) states,

$$| \psi > = 1/\sqrt{2}) | + - > - 1/\sqrt{2}) | - + > \quad (1)$$

The principles of quantum mechanics say that the prepared system is in a linear combination of these two states, and can provide only the probabilities of finding the entangled system in either the $| + - >$ state or the $| - + >$ state. Quantum mechanics does not describe the paths or the spins of the individual particles. Note that should measurements result in a $| ++ >$ or $| - - >$ state, that would violate the conservation of angular momentum.

EPR tests can be done more easily with polarized photons than with electrons, which require complex magnetic fields. The first of these was done in 1972 by STUART FREEDMAN and JOHN CLAUSER at UC Berkeley. They used oppositely polarized photons (one with spin = +1, the other spin = -1) coming from a central source. Again, the total photon spin of zero is conserved. Their data, in agreement with quantum mechanics, violated Bell's inequalities to high statistical accuracy, thus providing strong evidence against local hidden-variable theories and confirming quantum mechanics.

For more on superposition of states and the physics of photons, see the Dirac 3-polarizers experiment in appendix B.

Clauser, MICHAEL HORNE, ABNER SHIMONY, and RICHARD HOLT (known collectively as CHSH) and later ALAIN ASPECT did more sophisticated tests. The outputs of the polarization analyzers were fed to a coincidence detector that records the instantaneous measurements, described as + -, - +, + +, and - - . The first two (+ - and - +) conserve the spin angular momentum and are the only types ever observed in these nonlocality/entanglement tests.

A typical CHSH apparatus sends the signals from the polarization analyzers to a coincidence monitor.

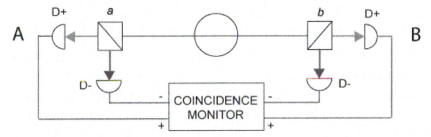

The coincidence monitor then counts four kinds of events, N++, N+-, N-+, and N--. Perfect correlation (and conservation of spin angular momentum) allows only + - and - + events.

Figure 21-21. The CHSH teams looked for perfect synchronization.

With the exception of some of Holt's early results that were later found to be erroneous, *no evidence has so far been found of any failure of standard quantum mechanics.* And as experimental accuracy has improved by orders of magnitude, quantum physics has correspondingly been confirmed to one part in 10^{16}, and the speed of any transfer of information between particles has a lower limit of 10^6 times the speed of light. There has been no evidence for local "hidden variables."

Nicolas Gisin and his colleagues have extended the polarized photon tests of EPR and the Bell inequalities to a separation of 18 kilometers near Geneva. They continue to find 100% correlation and no evidence of the "hidden variables" sought after by Einstein and David Bohm.

Nevertheless, wishful-thinking experimenters continue to look for possible "loopholes" in the experimental results, such as detector inefficiencies that might be hiding results favorable to Einstein's picture of "local reality."

Chapter 21

The Importance of Conservation Laws in Entanglement

Conservation laws are the consequence of extremely deep properties of nature that arise from simple considerations of symmetry. We regard these laws as "cosmological principles." Physical laws do not depend on the absolute place and time of experiments, nor their particular direction in space. Conservation of linear momentum depends on the translation invariance of physical systems, conservation of energy the independence of time, and conservation of angular momentum the invariance under rotations.

Recall that the EPR experiment starts with two electrons (or photons) prepared in an entangled state that is a linear combination of pure two-particle states, each of which conserves the total angular momentum and, of course, conserves the linear momentum as in Einstein's original EPR example. The initial information about the linear and angular momenta is established by the state preparation (a measurement).

Quantum mechanics describes the probability amplitude wave function ψ of the two-particle system as in a superposition of two-particle states. It is not separable into a product of single-particle states, and there is no information about the identical indistinguishable electrons traveling along distinguishable paths.

The probability amplitude wave function ψ travels from the source (at the speed of light or less). Let's assume that at t_1 observer A finds an electron (e_1) with spin up.

After the "first" measurement, new information comes into existence telling us that the wave function ψ has "collapsed" into the state $| + - >$. Just as in the two-slit experiment, probabilities have now become certainties. If the "first" measurement finds electron *1* is spin up, so the entangled electron *2* must be found by observer B to be in a "second" measurement with spin down to conserve angular momentum.

Notice that Einstein's intuition is in part correct that the "second" result seems already "determined" or "fixed" before the second measurement. The result is determined by the law of conservation of momentum that the total the spin must remain zero.

But the measurement by observer B was not pre-determined before observer A's measurement. It was simply *determined by her measurement*. And conservation of linear momentum tells us that at t_1 the second electron is equidistant from the source in the opposite direction.

As with any wave-function collapse, the probability amplitude information "travels" instantly.

But unlike the single particle in the two-slit experiment, where the collapse goes to a specific point in 3-dimensional configuration space, the "collapse" here is a "projection" into one of the two possible 6-dimensional two-particle quantum states $| + - >$ or $| - + >$.

Just as the single particle in the two-slit experiment did not have a position before the measurement, the two particles, which just before the measurement did not have positions, instantly acquire their positions in a space-like separation after the measurement.

This makes "visualization" (Schrödinger's *Anschaulichkeit*) more difficult, but the parallel with the collapse in the two-slit case provides an intuitive insight of sorts.

Schrödinger said that his "Wave Mechanics" provided more "*visualizability*" than the "damned quantum jumps" of the Copenhagen school, as he called them. He was right.

But we must focus on the probability amplitude wave function of the prepared two-particle state, and not attempt to describe the paths or locations of independent particles - which is only possible after some measurement has been made. We must also keep in mind the conservation laws that Einstein used to describe nonlocal behavior in the first place. Then we can see that the "mystery" of nonlocality for two particles is primarily the same mystery as the single-particle collapse of the wave function. But there is an extra mystery, one we might call an "enigma," of the *nonseparability* of identical indistinguishable particles.

In his 1935 paper (and his correspondence with Einstein), Schrödinger described the two particles in EPR as "entangled" in English, *verschränkt* in German, which means something like cross-linked. It describes someone standing with arms crossed.

In the time evolution of an entangled two-particle state according to the Schrödinger equation, we can visualize it (just as we visualize the single-particle wave function) as collapsing when a measurement is made. The discontinuous "jump" is also described as the "reduction of the wave packet." This is apt in the two-particle case, where the superposition of | + - > and | - + > states is "projected" or "reduced to one of these states, say | - + >, and then further reduced to the product of two independent one-particle states, | - >| + >.

Measurement of a two-particle wave function simultaneously measures both particles, reducing them to *separate* one-particle wave functions, after which they are no longer entangled.

When entangled, the particles are *nonseparable*. Once measured, they are separate quantum systems with their own wave functions. They are no longer entangled.

In the two-particle case (instead of just one particle making an appearance), when either particle is measured we know instantly the now determinate properties of the other particle. They are the properties that satisfy the conservation laws, including its location equidistant from, but on the opposite side of, the source, and the complementary spin.

In the one-particle case, it has no definite position before the experiment, then it appears somewhere. For two particles, neither one has a position, then both appear simultaneously (in an appropriate frame of reference and with required opposite spins).[3]

Can a Special Frame Resolve the EPR Paradox?

Almost every presentation of the EPR paradox begins with something like "Alice observes one particle..." and concludes with the question "How does the second particle get the information needed so that Bob's measurements correlate perfectly with Alice?"

There is a fundamental *asymmetry* in this framing of the EPR experiment. It is a surprise that Einstein, who was so good at seeing deep symmetries, did not consider how to remove the asymmetry.

---

3   For an animation of a two-particle measurement, see informationphilosopher. com/solutions/experiments/EPR/EPR-collapse.gif

Consider this reframing: Alice's measurement collapses the two-particle wave function. The two indistinguishable particles simultaneously appear at locations in a space-like separation. The frame of reference in which the source of the two entangled particles and the two experimenters are at rest is a *special frame* in the following sense.

As Einstein knew very well, there are frames of reference moving with respect to the laboratory frame of the two observers in which the time order of the events can be reversed. In some moving frames Alice measures first, but in others Bob measures first.

If there is a special frame of reference (not a *preferred frame* in the relativistic sense), surely it is the one in which the origin of the two entangled particles is at rest. Assuming that Alice and Bob are also at rest in this special frame and equidistant from the origin, we arrive at the simple picture in which any measurement that causes the two-particle wave function to collapse makes both particles appear simultaneously at determinate places with fully correlated properties (just those that are needed to conserve energy, momentum, angular momentum, and spin).

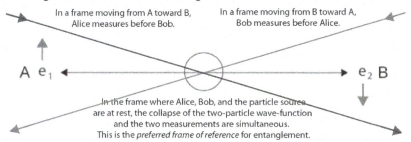

In a frame moving from A toward B, Alice measures before Bob.

In a frame moving from B toward A, Bob measures before Alice.

A e_1 e_2 B

In the frame where Alice, Bob, and the particle source are at rest, the collapse of the two-particle wave-function and the two measurements are simultaneous. This is the *preferred frame of reference* for entanglement.

Figure 21-22. In this special frame the source and measurements are at rest and both measurements are made at exactly the same time.

Clearly, the idea that different relativistic frames of reference change the order of the measurements throws doubt on claims by either observer to "measure first."

We can also ask what happens if Bob is not at the same distance from the origin as Alice. This introduces a positional asymmetry. But there is still no time asymmetry from the point of view of the two-particle wave function collapse.

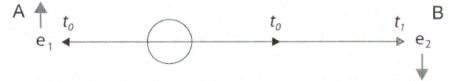

If observer A measures electron 1 with spin up at t_0, electron 2 *instantly* is spin down (Ψ collapses to $| + - >$).

Electron 2 is then *determined* to be found with spin down if measured by observer B at a later time t_1.

But this was not *predetermined* before A's measurement at t_0.

Figure 21-23. Here Alice measures long before Bob's measurement.

When Alice detects a particle (with spin up), at that instant the other particle also becomes determinate (with spin down) at the same distance on the other side of the origin. It continues, in that determinate state, to Bob's measuring apparatus.

Our idea of a special frame is not new.

Back in the 1960's, C. W. Rietdijk and Hilary Putnam independently, but mistakenly, argued that physical determinism could be proved true by considering the experiments and observers A and B in the diagram below to be moving at high speed with respect to one another. Roger Penrose developed a similar argument in his book *The Emperor's New Mind*, called the "Andromeda Paradox."

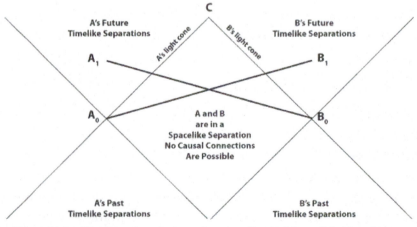

Figure 21-24. Physicists have known about our "special frame" for decades.

Nicolas Gisin's colleagues, Antoine Suarez and Valerio Scarani, used this idea of hyperplanes of simultaneity to make what they called "before-before" measurements.

Suarez and Scarani used the fact that for some relative speeds between the two observers A and B, observer A could "see" the measurement of observer B to be in his future, and vice versa. Because the two experiments have a "space-like" separation (neither is inside the causal light cone of the other), *each observer thinks he does his own measurement before the other.*

Gisin tested the limits on this effect by moving mirrors in the path to the birefringent crystals and showed that, like all other Bell experiments, the "before-before" suggestion of Suarez and Scarani did nothing to invalidate quantum mechanics.

But these experiments were able to put a lower limit on the speed with which the information about probabilities collapses, estimating it as at least thousands - perhaps millions - of times the speed of light and showed empirically that probability collapses are essentially instantaneous.

Despite all his experimental tests verifying quantum physics, including the "reality" of nonlocality and entanglement, Nicolas Gisin continues to explore the EPR paradox, considering the possibility that signals are coming to the entangled particles from "outside space-time."

Do We Need Superdeterminism?

During a mid-1980's interview by BBC Radio 3 organized by P. C. W. Davies and J. R. Brown, John Bell proposed the idea of a *"superdeterminism"* that could explain the correlation of results in entangled two-particle experiments without the need for faster-than-light signaling. The two experiments need only have been predetermined by causes reaching both experiments from an earlier time.

> Davies: I was going to ask whether it is still possible to maintain, in the light of experimental experience, the idea of a deterministic universe?
>
> Bell: You know, one of the ways of understanding this business is to say that the world is super-deterministic. That not only is inanimate nature

deterministic, but we, the experimenters who imagine we can choose to do one experiment rather than another, are also determined. If so, the difficulty which this experimental result creates disappears.[4]

Bell's superdeterminism would deny the important "free choice" of the experimenter (originally suggested by Bohr and Heisenberg) and later explored by JOHN CONWAY and SIMON KOCHEN. Conway and Kochen claim that the experimenters' free choice requires that atoms must have free will, something they call their *Free Will Theorem*.

In his 1996 book, *Time's Arrow and Archimedes' Point*, HUW PRICE proposes an Archimedean point "outside space and time" as a solution to the problem of nonlocality in the Bell experiments in the form of an "advanced action."

Rather than a "superdeterministic" common cause coming from "outside space and time" (as proposed by Bell, Gisin, Suarez, and others), Price argues that there might be a cause coming backwards in time from some interaction in the future. Penrose and STUART HAMEROFF have also promoted this idea of "backward causation," sending information backward in time in the Libet experiments and in the EPR experiments.

EPR "Loopholes" and Free Will

Investigators who try to recover the "elements of local reality" that Einstein wanted, and who hope to eliminate the irreducible randomness of quantum mechanics that follows from wave functions as probability amplitudes, often cite "loopholes" in EPR experiments. For example, the "detection loophole" claims that the efficiency of detectors is so low that they are missing many events that might prove Einstein was right.

Most all the loopholes have now been closed, but there is one loophole that can never be closed because of its metaphysical/philosophical nature. That is the "(pre-)determinism loophole."

---

4   *The Ghost in the Atom*, P.C.W. Davies and J. Brown, ch.3, p.47

If every event occurs for reasons that were established at the beginning of the universe, then all the careful experimental results are meaningless. Conway and Kochen have formalized this loophole in what they call the Free Will Theorem.

Although Conway and Kochen do not claim to have proven free will in humans, they assert that should such a freedom exist, then the same freedom must apply to the elementary particles.

What Conway and Kochen are really describing is nothing more than the indeterminism that quantum mechanics has introduced into the world. Although indeterminism is a requirement for human freedom, it is insufficient by itself to provide both "free" and "will" as we saw in chapter 4.

We also need the *adequate or statistical determinism* in the second stage of "free will" to ensure that whatever our "free choice" may be, it has been made consistent with our reasons for the choice.

There are no such considerations of reasons, motives, feelings, etc. going on at the quantum level for electrons. But Conway and Kochen are right about the fundamental connection between quantum indeterminism and free will.

Chapter 21

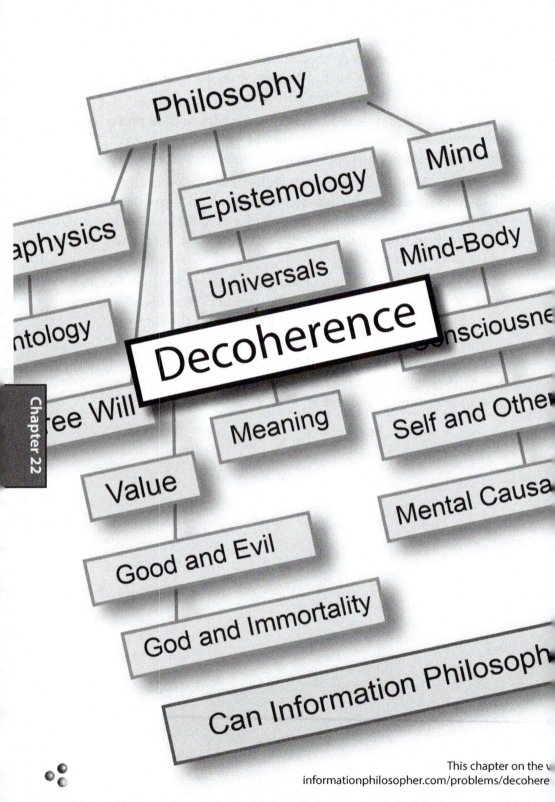

Decoherence

Decoherence is the study of interactions between a quantum system (generally a very small number of microscopic particles like electrons, photons, atoms, molecules, etc. - often just a single particle) and the larger macroscopic environment, which is normally treated "classically," that is, by ignoring quantum effects, but which decoherence theorists study quantum mechanically. Decoherence theorists attribute the absence of macroscopic quantum effects like interference (which is a coherent process) to interactions between a quantum system and the larger macroscopic environment.

They maintain that no system can be completely isolated from the environment. Decoherence, they say, accounts for the disappearance of macroscopic quantum effects, and is experimentally correlated with the loss of isolation.

Niels Bohr maintained that a macroscopic apparatus used to "measure" quantum systems must be treated classically. John von Neumann, on the other hand, assumed that everything is made of quantum particles, even the mind of the observer. This led him and Werner Heisenberg to say that a "cut" must be located somewhere between the quantum system and the mind, which would operate in a sort of "psycho-physical parallelism."[1]

A main characteristic of quantum systems is the appearance of wavelike interference effects. These only show up in large numbers of repeated identical experiments that make measurements on single particles at a time. Interference is never directly "observed" in a single experiment. When interference is present in a system, the system is called "coherent." Decoherence then is the loss or suppression of that interference.

Interference experiments require that the system of interest is extremely well isolated from the environment, except for the "measurement apparatus." This apparatus must be capable of recording the information about what has been measured. It can

---

1   Not to be confused with *panpsychism*.

be a photographic plate or an electron counter, anything capable of registering a quantum level event, usually by releasing a cascade of metastable processes that amplify the quantum-level event to the macroscopic "classical" world, where an "observer" can see the result.

This does not mean that specific quantum level events are determined by that observer (as noted by several of the great quantum physicists - MAX BORN, PASCUAL JORDAN, ERWIN SCHRÖDINGER, PAUL DIRAC, and textbook authors LANDAU and LIFSHITZ, ALBERT MESSIAH, and KURT GOTTFRIED, among others). Quantum processes are happening all the time. Most quantum events are never observed, let alone measured, though they can be inferred from macroscopic phenomenological observations.

To be sure, those quantum events that are "measured" in a physics experiment which is set up to measure a certain quantity are dependent on the experimenter and the design of the experiment. To measure the electron spin in a Stern-Gerlach experiment, for example, the experimenter is "free to choose" to measure the z-component of the spin, rather than the x- or y-component. This will influence quantum level events in the following ways:

The experimental outcome will produce a definite value for the z-component of the spin (either +1/2 or -1/2)

The x-component of the spin after the measurement will be in a linear combination/superposition of +1/2 or -1/2 states

$$| \psi > = (1/\sqrt{2}) | +1/2 > + (1/\sqrt{2}) | -1/2 >$$

It is in this sense that Bohr and Heisenberg described properties of the quantum world as not existing until we make a measurement. We have a "free choice" which experiment we perform, what we measure. If we measure position for example, the precise position value did not exist immediately before the measurement.

On the other hand, we can not create the particular value for the position. This is a *random choice made by nature,* as Dirac put it.

The Decoherence Program

The "decoherence program" of H. DIETER ZEH, ERICH JOOS, WOJCIECH ZUREK, JOHN WHEELER, MAX TEGMARK, and others has multiple aims -

• to show how classical physics emerges from quantum physics. They call this the "quantum to classical transition."

• to explain the failure to see any macroscopic superpositions of quantum states (e.g., Schrödinger's Cat as a superposition of live and dead cats).

• in particular, to identify the mechanism that suppresses ("decoheres") interference between states as something involving the "environment" beyond the system and measuring apparatus.

• to explain the *appearance* of particles following paths (they actually say there are no "particles," and maybe no paths).

• to explain the *appearance* of discontinuous transitions between quantum states (they say there are no "quantum jumps" either)

• to champion an Everett-style "universal wave function" (as a superposition of states) that evolves in a "unitary" fashion (i.e., deterministically) according to the Schrödinger equation.

• to clarify and perhaps solve the measurement problem, which they define as the lack of macroscopic superpositions.

• to explain the "arrow of time."

• to revise the foundations of quantum mechanics by changing some of its assumptions, notably challenging the "collapse" of the wave function.

Decoherence theorists say that they add no new elements to quantum mechanics (such as "hidden variables") but they do deny one of the three basic assumptions - namely Dirac's *projection postulate*. This is the method used to calculate the probabilities of various outcomes, which probabilities are confirmed to several significant figures by the statistics of large numbers of identically prepared experiments.

Decoherence theorists accept (even overemphasize) Dirac's *principle of superposition*. Some decoherence theorists also accept the *axiom of measurement*, although some of them question the link between eigenstates and eigenvalues.

The decoherence program hopes to offer insights into several other important phenomena:

• What Zurek calls the "einselection" (environment-induced superselection) of preferred states (the so-called "pointer states") in a measurement apparatus.

• The role of the observer in quantum measurements.

• Nonlocality and quantum entanglement (which is used to "derive" decoherence).

• The origin of irreversibility (by "continuous monitoring").

• The approach to thermal equilibrium.

The decoherence program finds unacceptable the following aspects of the standard quantum theory:

• Quantum "jumps" between energy eigenstates.

• The "apparent" collapse of the wave function.

• In particular, explanation of the collapse as a "mere" increase of information.

• The "appearance" of "particles."

• The "inconsistent" Copenhagen Interpretation - quantum "system," classical "apparatus."

• The "insufficient" Ehrenfest Theorems.

Decoherence theorists admit that some problems remain to be addressed, especially the "problem of outcomes." Without the collapse postulate, it is not clear how definite outcomes are to be explained.

As Tegmark and Wheeler put it:

> The main motivation for introducing the notion of wave-function collapse had been to explain why experiments produced specific outcomes and not strange superpositions of outcomes...it is embarrassing that

nobody has provided a testable deterministic equation specifying precisely when the mysterious collapse is supposed to occur.[2]

Some of the controversial positions in decoherence theory, including the denial of collapses and particles, come straight from the work of Schrödinger, for example his 1952 essays "Are There Quantum Jumps?" (Part I and Part II), where he denies the existence of "particles," claiming that everything can be understood as his waves alone.

Other important sources for decoherence theorists include: HUGH EVERETT III and his "relative state" or "many world" interpretation of quantum mechanics; EUGENE WIGNER's article on the problem of measurement; and JOHN BELL's reprise of Schrödinger's arguments against quantum jumps.

Decoherence advocates therefore look to other attempts to formulate quantum mechanics. Also called "interpretations," these are more often reformulations, with different basic assumptions about the foundations of quantum mechanics. Most assume the "universal" applicability of the unitary time evolution that results from the Schrödinger wave equation. They include these formulations::

- DeBroglie-Bohm "pilot-wave" or "hidden variables".
- Everett-DeWitt "relative-state" or "many worlds".
- Ghirardi-Rimini-Weber "spontaneous collapse".

Note that these "interpretations" are often in serious conflict with one another. Where Schrödinger thinks that waves alone can explain everything (there are no particles in his theory), DAVID BOHM thinks that particles not only exist but that every particle has a definite position that is a "hidden parameter" of his theory. H. Dieter Zeh, the founder of decoherence, sees

> one of two possibilities: a modification of the Schrödinger equation that explicitly describes a collapse (also called "spontaneous localization") or an Everett type interpretation, in which all measurement outcomes are assumed to exist in one formal superposition, but to be perceived separately as a consequence of their dynamical autonomy resulting from decoherence. It was John Bell who called Everett's many-worlds picture "extravagant," While this latter suggestion has been called "extravagant"

(as it requires myriads of co-existing quasi-classical "worlds"), it is similar in principle to the conventional (though nontrivial) assumption, made tacitly in all classical descriptions of observation, that consciousness is localized in certain semi-stable and sufficiently complex subsystems (such as human brains or parts thereof) of a much larger external world. Occam's razor, often applied to the "other worlds", is a dangerous instrument: philosophers of the past used it to deny the existence of the interior of stars or of the back side of the moon, for example. So it appears worth mentioning at this point that environmental decoherence, derived by tracing out unobserved variables from a universal wave function, readily describes precisely the apparently observed "quantum jumps" or "collapse events."[3]

The information interpretation of quantum mechanics[4] also has explanations for the measurement problem, the arrow of time, and the emergence of adequately, i.e., statistically determined classical objects. However, I-Phi does it while accepting the standard assumptions of orthodox quantum physics.

We briefly review the standard theory of quantum mechanics and compare it to the "decoherence program," with a focus on the details of the measurement process. We divide measurement into several distinct steps, in order to clarify the supposed "measurement problem" (mostly the lack of macroscopic state superpositions) and perhaps "solve" it.

The most famous example of probability-amplitude-wave interference is the two-slit experiment. Interference is between the probability amplitudes whose absolute value squared gives us the probability of finding the particle at various locations behind the screen with the two slits in it.

Finding the particle at a specific location is said to be a "measurement."[5]

In standard quantum theory, a measurement is made when the quantum system is "projected" or "collapsed" or "reduced" into a single one of the system's allowed states. If the system was "prepared" in one of these "eigenstates," then the measurement will find it in that state with probability one (that is, with certainty).

---

3   *Decoherence and the Appearance of a Classical World in Quantum Theory*, p.22
4   See chapter 17.
5   See chapter 18.

However, if the system is prepared in an arbitrary state ψ_a, it can be represented as being in a linear combination of the system's basic energy states φ_n:

$$\psi_a = \Sigma\, c_n \mid n >.$$

where

$$c_n = <\psi_a \mid \varphi_n >.$$

It is said to be in "superposition" of those basic states. The probability P_n of its being found in state φ_n is

$$P_n = <\psi_a \mid \varphi_n >^2 = c_n^{\,2}.$$

Between measurements, the time evolution of a quantum system in such a superposition of states is described by a unitary transformation $U(t_0, t_1)$ that preserves the same superposition of states as long as the system does not interact with another system, such as a measuring apparatus. As long as the quantum system is completely isolated from any external influences, it evolves continuously and deterministically in an exactly predictable (causal) manner.

Whenever the quantum system does interact however, with another particle or an external field, its behavior ceases to be causal and it evolves discontinuously and indeterministically. This acausal behavior is uniquely quantum mechanical. Nothing like it is possible in classical mechanics. Most attempts to "reinterpret" or "reformulate" quantum mechanics are attempts to eliminate this discontinuous acausal behavior and replace it with a deterministic process.

We must clarify what we mean by "the quantum system" and "it evolves" in the previous two paragraphs. This brings us to the mysterious notion of "wave-particle duality." In the wave picture, the "quantum system" refers to the deterministic time evolution of the complex probability amplitude or quantum state vector ψ_a, according to the "equation of motion" for the probability amplitude wave ψ_a, which is the Schrödinger equation,

$$ih/2\pi\; \delta\psi_a/\delta t = H\,\psi_a.$$

The probability amplitude looks like a wave and the Schrödinger equation is a wave equation. But the wave is an abstract quantity whose absolute square is the probability of finding a quantum particle somewhere. It is distinctly not the particle, whose exact position is unknowable while the quantum system is evolving deterministically. It is the probability amplitude wave that interferes with itself. Particles, as such, never interfere (although they may collide).

Note that we never "see" the superposition of particles in distinct states. There is no microscopic superposition in the sense of the macroscopic superposition of live and dead cats.[6]

When the particle interacts, with the measurement apparatus for example, we always find a whole particle. It suddenly appears. For example, an electron "jumps" from one orbit to another, absorbing or emitting a discrete amount of energy (a photon). When a photon or electron is fired at the two slits, its appearance at the photographic plate is sudden and discontinuous. The probability wave instantaneously becomes concentrated at the location of the particle.

There is now unit probability (certainty) that the particle is located where we find it to be. This is described as the "collapse" of the wave function.[7] Where the probability amplitude might have evolved under the unitary transformation of the Schrödinger equation to have significant non-zero values in a very large volume of phase space, all that probability suddenly "collapses" (faster than the speed of light, which deeply bothered ALBERT EINSTEIN in 1905) to the location of the particle.

Einstein said that some mysterious "spooky action-at-a-distance" must act to prevent the appearance of a second particle at a distant point where a finite probability of appearing had existed just an instant earlier.

Whereas the abstract probability amplitude moves continuously and deterministically throughout space, the concrete particle moves discontinuously and indeterministically to a particular point in space.

For this collapse to be a "measurement," the new information about which location (or state) the system has collapsed into must be recorded somewhere in order for it to be "observable" by a scientist. But the vast majority of quantum events - e.g., particle collisions that change the particular states of quantum particles before

---

6   See chapter 23.
7   See chapter 20.

and after the collision - do not leave an indelible record of their new states anywhere (except implicitly in the particles themselves).

We can imagine that a quantum system initially in state ψ_a has interacted with another system and as a result is in a new state φ, without any macroscopic apparatus around to record this new state for a "conscious observer."

H. D. Zeh describes how quantum systems may be "measured" without the recording of information.

> It is therefore a plausible experimental result that the interference disappears also when the passage [of an electron through a slit] is "measured" without registration of a definite result. The latter may be assumed to have become a "classical fact" as soon as the measurement has irreversibly "occurred". A quantum phenomenon may thus "become a phenomenon" without being observed. This is in contrast to Heisenberg's remark about a trajectory coming into being by its observation, or a wave function describing "human knowledge". Bohr later spoke of objective irreversible events occurring in the counter. However, what precisely is an irreversible quantum event? According to Bohr this event can not be dynamically analyzed.
>
> Analysis within the quantum mechanical formalism demonstrates nonetheless that the essential condition for this "decoherence" is that complete information about the passage is carried away in some objective physical form. This means that the state of the environment is now quantum correlated (entangled) with the relevant property of the system (such as a passage through a specific slit). This need not happen in a controllable way (as in a measurement): the "information" may as well form uncontrollable "noise", or anything else that is part of reality. In contrast to statistical correlations, quantum correlations characterize real (though nonlocal) quantum states - not any lack of information. In particular, they may describe individual physical properties, such as the non-additive total angular momentum J^2 of a composite system at any distance.[8]

The Measurement Process

In order to clarify the measurement process, we separate it into several distinct stages, as follows:

A particle collides with another microscopic particle or with a macroscopic object (which might be a measuring apparatus).

---

8   *Decoherence and the Appearance...*, pp.13-14

In this scattering problem, we ignore the internal details of the collision and say that the incoming initial state ψ_a has changed asymptotically (discontinuously, and randomly, viz., wave-function collapse) into the new outgoing final state φ_n.

Note that if we prepare a very large number of identical initial states ψ_a, the fraction of those ending up in the final state φ_n is just the probability

$$|< \psi_a \mid \varphi_n >|^2.$$

The information that the system was in state ψa has been lost (its path information has been erased; it is now "noise," as Zeh describes it). New information exists (implicitly in the particle, if not stored anywhere else) that the particle is in state φ_n.

If the collision is with a large enough (macroscopic) apparatus, it might be capable of recording the new system state information, by changing the quantum state of the apparatus into a "pointer state" correlated with the new system state.

"Pointers" could include the precipitated silver-bromide molecules of a photographic emulsion, the condensed vapor of a Wilson cloud chamber, or the cascaded discharge of a particle detector.

But this new information will not be indelibly recorded unless the recording apparatus can transfer entropy away from the apparatus greater than the negative entropy equivalent of the new information (to satisfy the second law of thermodynamics). This is the second requirement in every two-step creation of new information in the universe.

The new information could be meaningful to an information processing agent who could not only observe it but understand it. Now neurons would fire in the mind of the conscious observer that von Neumann and Wigner thought was necessary for the measurement process to occur at all.

Von Neumann (perhaps influenced by the mystical thoughts of Niels Bohr about mind and body as examples of his "complementarity") saw three levels in a measurement;

• the system to be observed, including light up to the retina of the observer.

• the observer's retina, nerve tracts, and brain

• the observer's abstract "ego."

JOHN BELL asked tongue-in-cheek whether no wave function could collapse until a scientist with a Ph.D. was there to observe it. He drew a famous diagram of what he called von Neumann's "shifty split."

Bell shows that one could place the arbitrary "cut" (Heisenberg called it the "Schnitt") at various levels without making any difference.

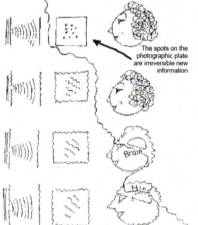

The spots on the photographic plate are irreversible new information

But an "objective" observer-independent measurement ends when irreversible new information has been indelibly recorded (in the photographic plate of Bell's drawing).

Von Neumann's physical and mental levels are perhaps better discussed as the mind-body problem.[9] It is not really the measurement problem in quantum physics.[10]

Figure 22-25. Bell's "shifty split."

The Measurement Problem

So what exactly is the "measurement problem?"

For decoherence theorists, the unitary transformation of the Schrödinger equation cannot alter a superposition of microscopic states. Why then, when microscopic states are time evolved into macroscopic ones, don't macroscopic superpositions emerge? According to H. D. Zeh:

> Because of the dynamical superposition principle, an initial superposition $\Sigma\, c_n \mid n >$ does not lead to definite pointer positions (with their empirically observed frequencies). If decoherence is neglected, one

---

9   See chapter 13.
10   See chapter 18.

obtains their entangled superposition $\Sigma c_n \mid n > \mid \Phi_n >$, that is, a state that is different from all potential measurement outcomes.[11]

And according to Erich Joos, another founder of decoherence:

It remains unexplained why macro-objects come only in narrow wave packets, even though the superposition principle allows far more "non-classical" states (while micro-objects are usually found in energy eigen-states). Measurement-like processes would necessarily produce nonclassical macroscopic states as a consequence of the unitary Schrödinger dynamics. An example is the infamous Schrödinger cat, steered into a superposition of "alive" and "dead".[12]

The fact that we don't see superpositions of macroscopic objects is the "measurement problem," according to Zeh and Joos.

An additional problem is that decoherence is a completely unitary process (Schrödinger dynamics) which implies time reversibility. What then do decoherence theorists see as the origin of irreversibility? Can we time reverse the decoherence process and see the quantum-to-classical transition reverse itself and recover the original coherent quantum world?

To "relocalize" the superposition of the original system, we need only have complete control over the environmental interaction. This is of course not practical, just as LUDWIG BOLTZMANN found in the case of JOSEF LOSCHMIDT's reversibility objection.[13]

Does irreversibility in decoherence have the same rationale - "not possible for all practical purposes" - as in classical statistical mechanics?

According to more conventional thinkers, the measurement problem is the failure of the standard quantum mechanical formalism (Schrödinger equation) to completely describe the nonunitary "collapse" process. Since the collapse is irreducibly indeterministic, the time of the collapse is completely unpredictable and unknowable. Indeterministic quantum jumps are one of the defining characteristics of quantum mechanics, both the "old" quantum theory, where Bohr wanted radiation to be emitted and absorbed discontinuously when his atom jumped between stationary states, and the

---

11   *Decoherence and the Appearance...* p.20
12   *Decoherence and the Appearance...* p.2. And see chapter 23.
13   See chapter 25.

modern standard theory with the Born-Jordan-Heisenberg-Dirac "*projection postulate.*"

To add new terms to the Schrödinger equation in order to control the time of collapse is to misunderstand the irreducible chance at the heart of quantum mechanics, as first seen clearly, in 1917, by Albert Einstein. When he derived his *A* and *B* coefficients for the emission and absorption of radiation, he found that an outgoing light particle must impart momentum hv/c to the atom or molecule, but the direction of the momentum can not be predicted! Neither can the theory predict the time when the light quantum will be emitted.

Such a random time was not unknown to physics. When ERNEST RUTHERFORD derived the law for radioactive decay of unstable atomic nuclei in 1900, he could only give the probability of decay time. Einstein saw the connection with radiation emission:

> It speaks in favor of the theory that the statistical law assumed for [spontaneous] emission is nothing but the Rutherford law of radioactive decay.[14]

But the inability to predict both the time and direction of light particle emissions, said Einstein in 1917, is "a weakness in the theory..., that it leaves time and direction of elementary processes to chance (Zufall, ibid.)." It is only a weakness for Einstein, of course, *because* his God does not play dice. Decoherence theorists too appear to have what WILLIAM JAMES called an "antipathy to chance."

We have several possible alternatives for eigenvalues. Measurement simply makes one of these actual, and it does so, said Max Born, in proportion to the absolute square of the probability amplitude wave function ψ_n. In this way, ontological chance enters physics, and it is partly this fact of quantum randomness that bothered Einstein (whose relativity theories are deterministic) and Schrödinger (whose equation of motion is deterministic).

What Decoherence Gets Right

Allowing the environment to interact with a quantum system, for example by the scattering of low-energy thermal photons or high-energy cosmic rays, or by collisions with air molecules, surely will suppress quantum interference in an otherwise isolated experiment.

---

14   Abraham Pais," "*Subtle is the Lord...*", p.411

But this is because large numbers of uncorrelated (incoherent) quantum events will "average out" and mask the quantum phenomena. It does not mean that wave functions are not collapsing. They are, at every particle interaction.

Decoherence advocates describe the environmental interaction as "monitoring" of the system by continuous "measurements."

Decoherence theorists are correct that every collision between particles entangles their wave functions, at least for the short time before decoherence suppresses any coherent interference effects of that entanglement.

But in what sense is a collision a "measurement." At best, it is a "pre-measurement."

It changes the path information that was present in the wave functions before the collision. But the new information may not be have been recorded anywhere (other than being implicit in the new state of the system).

All interactions change the state of a system of interest, but not all leave the "pointer state" of some measuring apparatus with new information about the state of the system.

So environmental monitoring, in the form of continuous collisions by other particles, is changing the specific information content of both the system, the environment, and a measuring apparatus (if there is one). But if there is no recording of new information (negative entropy created locally), the system and the environment may be in thermodynamic equilibrium.

Equilibrium does not mean that decoherence monitoring of every particle is not continuing.

It is. There is no such thing as a "closed system." Environmental interaction is always present.

If a gas of particles is not already in equilibrium, they may be approaching thermal equilibrium. This happens when any non-equilibrium initial conditions (Zeh calls these a "conspiracy") are being "forgotten" by erasure of path information during collisions. Information about initial conditions is implicit in the paths of all the particles. This means that, in principle, the paths could be reversed to return to the initial, lower entropy, conditions (the Loschmidt paradox).[15]

Erasure of path information could be caused by quantum particle-particle scattering (our standard view) or by decoherence "monitoring." How are these two related?

What Decoherence Gets Wrong

Decoherence makes no testable predictions that differ from standard quantum mechanics nor does it make calculations any easier. In short, decoherence is just a *way of talking* about quantum mechanics and especially the several interpretations that deny the collapse of the wave function.[16]

Quantum Interactions Do Not Create Lasting Information

The overwhelming number of collisions of microscopic particles like electrons, photons, atoms, molecules, etc, do not result in observable information about the collisions. The lack of observations and observers does not mean that there have been no "collapses" of wave functions. The idea that the time evolution of the deterministic Schrödinger equation continues forever in a unitary transformation that leaves the wave function of the whole universe undecided and in principle reversible at any time, is an absurd and unjustified extrapolation from the behavior of the ideal case of a single perfectly isolated particle.

The principle of microscopic reversibility applies only to such an isolated particle, something unrealizable in nature, as the decoherence advocates know with their addition of environmental "monitoring." Experimental physicists can isolate systems from the environment enough to "see" the quantum interference (but again, only in the statistical results of large numbers of identical experiments).

The Transition from Quantum to Classical World

In the standard quantum view, the emergence of macroscopic objects with classical behavior arises statistically for two reasons involving large numbers:

---

15   See chapter 25.
16   See chapter 20.

The law of large numbers (from probability and statistics)

When a large number of material particles is aggregated, properties emerge that are not seen in individual microscopic particles. These properties include, solidity, classical laws of motion, gravitational orbits, etc.

When a large number of quanta of energy (photons) are aggregated, properties emerge that are not seen in individual light quanta. These properties include continuous radiation fields with wavelike interference.

The law of large quantum numbers. This is Bohr's Correspondence Principle, which he used to show quantum mechanics approaches classical mechanics in the limit of large quantum numbers.

Decoherence and Standard Quantum Mechanics

Can we explain the following in terms of standard quantum mechanics?

• the decoherence of quantum interference effects by the environment

• their measurement problem, viz., the absence of macroscopic superpositions of states

• the emergence of "classical" adequately determined macroscopic objects

• the logical compatibility and consistency of two dynamical laws - the unitary transformation and the discontinuous "collapse" of the wave function

• the entanglement of "distant" particles and the appearance of "nonlocal" effects such as those in the Einstein-Podolsky-Rosen experiment

Let's consider these point by point.

The standard explanation for the decoherence of quantum interference effects by the environment is that when a quantum system interacts with the very large number of quantum systems in a macroscopic object, the averaging over independent phases cancels out (decoheres) coherent interference effects.[17]

---

17   *Quantum Mechanics*, Lev Landau and Evgeny Lifshitz, p.2

In order to study interference effects, a quantum system is isolated from the environment as much as possible. Even then, note that microscopic interference is never "seen" directly by an observer. It is *inferred* from probabilistic theories that explain the statistical results of many identical experiments. Individual particles are never "seen" as superpositions of particles in different states. When a particle is seen, it is always the whole particle and nothing but the particle. The absence of macroscopic superpositions of states, such as the infamous linear superposition of live and dead Schrödinger Cats, is therefore no surprise.[18]

The standard quantum-mechanical explanation for the emergence of "classical" adequately determined macroscopic objects is that they result from a combination of a) Bohr's correspondence principle in the case of large quantum numbers. together with b) the familiar law of large numbers in probability theory, and c) the averaging over the phases. Heisenberg indeterminacy relations still apply, but the individual particles' indeterminacies average out, and the remaining macroscopic indeterminacy is practically unmeasurable.

Perhaps the two dynamical laws would be inconsistent if applied to the same thing at exactly the same time. But the "collapse" of the wave function (von Neumann's **Process 1**, Pauli's measurement of the first kind) and the unitary transformation that describes the deterministic evolution of the probability amplitude wave function (von Neumann's **Process 2**) are used in a temporal sequence.

When you hear or read that electrons are *both* waves and particles, think "either-or" - first a wave of *possibilities*, then an *actual* particle. One process describes their continuous deterministic evolution (while isolated) along their mean free paths to the next collision or interaction. The other then describes what happens when quantum systems interact, in a collision or a measurement, when they make a discontinuous jump into a new state. One dynamical law applies to the wave picture, the other to the particle picture.

The paradoxical appearance of nonlocal "influences" of one particle on an entangled distant particle, at velocities greater than light

---

18   See chapter 23.

speed, are a consequence of a poor understanding of both the wave and particle aspects of quantum systems. The confusion usually begins with a statement such as "consider a particle A here and a distant particle B there."[19] When entangled in a two-particle probability amplitude wave function, the two identical particles are "neither here nor there," just as the single particle in a two-slit experiment does not "go through" one of the slits.

It is the single-particle probability amplitude wave that must "go through" both slits if it is to interfere. For a two-particle probability amplitude wave that starts its deterministic time evolution when the two identical particles are produced, it is only the probability of finding the particles that evolves according to the unitary transformation of the Schrödinger wave equation. It says nothing about where the particles "are."

Now if and when a particle is measured somewhere, we can then label it particle A. Conservation of energy and momentum tell us immediately that the other identical particle is now symmetrically located on the other side of the central source of particles. If the particles are electrons (as in DAVID BOHM's version of EPR), conservation of spin tells us that the now distant particle B must have its spin opposite to that of particle A, since they were produced with a total spin of zero.

Nothing is sent from particle A to B. The deduced properties are the consequence of conservation laws that are true for much deeper reasons than the puzzles of nonlocal entanglement. The mysterious instantaneous values for their properties is exactly the same mystery that bothered Einstein in 1905 about a single-particle wave function having values all over a photographic screen at one instant, then having values only at the position of the located particle in the next instant, apparently violating his then very new theory of special relativity.

To summarize: Decoherence by interactions with environment can be explained perfectly by multiple "collapses" of the probability amplitude wave function during interactions with environment particles. Microscopic interference is never "seen" directly by an

---

19   See chapter 21 for details.

observer. Interference is deduced from the statistical results of large numbers of experiments, each one of which has no superpositions.

We therefore never "see" macroscopic superpositions of live and dead cats. The "transition from quantum to classical" systems is the consequence of laws of large numbers. But there is only one world, the quantum world. The "classical world" is how the quantum world looks when there are a large number of particles, or even a single atomic system when it is in a state with large quantum numbers, according to Bohr's *correspondence principle*.

The quantum dynamical laws necessarily include two phases or processes, as John von Neumann showed, one needed to describe the continuous deterministic motions of probability amplitude waves and the other the discontinuous indeterministic motions of physical particles.

The attempt by decoherence theorists to ignore the discontinuous collapse of the wave function in a measurement is a failure, like all other attempts since Hugh Everett, though it is a very popular one.

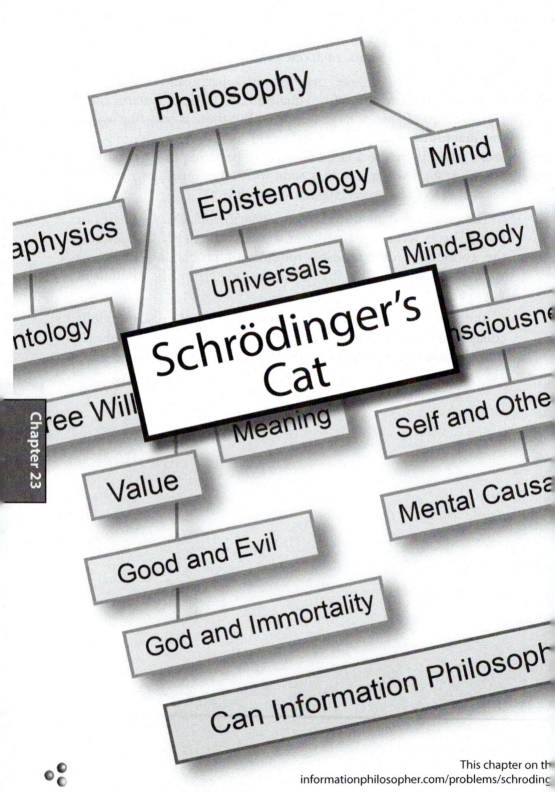

Schrödinger's Cat

Erwin Schrödinger's goal for his infamous cat-killing box was to discredit certain non-intuitive implications of quantum mechanics, of which his wave mechanics was the second formulation. Schrödinger's wave mechanics is continuous mathematically, and deterministic. Werner Heisenberg's matrix mechanics is discontinuous and indeterministic.

Schrödinger did not like Niels Bohr's idea of "quantum jumps" between Bohr's "stationary states" - the different "energy levels" in an atom. Bohr's "quantum postulate" said that the jumps between discrete states emitted (or absorbed) energy in the amount $h\nu = E_2 - E_1$.

Bohr himself did not accept Albert Einstein's 1905 hypothesis that the emitted radiation is a *discrete* quantum of energy $h\nu$, later known as a *photon*. Until well into the 1920's, Bohr and Max Planck, the original inventor of the quantum hypothesis believed radiation was a continuous wave of the kind defended by Schrödinger. This raised the question of wave-particle duality, which Einstein saw as early as 1909.

It was Einstein who originated the suggestion that the *superposition* of Schrödinger's wave functions implied that two different physical states could exist at the same time. This was a serious interpretational error that plagues the foundation of quantum physics to this day.

This error is found frequently in discussions of so-called "entangled" states (see chapter 20).

Entanglement occurs only for atomic level phenomena and over limited distances that preserve the coherence of two-particle wave functions by isolating the systems (and their eigenfunctions) from interactions with the environment.

We never actually "see" or measure any system (whether a microscopic electron or a macroscopic cat) in two distinct states. Quantum mechanics simply predicts a significant probability of the system being found in these different states. And these prob-

Chapter 23

ability predictions are borne out by the statistics of large numbers of identical experiments.

The Pauli Exclusion Principle says (correctly) that two identical indistinguishable (fermion) particles cannot be in the *same place at the same time*. Entanglement is often interpreted (incorrectly) as saying that a single particle can be in *two places at the same time*. Dirac's *principle of superposition* does not say that a particle is in two states at the same time, only that there is a non-zero probability of finding it in either state should it be measured.

Einstein wrote to Schrödinger with the idea that the random decay of a radioactive nucleus could be arranged to set off a large explosion. Since the moment of decay is unknown, Einstein argued that the superposition of decayed and undecayed nuclear states implies the superposition of an explosion and no explosion. It does not. In both the microscopic and macroscopic cases, quantum mechanics simply estimates the probability amplitudes for the two cases.

Many years later, RICHARD FEYNMAN made Einstein's suggestion into a nuclear explosion! (What is it about some scientists?)

Einstein and Schrödinger did not like the fundamental randomness implied by quantum mechanics. They wanted to restore determinism to physics. Indeed Schrödinger's wave equation predicts a perfectly deterministic time evolution of the wave function. But what is evolving deterministically is only abstract *probabilities - pure information*. And these probabilities are confirmed only in the *statistics* of large numbers of identically prepared experiments. Randomness enters only when a measurement is made and the wave function "collapses" into one of the possible states of the system.[1]

Schrödinger devised a variation on Einstein's idea in which the random radioactive decay would kill a cat. Observers could not know what happened until the box is opened.

---

1   See chapter 20.

The details of the tasteless experiment include:

• a Geiger counter which produces a macroscopic avalanche of electrons when an alpha particle passes through it,

• a bit of radioactive material with a decay half-life likely to emit an alpha particle in the direction of the Geiger counter during a time T,

• an electrical circuit, energized by the Geiger counter electrons, which drops a hammer,

• a flask of a deadly hydrocyanic acid gas, smashed open by the hammer.

The gas will kill the cat, but the exact time of death is unpredictable and random because of the irreducible quantum indeterminacy in the time of decay (and the direction of the decay particle, which might miss the Geiger counter!).

This thought experiment is widely misunderstood. It was meant (by both Einstein and Schrödinger) to suggest that quantum mechanics describes the simultaneous (and obviously contradictory) existence of a live and dead cat.

Here is the famous paradox with a cat both dead and alive.

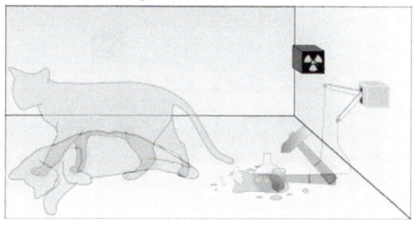

Figure 23-26. **What the statistics from multiple experiments give us is the probability of finding a live or dead cat, in this case half the cats are found dead and half alive, but we never see a macroscopic superposition of both.**

But quantum mechanics claims only that the time evolution of the Schrödinger wave functions will accurately predict the proportion of nuclear decays that will occur in a given time interval.

Quantum "probability amplitudes" do allow interference between the possible states of a quantum object, but not between macroscopic objects like live and dead cats More specifically, quantum mechanics provides us with the accurate prediction that if this experiment is repeated many times, half of the experiments will result in dead cats.

Note that this is a problem in epistemology. What knowledge is it that quantum physics provides?

If we open the box at the time T when there is a 50% probability of an alpha particle emission. The most a physicist can know is that there is a 50% chance that the radioactive decay will have occurred and the cat will be observed as dead or dying. Here is the famous diagram with a cat both dead and alive.

If the box were opened earlier, say at T/2, there is only a 25% chance that the cat has died. Schrödinger's superposition of live and dead cats would look like this.

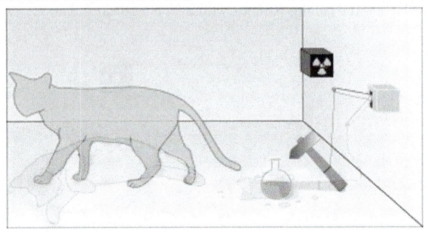

Figure 23-27. Here is the imaginary superposition of a mostly living cat and the pale shadow of a dead one.

If the box were opened later, say at 2T, there is only a 25% chance that the cat is still alive. Quantum mechanics is giving us only statistical information - knowledge about probabilities.

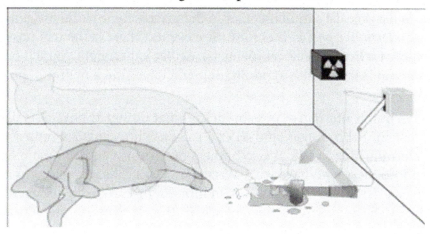

Figure 23-28. And here a mostlly dead cat, a vision of something that simply does not occur in macroscopic nature.

Schrödinger is simply wrong that the mixture of nuclear wave functions in the quantum world that accurately describes decay can be magnified to the macroscopic world to describe a similar mixture of live cat and dead cat wave functions and the simultaneous existence of live and dead cats.

The kind of coherent superposition of states needed to describe an atomic system as in a linear combination of states does not describe macroscopic systems (see Paul Dirac's explanation of the superposition of states using three polarizers in appendix C).

Instead of a linear combination of macroscopic quantum states, with quantum interference between the states, i.e.,

$$| Cat > = (1/\sqrt{2}) | Live > + (1/\sqrt{2}) | Dead >,$$

quantum mechanics tells us only that there is 50% chance of finding the cat in either the live or dead state, i.e.,

$$Cats = (1/2)\ Live + (1/2)\ Dead.$$

Just as in the quantum case, this probability prediction is confirmed by the statistics of repeated identical experiments, but no interference between these macroscopic states is ever seen.

What do exist simultaneously in the macroscopic world are genuine *alternative possibilities* for future events. There is the real possibility of a live or dead cat in any particular experiment. Which one is found is irreducibly random, unpredictable, and a matter of pure chance.

Genuine alternative possibilities is what bothered physicists like Einstein, Schrödinger, and MAX PLANCK who wanted a return to deterministic physics. It also bothers determinist and compatibilist philosophers who have what WILLIAM JAMES calls an "antipathy to chance." Ironically, it was Einstein himself, in 1916, who discovered the existence of irreducible chance, in the elementary interactions of matter and radiation.

Until the information comes into existence, the future is indeterministic. Once information is macroscopically encoded, the past is determined.

How Information Physics Resolves the Cat Paradox?

As soon as the alpha particle sets off the avalanche of electrons in the Geiger counter (an irreversible event with an entropy increase), new information is created in the world.

For example, a simple pen-chart recorder attached to the Geiger counter could record the time of decay, which a human observer could read at any later time. Notice that, as usual in information creation, energy expended by a recorder increases the entropy more than the increased information decreases it, thus satisfying the second law of thermodynamics.

Even without a mechanical recorder, the cat's death sets in motion biological processes that constitute an equivalent, if gruesome, recording. When a dead cat is the result, a sophisticated autopsy can provide an approximate time of death, because the cat's body is acting as an event recorder. There never is a superposition (in the sense of the simultaneous existence) of live and dead cats.

Chapter 23

The cat paradox points clearly to the information physics solution to the problem of measurement. Human observers are not required to make measurements. In this case, information is in the cat's body.

The cat is the observer.

In most physics measurements, any new information is captured by an apparatus well before any physicist has a chance to read any dials or pointers that indicate what happened. Indeed, in today's high-energy particle interaction experiments, the data may be captured but not fully analyzed until many days or even months of computer processing establishes what was observed. In this case, the experimental apparatus is the observer.

And, in general, the universe is its own observer, able to record (and sometimes preserve) the information created.

The basic assumption made in Schrödinger's cat thought experiments is that the deterministic Schrödinger equation describing a microscopic superposition of decayed and non-decayed radioactive nuclei evolves deterministically into a macroscopic superposition of live and dead cats.

But since the essence of a "measurement" is an interaction with another system (quantum or classical) that creates information to be seen (later) by an observer, the interaction between the nucleus and the cat is more than enough to collapse the wave function. Calculating the probabilities for that collapse allows us to estimate the probabilities of live and dead cats. These are probabilities, not probability amplitudes. They do not interfere with one another.

After the interaction, they are not in a superposition of states. We always have either a live cat or a dead cat, just as we always observe a complete photon after a polarization measurement and not a superposition of photon states, as P.A.M. DIRAC explains so simply and clearly[2] .

Chapter 23

---

2   see appendix C

The Arrow of Time

The laws of nature, except the second law of thermodynamics, are symmetric in time. Reversing the time in the dynamical equations of motion simply describes everything going backwards. The second law is different. Entropy must never decrease in time, except statistically and briefly, as Ludwig Boltzmann showed.

Many natural processes are apparently irreversible. Irreversibility is intimately connected to the direction of time. Identifying the physical reasons for the observed irreversibility, the origin of irreversibility, would contribute greatly to understanding the apparent asymmetry of nature in time, despite nature's apparently perfect symmetry in space.[1]

The Thermodynamic Arrow

In 1927, Arthur Stanley Eddington coined the term "Arrow of Time" in his book *The Nature of the Physical World*. He connected "Time's Arrow" to the one-way direction of increasing entropy required by the second law of thermodynamics.[2] This is now known as the "thermodynamic arrow."

In his later work, Eddington identified a "cosmological arrow," the direction in which the universe is expanding,[3] which was discovered by Edwin Hubble about the time Eddington first defined the thermodynamic arrow.

There are now a few other proposed arrows of time, including a psychological arrow (our perception of time), a causal arrow (causes precede effects), and a quantum mechanical arrow (electroweak decay asymmetries). We can ask whether one arrow is a "master arrow" that all the others are following, or perhaps time itself is just a given property of nature that is otherwise irreducible to something more basic, as is space.

Given the four-dimensional space-time picture of special relativity, and given that the laws of nature are symmetric in space, we may expect the laws to be invariant under a change in time direction. The laws do not depend on position in space or direction,

Chapter 24

---

1   See chapter 25.
2   Nature of the Physical World, 1927, p.328-9
3   New Pathways in Science, 1937, p.328-9

they are invariant under translations and rotations, since space is seen to be uniform and isotropic. But time is not just another spatial dimension. It enters into calculations of event separations as an imaginary term (multiplied by the square root of minus 1). Nevertheless, all the classical dynamical laws of motion are symmetric under time reversal.

So the basic problem is - how can macroscopic irreversibility result from microscopic processes that are fundamentally reversible?

Long before Eddington, scientists asked deep questions about the direction of time. Perhaps the first to explore the connection with physics was Boltzmann, who with JAMES CLERK MAXWELL investigated the statistical motions of the atoms and molecules of gases.

If the laws of nature are time symmetric, perhaps the "arrow of time" is to be found in the "initial" conditions, although this may be a circular concept, since "initial,"current," and "final" states are all defined with respect to time. Since the dynamical laws are time reversible, scientists as early as ISAAC NEWTON understood that one could calculate all the motions of a system by assuming "final conditions" and working backwards in time.

Nevertheless, many if not most physicists have assumed the universe must have begun in a highly ordered (low entropy) state and it has been "running down" (entropy or disorder increasing) ever since. In the nineteenth century, this was called the "heat death" of the universe. This view has the unfortunate implication that all the information in the current universe was present at the beginning, which is friendly to some theological ideas like predestination, but distinctly unfriendly to ideas of human free will.

Boltzmann assumed that the universe was infinitely old and that our current state is the consequence of a massive statistical fluctuation away from equilibrium and maximum entropy, a condition to which we must ultimately return.

Would time itself be reversed if we could make the entropy decrease? That is unlikely, since entropy decrease anywhere (creating negative entropy or negentropy, a term coined by LEON

BRILLOUIN) must be accompanied by an increase elsewhere, to satisfy the second law. Otherwise we could use the local reduction in the entropy to build a perpetual motion machine.

Put another way, if we could reverse the time, would entropy decrease? What can time reversal really mean? A thought experiment suggests not. Consider a closed perfume bottle inside a large empty container. Remove the bottle top and what would happen assuming that time is flowing backwards? It seems likely that the perfume molecules would leave the bottle whatever time is doing.

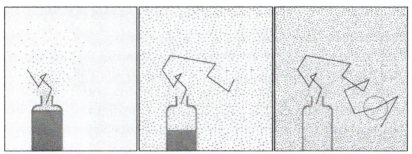

Figure 24-29. Information physics has shown that at each collision of a gas particle with another particle, the path information of where that particle has been is erased, so that time reversal would not return all the perfume to the bottle. .

For Aristotle, time was a measure of motion and change and for practical purposes, many scientists have thought that time reversal can be approximated by the reversal of all the velocities or momenta of material particles at an instant, starting from their current positions.

If we could perfectly reverse the motions of every material body (a practical impossibility, and perhaps a violation of Heisenberg's uncertainty principle), would that make the entropy decrease? Boltzmann agreed that it might, but only for a while. His intuition was that a system could not return to a highly ordered original state, such as every molecule getting back in the perfume bottle.

J. WILLARD GIBBS thought otherwise, if the detailed path information in all the macroscopic motions is still available as microscopic information (if information is a conserved quantity), then reversal of all the motions should be exactly like a movie played backwards.

The fundamental question of information philosophy is cosmological and ultimately metaphysical. What is the process that creates information structures in the universe?

Given the second law of thermodynamics, which says that any system will over time approach a thermodynamic equilibrium of maximum disorder or entropy, in which all information is lost, and given the best current model for the origin of the universe, which says everything began in a state of equilibrium some 13.75 billion years ago, how can it be that living beings are creating and communicating new information every day? Why are we not still in that state of thermal equilibrium?

It is perhaps easier for us to see the increasing complexity and order of information structures on the earth than it is to notice the increase in chaos that comes with increasing entropy, since the entropy is radiated away from the earth into the night sky, then away to the cosmic microwave background sink of deep space.

DAVID LAYZER is a Harvard cosmologist who in the early 1970's made it clear that in an expanding universe the entropy would increase, as required by the second law of thermodynamics, but that the maximum possible entropy of the universe might increase faster than the actual entropy increase. This would leave room for an increase of order or information at the same time the entropy is increasing![4]

Layzer pointed out that if the equilibration rate of the matter (the speed with which matter redistributes itself randomly among all the possible states) was slower than the rate of expansion, then the "negative entropy" or "order" (defined as the difference between the maximum possible entropy and the actual entropy) would also increase. CLAUDE SHANNON identified this negative entropy with information, though visible structural information in the universe may be much less than this "potential" information.

---

4   See appendix B for more on Layzer's work.

The Historical Arrow

Layzer called the direction of information increase the "historical arrow." In a 1975 article for *Scientific American* called "The Arrow of Time," he wrote:

> the complexity of the astronomical universe seems puzzling. Isolated systems inevitably evolve toward the featureless state of thermodynamic equilibrium. Since the universe is in some sense an isolated system, why has it not settled into equilibrium? One answer, favored by many cosmologists, is that the cosmological trend is in fact toward equilibrium but that too little time has elapsed for the process to have reached completion... I shall argue that this view is fundamentally incorrect. The universe is not running down, and it need not have started with a marked degree of disequilibrium; the initial state may indeed have been wholly lacking in macroscopic as well as microscopic information.

> Suppose that at some early moment local thermodynamic equilibrium prevailed in the universe. The entropy of any region would then be as large as possible for the prevailing values of the mean temperature and density. As the universe expanded from that hypothetical state the local values of the mean density and temperature would change, and so would the entropy of the region. For the entropy to remain at its maximum value (and thus for equilibrium to be maintained) the distribution of energies allotted to matter and to radiation must change, and so must the concentrations of the various kinds of particles. The physical processes that mediate these changes proceed at finite rates; if these "equilibration" rates are all much greater than the rate of cosmic expansion, approximate local thermodynamic equilibrium will be maintained; if they are not, the expansion will give rise to significant local departures from equilibrium.[5]

This is Layzer's seminal theory of the *growth of order* in the universe These departures represent macroscopic information; the quantity of macroscopic information generated by the expansion is the difference between the actual value of the entropy and the theoretical maximum entropy at the mean temperature and density.

---

5   Scientific American, December, 1975, p.68

In his 1989 book *The Emperor's New Mind*, ROGER PENROSE speculated on the connection between information, entropy, and the arrow of time.

> Recall that the primordial fireball was a thermal state — a hot gas in expanding thermal equilibrium. Recall, also, that the term 'thermal equilibrium' refers to a state of maximum entropy. (This was how we referred to the maximum entropy state of a gas in a box.) However, the second law demands that in its initial state, the entropy of our universe was at some sort of minimum, not a maximum!
>
> What has gone wrong? One 'standard' answer would run roughly as follows:
>
> True, the fireball was effectively in thermal equilibrium at the beginning, but the universe at that time was very tiny. The fireball represented the state of maximum entropy that could be permitted for a universe of that tiny size, but the entropy so permitted would have been minute by comparison with that which is allowed for a universe of the size that we find it to be today. As the universe expanded, the permitted maximum entropy increased with the universe's size, but the actual entropy in the universe lagged well behind this permitted maximum. The second law arises because the actual entropy is always striving to catch up with this permitted maximum.[6]

Penrose's "standard" answer is a clear reference to the pioneering work of David Layzer.

The Radiation Arrow

Whether they be electromagnetic waves or waves in water, we only observe wavelike disturbances that propagate outwards in space away from the disturbance. These waves are described by what is called the retarded potential. In his 1909 discussion of waves and particles, ALBERT EINSTEIN described the very remote possibility of incoming spherical waves:

> According to our prevailing theory, an oscillating electron generates a spherical wave that propagates outwards. The inverse process does not exist as an elementary process. A converging spherical wave is mathematically possible, to be sure; but to approach its realization requires

---

6   *The Emperor's New Mind*, p.328-9

Chapter 24

a vast number of emitting entities. The elementary process of emission is not invertible. In this, I believe, our oscillation theory does not hit the mark. Newton's emission theory of light seems to contain more truth with respect to this point than the oscillation theory since, first of all, the energy given to a light particle is not scattered over infinite space, but remains available for an elementary process of absorption.[7]

In 1945, JOHN WHEELER and his student RICHARD FEYNMAN attempted to symmetrize Maxwell's equations for electromagnetic fields with an "Absorber Theory of Radiation," that combined retarded potentials (outgoing spherical waves) and advanced potentials (incoming spherical waves) for radiation. They later described the theory as a mistake. There are no incoming spherical waves.

The Cosmological Arrow

We can define a cosmological direction of time as the direction in which the universe is expanding. There are excellent reasons for seeing this as the most fundamental of all arrows, even the one driving some of the others. Without expansion, a static universe would settle into thermal equilibrium and there would be no changes. There would be no entropy increase to show Eddington's thermodynamic arrow. There would be no information increase, as seen in Layzer's historical arrow.

Without the cosmological arrow, the thermodynamic, radiation, and historical arrows could not have been realized.

---

7   "On the Development of Our Views Concerning the Nature and Constitution of Radiation," *Einstein Collected Papers*, vol.6, p.213

Philosophy

Mind

Epistemology

Mind-Body

aphysics

Universals

Irreversibility

sciousne

ntology

Free Will

Meaning

Self and Othe

Value

Mental Causa

Good and Evil

God and Immortality

Can Information Philosoph

Chapter 25

Microscopic Irreversibility

In 1876, JOSEF LOSCHMIDT criticized his younger colleague LUDWIG BOLTZMANN's 1866 attempt to derive from classical dynamics the increasing entropy required by the second law of thermodynamics. Loschmidt's criticism was based on the simple idea that the laws of classical dynamics are time *reversible*. Consequently, if we just turned the time around, the time evolution of the system should lead to decreasing entropy.

This is the intimate connection between time and the second law of thermodynamics that ARTHUR STANLEY EDDINGTON later called the Arrow of Time.[1]

Microscopic time reversibility is one of the foundational assumptions of both classical mechanics and quantum mechanics. But a careful quantum analysis shows that reversibility fails even in the most ideal conditions - the case of two particles in collision - provided the quantum mechanical interaction with radiation is taken into account.

Our proof of microscopic irreversibility provides a new justification for Boltzmann's assumption of "molecular disorder" and strengthens his proof of *H*-Theorem.

In quantum mechanics, microscopic time reversibility is assumed to be true by some scientists because the deterministic linear Schrödinger equation itself is time reversible. But the Schrödinger equation only describes the deterministic time evolution of the probabilities of various quantum events.

When a quantum event occurs, if there is a record of the event (if new information enters the universe), the probabilities of multiple *possible* events collapse to the occurrence of just one *actual* event. This is the collapse of the wave function that JOHN VON NEUMANN called **process 1**.[2]

An irreversible event that leaves a record (stable new information) may become a measurement, if the new information is observed. Measurements are fundamentally and irreducibly irreversible.

---

1   See chapter 24
2   See chapter 20 and appendix C

Chapter 25

When particles collide, even structureless particles should not be treated as individual particles with single-particle wave functions, but as a single system with a two-particle wave function, because they are now entangled.[3]

Treating two atoms as a temporary molecule means we must use molecular, rather than atomic, wave functions. The quantum description of the molecule now transforms the six independent degrees of freedom for two atoms into three for the molecule's center of mass and three more that describe vibrational and rotational quantum states.

The possibility of quantum transitions between closely spaced vibrational and rotational energy levels in the "quasi-molecule' introduces indeterminacy in the future paths of the separate atoms. The classical path information needed to ensure the deterministic dynamical behavior has been partially erased. The memory of the past needed to predict the future has been lost.

Even assuming the practical impossibility of a perfect classical time reversal, in which we simply turn the two particles around, quantum physics requires two measurements to locate the two particles, followed by two state preparations to send them in the opposite direction.

Heisenberg indeterminacy puts calculable limits on the accuracy with which perfect reversed paths can be achieved.

Let us assume this impossible task can be completed, and it sends the two particles back along the reverse collision paths. On the return path, there is only a finite probability that a "sum over histories" calculation will produce the same (or reversed) quantum transitions between vibrational and rotational states that occurred in the first collision. Perfect reversal is not impossible but extremely improbable.

Thus a quantum description of a two-particle collision establishes the microscopic irreversibility that Boltzmann sometimes

Chapter 25

---

3   See chapter 21 on entanglement.

described as his assumption of "molecular disorder." In his second (1877) derivation of the H-theorem, Boltzmann used a statistical approach and the molecular disorder assumption to get away from the time-reversibility assumptions of classical dynamics.

The Origin of Irreversibility

The path information required for microscopic reversibility of particle paths is destroyed or erased by local interactions with radiation and other particles.

Boltzmann's dynamical H-Theorem (his 1872 *Stosszahlansatz*) correctly predicts the approach to equilibrium. But this apparent increase in entropy could be reversed, according to JOSEF LOSCHMIDT's time-reversibility objection and ERNST ZERMELO's recurrence objection. We show that the addition of electromagnetic radiation adds an irreducible element of randomness to atomic and molecular motions, erasing classical path information, just as the addition of a small speck of material can thermalize a non-equilibrium radiation field. Path erasure prevents reversibility and maintains a high entropy state indefinitely. Statistical fluctuations from equilibrium are damped by path erasure.

Photon emission and absorption during molecular collisions is shown to destroy nonlocal molecular correlations, justifying Boltzmann's assumption of "molecular chaos" (*molekular ungeordnete*) as well as Maxwell's earlier assumption that molecular velocities are not correlated. These molecular correlations were retained in WILLARD GIBBS formulation of entropy. But the microscopic information implicit in classical particle paths (which would be needed to implement Loschmidt's deterministic motion reversal) is actually *erased*. Boltzmann's physical insight was correct that his increased entropy is irreversible.

It has been argued that photon interactions can be ignored because radiation is isotropic and thus there is no net momentum transfer to the particles. The radiation distribution, like the distribution of particles, is indeed statistically isotropic, but, as we

Chapter 25

will show, each discrete quantum of angular momentum exchanged during individual photon collisions alters the classical paths sufficiently to destroy molecular velocity correlations.

Reversibility is closely related to the maintenance of path information forward in time that is required to assert that physics is *deterministic*. Indeterministic interactions between matter and radiation erase all path information. The elementary process of the emission of radiation is not time reversible, as first noted by ALBERT EINSTEIN in 1909. He argued that the elementary process of light radiation does not have reversibility ("*Umkehrbarkeit*"). The reverse process ("*umgekehrte Prozess*") does not exist as an elementary process, he said.

Macroscopic physics is only *statistically* determined. Macroscopic processes are adequately determined when the mass m of an object is large compared to the Planck quantum of action h (when there are large numbers of quantum particles).

But the information-destroying elementary processes of emission and absorption of radiation ensure that macroscopic processes are not individually reversible.

When interactions with a thermal radiation field and rearrangement collisions are taken into account, a quantum-mechanical treatment of collisions between material particles shows that a hypothetical reversal of all the velocities following a collision would only very rarely follow the original path backwards. Although the deterministic Schrödinger equation of motion for an isolated two-particle material system is time reversible (for conservative systems), the quantum mechanics of radiation interactions during collisions does not preserve particle path information, as does classical dynamics. Particle interactions with photons in the thermal radiation field and rearrangement collisions that change the internal states of the colliding particles are shown to be microscopically irreversible for all practical purposes. These quantum processes are equivalent to the irreversible "measurements" that von Neumann showed increase the entropy.[4]

---

4   See appendix C

In classical physics, if we time reverse a collision, two particles will reverse their vectors and go back along their original paths.

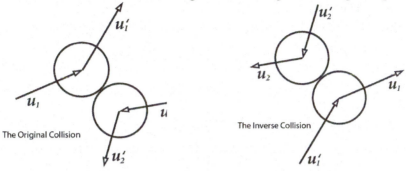

Figure 25-31. Classical particle collisions are perfectly time reversible.

Now consider a quantum collision between two atoms that results in the emission of a photon, deflecting the classical paths.

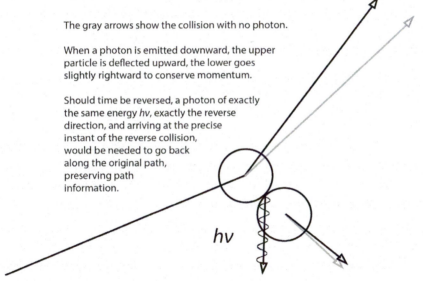

The gray arrows show the collision with no photon.

When a photon is emitted downward, the upper particle is deflected upward, the lower goes slightly rightward to conserve momentum.

Should time be reversed, a photon of exactly the same energy *hv*, exactly the reverse direction, and arriving at the precise instant of the reverse collision, would be needed to go back along the original path, preserving path information.

hv

Figure 25-30. Quantum particle collisions are not time reversible.

At some time *t* after the collision, let's assume we can reverse the separating atoms, sending them back toward the reverse collision. If there had been no photon emission, the most likely path is an exact traversal of the original path. But since a photon was emitted, traversing the original path requires us to calculate the probability that at precisely the right time a photon of the same frequency is absorbed by the quasi-molecule, corresponding to a quantum jump back to the original rotational-vibrational state (conserving energy), with the photon direction exactly opposite to the original absorption (conserving momentum), allowing the colliding atoms to reverse its original path. While this is not impossible, it is extraordinarily improbable.

The uncertainty principle would prevent an experimenter from preparing the two material particles with the precise positions and reverse momenta needed to follow the exact return paths to the collision point. Moreover, the Schrödinger equation of motion for the two particles would only provide a probability that the particles would again collide.

As to the photon, let us assume with Einstein that a light quantum is "directed" and so could be somehow aimed perfectly at the collision point. Even so, there is only a probability, not a certainty, that the photon would be absorbed.

We conclude that collisions of particles that involve radiation are *not microscopically reversible.*

Detailed Balancing

It is mistakenly believed that the detailed balancing of forward and reverse chemical reactions in thermal equilibrium, including the Onsager reciprocal relations, for example, depend somehow on the principle of microscopic reversibility.

Einstein's work is sometimes cited as proof of detailed balancing and microscopic reversibility. (The Wikipedia article, for example.) In fact, Einstein started with Boltzmann's assumption of detailed balancing, along with the "Boltzmann principle" that the probability of states with energy E is reduced by the exponential "Boltzmann factor," $f(E) \sim e^{-E/kT}$, to derive the transition probabilities for emission and absorption of radiation. Einstein also derived Planck's radiation law and Bohr's two "quantum postulates." But Einstein distinctly denied any symmetry in the elementary processes of emission and absorption.

Chapter 25

As early as 1909, he noted that the elementary process is not "invertible." There are outgoing spherical waves of radiation, but incoming spherical waves are never seen.

> "In the kinetic theory of molecules, for every process in which only a few elementary particles participate (e.g., molecular collisions), the inverse process also exists. But that is not the case for the elementary processes of radiation. According to our prevailing theory, an oscillating ion generates a spherical wave that propagates outwards. The inverse process does not exist as an elementary process. A converging spherical wave is mathematically possible, to be sure; but to approach its realization requires a vast number of emitting entities. The elementary process of emission is not invertible."[5]

The elementary process of the emission and absorption of radiation is asymmetric, because the process is "directed." The apparent isotropy of the emission of radiation is only what Einstein called "pseudo-isotropy" (*pseudoisotropie*), a consequence of time averages over large numbers of events. Einstein often substituted time averages for space averages, or averages over the possible states of a system in statistical mechanics.

Detailed balancing is thus a consequence of averaging over extremely large numbers of particles in equilibrium. This is the same limit that produces the so-called "quantum to classical" transition. And it is the same condition that gives us the "adequate" statistical determinism in the macroscopic, everyday world.

Neither detailed balancing nor the adequate determinism that we see in classical Newtonian experiments does anything to deny that at the microscopic quantum level, events are completely statistical, involving ontological chance. The interaction of radiation with matter has "a 'chance'-dependent value and a 'chance'-dependent sign" (emission or absorption), said Einstein in 1917.[6]

Chapter 25

---

5   "On the Development of Our Views Concerning the Nature and Constitution of Radiation," 1909, *Einstein Collected Papers*, vol.2, p.387

6   "On the Quantum Theory of Radiation," *Einstein Collected Papers*, vol.6, p.213

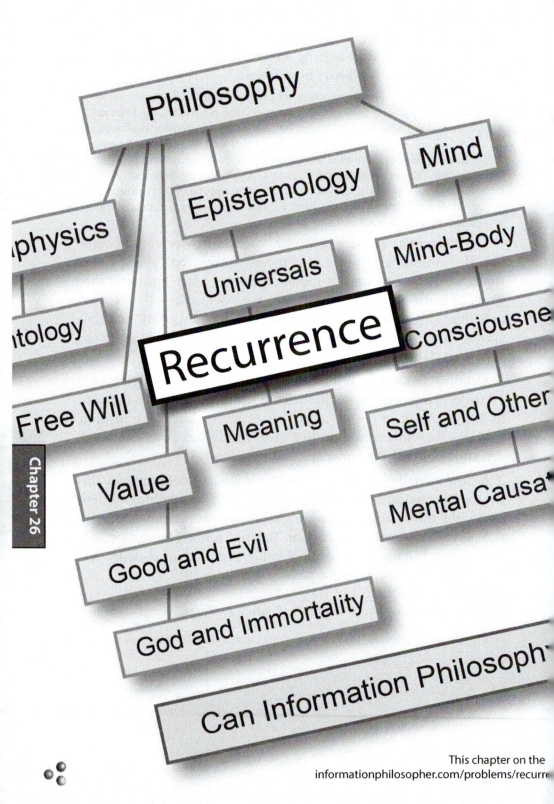

Philosophy

Mind

Epistemology

Mind-Body

physics

Universals

ntology

Recurrence

Consciousne

Free Will

Meaning

Self and Other

Value

Mental Causa*

Good and Evil

God and Immortality

Can Information Philosoph

The Recurrence Problem

The idea that the macroscopic conditions in the world will repeat after some interval of time is an ancient idea, but it plays a vital role in modern physics as well.

Ancient middle eastern civilizations called it the Great Year. They calculated it as the time after which the planets would realign themselves in identical positions in the sky.

The Great Year should not be confused with the time that the precession of the equinoxes takes to return the equinoxes to the same position along the Zodiac - although this time (about 26,000 years) is of the same order of magnitude as one famous number given by Babylonian astronomers for the Great Year (36,000 years).

Many societies have the concept of the Great Year, but none did calculations as carefully as the Babylonians. But since the planets orbital periods are not really commensurate, they kept increasing the time for the Great Year searching for a better recurrence time.

The Greek and Roman Stoics thought the Great Year was proof of law in nature and the God of reason that lies behind nature.

In modern philosophy, FRIEDRICH NIETZSCHE described an eternal return in his *Also Sprach Zarathustra*.

Zermelo's Paradox

ERNST ZERMELO' criticized LUDWIG BOLTZMANN's *H*-Theorem, the attempt to derive the increasing entropy required by the second law of thermodynamics from basic statistical mechanics.

It was the second "paradox" attack on Boltzmann. The first was JOSEF LOSCHMIDT's claim that entropy would be reduced if time were reversed. This is the problem of microscopic reversibility.[1]

Zermelo was an extraordinary mathematician. He was (in 1908) the founder of axiomatic set theory, which with the addition of the axiom of choice (also his work, in 1904) is the most common foundation of mathematics. The axiom of choice says that given any collection of sets, one can find a way to unambiguously select one object from each set, even if the number of sets is infinite.

---

1   See chapter 25 on irreversibility.

Chapter 26

Before this amazing work, Zermelo was a young associate of MAX PLANCK in Berlin, one of many German physicists who opposed the work of Boltzmann to establish the existence of atoms.

Zermelo's criticism was based on the work of HENRI POINCARÉ, an expert in the three-body problem, which, unlike the two-body problem, has no exact analytic solution.

Poincaré had been able to establish limits or bounds on the possible configurations of the three bodies from conservation laws. Planck and Zermelo applied some of Poincaré's thinking to the n particles in a gas. They argued that given a long enough time, the particles would return to a distribution in "phase space" (a 6n-dimensional space of possible velocities and positions) that would be indistinguishable from the original distribution.

Thus, they argued, Boltzmann's formula for the entropy would at some future time go back down, vitiating Boltzmann's claim to have proved that entropy always increases - as the second law of thermodynamics requires.

Boltzmann replied that his argument was statistical. He only claimed that entropy increase was overwhelmingly more probable than Zermelo's predicted decrease. Boltzmann calculated the probability of a decrease of a very small gas of only a few hundred particles and found the time needed to realize such a decrease is many orders of magnitude larger than the presumed age of the universe.

The idea that a macroscopic system can return to exactly the same physical conditions is closely related to the idea that an agent may face "exactly the same circumstances in making a decision. Determinists maintain that given the "fixed past" and the "laws of nature" that the agent would have to make exactly the same decision again.[2]

---

2   See chapter 5

The Extreme Improbability of Perfect Recurrence

In a classical deterministic universe, given enough time, the universe can return to the exact circumstance of any earlier instant of time, because it contains the same amount of matter, energy, and information.

But, in the real universe, information expands from a minimum at the origin, to ever larger amounts of information.

ARTHUR STANLEY EDDINGTON was probably the first to see that the expanding universe with increasing information provides a resolution to Zermelo's objection to Boltzmann.

> "By accepting the theory of the expanding universe we are relieved of one conclusion which we had felt to be intrinsically absurd. It was argued that every possible configuration of atoms must repeat itself at some distant date. But that was on the assumption that the atoms will have only the same choice of configurations in the future that they have now. In an expanding space any particular congruence becomes more and more improbable. The expansion of the universe creates new possibilities of distribution faster than the atoms can work through them, and there is no longer any likelihood of a particular distribution being repeated. If we continue shuffling a pack of cards we are bound sometime to bring them into their standard order — but not if the conditions are that every morning one more card is added to the pack."[3]

And note that it is the failure of recurrence that makes all the arrows of time of chapter 24 into one-way arrows.

---

3   *New Pathways in Science*, 1939, p.68

Emergence

Information philosophy explains the reality of emergence, because what emerges is *new information*. The universe began with minimal information. For hundreds of thousands of years, the only information structures were fundamental particles. These were only the simplest matter and energy, and they are *conserved quantitities*. In a *deterministic* universe, that initial information would be all the information in the universe today and in the future, because information would be conserved.

But information is not conserved. Because it is neither matter not energy, information is *immaterial*. Matter can be converted to energy ($E = mc^2$), but their total is a constant. The only thing that is new is information. *Information is the only emergent.*

A complex physical world of galaxies, stars, and planets has emerged, a diverse biological world has emerged, and a mental world of ideas has emerged, including the *idea of emergence* itself. Emergence is the result of the **cosmic creation process**.[1]

And this process is fundamentally a rearrangement and transformation of the fundamental particles of matter and energy.

The basic idea of emergence is that there are properties - perhaps even "laws" - at the upper hierarchical levels of nature that are not derivable from or reducible to the properties and laws of the lower levels. Thus chemistry has properties not derivable from physics, biology has properties not derivable from chemistry, and psychology has properties not derivable from biology.

Emergence or Reduction?

Reductionism, by contrast, argues that everything can be explained by (reduced to) the basic laws of physics. The world is said to be "causally closed." "Physicalism" is the idea that everything that is caused has a physical cause, that everything that happens is caused by material particles in motion

Causal control is assumed to work "bottom-up." The motions and forces between the material particles are said to determine

---

1   See appendix F.

everything chemical, biological, and psychological. Information theory would then require that the information content of everything being done at the higher biological and mental levels is actually contained in the structure and motions of the atoms and molecules. We shall show that this reductionism is implausible

Causal closure implies that every thought in the mind is somehow present in the paths or positions of the atomic particles themselves. Mental causation is then redundant. Mental events are epiphenomenal, non-existent, just an illusion.

Genuine emergence of new properties at the higher biological and psychological levels, on the other hand, requires that those properties can exert "top-down" causal control on the motions of particles in lower levels. This is the notion of *downward causation*, the highest version of which is mental causation.[2] It means motions of the atomic particles must effectively be controlled by the mind, which strikes many biologists and psychologists, who are uncomfortable making claims about physics, as extravagant.

If the laws of nature control everything in the visible universe, they say, how can they fail to control the mind?

Proving this "top-down" or mental causation is made doubly difficult, since we would like to show that "bottom-up" causes on the body and mind can somehow be blocked. It seems illogical or even impossible to show that causation can flow downward but not upward.

But we can demonstrate emergent phenomena at the biological and mental (neural) level that have exactly this emergent property of what we can call "one-way causality."

History of the Idea of Emergence

The idea of emergence was implicit in the work of JOHN STUART MILL and explicit in the work of "emergentists" like GEORGE HENRY LEWES, SAMUEL ALEXANDER, C. LLOYD MORGAN, and

---

2   See chapter 15.

Chapter 27

C. D. Broad. Some wanted to explain the direct emergence of mind from matter, to solve the mind-body problem, but as Alexander put it, there are at least two distinct steps - mind emerges from life, just as life emerges from the physical-chemical.

Mill discusses the Laws of Nature in his System of Logic, Book III. Although Mill did not use the term "emergent," he makes the concept clear enough:

> The chemical combination of two substances produces, as is well known, a third substance with properties different from those of either of the two substances separately, or of both of them taken together. Not a trace of the properties of hydrogen or of oxygen is observable in those of their compound, water. The taste of sugar of lead is not the sum of the tastes of its component elements, acetic acid and lead or its oxide; nor is the colour blue vitriol a mixture of the colours of sulphuric acid and copper...If this be true of chemical combinations, it is still more true of those far more complex combinations of elements which constitute organized bodies; and in which those extraordinary new uniformities arise, which are called the laws of life... To whatever degree we might imagine our knowledge of the properties of the several ingredients of a living body to be extended and perfected, it is certain that no mere summing up of the separate actions of those elements will ever amount to the action of the living body itself.[3]

Lewes also used Mill's example of the properties of water not being reducible to those of oxygen and hydrogen. He coined the term "emergent" in 1875:

> Although each effect is the resultant of its components, the product of its factors, we cannot always trace the steps of the process, so as to see in the product the mode of operation of each factor. In the latter case, I propose to call the effect an emergent. It arises out of the combined agencies, but in a form which does not display the agents in action.[4]

In his 1920 book *Space, Time, and Deity,* Samuel Alexander cited Lloyd Morgan as his source of emergentism, and wrote:

> much of what I have to say has been already said by Mr. Lloyd Morgan in the concluding chapter of his work on Instinct and Experience. The argument is that mind has certain specific characters to which there is or even can be no neural counterpart...

---

3   *A System of Logic,* Book III, chapter VI
4   *Problems of Life and Mind,*(1875), vol. 2, p. 412

> Mind is, according to our interpretation of the facts, an 'emergent' from life, and life an emergent from a lower physico-chemical level of existence.[5]

Later, in his 1922 Gifford Lectures and 1923 book *Emergent Evolution*, LLOYD MORGAN saw even atoms and molecules as emergent entities and introduced the related "top-down" concept of hierarchical *supervenience*:

> ...in the physical world emergence is no less exemplified in the advent of each new kind of atom, and of each new kind of molecule. It is beyond the wit of man to number the instances of emergence. But if nothing new emerge - if there be only regrouping of pre-existing events and nothing more - then there is no emergent evolution.
>
> Under emergent evolution there is progressive development of stuff which becomes new stuff in virtue of the higher status to which it has become raised under some supervenient kind of substantial gotogetherness.[6]

Vitalists like HENRI BERGSON and HANS DRIESCH may not have used the term emergence, but they strongly supported the idea of teleological (purposeful), likely non-physical, causes, without which they thought that life and mind could not have emerged from physical matter.

C. D. BROAD's view of the mind was emergentist and vitalist.

But Broad distinguished between what he called "Substantial Vitalism" (a dualist theory of an immaterial substance as a vital force, for example, Bergson's *élan vital*) and what Broad called "Emergent Vitalism" (some kind of non-reductive materialism, in which the vital property emerges from the body, and in the case of mind, from the highest bodily level - the brain).

Broad says he borrowed the adjective "emergent" from Lloyd Morgan and Alexander.

Broad contrasted the two forms of Substantial and Emergent Vitalism with what he called "Biological Mechanism," which is essentially a reduction of biology to physics and chemistry. All the emergentists were of course anti-mechanists or anti-reductionists.

---

5   *Space, Time, and Deity* (1920), vol. 2, p. 14
6   *Emergent Evolution* (1923), pp. 1-6

Broad also mentioned Driesch, an anti-mechanist who developed a sophisticated form of vitalism that he called "neovitalism."

Driesch saw clear evidence of a kind of teleology in the ability of lower organisms to rebuild their lost limbs and other vital parts. He used Aristotle's term "*entelechy*" (loosely translated as "having the final cause in") to describe the organism's capacity to rebuild itself. Driesch said this disproved the theory of *preformation* from a single original cell. Driesch studied the original cells of a sea urchin, after they had divided into two cells, then four, then eight. At each of these stages, Driesch separated out single cells and found that the separated cells went on to develop into complete organisms. This is regarded as the first example of biological cloning.

Broad rejected Driesch's idea of *entelechy* as a non-material, non-spatial agent that is neither energy nor a material substance of a special kind, but we should note that Driesch's entelechy well describes the information content of any cell by which it develops into a complete organism. Driesch himself maintained that his entelechy theory was something very different from the substance dualism of older vitalisms. So what was Broad's criticism of Driesch? Neither thinker could produce a clear description of their vital element.

Broad was sophisticated in his discussion of emergence. He saw that the kind of emergence that leads to water and its unique chemical properties, when compared to the properties of its molecular components hydrogen and oxygen, has no element of purpose or teleology. The emergence of life (and mind) from physics and chemistry, however, clearly introduces a kind of design or purpose. Modern biologists call it *teleonomy*, to distinguish it from a metaphysical *telos* that pre-exists the organism. It comes as an essential part of the organism.

It seems likely that both Driesch and Broad were trying to grasp this teleonomy, which can be simply described as the built-in purpose of each living cell to replicate its information. "The goal of every cell is to become two cells."

Chapter 27

Three Kinds of Information Emergence

Note there are three distinct kinds of emergence, at the material, biological, and mental levels:

1. the *order out of chaos* when the randomly distributed matter in the early universe first gets organized into information structures.

This was not possible before the first atoms formed about 400,000 years after the Big Bang. Information structures like the stars and galaxies did not exist before about 400 million years. As we saw, gravitation was the principal driver creating information structures.

Nobel prize winner ILYA PRIGOGINE discovered another ergodic process that he described as the "self-organization" of "dissipative structures." He popularized the slogan "order out of chaos" in an important book.[7] Unfortunately, the "self" in self-organization led to some unrealizable hopes in cognitive psychology. There is no self, in the sense of a person or agent, in physical phenomena like convection cells and whirlpools.

Both gravitation and Prigogine's dissipative systems produce a purely physical/material kind of order. The resulting structures contain information, with a "steady state" flow of information-rich matter and energy through them. But they do not process or communicate information. They have no purpose, no "telos."

Order out of chaos can explain the emergence of downward causation on their atomic and molecular components. But this is a gross kind of downward causal control. Explaining life and mind as "complex adaptive systems" has not been successful. We need to go beyond "chaos and complexity" theories to *teleonomic* theories.

2. the *order out of order* when the material information structures form self-replicating biological information structures. Some become information processing systems.

---

7   *Order Out of Chaos.* Shambhala, 1984.

In his famous essay, "What Is Life?," Erwin Schrödinger noted that life "feeds on negative entropy" (or information). He called this "order out of order."

This kind of biological processing of information first emerged about 3.5 billion years ago on the earth. It continues today on multiple emergent biological levels, e.g., single-cells, multi-cellular systems, organs, etc., each level creating new information structures and information processing systems not reducible to (caused by) lower levels and exerting downward causation on the lower levels.

And this downward causal control is extremely fine. Biological systems control the motions and arrangements of individual atoms and molecules.

Biological systems are cognitive systems, using internal "subjective" knowledge to recognize and interact with their "objective" external environment, communicating meaningful messages to their internal components and to other individuals of their species with a language of arbitrary symbols, taking actions to maintain themselves and to expand their populations by learning from experience.[8]

With the emergence of life, "purpose" also entered the universe. It is not the pre-existent "teleology" of many idealistic philosophies (the idea of "essence" before "existence"), but it is the "entelechy" of Aristotle, who saw that living things have within them a purpose, an end, a "telos." To distinguish this evolved telos in living systems from teleology, modern biologists use the term "teleonomy."

Chapter 27

3. the pure *information out of order* when organisms with minds generate, store (in the brain), replicate, utilize, and then externalize some non-biological information, communicating it to other minds and storing it in the environment. Communication can be by hereditary genetic transmission or by an advanced organism capable of learning and then teaching its contemporaries directly by signaling, by speaking, or indirectly by writing and publishing the knowledge for future generations.

---

8   See appendix G on Biosemiotics.

This kind of information can be highly abstract mind-stuff, pure Platonic ideas, the stock in trade of philosophers. It is neither matter nor energy (though embodied in the material brain), a kind of pure spirit or ghost in the machine. It is a candidate for the immaterial dualist "substance" of RENÉ DESCARTES, though it is probably better thought of as a "property dualism," since information is an immaterial property of all matter.

The information stored in the mind is not only abstract ideas. It contains a recording of the experiences of the individual. In principle every experience may be recorded, though not all may be reproducible/recallable. Information philosophy claims that everything created since the origin of the universe over thirteen billion years ago has involved just two fundamental physical processes that combine to form the core of all creative processes at all three levels.[9]

This core creative process underlies the formation of microscopic objects like atoms and molecules, as well as macroscopic objects like galaxies, stars, and planets. (Note that the formation of self-organizing material systems in conditions far from equilibrium that are the subjects of chaos and complexity theories are this basic, non-teleonomic form of emergence.)

With the emergence of teleonomic (purposive) information in self-replicating systems, the same core process underlies all biological creation. But now some random changes in information structures are rejected by natural selection, while others reproduce successfully.

Finally, with the emergence of self-aware organisms and the creation of extra-biological information stored in the environment, the same information-generating core process underlies communication, consciousness, free will, and creativity.

The physical processes in the core creative process are quantum cooperative phenomena (involving the mysterious "collapse" of the wave function necessary for the appearance of particles - see chapter

---

9   See appendix F for details on the cosmic creation process

20) and thermodynamics, which requires the transfer of entropy away from newly emergent information structures to ensure their stability.[10]

Emergence in the Body

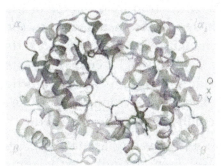

Figure 27-32. Four protein chains of hemoglobin.

When a ribosome assembles 330 amino acids in four symmetric polypeptide chains (globins), each globin traps an iron atom in a heme group at the center to form the hemoglobin protein. This is *downward causal control* of the amino acids, the heme groups, and the iron atoms by the ribosome. The ribosome is an example of ERWIN SCHRÖDINGER's emergent "order out of order," life "feeding on the negative entropy" of digested food.

When 200 million of the 25 trillion red blood cells in the human body die each second, in each of the new cells 100 million hemoglobins cell must be assembled. With the order of a few thousand bytes of information in each hemoglobin, this is 10 thousand x 100 million x 200 million = 2 x 10^{20} bits of information per second, a million times more information processing than today's fastest computer CPU. Red blood cells are 25% of body weight. Twenty percent of these are working in the brain to support mental information processing.

When a ribosome produces a protein that does not fold properly, a chaperone enzyme, shaped like a tiny trash can, opens its lid and captures the protein. It then closes the lid and squeezes the protein. Upon release, the protein then frequently folds properly. If it does not, the chaperone captures it again and disassembles it back to its amino acids. The chaperone is an emergent agent that is in no way the result of "bottom-up" processes from its amino acid components. It is also an extraordinary example of biological error detection and correction.

---

10   See appendix B on entropy and the second law

Emergence in the Brain

When a single neuron fires, the active potential rapidly changes the concentration of sodium (Na+) ions inside the cell and potassium (K+) ions outside the cell. Within milliseconds, thousands of sodium-potassium ion channels in the thin lipid bilayer of the cell wall must move billions of those ions from one side to the other. They do it with emergent biological machinery that exerts downward causation on the ions, powered by ATP energy carriers (feeding on negative entropy). Random quantum indeterministic motions of the ions put some near the pump opening, where quantum collaborative forces capture them in a lock-and-key structure.[11]

When many motor neurons fire, innnervating excitatory post-synaptic potentials (EPSPs) that travel down through the thalamus and the spinal cord and cause muscles to contract, that is as literal as downward causation gets in the body.

When the emergent mind decides to move the body, that mental causation is realized as downward causation.

When an emergent philosopher rearranges and communicates ideas, verbally in lectures, or as written words in a published paper, or as the bits of information in a computer memory, this is "information out of order," ultimately dependent on the body digesting food, producing energy with negative entropy ("order out of order"), but in no way controlled "bottom-up" by the molecules of body or food material, or by the energy consumed.

The Emergence of Immaterial Information Processing

Can information provide the basis for a different kind of mental substance, one that emerged?

Abstract information is neither matter nor energy, yet it needs matter for its concrete embodiment and energy for its communication. Information is *immaterial*.

It is the modern spirit, the ghost in the machine.

Immaterial information is perhaps as close as a physical or biological scientist can get to the idea of a soul or spirit that departs the body at death. When a living being dies, it is the maintenance of biological and mental information that ceases. The matter remains.

---

11   See "Ion Pumps in Neurons Select Individual Atoms" on page 183

Information philosophy proposes a mind-body dualism in which thoughts (pure information processing) in our minds have genuine causal power over the body. This might be considered a *metaphysical* mind, but it is purely biological and entirely dependent on the brain. There are *multiple realizations* of physical/material "hardware" that can implement the "software" of our ideas.

For example, when one person teaches another some new technique, or transmits some purely intellectual knowledge, the other person is another physical realization, different hardware now running the same software.

To make this case, we need to establish the following:

• that the information in a mind can be regarded as an *immaterial* substance.[12]

• that the information in a mind, while dependent on the body, has genuine causal (adequately determined) power over the body.[13]

• that the information in a mind has not been pre-determined by the sum of genetic inputs and life experiences, but has at least in part been created by the agent, with inputs from some indeterministic processes.[14]

The Emergence of Determinism

When small numbers of atoms and molecules interact, their motions and behaviors are indeterministic, governed by the rules of quantum mechanics. But when large numbers of particles gather into large material objects, they are statistically determined. This is called the "quantum to classical transition."

WERNER HEISENBERG's principle of indeterminacy (mistakenly called "uncertainty," as if the problem is epistemic/subjective and not ontological/objective) gives us the minimum error in simultaneous measurements of position x and momentum p, for any object, large or small,

$$\Delta p \, \Delta x \geq h,$$

where h is Planck's constant of action.

---

12   See appendix A on information
13   See chapter 16 on mental causation
14   See chapter 4 on the two-stage model of free will.

To see how "adequate" determinism emerges for large numbers of particles, note that the momentum $p = mv$ (the product of mass and velocity), so we can write the indeterminacy principle in terms of velocities and positions as

$$\Delta v \, \Delta x \geq h / m.$$

When large numbers of microscopic particles get together in massive aggregates, the mass increases and h / m approaches zero, the indeterminacy of the individual particles gets averaged over and macroscopic "adequately" deterministic laws "emerge." The positions and velocities of large massive objects can therefore be "determined" to a high degree of accuracy, in fact beyond our ability to measure.

Determinism is thus an emergent property for an object made up of large numbers of material particles,.

The "laws of nature," such as Newton's laws of motion, are all statistical in nature. They also "emerge" when large numbers of atoms or molecules get together. For large enough numbers, the probabilistic laws of nature approach practical certainty. But the fundamental indeterminism of component atoms never completely disappears.

There Was a Time with No Determinism

So determinism "emerges" today from microscopic quantum systems as they become a part of larger and more classical systems. But we can say that determinism also emerged in time. In the earliest years of the universe, large massive objects did not yet exist. All matter was microscopic and quantal.

We can now identify that time in the evolution of the universe when determinism first could have emerged. Before the so-called "recombination era" at about 380,000 years, when the universe cooled to a few thousand degrees Kelvin, a temperature at which atoms could form out of sub-atomic particles (protons, helium nuclei, and electrons), there were no "macroscopic objects" to exhibit deterministic behavior.

The early universe was filled with positive ions and negatively charge electrons. The electrons scattered light photons, preventing them from traveling very far. The universe was effectively opaque past very short distances. When the temperature fell to about 3000 degrees K, the charged particles combined to form neutral atoms (hydrogen and helium). With the scattering electrons now bound into atoms, the photons suddenly could "see" (travel) to enormous distances. This produced the transparent universe that we take for granted today (on cloudless nights).

Those 3000 degrees K photons have been red-shifted as a result of the universe expansion and now appear to us as the 2.7 degree K "cosmic microwave background" radiation left over from the big bang. We are looking at a moment in time when "classical" objects obeying apparently deterministic causal laws did not yet exist.

After a few hundred million years, large material objects could begin to form. Only then could anything "classical"" or "deterministic" come into existence, could "emerge."

Emergence Denied

Some prominent philosophers of science, logical empiricists who were committed to the ability of physical science to explain everything as "unified science," were confident that "emergence" would go the way of "holism" and "vitalism."

For example, the former member of the Vienna Circle and leading reductionist HERBERT FEIGL wrote in 1958:

> Inseparably connected with holism and the Gestalt philosophy is the doctrine of emergence. This is indeed my own, admittedly risky and speculative, guess; that is to say, I believe that once quantum dynamics is able to explain the facts and regularities of organic chemistry (i.e. of non-living, but complex compounds) it will in principle also be capable of explaining the facts and regularities of organic life.[15]

Chapter 27

---

15   "The 'Mental' and the 'Physical'", in *Concepts, Theories, and the Mind-Body Problem*, Minnesota Studies in the Philosophy of Science, vol.2, p. 414

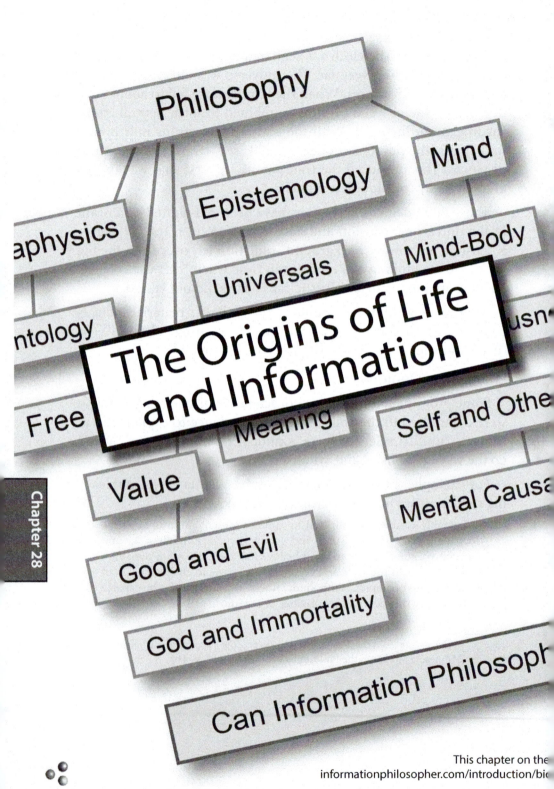

Philosophy

Mind

Epistemology

Mind-Body

aphysics

Universals

The Origins of Life
and Information

usn

ntology

Free

Meaning

Self and Othe

Value

Mental Causa

Good and Evil

God and Immortality

Can Information Philosoph

Origins of Life and Information

Despite many controversies about the role of information in biology over the past several decades, we can now show that the creation of information is not only necessary to understand biology, but that biology is a proper subset of information creation in the universe, including the evolution of human minds, which have created the knowledge about how abstract *immaterial* information and concrete information structures (matter and energy with low entropy) have been and are now being created in the universe.

A new story of biological evolution is needed, integrating it into the cosmological story and illustrating the total dependence of life on cosmological sources of negative entropy (information). We cannot appreciate the origin of life without first understanding the origin of information.

The first information *structures* formed in the early universe. Elementary particles, atoms and molecules, galaxies, stars, and planets, are all the result of microscopic quantum cooperative phenomena and macroscopic gravitational forces. These are the very special anti-entropic processes that we call *ergodic* (information *creating*) .

But it is not until the *emergence* of life that information *replication*, information *processing,* and information *communication* begins. Living things are *biological information processors*, forms through which matter and energy flows, with capabilities far beyond the electronic digital computers that cognitive scientists think provides a "computational theory of mind."

Most important, living things have "purposes." They engage in high level communications of information with other living things and with the environment. Their messaging is meaningful, allowing them to be active users of information, compared to passive material things, whose structural information is largely inert and meaningless. Living things also have *histories*, unlike physics and chemistry.

History and Evolution in the Universe

Long before there was life, the galaxies, stars, and planets had a rich developmental or evolutionary history of their own. Astrophysics tells us that stars radiated energy into space as they dissipated the energy of gravitational collapse (the photons carried away positive entropy to balance the new spherically symmetric order). The stars paused their collapsing when their interiors reached temperatures high enough to initiate thermonuclear reactions, which convert the lightest elements (hydrogen and helium) into heavier elements. When the fuel is exhausted, the stars resume collapsing, some exploding catastrophically and spewing out into interstellar space their newly formed elements, especially the heavy elements needed for life.

Geophysics tells us that the surfaces of planets also go through heating, then cooling, as they radiate away the energy of gravitational binding. Chemical processes produce ever more complex molecules on planetary surfaces, and astrobiology now finds pre-biological organic molecules everywhere in space.

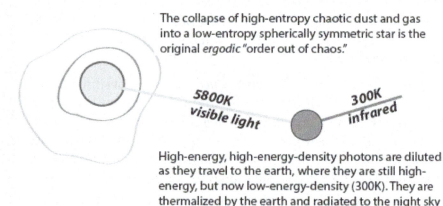

The collapse of high-entropy chaotic dust and gas into a low-entropy spherically symmetric star is the original *ergodic* "order out of chaos."

5800K
visible light

300K
infrared

High-energy, high-energy-density photons are diluted as they travel to the earth, where they are still high-energy, but now low-energy-density (300K). They are thermalized by the earth and radiated to the night sky

Figure 28-1. Photons are the major source of negative entropy on the earth.

When a planet is bathed by radiation from a nearby star, the radiation field is far from equilibrium. The high-temperature photons leaving the solar surface (5800K) are spread out over a huge volume of space. The energy density of the radiation falling on the Earth corresponds to a much lower temperature (300K), but the high-color-temperature photons cannot cool down without interacting with matter.

When they do interact with the planetary surface, photons provide the necessary stream of free energy to form even more complex information structures, the macromolecules that are the chemical basis for life. An alternative stream of free energy with negative entropy comes from inside the cooling planet.

Whether from the Sun or high-temperature vents in the planetary surface, it is these out-of-equilibrium conditions that lead to the first living things. They are negative entropy flows which are potential new information generators.

The Origin of Life

Early theories of the origin of life were based solely on physics and chemistry, from the 1920's hypotheses of A.I. OPERIN and J.B.S. HALDANE that the early atmosphere of the Earth was reducing (hydrogen and not oxidizing), to MELVIN CALVIN's 1930's suggestion for autocatalytic cycles, and the famous 1950's experiments of HAROLD UREY and STANLEY MILLER that showed many organic molecules could form spontaneously (especially critical amino acids, the building blocks of proteins) in Haldane's "prebiotic soup."

In the last several decades, theories of chaos and complexity have led to the idea of "self-organizing" complex adaptive systems that combine various autocatalytic cycles, for example, the hypercycles of MANFRED EIGEN. The Nobel-prize-winning physical chemist ILYA PRIGOGINE identified irreversible processes in systems away from thermal equilibrium that he called "dissipative."

Examples of "dissipative systems" include whirlpools and Bénard convection cells. They exhibit what Prigogine called "order out of chaos" and are an example of "emergence."[1] All living systems are "dissipative," so Prigogine and the complex adaptive system advocates thought they might explain the nature of life.

Complexity theories were popular because they added an element of *unpredictability* to otherwise deterministic physics, without accepting the *indeterminism* and ontological chance of quantum physics.

Chapter 28

---

1   See chapter 27 for the three kinds of emergence.

All these complex, dissipative, autocatalytic processes depend on a stream of free energy and negative entropy for their operation. But if all that they produce is a "passive" information structure, it is the just the same kind of "order out of chaos" that gravitation produces in the galaxies, stars, and planets. It is not yet life.

The most sophisticated example of an autocatalytic system is one that can generate large quantities of prebiotic molecules, such as the amino acids that combine to form proteins. This is the citric acid cycle (or Krebs cycle) used by all living systems today. It was almost certainly a precursor of life, before the information replication we associate with complex nucleotides and genetic code (DNA and RNA).

Metabolic cycles do not *use* information in the sense of processing it, but they do use the negative entropy flow to increase information in the form of the amino acids. A large quantity of amino acids can create proteins, but only randomly. Proteins cannot recreate themselves precisely. They cannot transfer hereditary information.

So alongside a working metabolic cycle we need information replication. The earliest such information structures were probably duplicated on an external template (a catalyst). Before DNA appeared, there was an RNA world in which RNA could perform the enzyme functions that proteins perform today, as well as the self-replication that DNA gives us.

The central dogma of biology today is that DNA generates RNA which generates the proteins from amino acids. And today we see the clear central role of information, specifically the messaging and processing of information via "messenger RNA" and "transfer RNA."

To be considered life, information philosophy expects an "active" information structure that is *processing* information, communicating messages among the components to maintain its structure.

The first person to articulate the information processing aspect of life was LILA GATLIN, who wrote in 1971

> Life may be defined operationally as an information processing system—
> a structural hierarchy of functioning units—that has acquired through
> evolution the ability to store and process the information necessary for

its own accurate reproduction. The key word in the definition is information.[2]

At some moment, a primitive macromolecule replicated itself. To do this, it created new (duplicate) information, so positive entropy equal to or greater than the new negative entropy must have been carried away from the new information structure (for it to be stable).

Mere replication should not yet be seen as life. And anything like metabolism would just be the flows of the low entropy solar photons or geothermal free energy that get degraded in the process of providing the available energy needed to form the new molecule. But we might anthropomorphize a bit and say that the *apparent* purpose of the molecule appears to be replicating itself, increasing *its own kind* of information structure in the universe.

Now at some point the replication might have been less than perfect (note the element of *chance* here).

Imagine now that the new molecule might be even more efficient than the original molecule at replicating itself (it has greater reproductive success). Note that the new molecule has more, or at least *different*, information in it than the original. Now we might say that this is the beginning of Darwinian evolution, which *appears* to have a goal of building richer, more robust, living information structures.

We now have both primitive inheritance (of the information) and a form of variability. Some of these molecules might not only be more successful replicators, they might have chemical properties that allow them to resist being destroyed by environmental conditions. The energetic extreme-ultraviolet photons, for example, or destructive cosmic rays, which might have been the source of the original variations.

The result might be a runaway exponential explosion of the concentration of those molecules (an important characteristic of living systems) as well as alteration of their environment. Early life generated an oxygen atmosphere that protected it from the ionizing ultraviolet rays that may have led to life in the first place.

Replication could lead to populations of the molecule that are well beyond the normal populations that would be expected in chemical

---

2   *Information Theory and the Living System*, p.1

equilibrium. Chemists might view this as simply an autocatalytic process, in which the molecule catalyzes its own production. But because it is *information* replicating itself, it is qualitatively different from mere chemical autocatalysis.

At the atomic level, it will be quantum cooperative phenomena that pull the constituent atoms into the desired molecular positions. It is the overall shape (form, information) that produces a dynamical interactive constraint well beyond the mere *aggregation* of individual atoms.

Loosely speaking, the new, more successful species of molecule has "learned" something, storing the new information internally and passing it on to the next generation.

Jumping now to human evolution, we see a species of multi-molecular, multi-cellular organism that has found a way to externalize information, storing it in the environment (culture), where it can be shared with new generations of humans, who continue to add to this external store of knowledge we call the *Sum*, enabling them to dominate the planet, for better or worse.

The Origin of Information

Passive information structures formed in the universe from the first few moments of time. But these elementary particles could not even form a lasting atomic structure until nearly 400,000 years after the expansion of the universe had begun. The universe had to cool significantly more, taking millions of years, before the galaxies, stars, and planets could form.

Although these magnificent astronomical bodies are the dominant contents of the universe, their information is essentially inert and meaningless until astronomers have appeared to study them, *extracting* their information. It is said that an astronomer is one galaxy's way of knowing about other galaxies, the universe's means of self-contemplation. These of course are mere metaphors, because the flow of information is one way, from the passive structures to the information-processing minds.

Claude Shannon[3] analyzed the communication of information in terms of senders and receivers, exchanging coded messages through noisy channels. It applies to the extraction of any kind of information, for example the yes/no answers to questions put to the physical world by scientists making quantum measurements.[4]

We can think of the Sun as sending its photons to Earth, although since they go out in all directions, less than one in a billion is received here. But where astronomers do not return any information to the stars and galaxies they study, even the smallest organism *interacts* with its environment and *exchanges* information in meaningful ways. All organisms and their components are "interactors" exchanging information.

All life draws its nourishment from the stream of negative entropy, the matter and free energy that flows though every organism. But living things also excrete matter and degraded energy into their environment, a return information flow that alters, in many ways creates, their local world - the biosphere.

Information in Biology

The major question for information in biology is this, are the communications between biological systems (organisms) and between their components (cells, organelles, macromolecules) *semiosis*, the exchange of signs?

Major textbooks on biology have always used terms like signaling, coding, transcribing, translating, communicating, messengers, recognition, even language, but they almost always insist that these are only metaphors, that they are not the kind of intentional and meaningful exchanges of signs that humans use.[5]

Consider what happens in a cell when a particular protein or enzyme is in short supply. A messenger enters the nucleus with a signal that more of the protein is needed. Responding to the signal, an enzyme (synthetase) travels to the exact segment of the DNA that contains the sequence of nucleotides for the needed protein.

---

3   *The Mathematical Theory of Communication*, 1948
4   See "Meaning in the Theory of Information" on page 142
5   See appendix G for the story of Biosemiotics.

The synthetase moves along the DNA, transcribing the sequence of nucleotide triplets (called codons) into a growing RNA with a message intended for the ribosome that manufactures proteins. Each codon refers to a specific amino acid in the protein.

The "messenger RNA" detaches itself from the DNA and travels through the nuclear membrane into the cell cytoplasm where ribosomes and a supply of amino acids is located. The amino acids are moving about randomly and very rapidly as a result of thermal and quantal noise. The long thread of mRNA enters the ribosome, which stops it to wait for the arrival of a "transfer RNA" carrying an amino acid and the three-letter "anticodon" that matches the codon in the mRNA for the next amino acid needed in the polypeptide chain.

When the one-dimensional linear protein leaves the ribosome, it folds itself into a three-dimensional shape that has enzymatic activity. If it does not fold correctly, it is swallowed by tiny "trashcan" shaped structures called "chaperones." The chaperone closes its cover and squeezes the protein, encouraging it to fold correctly.

If it does not, the protein is broken up into its amino acids. This is an amazing degree of error detection and correction.

The whole chain of communications between the signal that entered the nucleus, the syntax of the message, the semantic decoding of the mRNA by the ribosome, which refers to exactly the right amino acids as they fly around at high speeds connected to transfer RNA, looks like interpretation of the message, with reference to the amino acids. The message has pragmatic significance, leading to meaningful action (production of the protein). The later Wittgenstein tells us that "meaning is use." The cell is using all this communication of information for the purpose of staying alive!

Information philosophy looks at all this as the primitive prototype of the information communication and processing that we have today in human beings. In human language, the fundamental elements are syntax, semantics, pragmatics, and morphology (the shapes of the signs). Are not all of these already present in our smallest organisms?

Chapter 28

Despite many calls to recognize the reality of information in biology, the reductionist view that biology is nothing but the result of physics and chemistry has prevented it. Here are some important calls over the years to accept information in biology.

"Life may be defined operationally as an information processing system—a structural hierarchy of functioning units—that has acquired through evolution the ability to store and process the information necessary for its own accurate reproduction. The key word in the definition is information. This definition, like all definitions of life, is relative to the environment. My reference system is the natural environment we find on this planet. However, I do not think that life has ever been defined even operationally in terms of information. This entire book constitutes a first step toward such a definition."[6]

"Evidently nature can no longer be seen as matter and energy alone. Nor can all her secrets be unlocked with the keys of chemistry and physics, brilliantly successful as these two branches of science have been in our century. A third component is needed for any explanation of the world that claims to be complete. To the powerful theories of chemistry and physics must be added a late arrival: a theory of information. Nature must be interpreted as matter, energy, and information."[7]

"A central and fundamental concept of this theory is that of 'biological information,' since the material order and the purposiveness characteristic of living systems are governed completely by information, which in turn has its foundations at the level of biological macromolecules . The question of the origin of life is thus equivalent to the question of the origin of biological information."[8]

"Information as the central concept in molecular biology:...Information, transcription, translation, code, redundancy, synonymous, messenger, editing, and proofreading are all appropriate terms in biology. They take their meaning from information theory (Shannon, 1948) and are not synonyms, metaphors, or analogies."[9]

Biological Machines

We have seen that biological communications, the information exchanged in messages between biological entities, is far more important than the particular physical and chemical entities themselves. These material entities are used up and replaced many

Chapter 28

---

6   *Information Theory and the Living System*, (1971) Lila Gatlin, p.1
7   *Grammatical Man*, (1982) Jeremy Campbell, p.16, inspired by Gatlin
8   *Information and the Origin of Life*, (1990) Bernd-Olaf Küppers, p.xvii
9   *Information Theory, Evolution, and the Origin of Life*, (2005) H. Yockey, p.6

times in the life cycle of a whole organism, while the messaging has remained constant, not just over the individual life cycle, but that of the whole species.

In fact most messages, and the specific molecules that embody and encode those messages, have been only slowly varying for billions of years.

As a result, the sentences (or statements or "propositions") in biological languages may have a very limited vocabulary compared to human languages. Although the number of words added to human languages in a typical human lifetime is remarkably small.

Biological information is far more important than matter and energy for another reason. Beyond biological information as "ways of talking" in a language, we will show that the messages do much more than send signals, they *encode* the architectural plans for biological machines that have exquisite control over individual molecules, atoms, and their constituent electrons and nuclei.

Far from the materialist idea that fundamental physical elements have "causal control" over living things, we find that biological information processing systems are machines, intelligent robotic machines, that assemble themselves and build their own replacements when they fail, and that use the flow of free energy and material with negative entropy to manipulate their finest parts.

Coming back to the great philosopher of logic and language LUDWIG WITTGENSTEIN, who briefly thought of "models" as explanatory tools that can "show" what is difficult or impossible to "say" in a language, we offer still pictures of a few biological machines, with links to dynamic animated models on the I-Phi website.

The amazing operations of these machines are so far beyond man-made machines that it has called into question the ability of Darwinian evolution to create them by random trials and errors. But the most complex of these machines have been shown to be composed of dozens of smaller and simpler parts that did and still do much simpler tasks in the cell.

The five biological machines that we chose are

- the *ribosome*, a massive factory that manufactures thousands of different possible proteins when messenger RNA carries a request for one of them from the nuclear DNA,

- *ATP synthase*, which packages small amounts of energy into a nucleotide molecule that carries energy to any place in the organism that needs power to perform its function,

- the *flagellum*, a high-speed motor that moves bacterial cells to sources of matter and energy in their environment,

- the *ion pump*, which moves calcium and potassium ions to rapidly recharge the activation potential of a neuron so it is ready to fire again in a fraction of a second so the mind can make its decisions and take actions to move the body,

- the *chaperone*, an error detection and correction system beyond the ability of our finest computers to protect memories from noise.

Biology cannot prevent the occurrence of random errors. Indeterministic chance is the original source of variability in our genes that led to the incredible diversity of life forms, including us humans.

But the nearly perfect operation of our biological machines and the phenomenal fidelity of copying our many genetic codes over billions of years shows the stability and "adequate determinism" of biology in the presence of ontological chance, a consequence of the noise-immune *digital* nature of biological information.

Ribosomes

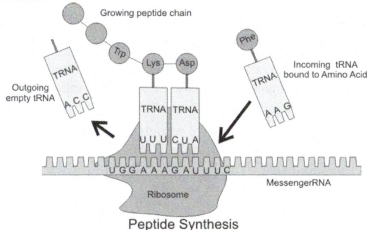

Peptide Synthesis

Figure 28-2. The ribosome waits for the right tRNA and amino acid to collide, then captures it to be added to the growing protein

Chapter 28

The linear messenger RNA is a sequence of three-letter nucleotide "codons," each of which codes for one of twenty possible amino acids. The transfer RNAs are flying around randomly in the cell carrying an amino acid with the complementary anti-codon. When an incoming tRNA colliding with the ribosome is a match, the mRNA captures it and moves three letters into the ribosome. The amino acid is detached from the tRNA and attached to the growing peptide chain, and the mRNA advances three more letters, releasing the outgoing, now empty tRNA, who will capture a replacement amino acid.

Notice that the tRNAs are moving quickly and randomly, so a large number of incorrect tRNAs bang into the next position on the mRNA while it waits for the correct match. Nothing in the path of the tRNA is *determining* the new sequence, as some physical chemists think. Which particular tRNA and amino acid of the right kind is added next is pure chance.

The ribosome is an ancient machine, going back to the last universal common ancestor (LUCA) of the three domains of life - bacteria, archaea, and eukaryotes. It is built from a few RNA molecules that self-fold to become enzymes (ribozymes) and a number of proteins that provide a supporting structure for the RNA. The longest of these RNAs is at the middle step when the amino acid is released from the tRNA and attached to the growing peptide chain.

Comparing modern ribosomes in the three domains, the microbiologist GEORGE FOX, who with CARL WOESE identified the archaea domain, reconstructed the likely earliest version of the ribosome, an important component of the RNA world's transition to DNA.

We shall see that reconstructing the earliest versions of important biological components, especially the biological machines, can provide deep insights into the origin of life.

By comparison, the efforts of complex adaptive systems theorists to guess at the earliest auto-catalytic chemical systems have largely been fruitless, since chemical systems do not process information about the different chemicals.

ATP Synthase

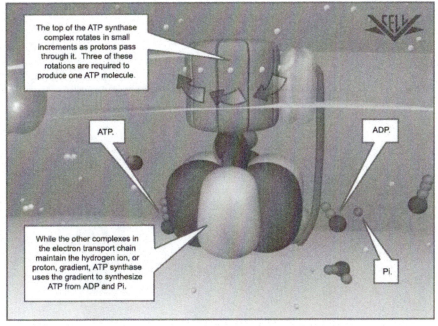

The top of the ATP synthase complex rotates in small increments as protons pass through it. Three of these rotations are required to produce one ATP molecule.

ATP.

ADP.

While the other complexes in the electron transport chain maintain the hydrogen ion, or proton, gradient, ATP synthase uses the gradient to synthesize ATP from ADP and Pi.

Pi.

Figure 28-3. The rotating motor embedded in the membrane spins at 10,000 rpm.

The source of power for most biological machines is the ATP (adenosine triphosphate) molecule. Adenosine is one of the four nucleotides in the genetic code (G, C, A, T). The ATP synthase machine above adds an inorganic phosphate group Pi back to a depleted diphosphate ADP, powered by "chemiosmosis," a flow of protons (hydrogen ions) across the semi-permeable cell membrane.

As each proton enters the top of the synthase complex, the top rotates by one of its segments. A fixed shaft (on the right) holds the lower part of the synthase in place while the rotating center shaft pushes lower segments to open and close, providing the energy to add back a Pi to the ADP.

ATP contributes a jolt of power to other machines (see the ion pumps below) when the third phosphate group is detached and energetic ATP becomes depleted ADP.

But what was the basic power source before complex biological machines like ATP came into existence?

The Flagellum

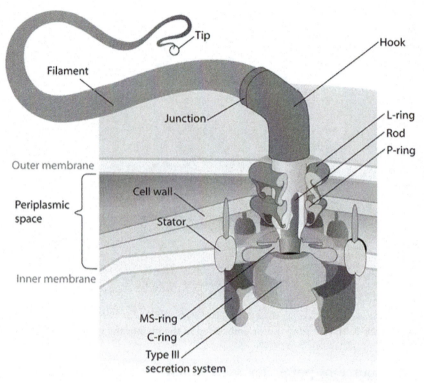

Figure 28-4. **This motor can instantly switch into reverse, the bacterium tumbles randomly, then switches back to forward motion in a new direction.**

Another rotating system embedded in a cell wall is the reversible motor that drives the flagella of mobile bacteria. The rotor has been measured at an incredible tens of thousands of rotations per minute. This system is so amazing it is considered the "poster child" of intelligent design advocates, but of its fifty protein parts, over forty have been identified as having simpler, but similar, functions that have "exadapted " for their role in the flagellum motor.

Bacterial flagella are powered by a flow of protons just like the rotating part of the ATP synthase, others by a flow of sodium ions, and some are powered by ATP flows. Some organisms have flagella only in their earliest development phase, for example, spermatazoa. But we can ask what produced the flow of protons before there was a molecule as advanced as ATP?

Ion Pumps

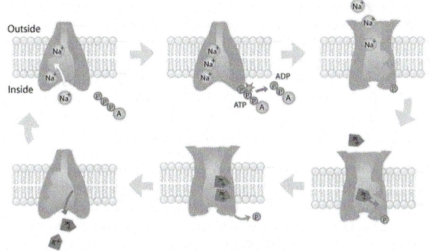

Figure 28-7. The ion pump uses ATP as its power source.

When a single neuron fires, the active potential rapidly changes the concentration of sodium (Na+) ions inside the cell and potassium (K+) ions outside the cell. Within milliseconds, thousands of sodium-potassium ion channels in the thin lipid bilayer of the cell wall must move billions of those ions from one side to the other. They do it with emergent biological machinery that exerts downward causation on the ions, powered by ATP energy carriers (feeding on negative entropy). Random quantum indeterministic motions of the amino acids drive them near the pump opening, and quantum collaborative forces capture them in a lock-and-key structure.

ATP hydrolysis provides the energy for a full cycle of opening and closing the pump, which pumps three sodium ions out of the cell for every two potassium ions pumped in. In neurons, the pump uses about 2/3 of the energy expenditure in the cell.

Before there were ion channels powered by ATP, could some primitive proteins have evolved to move specific ions across a membrane and create an electrochemical potential?

Chaperones

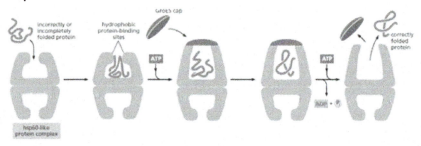

Figure 28-5. The error-correcting chaperone also uses ATP.

When a newly manufactured protein leaves the ribosome, it sometimes fails to fold properly to become an active enzyme that carries out its proper function in the cell. A well-folded protein hides away all its oily hydrophobic sites, exposing it hydrophylic sites to the water-based solution in the cell.

The incorrectly folded protein's hydrophobic sites are attracted to hydrophobic locations inside a chaperone. Once inside a cap is attached to the top and forces inside the chaperone encourage it to fold properly, in which case the cap opens and the normal protein is released. Once again, it is ATP that powers the chaperones.

Motive Power?

What ultimately powers all these machines? Of course it is ultimately free energy in a negative entropy flow, but what is the specific chemistry? If it starts with sunlight, it will be photosynthesis that extracts energy in the photons via redox reactions (simultaneous reduction and oxidation) that produce electrons and ions. For example water becomes H^+ and OH^-, with transfer of H+ ions (protons) across plant cell membranes. In mitochondria, it is the breakdown of food (sugars) in the citric acid cycle, with transfer of protons across the inner mitochondrial membrane.

In either case, an electrochemical gradient across a membrane is like a battery voltage (a tiny tenth of a volt) that powers all of life. It may have originated with amino acids randomly assembled into proteins that penetrated the bilayer phospholipids of proto-cells to act as proto-ion-pumps.

Chapter 28

Life, Love, and Death

A few speculations about three topics - *bios*, *eros*, and *thanatos*[10] - that often raise origin questions - why are we living?, why sex?, and why do we die?

From the standpoint of information philosophy, biology seems to have been a series of cosmic accidents, some of which in retrospect can be seen as highly unlikely. Against the arguments that given the right conditions, life is highly probable, we can note that life remained unicellular for the first few billion years. The endosymbiosis of bacterial cells being hosted by an archeon, to form the eukaryotes who became multicellular, suggests that this critical step for the possibility of intelligent life was highly improbable.

The importance of chance is evident from the evolution of the deliberate randomization of genes in sexual reproduction, which seems to aim at creating unique individuals.

As human life is about to take control of the evolution of the human genome, a major objective may be to eliminate the chance elements that lead to cell death.

Working Backwards in Time

We saw in chapters 12 to 16 how *philosophers of mind* attempt to *reduce* mental states to bottom-up deterministic causation by the laws of physics and chemistry at work in the brain.

Most biologists today are also reductionists, feeling more comfortable with the materialist laws of the physical sciences than with *immaterial* ideas like emergence, purpose, and information. Most cognitive scientists and neuroscientists share this traditional and conservative view.

But information philosophers and scientists today should make the strong case that life is more than the conserved quantities of matter and energy, and more than the deterministic laws of classical physics and chemistry.

Life is matter and energy - plus *information*. Life is quantum physics and chemistry - plus the *new information* in the universe that would be impossible without the ontological chance of quantal indeterminism.

Chapter 28

---

10   Or at the cellular level - *mitosis, meiosis, and apoptosis.*

Unlike physics and chemistry, life has a history - an information history. We are more likely to figure out the origin of life by working backwards to guess the most primitive elements of today's most universal parts (e.g., the citric acid cycle), than by trying to work forward from primitive chemical reactions of atoms and molecules that know nothing, that always lose any information about where they have been in the past.

We consider the origins of four increasingly sophisticated information-controlled processes - the metabolic cycle, chemiosmosis, the ribosome, and the genetic code. Our technique will be to strip them down to their primitive core elements. By reducing the amount of information in each process, we are working backward in time.

The current eight-step metabolic cycle uses sophisticated ATP as a catalyst. The earliest cycle would eliminate those steps.

Chemiosmosis moves protons or other ions across a membrane to create electrochemical potentials. This is done by multiple protein complexes in the current electron transfer chain. Today's proteins are produced by the ribosome, with RNA messages from the DNA. Let's work back to a time without either of these. It will still be proteins separating the electrons from the protons. They must do it without ATP, because they provide the power to create ATP. So let's look for the simplest components of today's proteins that can do this.

There are several different such complexes. The largest one uses a string of connected iron-sulfur clusters, each of which takes a small amount of energy from the electron and passes it, perhaps by quantum tunneling, to the next cluster. The presence of these FeS_2 clusters points to GÜNTER WÄCHTERSHÄUSER's iron-sulfur world hypothesis of life forming on mineral surfaces near hydrothermal vents in the deep sea. Membranes over pores in rock surfaces would later become modern cells in the RNA world.

It was a study of the different ribosomes in bacteria, archaea, and eukaryotes that led to CARL WOESE's discovery of the three domains of life. Woese's colleague GEORGE FOX and HYMAN HARTMAN of MIT have worked backward in time to the most ancient parts of the ribosome, specifically a central RNA molecule that encloses the center where a new amino acid is added to the growing peptide (protein) chain.

The current genetic code uses three nucleotides out of four RNA possibilities (G, C, A, U), giving 64 codes to choose one of twenty amino acids. But the third nucleotide often has no relevance for the amino acid. As long as the first two are GG, any one of the four will still code for glycine. GCx codes for alanine, CGx for arginine, and CCx for proline. All four of these amino acids are very common. Could there have been an early time when there was a simpler, two-base code and only four amino acids in the first proteins to be coded for, probably in a ribozyme with the hereditary information?

Hartman has connected this hypothesis back to the *reversed* citric acid cycle that was likely in the early earth's reducing atmosphere. He estimated the number of extra steps beyond the metabolic cycle needed to produce each amino acid, identifying the easiest to manufacture. Alanine, glycine, aspartic acid, and glutamic acid are one step away. Glutamine, asparagine, and serine are two steps away. Between those with the simplest codes and those with the mini mum number of steps to produce them, glycine and alanine were likely the earliest amino acids to enter the genetic code.

Second Codon Position

	G	C	A	U	
G	Gly	Ala	Glu / Asp	Val	G A C U
C	Arg	Pro	Gln / Hist	Leu	G A C U
A	Arg / Ser	Thr	Lys / Asn	Met / ILeu	G A C U
U	Trp / Term / Cys	Ser	Term / Tyr	Leu / Phe	G A C U

First Codon Position (rows: G, C, A, U) — *Third Codon Position* (columns at right)

Figure 28-6. Was there an earlier time when only two nucleotides coded for fewer amino acids?

Chapter 28

Philosophy

Mind

Epistemology

Metaphysics

Mind-Body

Universals

Ontology

Information

Consciousn

Free Will

Meaning

Self and Othe

Value

Mental Causa

Good and Evil

God and Immortality

Can Information Philosoph

Appendix A

Information

Information is the fundamental metaphysical connection between *idealism* and *materialism.*

Information is the *form* in all concrete objects as well as the *content* in non-existent, merely possible, *abstract entities.* It is the disembodied, de-materialized *essence* of anything.

Information philosophy goes beyond *a priori* logic and its puzzles, beyond *analytic* language and its games and paradoxes, beyond philosophical claims of *necessary* truths, to a *contingent* physical world that is best represented as made of dynamic, inter-acting *information structures.* Models of these structures can best represent the fundamental metaphysical nature of reality.

Knowledge begins with information structures in minds that are partial *isomorphisms* (mappings) of the information structures in the external world. Information philosophy is the ultimate *correspondence* theory.

But I-Phi shows that there is no isomorphism, no information in common, no necessary connection, between *words and objects.* Although language is an excellent tool for human communica-tion, its arbitrary and ambiguous nature makes it ill-suited to rep-resent the world directly. Language does not picture reality. Is is not the best tool for solving philosophical problems.

The extraordinarily sophisticated connection between words and objects is made in human minds, mediated by the brain's experience recorder and reproducer (ERR).[1] Words stimulate neurons to start firing and to play back relevant experiences that include the objects.

By contrast, a dynamic information model of an information structure in the world is presented immediately to the mind as a look-alike and act-alike simulation, which is experienced for itself, not mediated through words.

---

1   See appendix E on the experience recorder and reproducer..

Without words and related experiences previously recorded in your mental experience recorder, you could not comprehend spoken or written words. They would be mere noise, with no meaning. Compare these two representations of a cat.

CAT

Compared to a spoken or printed word, a photograph or a moving picture with sound can be seen and mostly understood by human beings, independent of their native tongue.

The elements of information philosophy, *dynamical models of information structures*, go far beyond logic and language as a representation of the fundamental, metaphysical, nature of reality.

Models "write" directly into our mental experience recorders. They are not *mediated* through ambiguous language.

Computer animated models must incorporate all the laws of nature, from the differential equations of quantum physics to the myriad processes of biology. At their best, simulations are not only our most accurate knowledge of the physical world, they are the best teaching tools ever devised. We can transfer knowledge nonverbally to coming generations and most of the world's population via the Internet and ubiquitous smartphones.

If you think about it, everything you know is pure abstract information. Everything you are is an "information structure," a combination of matter and energy that embodies and communicates your information. And everything that you value contains information.

You are a creator of information, part of a cosmic creation process. Your free will depends on your unique ability to create alternative possibilities for your willed decisions and responsible actions.

The simple definition of information is the act of informing - the communication of knowledge from a sender to a receiver that informs (literally shapes) the receiver.

By information we mean a quantity that can be understood mathematically and physically. It corresponds to the common-sense meaning of information, in the sense of communicating or informing. It is like the information stored in books and computers. But it also measures the information in any physical object, like a snow crystal or a star like our sun, as well as the information in biological systems, including the genetic code, the cell structure, and the developmental learning of the phenotype.

Although some commentators would like to limit the term "information" to messages sent with an *intended* purpose, physical scientists have long included the structure in physical objects as something that can be measured by an observer and thus is also information. Information philosophy recognizes material objects as "information structures," from which pure information content can be abstracted as meaningful knowledge, even though the object itself may have no purpose.

The sender of information need not be a person, an animal, or even a living thing. It might be a purely material object, a rainbow, for example, sending color information to your eye.

The receiver, too, might be merely physical, a molecule of water in that rainbow that receives too few photons and cools to join the formation of a crystal snowflake, increasing its information content.

Information theory, the mathematical theory of the communication of information, says little about meaning in a message, which is roughly the use to which the information received is put. Information philosophy extends the information flows in human communications systems and digital computers to the natural information carried in the energy and material flows between all the information structures in the observable universe.

A message that is certain to tell you something you already know contains no new information. It does not increase your knowledge, or reduce the uncertainty in what you know, as information theorists put it.

Appendix A

Information in the Universe

Information in physical systems was connected to a measure of the structural order in a system as early as the nineteenth century by WILLIAM THOMSON (later Lord Kelvin) and LUDWIG BOLTZMANN, who described an increase in the thermodynamic entropy as "lost information."

In 1877, Boltzmann proved his "*H*-Theorem" that the entropy or disorder in the universe always increases.[2]

He defined entropy *S* as the logarithm of the number *W* of possible microscopic states of a physical system, an equation now known as Boltzmann's Principle,

$S = k \log W.$

In 1929, LEO SZILARD showed the mean value of the quantity of information produced by a 1-bit, two-possibility ("yes/no") measurement as $S = k \log 2$, where *k* is Boltzmann's constant, connecting information directly to entropy.

Following Szilard, LUDWIG VON BERTALANFFY, ERWIN SCHRÖDINGER, NORBERT WIENER, CLAUDE SHANNON, WARREN WEAVER, JOHN VON NEUMANN, and LEON BRILLOUIN, all expressed similar views on the connection between physical entropy and abstract "bits" of information.

Schrödinger said the information in a living organism is the result of "feeding on negative entropy" from the sun. Wiener said "The quantity we define as amount of information is the negative of the quantity usually defined as entropy in similar situations."

Brillouin created the term "negentropy" because he said, "One of the most interesting parts in Wiener's *Cybernetics* is the discussion on "Time series, information, and communication," in which he specifies that a certain "amount of information is the negative of the quantity usually defined as entropy in similar situations."

Shannon, with a nudge from von Neumann, used the term entropy to describe his estimate of the amount of information that can be

Appendix A

---

2   Boltzmann's critics objected to his proof, but we have shown how to overcome their objections in chapters 24 and 25.

communicated over a channel, because his mathematical theory of the communication of information produced a mathematical formula identical to Boltzmann's equation for entropy, except for a minus sign (the negative in negative entropy).

Shannon described a set of i messages, each with probability pi. He then defined a quantity H,

$H = k \, \Sigma \, p_i \, log \, p_i$

where k is a positive constant. Since H looked like the H in Boltzmann's H-Theorem, Shannon called it the entropy of the set of probabilities $p_1, p_2, \ldots, p_n$.

To see the connection, we can note that Boltzmann assumed that all his probabilities were equal. For n equal states, the probability of each state is $p = 1/n$. The sum over n states, $\Sigma \, p_i \, log \, p_i$, is then $n \times 1/n \times log \, (1/n) = log \, (1/n) = -log \, n$. If we set $n = W$, we get Boltzmann's entropy with a minus sign,

$H = - k \, log \, W.$

Shannon's entropy H is simply the negative of Boltzmann's S.

Shannon showed that a communication that is certain to tell you something you already know (one of the messages has probability unity) contains no new information. The logarithm of 1 is 0.

If everything that happens was certain to happen, as determinist philosophers claim, no new information would ever enter the universe. Information would be a universal constant. There would be "nothing new under the sun." Every past and future event could in principle be known (as PIERRE-SIMON LAPLACE suggested[3]) by a super-intelligence with access to such a fixed totality of information.

It is of the deepest philosophical significance that information is based on the mathematics of probability. If all outcomes were certain, there would be no "surprises" in the universe. Information would be conserved and a universal constant, as some mathematicians mistakenly believe it is. Information philosophy requires the ontological chance and probabilistic outcomes of modern quantum physics to create new information structures.

Appendix A

---

3   See "Laplace's Demon" on page 28

But at the same time, without the extraordinary stability of quantized information structures over cosmological time scales, life and the universe we know would not be possible. Quantum mechanics reveals the architecture of the universe to be *discrete* rather than continuous, to be digital rather than analog. And digital provides extraordinary stability.

Creation of information structures means that in parts of the universe local entropy is actually going down. Creation of a low-entropy system is always accompanied by radiation of energy and entropy away from the local structure to the night sky and the cosmic background radiation.

From Newton's time to the start of the 19th century, the Laplacian view coincided with the notion of the divine foreknowledge of an omniscient God. On this view, complete, perfect and constant information exists at all times that describes the designed evolution of the universe and of the creatures inhabiting the world.

In this God's-eye view, information is a constant of nature. Some mathematicians argue that information must be a conserved quantity, like matter and energy. They are wrong. In Laplace's view, information would be a constant straight line over all time, as shown along the top of the figure.

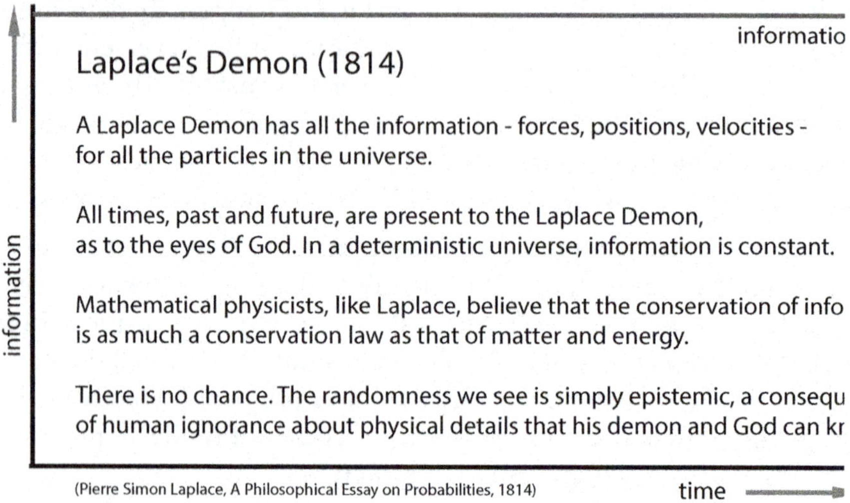

informatio

Laplace's Demon (1814)

A Laplace Demon has all the information - forces, positions, velocities - for all the particles in the universe.

All times, past and future, are present to the Laplace Demon, as to the eyes of God. In a deterministic universe, information is constant.

Mathematical physicists, like Laplace, believe that the conservation of info is as much a conservation law as that of matter and energy.

There is no chance. The randomness we see is simply epistemic, a consequ of human ignorance about physical details that his demon and God can kr

information

(Pierre Simon Laplace, A Philosophical Essay on Probabilities, 1814)   time

Figure 29-1. Constant information in a deterministic universe

If information were a universal constant, there would be "nothing new under the sun." Every past and future event can in principle be known by Laplace's super-intelligent demon, with its access to such a fixed totality of information.

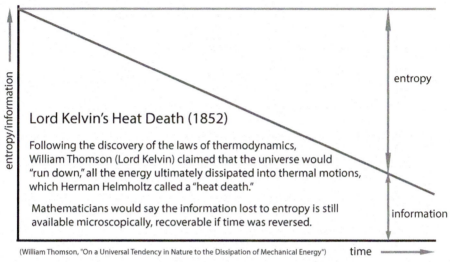

Figure 29-2. The second law predicts a heat death of the universe

But midway through the nineteenth century, Lord Kelvin (William Thomson) realized that the newly discovered second law of thermodynamics required that information could not be constant, but would be destroyed as the entropy (disorder) increased. HERMANN HELMHOLTZ described this as the "heat death" of the universe.

Mathematicians who are convinced that information is always conserved argue that macroscopic order is disappearing into microscopic order, but the information could in principle be recovered, if time could only be reversed.

This raises the possibility of some connection between the increasing entropy and what ARTHUR STANLEY EDDINGTON called "Time's Arrow." [4]

Kelvin's claim that information must be destroyed when entropy increases would be correct if the universe were a closed system. But in our open and expanding universe, my Harvard colleague DAVID LAYZER showed that the maximum possible entropy is increasing

Appendix A

4   See chapter 24.

faster than the actual entropy. The difference between maximum possible entropy and the current entropy is called negative entropy, opening the possibility for complex and stable information structures to develop.

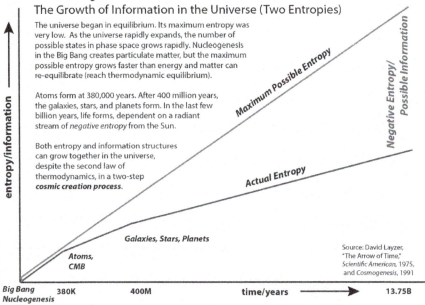

The Growth of Information in the Universe (Two Entropies)

The universe began in equilibrium. Its maximum entropy was very low. As the universe rapidly expands, the number of possible states in phase space grows rapidly. Nucleogenesis in the Big Bang creates particulate matter, but the maximum possible entropy grows faster than energy and matter can re-equilibrate (reach thermodynamic equilibrium).

Atoms form at 380,000 years. After 400 million years, the galaxies, stars, and planets form. In the last few billion years, life forms, dependent on a radiant stream of *negative entropy* from the Sun.

Both entropy and information structures can grow together in the universe, despite the second law of thermodynamics, in a two-step **cosmic creation process.**

Maximum Possible Entropy

Negative Entropy/ Possible Information

Actual Entropy

Galaxies, Stars, Planets

Atoms, CMB

Source: David Layzer, "The Arrow of Time," *Scientific American,* 1975, and *Cosmogenesis,* 1991

entropy/information

Big Bang Nucleogenesis   380K   400M   **time/years** →   13.75B

Figure 29-3. Growth of information and entropy in the universe

We can see from the figure that it is not only entropy that increases in the direction of the arrow of time, but also the information content of the universe. We can describe the new information as "*emerging.*" [5]

The expanding universe is the source of possibilities

Despite the second law of thermodynamics, stable and lawlike information structures evolved out of the initial chaos. First, quantum processes formed microscopic particulate matter – baryons, nuclei - from the fundamental quarks and electrons. Eventually these became atoms. Later, under the influence of gravitation, they coalesced into macroscopic galaxies, stars, and planets.

---

5   See chapter 27.

Every new information structure reduces the entropy locally, so the second law requires an equal (or generally much greater) amount of entropy to be carried away. Without the expansion of the universe, this would be impossible.

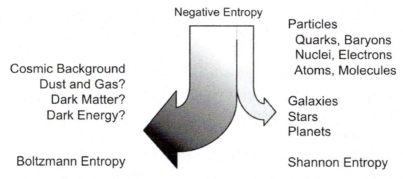

Figure 29-4. Two entropy flows

The positive entropy carried away (the big dark arrow on the left) is always greater than and generally orders of magnitude larger than the negative entropy in the created information structure (the smaller light arrow on the right).

See appendix B for the other negative entropy flows that ultimately lead to human life.

Information is *emergent*, because the universe began with minimal, essentially zero, information. It was in a state of thermodynamic equilibrium, maximum disorder.

And there are three distinct kinds of information emergence:

• the "order out of chaos" when the matter in the universe formed cosmic information structures. This is also ILYA PRIGOGINE's chaos and complexity theory.

• the "order out of order" when the material information structures form self-replicating biological information processing systems. This is what ERWIN SCHRÖDINGER described as life "feeding on negative entropy."

Appendix A

• the pure "information out of order" when organisms with minds create, process, and externalize information, communicating it to other minds and storing it in the environment, sharing it with all humanity as the *Sum* of human knowledge.

Information philosophy explains how new information is constantly being created, by nature and by humanity. We are co-creators of our universe.

Information theory is the mathematical quantification of communication to describe how information is transmitted and received, in human language, for example.

Information science is the study of the categorization, classification, manipulation, storage, and retrieval of information.

Cognitive science is the study of the mental acquisition, retention, and utilization of knowledge, which we can describe as the recording and reproduction of experiences as guides for action.

Information philosophy is an attempt to examine some classic problems in philosophy from the standpoint of information.

What is information that merits its use as the foundation of a new philosophical method of inquiry?

Abstract information is neither matter nor energy, yet it needs matter for its concrete embodiment and energy for its communication. Information is immaterial.

Information is the modern spirit, the ghost in the machine.

Immaterial information is perhaps as close as a physical or biological scientist can get to the idea of a soul or spirit that departs the body at death. When a living being dies, it is the maintenance of biological information that ceases. The matter remains.

Biological systems are different from purely physical systems primarily because they create, store, and communicate information. Living things store information in a memory of the past that they use to shape their future. Fundamental physical objects like atoms have no history.

And when human beings export some of their personal information to make it a part of human culture, that information moves closer to becoming immortal.

Human beings differ from other animals in their extraordinary ability to communicate information and store it in external artifacts. In the last decade the amount of external information per person may have grown to exceed an individual's purely biological information.

Information is an excellent basis for philosophy, and for science as well, capable of answering questions about metaphysics (the ontology of things themselves), epistemology (the existential status of ideas and how we know them), idealism (pure information), the mind-body problem, the problem of free will, and the "hard" problem of consciousness.

Actionable information has pragmatic value.

In our information philosophy, knowledge is the sum of all the information created and preserved by humanity. It is all the information in human minds and in artifacts of every kind - from books and internetworked computers to our dwellings and managed environment.

We shall see that all information in the universe is created by a single two-part cosmic creation process, the only one capable of generating and maintaining information in spite of the dread second law of thermodynamics, which describes the irresistible increase in disorder or entropy. We call this anti-entropic process ergodic. It should be appreciated as the creative source of everything we can possibly value, and of everything distinguishable from chaos and therefore interesting.

Enabled by the general relativistic expansion of the universe, the cosmic creative process has formed the macrocosmos of galaxies, stars, and planets. It has also generated the particular forms of microscopic matter - atoms, molecules, and the complex macromolecules that support biological organisms. It includes all quantum cooperative phenomena.

Appendix A

Quantum phenomena control the evolution of life and human knowledge. They help bring new information into the universe in a fundamentally unpredictable way. They drive biological speciation. They facilitate human creativity and free will.

Although information philosophy looks at the universe, life, and intelligence through the single lens of information, it is far from mechanical and reducible to a deterministic physics. The growth of information over time - our principle of increasing information - is the essential reason why time matters and individuals are distinguishable.

Information is the principal reason that biology is not reducible to chemistry and physics. Increasing information (a combination of perfect replication with occasional copying errors) explains all emergent phenomena."

In information philosophy, the future is unpredictable for two basic reasons. First, quantum mechanics shows that some events are not predictable. The world is causal, but not pre-determined. Second, the early universe does not contain the information of later times, just as early primates do not contain the information structures for intelligence and verbal communication, and infants do not contain the knowledge and remembered experience they will have as adults.

In the naive world of Laplace's demon and strict determinism, all the information in the universe is constant at all times. But "determinism" itself is an emergent idea, realized only when large numbers of particles assemble into bodies that can average over the irreducible microscopic indeterminacy of their component atoms.

Information and Entropy

In our open and expanding universe, the maximum possible entropy is increasing faster than the actual entropy. The difference between maximum possible entropy and the current entropy is called negative entropy. There is an intimate connection between the physical quantity negative entropy and information.6

6   See appendix B for more on entropy and the second law.

To give this very positive quantity of "negative" entropy a positive name, we call it "Ergo" and describe processes capable of generating negative entropy "ergodic."

Ergodic processes provide room to increase the information structures in the universe. As pointed out by David Layzer, the Arrow of Time[7] points not only to increasing disorder but also to increasing information.

The increase of biological information is primarily by perfect replication of prior existing information, but it is critically important that replication errors occur from time to time. They are the source of new species and creative new ideas.

The universe is creative. Information structures and processes are emergent. Some laws of nature are emergent. Adequately deterministic phenomena are emergent. The very idea of determinism is emergent.[8] Knowledge of the present did not all exist in the past. We have only a rough idea of the exact future.

The creative process continues. Life and humanity are a part of the process. What gets created is in part our responsibility. We can choose to help create and preserve information. Or we can choose to destroy it. We are free to create our own futures.

Why Information?   Information is neither Matter nor Energy,

But it needs Matter for its Embodiment,
And it needs Energy for its Communication.
Information is the modern Spirit.
It is the Ghost in the Machine.
It is the Mind in the Body.
It is the Soul, and when we Die,
It is our Information that Perishes,
unless we Publish it to the World and Posterity.

Therefore, we publish this book and the accompanying website, whose contents are freely usable according to a Creative Commons license, because *information wants to be free.*

---

7   See chapter 24 for the arrow of time.
8   See chapter 27 on emergence.

Philosophy

Mind

Epistemology

aphysics

Mind-Body

Universals

ntology

Entropy and
Second Law

onsciousn

Free Will

Self and Othe

Value

Mental Causa

Good and Evil

God and Immortality

Can Information Philosopl

pendix B

Entropy and the Second Law

Every scientist who made a major contribution to the probabilistic nature of the world had some doubts as to whether the use of probability implies that chance is real. Is the appearance of randomness just a consequence of the limits on human knowledge and merely epistemological? Or is randomness a fundamental part of the external world and thus ontological? Quantum physics says chance is ontological and the laws of physics are statistical.

In 1860, JAMES CLERK MAXWELL was the first physicist to use statistics and probability. He discovered the distribution of velocities of atoms or molecules in a gas. Although there was no real evidence for the existence of atoms until ALBERT EINSTEIN's work on Brownian motion in 1905, Maxwell and LUDWIG BOLTZMANN showed that the macroscopic laws of thermodynamics could be explained if gases consist of microscopic atoms in motion. They used the *calculus of probabilities* to reduce thermodynamics to statistical mechanics.

This is despite the fact that they knew next to nothing about the details of processes at the atomic level.

Paradoxically, ignorance of microscopic details is overcome by the power of averages over large numbers of cases. The average value of any property gets more and more accurate as the number of independent events gets large. The number of gas particles in a cubic centimeter of air is truly astronomical, close to the number of stars in the observable universe. For this reason, thermodynamic gas laws like $PV = NkT$ derived from statistical mechanics are highly accurate, well beyond experimental error. This accuracy suggests the laws are deterministic. But they are only adequately or *statistically* deterministic. Determinism is an illusion.[1]

Discrete Particles

To refine a famous comment by RICHARD FEYNMAN, if there is just one fact that could survive the destruction of knowledge, so as to give future scientists the fastest recovery of physics, it would be

---

1   See chapter 19.

that the contents of the universe are made up of discrete particles, not fields. This is now the standard model of particle physics. It grew out of the study of ordinary gases.

Figure 30-5. The perfume molecules dissipate until they are uniformly distributed. Classical statistical physics mistakenly claims that if the velocities of all the particles were reversed at an instant, the molecules would return to the bottle. It assumes that the complete path information needed to return to the bottle is preserved. But information is not conserved. It can be created and it can be destroyed. We shall show why such microscopic reversibility is extremely unlikely.

Gas particles are distributed in ordinary coordinate space (x, y, z) and in a conjugate momentum $(p = mv$, mass times velocity) space (p_x, p_y, p_z).

These two spaces are combined to form a six-dimensional space called a "phase space," one element of which is $\Delta x\, \Delta y\, \Delta z\, \Delta p_x\, \Delta p_y\, \Delta p_z$. At equilibrium, when average density is the same everywhere, particles are found distributed in proportion to the volume of those spaces. But phase space elements are weighted by an exponential factor that reduces the probability of particles being found in higher energy spaces. The factor is

$e^{-p^2/2mkT} = e^{-E/kT}$, today known as the "Boltzmann factor," though it was first found by Maxwell.

E is the particle energy, p is the particle momentum, T is the absolute temperature (in degrees Kelvin), e is the base of natural logarithms, and k is Boltzmann's constant (so named by MAX PLANCK). As E increases, the probability of finding particles with that energy decreases exponentially. But as the temperature T rises, the probability of finding particles with any given energy E increases.

Appendix B

With the hindsight of quantum physics, we can envision the distribution of particles as the integer number ("occupation number") of particles in the smallest possible volumes of this 6-dimensional "phase space" allowed by quantum mechanics. These have the dimensions of h^3, where h is Planck's constant. h has the dimensions of action (momentum times position). It's called the "quantum of action."

This minimum phase space volume of h^3 can be understood as the result of Heisenberg's uncertainty principle for each dimension, $\Delta p\, \Delta x = h$. It is as if space itself is divided into these small "cells." But space is continuous, like time. Space and time are abstract tools for assigning numbers to particle properties like location and motion. The minimum volume h^3 corresponds to locations and momenta where there is a non-zero probability of finding a discrete particle.

Although classical statistical mechanics did not include these quantum volumes, Boltzmann did divide phase space into discrete "coarse-grained" volumes for calculation purposes. This important new insight of classical statistical mechanics was accepting the radical idea of the ancient Greeks DEMOCRITUS and LEUCIPPUS that matter comes in indivisible discrete discontinuous lumps.

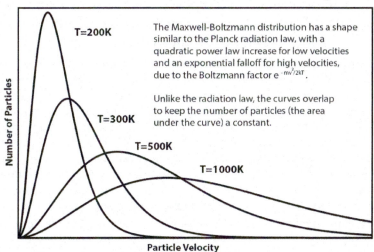

T=200K

The Maxwell-Boltzmann distribution has a shape similar to the Planck radiation law, with a quadratic power law increase for low velocities and an exponential falloff for high velocities, due to the Boltzmann factor $e^{-mv^2/2kT}$.

Unlike the radiation law, the curves overlap to keep the number of particles (the area under the curve) a constant.

T=300K

T=500K

T=1000K

Number of Particles

Particle Velocity

Figure 30-6. The number of particles with a given velocity at different temperatures.

Maxwell not only accepted the idea of atoms and molecules, he deduced their distribution among different velocities,

$N(v) = (2\pi mkT)^{-3/2} 4\pi v^2 e^{-mv^2/2kT}$

When heat is added and the temperature rises, the average velocity gets higher and there are fewer particles with low velocities, since the total number of molecules is a constant. Note that it was Maxwell who first found the exponential decay at higher energies $e^{-mv^2/2kT}$, now called the "Boltzmann factor."

Maxwell did not know about the future Boltzmann's constant k and its relationship to temperature, but he knew that the exponential term is a measure of the average velocity squared, and so of the average energy ($mv^2/2$).

The Maxwell-Boltzmann velocity distribution has two distinct regions which were critically important in MAX PLANCK's attempt to discover the distribution of electromagnetic radiation. For very low energies, the number rises as the square of the velocity. It turns around at a maximum near the average velocity. It then declines slowly like the long exponential tail of the normal distribution of errors because of the Boltzmann factor.

Boltzmann explained that probabilities can give definite results because of the large number of particles in a gas, but that the use of probabilities does not imply any uncertainty. He wrote:

> The mechanical theory of heat assumes that the molecules of a gas are not at rest, but rather are in the liveliest motion. Hence, even though the body does not change its state, its individual molecules are always changing their states of motion, and the various molecules take up many different positions with respect to each other. The fact that we nevertheless observe completely definite laws of behaviour of warm bodies is to be attributed to the circumstance that the most random events, when they occur in the same proportions, give the same average value. For the molecules of the body are indeed so numerous, and their motion is so rapid, that we can perceive nothing more than average values.

Boltzmann refers to the social statistics of Buckle and Quételet

> One might compare the regularity of these average values with the amazing constancy of the average numbers provided by statistics, which are also derived from processes each of which is determined by a completely unpredictable inter-

Appendix B

action with many other factors. The molecules are likewise just so many individuals having the most varied states of motion, and it is only because the number of them that have, on the average, a particular state of motion is constant, that the properties of the gas remain unchanged. The determination of average values is the task of probability theory. Hence, the problems of the mechanical theory of heat are also problems of probability theory.

It would, however, be erroneous to believe that the mechanical theory of heat is therefore afflicted with some uncertainty because the principles of probability theory are used. One must not confuse an incompletely known law, whose validity is therefore in doubt, with a completely known law of the calculus of probabilities; the latter, like the result of any other calculus, is a necessary consequence of definite premises, and is confirmed, insofar as these are correct, by experiment, provided sufficiently many observations have been made, which is always the case in the mechanical theory of heat because of the enormous number of molecules involved.[2]

> In the 1870's, Boltzmann clearly saw probability as completely deterministic.

The Second Law of Thermodynamics

Beyond his ability to visualize the above "liveliest states of motion" for atoms, Boltzmann's greatest work was his attempt to prove the second law of thermodynamics. The second law says that isolated systems always approach thermal equilibrium. Entropy or disorder always increases. Boltzmann showed that if the velocities of gas molecules were initially not in the Maxwell distribution above, they would always approach that distribution, and do it rapidly at standard temperatures and pressures (as we all know from experience).

Boltzmann then developed a mathematical expression for entropy (he called it H), the quantity in classical thermodynamics that is a maximum for systems in thermal equilibrium.

At first Boltzmann tried to do this with the dynamical theories of classical mechanics. The particles in his system would move around in phase space according to deterministic Newtonian laws. They collide with one another as hard spheres (elastic collisions). He included only two-particle collisions, assuming three-particle collisions are rare. As it turns out, three-particle collisions are essential for proving Boltzmann's insights, but calculations are difficult.

Appendix B

---

2   "Further Studies on the Thermal Equilibrium of Gas Molecules," Vienna Academy of Sciences, 1872

But Boltzmann's mentor, JOSEF LOSCHMIDT, criticized the results. Any dynamical system, he said, would move in reverse if all the particles could have their velocities reversed. Apart from the practical impossibility of doing this, Loschmidt had shown that systems could exist for which the entropy should decrease instead of increasing. This is called Loschmidt's Reversibility Objection, or the problem of microscopic reversibility.[3]

Loschmidt's criticism forced Boltzmann to reformulate his proof of the second law with purely statistical considerations based on probability theory.

He looked at all the possible distributions for particles in phase space consistent with a given total energy. Since phase space is continuous, there is an infinity of positions for every particle. So Boltzmann started by limiting possible energy values to discrete amounts ε, 2ε, 3ε, etc. He thought he would eventually let ε go to zero, but his discrete "coarse-graining" gets him much closer to modern quantum physics. He replaced all his integrals by discrete sums (something the "founders of quantum mechanics" in the nineteen-twenties would do).

Boltzmann then found the following expression that when summed over all the possible discrete energy states has the desired property of irreversible statistical increase,

$\Sigma f(E) \log f(E)$, where $f(E)$ is the fraction of states with energy E.

In 1948, CLAUDE SHANNON found a similar expression to describe the amount of information, $\Sigma_i p_i \log p_i$, thus connecting his communication of information to Boltzmann's entropy

Today scientists identity Boltzmann's expression with the thermodynamic entropy S, defined as the change of heat Q added to a system, divided by the temperature T,

$dS = dQ/T.$

---

3   See chapter 25 on irreversibility.

In terms of a sum over possible states, S is now written as the logarithm of the total number of possible states W multiplied by Boltzmann's constant,

$S = k \log W.$

Boltzmann was discouraged to find that a group of scientists, who still hoped to deny the existence of atoms, continued to criticize his "H-Theorem." They included HENRI POINCARÉ, an expert on the three-body problem, MAX PLANCK, who himself hoped to prove the second law is not statistical but *absolute*, and a young student of Planck's named ERNST ZERMELO who was an extraordinary mathematician, later the founder of axiomatic set theory.

Poincaré's work on the three-body problem suggested that, given enough time, a bounded world, governed only by the laws of mechanics, will always pass through a state very close to its initial state. Zermelo accepted Boltzmann's claim that a system will most likely be found in a macrostate with the largest number of microstates, but he argued that given enough time it would return to a less probable state. Boltzmann's H-Theorem of perpetual increase of entropy would therefore be incorrect sometime in the long run.

Information physics has shown that, when quantum physics and the interaction of electromagnetic radiation with matter are taken into account, Loschmidt's reversibility objection and Zermelo's recurrence objection fail to prevent entropy from increasing indefinitely in our open universe.[4]

Unfortunately for Boltzmann, he died just before the significance of radiation and the quantum were appreciated, and just as Einstein proved the existence of his atoms. And ironically, it was Max Planck, Zermelo's mentor and one of those strongly opposing both Boltzmann's ideas of atoms and his use of statistics, who was to correctly guess the distribution law for electromagnetic radiation.

Adding to the injustice, to develop his radiation law, Planck used Boltzmann's own statistical ideas, his assumption about discrete

Appendix B

---

4   See chapter 25 on irreversibility and 26 on the recurrence problem.

energies, coarse graining, and his ideas about entropy. The radiation distribution has almost exactly the same shape as the Maxwell-Boltzmann distribution for particle velocities. You can see the initial rise as the square of the radiation frequency v, and after the maximum the decline according to the Boltzmann factor $e^{-hv/kT}$, where the energy $E = hv$ is Planck's new constant h times the radiation frequency. The reason for the similarity is profound, electromagnetic radiation - light is also made of particles, as Einstein brilliantly hypothesized in 1905.

$$B(v) = 8\pi hv^3/ c^3 (e^{hv/kT} -1)^{-1}$$

Figure 30-5 shows the number of photons with a given frequency at different temperatures. When heat is added and the temperature rises, the average energy gets higher at all frequencies. The frequency at which energy is a maximum moves to higher frequencies. Unlike the Maxwell-Boltzmann distribution above (Figure 30-4), where the total number of molecules is a constant, additional heat shows up as more photons at all frequencies. The number of photons is not conserved. So the area under the radiation curve grows with temperature, where the area under the particles curve is a constant.

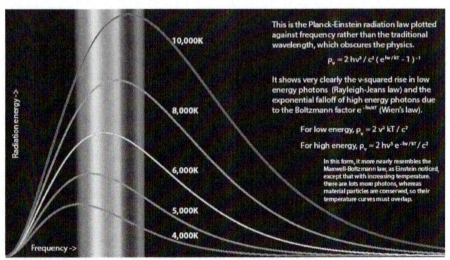

Figure 30-7. Planck's radiation distribution law is often presented as a function of wavelength rather than frequency, but this masks the similarity with the Maxwell-Boltzmann distribution of particles.

Appendix B

Compounding the irony and injustice for Boltzmann still further, Planck, who was long the opponent of discrete particles and statistical mechanics, used Boltzmann's assumption that energies come in discrete amounts, ε, 2ε, 3ε, etc. Planck called them *quanta* of energy $h\nu$, $2h\nu$, $3h\nu$, proportional to frequency ν, where h is a new constant, now named for Planck. He thereby named and launched the twentieth-century development of quantum mechanics, without really understanding the full implications of quantizing the energy. Planck thought quantization was just a mathematical trick to get the right formula for the blackbody radiation law.

Albert Einstein said that "the formal similarity between the curve of the chromatic distribution of thermal radiation and the Maxwellian distribution law of velocities for gas particles is so striking that it could not have been hidden for long." But for over twenty years few others than Einstein saw so clearly the implication that light itself is a localizable quantized discrete particle just as any particle of matter! Planck refused to believe this for many years.

So did Niels Bohr, despite his famous 1913 work that quantized the energy levels for electrons in his Bohr model of the atom.

Bohr postulated two things, 1) that the energy levels in the atom are discrete and 2) that when an electron jumps between levels it emits or absorbs energy $E = h\nu$, where the radiated energy E is the difference between the two energy levels in the atom, $E = E_n - E_m$.

After independently developing the theory of statistical mechanics in 1902-1904, extending it well beyond Boltzmann, Einstein hypothesized in 1905 that light comes in bundles of localized energy that he called light quanta (now known as photons). Although it is hard to believe, Bohr denied the existence of discrete photons well into the nineteen-twenties, although today's textbooks teach that quantum jumps in the Bohr atom emit or absorb photons (a grave this case an injustice to Einstein. Bohr insisted until the middle 1920's that the radiation in his discrete quantum jumps is a *continuous* wave. He was most reluctant to accept Einstein's work, to depart from Maxwell's classical laws of electromagnetism.

Appendix B

Einstein had told friends that his hypothesis of light quanta was more revolutionary than his theory of special relativity published the same year. It was Einstein, not Planck or Bohr or Heisenberg, who should be recognized as the *father of quantum theory*. He first saw mysterious aspects of quantum physics like wave-particle duality, nonlocality, entanglement, and the ontological nature of chance, perhaps more deeply than any other physicist has ever seen them.

Einstein famously abhorred chance ("God does not play dice"), but he did not hesitate to tell other physicists that chance seems to be an unavoidable part of quantum theory.

Entropy Flows in the Universe

Creation of information structures means that in parts of the universe the local entropy is actually going down. Creation of a low entropy system is always accompanied by transfer of positive entropy away from the local structures to distant parts of the universe, into the night sky for example.

My Harvard colleague ERIC CHAISSON studied energy rather than entropy. He saw energy consumption or production per gram a better measure of complexity in cosmic evolution. He wrote,

> When examined on a system-by-system basis, information content can be a slippery concept full of dubious semantics, ambivalent connotations, and subjective interpretations. Especially tricky and controversial is meaningful information, the value of information...The conceptual idea of information has been useful, qualitatively and heuristically, as an aid to appreciate the growth of order and structure in the Universe, but this term is too vague and subjective to use in quantifying a specific, empirical metric describing a whole range of real-world systems. [5]

But information philosophy sees matter and energy as conserved quantities that need information concepts to explain how they do what they do. As the universe expands, both positive and negative entropy are generated.[6] The normal thermodynamic entropy is known as the Boltzmann Entropy. The negative entropy, often called the Shannon Entropy, is a measure of the information content in the *open* and evolving universe.

Appendix B

---

5   *Cosmic Evolution: The Rise of Complexity in Nature*, p.132.
6   As shown by our common mentor at Harvard, David Layzer.

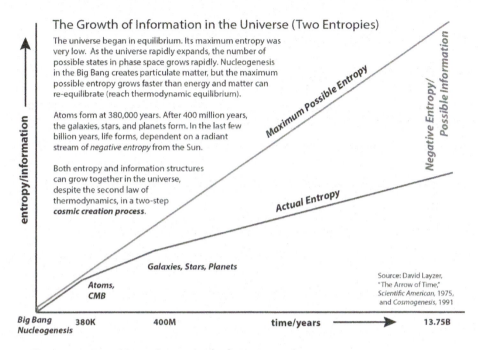

The Growth of Information in the Universe (Two Entropies)

The universe began in equilibrium. Its maximum entropy was very low. As the universe rapidly expands, the number of possible states in phase space grows rapidly. Nucleogenesis in the Big Bang creates particulate matter, but the maximum possible entropy grows faster than energy and matter can re-equilibrate (reach thermodynamic equilibrium).

Atoms form at 380,000 years. After 400 million years, the galaxies, stars, and planets form. In the last few billion years, life forms, dependent on a radiant stream of *negative entropy* from the Sun.

Both entropy and information structures can grow together in the universe, despite the second law of thermodynamics, in a two-step **cosmic creation process**.

Maximum Possible Entropy

Actual Entropy

Negative Entropy/ Possible Information

entropy/information

Negative Entropy/ Possible Information

Galaxies, Stars, Planets

Atoms, CMB

Source: David Layzer, "The Arrow of Time," *Scientific American*, 1975, and *Cosmogenesis*, 1991

Big Bang Nucleogenesis   380K   400M   **time/years** ⟶   13.75B

Figure 30-8. David Layzer's growth of information in the universe

"Negative entropy" is simply the difference between the maximum possible entropy (where all the particles in a physical system would be in a maximum state of disorder, there would be no visible structure) and the actual entropy.

For matter in thermodynamic equilibrium, there is only motion of the microscopic constituent particles ("the motion we call heat"). The existence of macroscopic structures, such as the stars and planets, and their motions, is a departure from thermodynamic equilibrium. And that departure we call the "negative entropy."

The second law of thermodynamics says that the entropy (or disorder) of a *closed* physical system increases until it reaches a maximum, the state of thermodynamic equilibrium. It requires that the entropy of the universe is now and has always been increasing. This established fact of increasing entropy led many scientists and philosophers to assume that the universe we have is "running down" to a "heat death." They think that means the universe began in a very high state of information, since the second law requires that any

Appendix B

organization or order is susceptible to decay. The information that remains today, in their view, has always been here.

But Harvard cosmologist DAVID LAYZER showed that the universe is not a closed system (see Figure 30-4). It is in a dynamic state of expansion that is moving away from thermodynamic equilibrium faster than entropic processes can keep up. The maximum possible entropy is increasing much faster than the actual increase in entropy. The difference between the maximum possible entropy and the actual entropy is potential information.

Positive and Negative Flows

There are two information/entropy flows. In any process, the positive entropy increase is always at least equal to, and generally orders of magnitude larger than, the negative entropy in any created information structures, to satisfy the second law of thermodynamics.

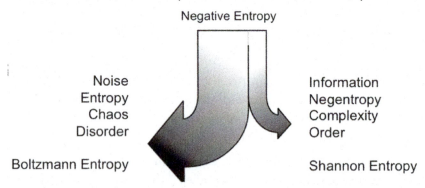

Negative Entropy

Noise
Entropy
Chaos
Disorder

Information
Negentropy
Complexity
Order

Boltzmann Entropy

Shannon Entropy

Figure 30-9. Information flows into Boltzmann and Shannon Entropy.

Material particles are the first information structures to form in the universe from the primordial quarks and electrons. They are baryons, the protons and neutrons of atomic nuclei, which combine with electrons to form atoms and eventually molecules, when the temperature is low enough. After hundreds of millions of years, these particles are attracted by the force of gravitation to form the gigantic information structures of the galaxies, stars, and planets.

Appendix B

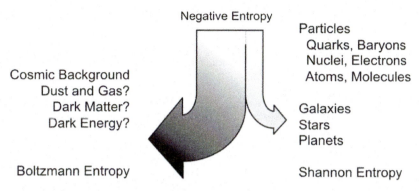

Negative Entropy

Cosmic Background
Dust and Gas?
Dark Matter?
Dark Energy?

Particles
Quarks, Baryons
Nuclei, Electrons
Atoms, Molecules

Galaxies
Stars
Planets

Boltzmann Entropy

Shannon Entropy

Figure 30-10. Cosmological information flows.

Microscopic quantum mechanical particles and huge self-gravitating systems are stable and have extremely long lifetimes, thanks in large part to quantum stability.

Stars are another source of radiation, after the original Big Bang cosmic source, which has cooled down to 3 degrees Kelvin (3K) and shines as the cosmic microwave background radiation.

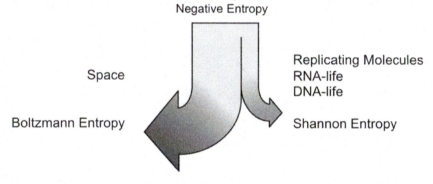

Negative Entropy

Space

Replicating Molecules
RNA-life
DNA-life

Boltzmann Entropy

Shannon Entropy

Figure 30-11. Sun to Earth information flow.

Our solar radiation has a high color temperature (5000K) and a low energy-content temperature (273K). It is out of equilibrium and it is the source of all the information-generating negative entropy that drives biological evolution on the Earth. Note that the fraction of the light falling on Earth is less than a billionth of that which passes by and is lost in space.

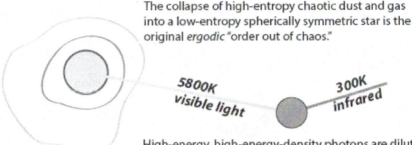

The collapse of high-entropy chaotic dust and gas into a low-entropy spherically symmetric star is the original *ergodic* "order out of chaos."

5800K visible light

300K infrared

High-energy, high-energy-density photons are diluted as they travel to the earth, where they are still high-energy, but now low-energy-density (300K). They are thermalized by the earth and radiated to the night sky

A tiny fraction of the solar energy falling on the earth gets converted into the information structures of plants and animals. Most solar energy is radiated away as waste energy to the night sky.

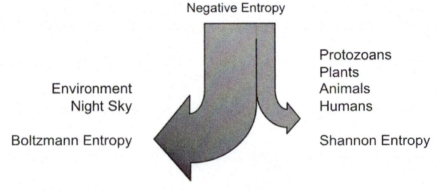

Negative Entropy

Environment
Night Sky

Boltzmann Entropy

Protozoans
Plants
Animals
Humans

Shannon Entropy

Appendix B

Figure 30-12. Information flows into life.

Every biological structure is a quantum mechanical structure. DNA has maintained its stable information structure over billions of years in the constant presence of chaos and noise.

The extraordinarily stable information content of a human being, from the DNA in every cell to the memories in the *Experience Recorder and Reproducer*,[7] survives many changes in the material content of the body during a person's lifetime. Only with death does the mental information (spirit, soul) dissipate - unless it is saved somewhere. [8]

---

7   See appendix E for the ERR
8   See chapter 2 for identity over time.

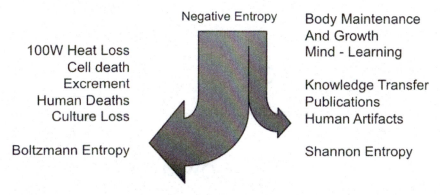

Negative Entropy

Body Maintenance
And Growth
Mind - Learning

100W Heat Loss
Cell death
Excrement
Human Deaths
Culture Loss

Knowledge Transfer
Publications
Human Artifacts

Boltzmann Entropy

Shannon Entropy

Figure 30-13. Information flows in a human being.

The total mental information in a living human is orders of magnitude less than the information content and information processing rate of the body. But the information structures created by humans outside the body, in the form of external knowledge like this book, and the enormous collection of human artifacts, rival the total biological information content of one individual human.

Information increases and we are co-creators of the universe Creation of information structures means that today there is more information in the universe than at any earlier time. This fact of increasing information fits well with an undetermined universe that is still creating itself. In this universe, stars are still forming, biological systems are creating new species, and intelligent human beings are co-creators of the world.

All this creation is the result of the two-step core process that creates all information.[9] It is a combination of two distinct physical processes, one quantum mechanical, the other thermodynamic.

Understanding this core creative process is as close as we are likely to come to understanding the reality behind the popular idea of an anthropomorphic creator of the universe, a still-present divine providence, the cosmic source of everything good and evil.

Information philosophy hopes to replace beliefs with knowledge. The "miracle of creation" is happening now, in the universe and in you and by you.

---

9   See appendix F on the cosmic creation process.

Appendix B

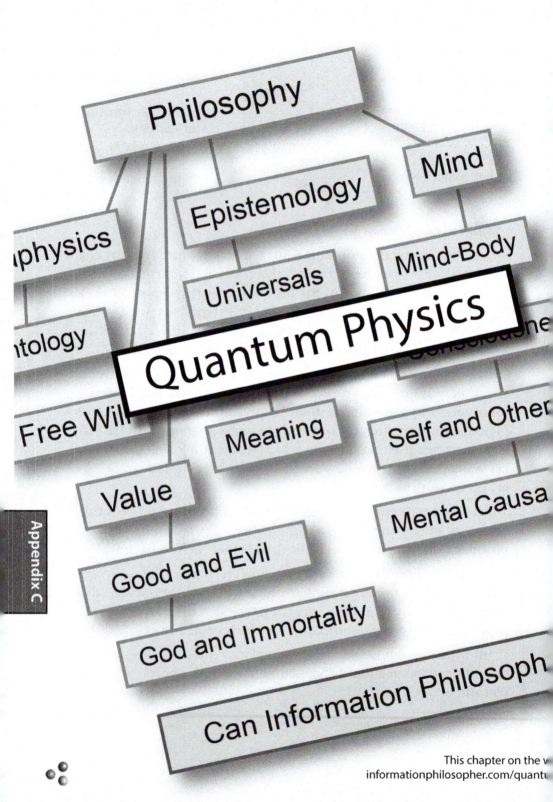

This chapter on the w
informationphilosopher.com/quantu

Quantum Physics

In the classical Newtonian picture of matter in motion, there is only one possible future, determined completely by the distribution and motion of matter at any moment. The future is *certain* and "causally closed." Complete information about the future exists today, even if unknowable.

In the quantum picture, there are many possible futures. Quantum mechanics lets us exactly calculate the probability for the different futures, but it cannot tell us the actual future that will be realized. The actual future is uncertain. New information about the future is being created every day and we are co-creators of that information. The future is open.

It is important to understand that new information generated by quantum mechanics is not necessarily permanent. New information must be stably recorded and protected from erasure by the destructive forces of entropy.

As we saw in appendix B, this requires that more positive entropy must be transferred away from the information structure than its new negative entropy, to satisfy the second law.

MAX PLANCK derived the distribution of radiation at different frequencies (or wavelengths) just as Maxwell and Boltzmann had derived the distribution of velocities (or energies) of the gas particles.[1] Both curves have a power law increase on one side up to a maximum and an exponential decrease down the other side from the maximum (the "Boltzmann factor" of $e^{-E/kT}$). This is because both curves describe particles, one matter, the other light.

Planck's assumption that the energy of the oscillators is "quantized" was the beginning of quantum mechanics, but he did not actually believe that radiation came in the form of discrete particles, as we do today. It was ALBERT EINSTEIN in 1905 who made the hypothesis that light comes in highly localized discrete particles, subsequently called "photons." Later, Einstein showed that each photon, although massless, must have an associated momentum $p = h\nu/c = h/\lambda$, another fundamental connection between matter and light deriving from his most famous equation, $E = mc^2$.

---

1   See Figure 30-2 in appendix B.

Appendix C

But Einstein was puzzled and deeply concerned about the connection between the wave properties of light and his new insight that light consists of particles. In classical electrodynamics, electromagnetic radiation (light, radio) is well known to have wave properties, such as interference. When the crest of one wave meets the trough of another, the two waves cancel one another. How, he wondered, could discrete particles show interference effects?

Like water surface waves, light goes off in all directions as outgoing spherical waves. But if the energy of light fills a large spherical volume, Einstein wondered, how does the energy get itself collected together instantaneously to be absorbed by a single electron in a particular atom? Does the widely distributed energy move faster than the speed of light when it collapses to a single point?

In 1905, Einstein published his special theory of relativity denying that possibility. That same year he proved the existence of Boltzmann's atoms with his explanation that the Brownian motions of visible particles in a liquid are caused by invisible atoms or molecules. His concerns about light waves versus light particles also appeared the same year, in his paper on the photoelectric effect (for which he was awarded the Nobel prize).

When ultraviolet light shines on a metal surface and ejects a single electron from one of the atoms in that metal, Einstein showed that some energy in the light beam acts like a single particle of light getting absorbed by a single ejected electron.

Appendix C

Einstein assumed there is a "work function" or potential energy P that must be overcome to release an electron and that the energy of a photon must exceed that energy. Any excess energy E_e should show up as kinetic energy in the liberated electron.

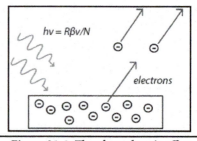

Figure 31-1. The photoelectric effect

$$E_e = hv - P.$$

Some part of the incoming photon energy, P, is used to release the electron. Einstein predicted the other part would show a linear relationship between the kinetic energy E_e of the electron and the frequency v. It was over ten years before Einstein's predictions were experimentally confirmed.

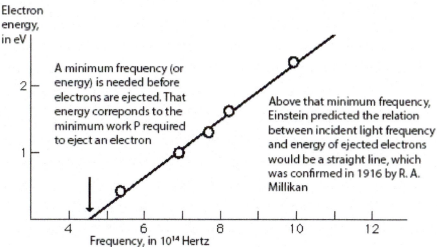

Electron energy, in eV

A minimum frequency (or energy) is needed before electrons are ejected. That energy correponds to the minimum work P required to eject an electron

Above that minimum frequency, Einstein predicted the relation between incident light frequency and energy of ejected electrons would be a straight line, which was confirmed in 1916 by R. A. Millikan

Frequency, in 10^{14} Hertz

Figure 31-2. Millikan confirmed Einstein's relation between the photon energy hv and the energy of the ejected electron.

Turning up the intensity (more photons) of light with less energy (longer wavelengths) cannot eject an electron. And once the light has high enough frequency (energy), it does not matter how low the intensity of the light, electrons continue to be ejected.

It is thus the energy of a single quantum of light that becomes energy in a single electron. At this moment in 1905, Einstein was grappling with two problems that the "founders" of quantum mechanics would themselves not see for another twenty years.

The first problem is the apparent "collapse" of the light wave. The second is called "nonlocal" behavior. Einstein's great field theories like gravitation require what he called "local reality."

If we can see these problems through Einstein's young eyes, which many great quantum physicists could not, we may also see the most plausible solutions to those two problems and perhaps more. A third Einstein insight will help us understand "wave-particle duality." A fourth will clarify "entanglement."

In 1913, NIELS BOHR developed his radical model of the atom incorporating Planck's quantum conditions. Where classical electrodynamic theory says that electrons orbiting a central nucleus would continuously radiate energy at the orbital frequency (and the loss of energy would cause the electron to spiral in to the nucleus), Bohr postulated the atom has "stationary states" and that transitions (discontinuous "quantum jumps") between those states result in the emission or absorption of energy with a frequency v, according to Planck's relation $hv = E_m - E_n$, where E_m and E_n are the energies of the two states.

Einstein had confirmed the relation $E = hv$ in his photoelectric paper, *but Bohr did not mention it.* Bohr's theory agreed perfectly with the frequencies of known spectral lines in the hydrogen atom and predicted many more lines that were subsequently found.

Einstein called Bohr's theory an "enormous achievement" and "one of the greatest discoveries," but Bohr did not accept Einstein's hypothesis of discrete light particles. The quantum jumps are discontinuous, but the emitted radiation is continuous, said Bohr.

Bohr was asked in 1913 by Lord Rutherford how we know to which other state a quantum jump will go. He replied that we do not know. A few years later, Einstein calculated the probabilities for electronic transitions between Bohr's energy levels. He confirmed that it quantum jumps are a matter of chance, just as we cannot predict the time or direction of a particle ejected from a decaying radioactive nucleus. Quantum theory is a *statistical* theory.

In the 1920's, LOUIS DE BROGLIE argued that if photons, with their known wavelike properties, could be described as particles, perhaps particles like electrons might show wavelike properties with a wavelength λ inversely proportional to their momentum $p = m_e v$. De Broglie's formula for a particle's wavelength, $\lambda = h/p$, is the same as Einstein's formula for the momentum of a photon, $p = hv/c$, because $\lambda v = c$.

Experiments confirmed de Broglie's assumption and led ERWIN SCHRÖDINGER to derive a "wave equation" to describe the motion of de Broglie's waves. For elementary particles, Schrödinger's quantum equation replaces the classical Newton equations of motion.

Note that Schrödinger's equation describes the motion of only the wave aspect, not the particle aspect, and so it includes interference effects in the waves. Note also that it is fully deterministic and continuous, just like Newton's equations. Schrödinger thought particles are not real, but could be explained as point-like singularities in his continuous waves.

There was some hope, particularly by Einstein, that Schrödinger's continuous equation would return determinism to physics, eliminating chance. It was not to be.

Schrödinger attempted to interpret his "wave function" for the electron as a probability density for electrical charge, but charge density would be positive everywhere and thus unable to interfere with itself. Moreover, fractions of the electron spread out in the wave are never found. Fractions of the energy would have different (lower) energies and frequencies.

Long before the work of de Broglie and Schrödinger, Einstein had suggested that light waves might be thought of as a "ghost field" (*Gespensterfeld*) or a "leading field (*Führungsfeld*) that guides the motion of the light particles. Einstein suggested that waves indicate the probable locations of his light quanta, although few physicists accepted his radical hypothesis.

The information about probabilities and possibilities in the wave function is *immaterial*, but that abstract information has real causal powers. The wave's interference with itself predicts null points where no particles should be found. And experiments confirm that no particles are found there. Information philosophy views information as a kind of modern "spirit."

MAX BORN applied Einstein's suggestion about light to matter. He shocked the world of physics by suggesting that the absolute values of the square of the wave function ψ ($|\psi|^2$) can be interpreted as the probability of finding an electron in various position and momentum states - if a measurement is made. This allows the probability amplitude ψ to interfere with itself, producing non-intuitive phenomena such as the two-slit experiment. It is an *immaterial* wave of information about possible locations that passes through both slits.

Despite the *immaterial* probability amplitude going through two slits and interfering with itself, experimenters never find parts of electrons. They are always found whole.

Born's statistical interpretation of the wave function ("Born rule") says that the motion of the *immaterial* probabilities wave function is continuous and deterministic, but the motion of the material particles themselves is discontinuous and probabilistic.

Einstein and Schrödinger could never accept this.

Interpreters of quantum mechanics have found it hard to reconcile this combination of determinism and indeterminism, of continuous wavelike possibilities and discontinuous particle-like actualizations. The information interpretation of quantum mechanics attempts that reconciliation. (See chapter 16.)

Note the connection between alternative possibilities for action in the mind and adequately determined actions. (Chapter 4.)

Basic Quantum Mechanics

The basic ideas of quantum mechanics are hopelessly non-intuitive. They describe quantum phenomena that are simply impossible to imagine in classical physics. This does not mean that they cannot be *visualized*, by which we mean illustrated, even animated with tools now available for web pages, which are much more powerful than images on a static printed page.

We hope that watching the animations will help you to develop new intuitions about the way the quantum world works. The classical world we experience is just the quantum world as seen at our macroscopic level, where it is averaged over a vast number of indeterministic quantum events to produce an adequately (or statistically) determined world.

We present the fundamental ideas of quantum mechanics following two great mathematical physicists, PAUL DIRAC and JOHN VON NEUMANN. Von Neumann proposed that quantum mechanics consists of just two basic processes. Dirac said the basics can be summarized in just three definitions, a *principle of superposition*, an *axiom of measurement*, and a *projection postulate.* Let's start with Dirac's three definitions, then see how they are realized in von Neumann's processes.

Finally, we present Dirac's application of the three definitions in the very simple case of a quantum system in a superposition of just two quantum states. This example of three polarizers also demonstrates von Neumann's two processes.

Almost all the conflicting interpretations of quantum mechanics today depend on either denying one or more of these basic elements of quantum mechanics or extending them to situations where they do not apply.

These three definitions and two processes are used throughout the physics chapters in support of the proposed solutions to great problems in physics.

The Principle of Superposition

The fundamental equation of motion in quantum mechanics is Schrödinger's famous wave equation that describes the evolution in time of his wave function ψ,

$ih/2\pi \, \delta\psi/\delta t = H\psi.$

For a single particle in idealized complete isolation, and for a Hamiltonian H that does not involve magnetic fields, the Schrödinger equation is a unitary transformation that is time-reversible.[2]

MAX BORN interpreted the square of the absolute value of Schrödinger's wave function as providing the probability of finding a quantum system in a certain state ψ_n (the "Born rule").

The quantum (discrete) nature of physical systems results from there generally being a large number of solutions ψ_n (called eigenfunctions) of the Schrödinger equation in its time-independent form, with energy eigenvalues E_n.

$H\psi_n = E_n\psi_n,$

endix C

---

2   See the principle of microscopic reversibility in chapter 24.

The discrete energy eigenvalues E_n limit interactions (for example, with photons) to the energy differences $E_n - E_m$, as assumed by Bohr. Eigenfunctions ψ_n are orthogonal to one another,

$$< \psi_n | \psi_m > = \delta_{nm},$$

where δ_{nm} is the Dirac delta-function, equal to 1 when $n = m$, and 0 otherwise. The sum of the diagonal terms in the matrix $< \psi_n | \psi_m >$, when $n = m$, must be normalized to 1 to be meaningful as Born rule probabilities.

$$\Sigma P_n = \Sigma < \psi_n | \psi_n >^2 = 1.$$

The off-diagonal terms in the matrix, $< \psi_n | \psi_m >$, are interpretable as interference terms. When the matrix is used to calculate the expectation values of some quantum mechanical operator O, the off-diagonal terms $< \psi_n | O | \psi_m >$ are interpretable as transition probabilities - the likelihood that the operator O will induce a transition from state ψ_n to ψ_m.

The Schrödinger equation is a *linear* equation. It has no quadratic or higher power terms, and this introduces a profound - and for many scientists and philosophers a disturbing - feature of quantum mechanics, one that is impossible in classical physics. This is the *principle of superposition* of quantum states. If ψ_a and ψ_b are both solutions of the equation, then an arbitrary linear combination of these, $\psi = c_a \psi_a + c_b \psi_b$, with complex coefficients c_a and c_b, is also a solution.

Together with Born's statistical interpretation of the wave function (remember this was Einstein's original idea), the principle of superposition accounts for the major mysteries of quantum theory, some of which we hope to resolve, or at least reduce, with an objective (observer-independent) explanation of information creation during quantum processes, which can often be interpreted as measurements.

The Axiom of Measurement

The *axiom of measurement* depends on the idea of "observables," physical quantities that can be measured in experiments. A physical observable is represented as a Hermitean operator A that is self-adjoint (equal to its complex conjugate, $A^* = A$).

The diagonal elements $< \psi_n \mid A \mid \psi_n >$ of the operator's matrix are interpreted as giving the expectation value for A_n (when we make a measurement). The off-diagonal n, m elements describe the uniquely quantum property of interference between wave functions and provide a measure of the probabilities for transitions between states n and m.

It is these intrinsic quantum probabilities that provide the ultimate source of indeterminism, and consequently of irreducible irreversibility (see chapter 25). The axiom of measurement is then that a large number of measurements of the observable A, known to have eigenvalues A_n, will result in the number of measurements with value A_n being proportional to the probability of finding the system in eigenstate ψ_n with eigenvalue A_n.

The Projection Postulate

The third novel idea of quantum theory is often considered the most radical. It has certainly produced some of the most radical ideas ever to appear in physics, in attempts to deny it (as the decoherence program appears to do, as do also Everett relative-state interpretations, many worlds theories, and Bohm-de Broglie hidden variables). The *projection postulate* is actually very simple, and arguably intuitive as well. It says that when a measurement is made, the system of interest will be found in one of the possible eigenstates ψ_n of the measured observable, with the eigenvalue A_n.

We have several possible alternatives for eigenvalues A_n. Measurement simply makes one of these eigenvalues actual, and it does so, said Max Born, in proportion to the absolute square of the probability amplitude wave function $|\psi_n|^2$. In this way, ontological chance enters physics, and it is partly this fact of quantum randomness that bothered Einstein ("God does not play dice") and Schrödinger (whose equation of motion is deterministic).

When Einstein derived the expressions for the probabilities of emission and absorption of photons in 1916, he lamented that the theory seemed to indicate that the direction of an emitted photon was a matter of pure chance (*Zufall*), and that the time of emission was also statistical and random, just as ERNST RUTHERFORD had

Appendix C

found for the time of decay of a radioactive nucleus. Einstein called it a "weakness in the theory."

Most "interpreters" of quantum mechanics do not accept this postulate, with its idea of a "collapse." [3]

Von Neumann's Two Processes

In 1932, JOHN VON NEUMANN explained that two fundamentally different processes are going on in quantum mechanics.

Process 1: A *non-causal* process, in which a measured electron winds up randomly in one of the possible physical states (eigenstates) of the measuring apparatus plus electron.

The probability for each eigenstate is given by the square of the coefficients c_n of the expansion of the original system state (wave function ψ) in a set of wave functions φ_n that represent the eigenfunctions of the measuring apparatus plus electron.

$$\psi = \Sigma_n c_n \mid \varphi_n >$$
$$c_n = < \varphi_n \mid \psi >$$

Process 1 corresponds exactly to Dirac's projection postulate. It also describes the "collapse" of the wave function. It introduces indeterminism and ontological chance.

This is as close as we get to a description of the discontinuous motion of the particle aspect of a quantum system. According to von Neumann, the particle simply "shows up" somewhere as a result of a measurement. The information interpretation of quantum physics says it can only "show up" if a new stable information structure is created that can be seen by an observer, after which it may constitute a measurement.

PAUL DIRAC explained process 1 with a very simple quantum system that has only two states, horizontal and vertical polarization. We will describe it below.[4] It exhibits properties of quantum mechanics that are impossible for a classical system.

Process 2: A *causal* process, in which the electron wave function ψ evolves deterministically according to Schrödinger's equation of motion for the wavelike aspect. This evolution describes the

Appendix C

---

3   See chapter 19.
4   See p.374.

continuous motion of the probability amplitude wave ψ between discontinuous measurements,

$(ih/2\pi) \, \partial\psi/\partial t = H\psi.$

Von Neumann claimed there is another major difference between these two processes. He said Process 1 is thermodynamically *irreversible*. (See chapter 24.) Process 2 is *reversible*. This confirms the fundamental connection between quantum mechanics and thermodynamics that is explainable by the information interpretation of quantum physics.

Information physics establishes that an experiment may create *irreversible* new information. If it does not, no observation and thus no measurement is possible. Most processes in the universe that create new information are never observed. Process 2 is in principle *reversible*, in practice maybe not. If so, it preserves information. The figure is an example of a reversible process.

Dirac's Three Polarizers

In his 1930 textbook *The Principles of Quantum Mechanics*, Dirac introduced the uniquely quantum concepts of superposition, measurement, projection/collapse, and indeterminacy using polarized photons. Einstein said of Dirac,

> "Dirac, to whom, in my opinion, we owe the most perfect exposition, logically, of this [quantum] theory, rightly points out that it would probably be difficult, for example, to give a theoretical description of a photon such as would give enough information to enable one to decide whether it will pass a polarizer placed (obliquely) in its way or not."[5]

Dirac's example with an "oblique" polarizer suggests a very simple and inexpensive experiment to demonstrate the superpositions of quantum states, the projection or representation of a given state vector in another basis set of vectors, the preparation of quantum systems in states with known properties, and the measurement of various properties.

Any measuring apparatus is also a state preparation system. We know that after a measurement of a photon which has shown it to be in a state of vertical polarization, for example, a second measurement with the same (vertical polarization detecting) capability will show the photon to be in the same state with probability unity. Quantum mechanics is not always uncertain. There is also no uncertainty if we measure a vertically polarized photon with a horizontal polarization detector. There is zero probability of finding the vertically polarized photon in a horizontally polarized state.

Since any measurement increases the amount of information, there must be a compensating increase in entropy absorbed by or radiated away from the measuring apparatus.

The natural basis set of vectors is usually one whose eigenvalues are the observables of our measurement system. In Dirac's bra and ket notation, the orthogonal basis vectors in our example are $| v >$, the photon in a vertically polarized state, and $| h >$, the photon in a horizontally polarized state. These two states are eigenstates of our measuring apparatus.

The interesting case to consider is a third measuring apparatus that prepares a photon in a diagonally polarized state 45° between $| v >$ and $| h >$, the "oblique" polarizer.

Dirac tells us this diagonally polarized photon can be represented as a *superposition* of vertical and horizontal states, with complex number coefficients that represent "probability amplitudes," as shown in equation 1.

$$| d > = (1/\sqrt{2}) | v > + (1/\sqrt{2}) | h > \qquad (1)$$

Note that vector lengths are normalized to unity, and the sum of the squares of the probability amplitudes is also unity. This is the orthonormality condition needed to interpret the (squares of the) wave functions as probabilities, as proposed by Max Born, following Einstein's idea that waves show the probable locations for light quanta.

When these complex number coefficients are squared (actually when they are multiplied by their complex conjugates to produce positive real numbers), the numbers represent the probabilities of finding the photon in one or the other state, should a measurement be made. Dirac's bra vector $< |$ is the complex conjugate of the corresponding ket vector $| >$.

Appendix C

It is the probability amplitudes that interfere in the two-slit experiment. To get the probabilities of finding a photon, we must square the probability amplitudes. Actually we must calculate the expectation value of some operator that represents an observable. The probability P of finding the photon in state $|\psi>$ at a position (in configuration space) r is

$P(r) = < \psi \,|\, r \,|\, \psi >.$

No single experiment can convey all the wonder and non-intuitive character of quantum mechanics. But we believe Dirac's simple examples of polarized photons can teach us a lot. He thought that his simple examples provide a good introduction to quantum physics and we agree.

We use three squares of polarizing sheet material with white labels A, B, and C to illustrate Dirac's explanation of quantum superposition of states and the collapse of a mixture of states to a pure state upon measurement or state preparation.

Here are the three polarizing sheets. They are a neutral gray color because they lose half of the light coming though them. The lost light is absorbed by the polarizer, converted to heat, and this accounts for the (Boltzmann) entropy gain required by our new information (Shannon entropy) about the exact polarization state of the transmitted photons.

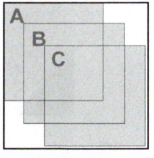

Here polarizers A and B are superimposed to show that the same amount of light comes through two polarizers, as long as the polarizing direction is the same. The first polarizer prepares the photon in a given state of polarization. The second is then certain to find it in the same state. Let's say the direction of light polarization is vertical when the letters are upright.

If one polarizer, say B, is turned 90°, its polarization direction will be horizontal and if it is on top of vertical polarizer A, no light will pass through it, as we see in figure 3. We can still see half of the unpolarized light from letter A.

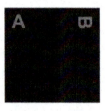

The Wonder and Mystery of the Oblique Polarizer

As you would expect, any quantum mechanics experiment must contain an element of "Wow, that's impossible!" or we are not getting to the non-intuitive and unique difference between quantum mechanics and the everyday classical mechanics. So let's look at the amazing aspect of what Dirac is getting to, and then we will see how quantum mechanics explains it.

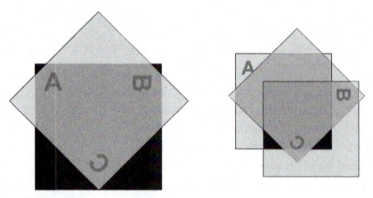

We turn the third polarizer C so its polarization is along the diagonal. Dirac tells us that the wave function of light passing through this polarizer can be regarded as in a mixed state, a superposition of vertical and horizontal states. As Einstein agreed, the information as to the exact state in which the photon will be found following a measurement does not exist.

We can make a measurement that detects vertically polarized photons by holding up the vertical polarizer A in front of the oblique polarizer C. Either a photon comes through A or it does not. Similarly, we can hold up the horizontal polarizer B in front of C. If we see a photon, it is horizontally polarized.

Appendix C

From equation (1) we see that the probability of detecting a photon diagonally polarized by C, if our measuring apparatus (polarizer B) is measuring for horizontally polarized photons, is 1/2. Similarly, if we were to measure for vertically polarized photons, we have the same 50% chance of detecting a photon.

Going back to polarizers A and B crossed at a 90° angle, we know that no light comes through.

And if we hold up polarizer C along the 45 degree diagonal and place it in front of (or behind) the crossed polarizers, nothing changes. Still no light is getting through.

But here is the amazing, impossible part. If you insert polarizer C *between* A and B at that 45 degree angle, some light now gets through. Note that C is slipped between A (in the rear) and B (in front).

If B, crossed 90° with A, blocks all light, how can *adding* another polarization filter add light? It is somewhat less light than through C alone, and we shall see why.

The Quantum Physics Explanation

Let's start with the A polarizer in the back. It *prepares* the photons in the vertical polarization state $| v >$. If we now had just polarizer B, it would measure for horizontal photons. None through A are horizontal, so no photons get through B.

Measurements are von Neumann **process 1**.

When we interpose C at the oblique angle, it measures for diagonal photons. The vertically polarized photons coming through A can be considered in a superposition of states at a 45 degree angle and a -45 degree angle. Photons at -45 degrees are absorbed by C. Those at +45 degrees pass through C.

C makes a *measurement* of 45 degree photons. It can also be viewed as a *preparation* of 45 degree photons. Only half the photons come through polarizer C, but they have been prepared in a state of diagonal polarization $| d >$.

The original vertical photons coming through A had no chance of getting through B, but the diagonal photons passing through C (half the original photons) can now be regarded as in a linear superposition of vertical and horizontal photons, and the horizontal photons can now pass through B. Those vertically polarized will get absorbed by B, as usual.

Recall from equation (1) that | d > is a superposition of the basis vectors | v > and | h >, with coefficients $1/\sqrt{2}$, which when squared give us probabilities $1/2$. Fifty percent of these photons emerging from C will pass though B. One quarter or 25% of the original A photons make it through.

This happens if we send just one photon through at a time, just as with the two-slit experiment. Just as we can not say that the photon passes through slit A or B (only probabilities are moving in von Neumann's process 2), we cannot say that our photons are in one state or another. They are in the mysterious linear combination that can collapse instantaneously into one state when a measurement is made.

Einstein and Quantum Physics

It was ALBERT EINSTEIN in 1916 who first saw that quantum mechanics involves chance. Because he did not like chance ("God does not play dice" was his oft-repeated claim), he called it a "weakness in the theory." But his insight into chance is much clearer than that of Werner Heisenberg and Max Born. Seeing chance through Einstein's eyes may convince many philosophers and scientists who are now confused by disagreements between the various "interpretations" of quantum mechanics.[6]

Paradoxically, ironically perhaps, and even tragically, almost no scientists and philosophers recognize the full range of Einstein's contributions to quantum mechanics, primarily because he disavowed his own quantum discoveries as contrary to his fundamental beliefs about the workings of the universe.

Besides quantizing light energy and seeing its interchangeability with matter, $E = mc^2$, Einstein was the first scientist to see many of the most fundamental aspects of quantum physics - the quantal derivation of the blackbody radiation law, nonlocality and instanta-

Appendix C

neous action-at-a-distance (1905), the internal structure of atoms (1906), wave-particle duality and the "collapse" of the wave aspect (1909), transition probabilities for emission and absorption processes that introduce indeterminism whenever matter and radiation interact, making quantum mechanics a statistical theory (1916-17), the indistinguishability of elementary particles with their strange quantum statistics (1925), and the nonseparability and entanglement of interacting identical particles (1935).

It took the physics community eighteen years to accept Einstein's light-quantum hypothesis. He saw wave-particle duality fifteen years before deBroglie, Schrödinger, Heisenberg, and Bohr. He saw indeterminism a decade before the Heisenberg uncertainty principle. He saw nonlocality as early as 1905, presenting it formally in 1927, but was ignored. In the 1935 Einstein-Podolsky-Rosen paper, he added nonseparability, which was dubbed "entanglement" by Schrödinger.

Information philosophy sees *immaterial* information as a kind of modern "spirit." Einstein himself described the wave as a "ghostly field" (*Gespensterfeld*) and as a "guiding field" (*Führungsfeld*). This idea was taken up later by Louis de Broglie as "pilot waves" and by Erwin Schrödinger, who developed the linear equation that describes how the probability wave function moves through space deterministically. This restoration of some determinism was a brief bright moment for Einstein. He saw a possible return to a deterministic theory for quantum mechanics and his continuous field theory. But it was not to be, despite the large number of present-day physicists who are still pursuing Einstein's and Schrödinger's dreams, by denying indeterminism and "quantum jumping."

Einstein even made the original suggestion to Schrödinger that a microscopic superposition might become a macroscopic superposition, the idea that Schrödinger made famous as his cat paradox.

The problems raised by Einstein are usually presented as arising *after* the "founders" of quantum mechanics and their Copenhagen Interpretation in the late 1920's. Modern attention to Einstein's work on quantum physics often starts with the EPR paper of 1935, when his mysteries of nonlocality, nonseparability, and entanglement were first being clearly understood by his opponents.

Appendix C

Philosophy

Mind

Epistemology

Metaphysics

Mind-Body

Universals

Ontology

Chance

Consciousn

Free Will

Meaning

Self and Othe

Value

Mental Causa

Appendix D

Good and Evil

God and Immortality

Can Information Philosoph

Chance

Is chance *ontological* and real or *epistemic* and the result of human ignorance. Information philosophy answers this question.

For most of the history of philosophy, ontological chance has been strictly denied. LEUCIPPUS (440 BCE) stated the first dogma of determinism, an absolute necessity.

> "Nothing occurs by chance (*maton*), but there is a reason (*logos*) and necessity (*ananke*) for everything."

Chance is regarded as inconsistent with causal determinism and with physical or mechanical determinism.

The first thinker to suggest a physical explanation for chance in the universe was EPICURUS. Epicurus was influenced strongly by ARISTOTLE, who regarded chance as a fifth cause. Epicurus said there must be cases in which the normally straight paths of atoms in the universe occasionally bend a little and the atoms "swerve" to prevent the universe and ourselves from being completely determined by the mechanical laws of DEMOCRITUS.

For Epicurus, the chance in his atomic swerve was simply a means to deny the fatalistic future implied by determinism (and necessity). As the Epicurean Roman LUCRETIUS explained the idea,

> "...if all motion is always one long chain, and new motion arises out of the old in order invariable, and if the first-beginnings do not make by swerving a beginning of motion such as to break the decrees of fate, that cause may not follow cause from infinity, whence comes this freedom in living creatures all over the earth."[1]

Epicurus did not say the swerve was directly involved in decisions so as to make them random. His critics, ancient and modern, have claimed mistakenly that Epicurus did assume "one swerve - one decision." Some recent philosophers call this the "traditional interpretation" of Epicurean free will, an unfortunate error.

On the contrary, following ARISTOTLE, Epicurus thought human agents have an autonomous ability to transcend the necessity and chance of some events. He stated clearly that this special ability makes us morally responsible for our actions.

Appendix D

---

1   *De Rerum Natura*, Book 2, lines 251-256

Epicurus, again following Aristotle, finds a *tertium quid*, between and beyond the other two options, necessity (Democritus' determinism) and chance (Epicurus' swerve).

The *tertium quid* is agent autonomy. Epicurus wrote:

> "...some things happen of necessity (ἀνάγκη), others by chance (τύχη), others through our own agency (παρ' ἡμᾶς)...necessity destroys responsibility and chance is uncertain; whereas our own actions are autonomous, and it is to them that praise and blame naturally attach."[2]

Despite abundant evidence, many philosophers deny that real chance exists. If a single event is determined by chance, then indeterminism would be "true," they say, and undermine the very possibility of certain knowledge. Some go to the extreme of saying that chance makes the state of the world totally independent of any earlier states,[3] which is nonsense, but it shows how anxious they are about chance.

The Stoic CHRYSIPPUS (200 BCE) said that a single uncaused cause could destroy the universe (cosmos), a concern shared by some modern philosophers, for whom reason itself would fail. He wrote:

> "Everything that happens is followed by something else which depends on it by causal necessity. Likewise, everything that happens is preceded by something with which it is causally connected. For nothing exists or has come into being in the cosmos without a cause. The universe will be disrupted and disintegrate into pieces and cease to be a unity functioning as a single system, if any uncaused movement is introduced into it."

The core idea of chance and indeterminism is closely related to the idea of causality. Indeterminism for some is simply an event without a cause, an uncaused cause or *causa sui* that starts a new causal chain. If we admit some uncaused causes, we can have an adequate (statistical) causality without the physical necessity of strict determinism - which implies complete predictability of events and only one possible future.

---

2   Letter to Menoeceus, §133
3   Compare perdurantism on p.40

An example of an event that is not strictly caused is one that depends on chance, like the flip of a coin. If the outcome is only probable, not certain, then the event can be said to have been caused by the coin flip, but the head or tails result itself was not predictable. So this "soft" causality, which recognizes prior uncaused events as causes, is undetermined and the result of chance alone.

The Calculus of Probabilities

The great mathematical theorists of games of chance found ways to argue that the chance they described was somehow necessary, that chance outcomes were actually determined by "laws." The greatest of these, PIERRE-SIMON LAPLACE, preferred to call his theory the "calculus of probabilities." With its connotation of approbation, *probability* is a more respectable term than chance, which has associations of gambling and lawlessness. For Laplace, the random outcomes were not predictable only because we lack the detailed information needed to predict. As did the ancient Stoics, Laplace explained the appearance of chance as the result of human ignorance. He said,

> "The word 'chance,' then expresses only our ignorance of the causes of the phenomena that we observe to occur and to succeed one another in no apparent order."

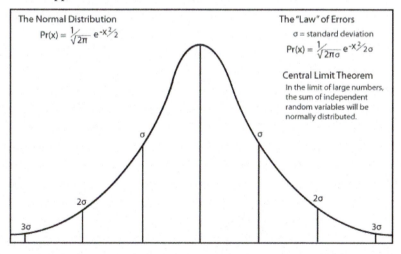

The Normal Distribution

$$Pr(x) = \frac{1}{\sqrt{2\pi}} e^{-x^2/2}$$

The "Law" of Errors

σ = standard deviation

$$Pr(x) = \frac{1}{\sqrt{2\pi\sigma}} e^{-x^2/2\sigma}$$

Central Limit Theorem
In the limit of large numbers, the sum of independent random variables will be normally distributed.

Figure 32-1. C.S.Peirce called the distribution of random events "normal."

Decades before Laplace, ABRAHAM DE MOIVRE discovered the normal distribution (the bell curve) of outcomes for ideal random processes, like the throw of dice. Perfectly random processes produce a *regular* distribution pattern for many trials (the law of large numbers). Inexplicably, the discovery of these regularities in various social phenomena led the great thinkers to conclude that the phenomena were determined, not random. They simply denied the existence of chance in the world.

In 1718 De Moivre wrote a book called *The Doctrine of Chances*. It was very popular among gamblers. In the second edition (1738) he derived the mathematical form of the normal distribution of probabilities, but he denied the reality of chance. Because it implied events that God could not know, he labeled it *atheistic*.

> "Chance, in atheistical writings or discourse, is a sound utterly insignificant: It imports no determination to any mode of existence; nor indeed to existence itself, more than to non existence; it can neither be defined nor understood."

As early as 1784, IMMANUEL KANT had argued that the regularities in social events from year to year showed that they must be the consequence of underlying deterministic laws.

> "Thus marriages, the consequent births and the deaths, since the free will seems to have such a great influence on them, do not seem to be subject to any law according to which one could calculate their number beforehand. Yet the annual (statistical) tables about them in the major countries show that they occur according to stable natural laws."

In the early 1800's ADOLPHE QUÉTELET and HENRY THOMAS BUCKLE argued that these regularities in "social physics" proved that individual acts like marriage and suicide were not "free," but determined by an unknown natural law.

The possibility that chance is more than human ignorance entered physics when LUDWIG BOLTZMANN showed in 1877 that random collisions between atomic particles in a gas could explain the increase in entropy that is the Second Law of Thermodynamics.

In 1866, when Boltzmann first derived Maxwell's velocity distribution of gas particles, he did it assuming that the physical motion of each particle (or atom) was *determined* exactly by Newton's laws. And in 1872, when he attempted to show how his kinetic theory of gases could explain the increase in entropy, he again used strictly deterministic physics. But Boltzmann's former teacher JOSEF LOSCHMIDT objected to this derivation of the second law. Loschmidt said that if time was reversed, the deterministic laws of classical mechanics require that the entropy would then go down, not up.[4]

So in 1877 Boltzmann reformulated his derivation, assuming that each collision of gas particles was not determined, but statistical and random. He assumed that the directions and velocities of particles after a collision depended on chance, as long as energy and momentum were conserved. He could then argue that the particles would be located randomly in "phase space" based on the statistical assumption that individual cells of phase space were equally probable. His *H*-Theorem produced a quantity which would go only up, independent of the time direction. Laws of nature became statistical.

Boltzmann's student FRANZ S. EXNER defended the idea of absolute chance and indeterminism as a hypothesis that could not be ruled out on the basis of observational evidence. Exner did this in his 1908 inaugural lecture at Vienna University as rector (two years after Boltzmann's death), and ten years later in a book written during World War I. But Exner's view was not the standard view. Ever since the eighteenth-century development of the calculus of probabilities, scientists and philosophers assumed that probabilities and statistical phenomena, including social statistics, were completely determined. They thought that our inability to predict individual events was due simply to our ignorance of the details.

In his own 1922 inaugural address at the University of Zurich, *What Is a Law of Nature?*, ERWIN SCHRÖDINGER said about his favorite teacher,

> "It was the experimental physicist, Franz Exner, who for the first time, in 1919, launched a very acute philosophical criticism against the taken-for-granted manner in which the absolute determinism of molecular processes was accepted by everybody. He came to the conclusion that

4   See chapter 25.

the assertion of determinism was certainly possible, yet by no means necessary, and when more closely examined not at all very probable.

"Exner's assertion amounts to this: It is quite possible that Nature's laws are of thoroughly statistical character. The demand for an absolute law in the background of the statistical law — a demand which at the present day almost everybody considers imperative — goes beyond the reach of experience."

Ironically, just four years later, after developing his continuous and deterministic wave theory of quantum mechanics, Schrödinger would himself "go beyond the reach of experience." He searched for deterministic laws underlying the discontinuous, discrete, statistical and probabilistic indeterminism of the Bohr-Heisenberg school, to avoid the implications of absolute chance in quantum mechanics. Planck and Einstein too were repulsed by randomness and chance. "God does not play dice," was Einstein's famous remark.

A major achievement of the Ages of Reason and Enlightenment was to banish absolute chance as *unintelligible* and *atheistic*. Newton's Laws provided a powerful example of deterministic laws governing the motions of everything. Surely Leucippus' and Democritus' original insights had been confirmed?

Franz Exner was not alone in defending chance before quantum physics. In the nineteenth century in America, CHARLES SANDERS PEIRCE coined the term "tychism" for his idea that absolute chance was the first step in three steps to "synechism" or continuity.

Peirce was influenced by the social statisticians, Buckle and Quételet, by French philosophers CHARLES RENOUVIER and ALFRED FOUILLÉE, who also argued for some absolute chance, by the physicists Maxwell and Boltzmann, but most importantly Peirce was influenced by the philosophers Kant and Hegel, who saw things arranged in the *triads* that Peirce so loved.

Quételet and Buckle thought they had established an absolute deterministic law behind all statistical laws. Buckle went so far as to claim it established the lack of free will.

Renouvier and Fouillée introduced chance or indeterminism simply to contrast it with determinism, and to discover some way, usually a dialectical argument like that of Hegel, to reconcile the opposites. Renouvier argues for human freedom, but nowhere explains exactly how chance might contribute to that freedom, other than negating determinism.

Maxwell may have used the normal distribution of Quételet and Buckle's social physics as his model for the distribution of molecular velocities in a gas. Boltzmann also was impressed with the distribution of social statistics, and was initially convinced that individual particles obeyed strict and deterministic Newtonian laws of motion.

Peirce does not explain much with his tychism. And, with his view that continuity and evolutionary love is supreme, may have had doubts about the importance of chance. He did not propose chance as directly or indirectly providing free will. He never mentions the ancient criticisms that we cannot accept responsibility for chance decisions. And he does not really care for chance as the origin of species, preferring a more deterministic and continuous lawful development, under the guidance of evolutionary love. He called Darwinism "greedy? But Peirce does say clearly, well before Boltzmann and Exner, that the observational evidence simply does not establish strict determinism.

It remained for WILLIAM JAMES, Peirce's close friend, to assert that chance can provide random unpredictable alternatives from which the will can choose or "determine" one alternative. James was the first thinker to enunciate clearly a two-stage decision process, with chance in a *present* time of random alternatives, leading to a choice which selects one alternative and transforms an equivocal ambiguous *future* into an unalterable determined *past*.

Free will consists of undetermined alternatives followed by adequately but statistically determined choices.

"The stronghold of the determinist argument is the antipathy to the idea of chance...This notion of alternative possibility, this admission that any one of several things may come to pass is, after all, only a roundabout name for chance...

Appendix D

"What is meant by saying that my choice of which way to walk home after the lecture is ambiguous and matter of chance?...It means that both Divinity Avenue and Oxford Street are called but only one, and that one either one, shall be chosen."[5]

Chance is critically important for the question of free will because strict necessity implies just one possible future. Absolute chance means that the future is fundamentally unpredictable at the levels where chance is dominant. Chance allows alternative futures and the question becomes how the one actual present is realized from these potential alternative futures.

The amount of chance and the departure from strict causality required for free will is very slight compared to the miraculous ideas often associated with the "causa sui" (self-caused cause) of the ancients. For medieval philosophers, only God could produce a *causa sui*, a miracle. Modern quantal randomness, unless amplified to the macroscopic world, is often insignificant, not a miracle at all.

Despite DAVID HUME's critical attack on causality, many philosophers embrace causality strongly, including Hume himself in his other writings, where he dogmatically asserts *"'tis impossible to admit of any medium betwixt chance and an absolute necessity."*

Since Chrysippus twenty-two centuries ago, philosophers still connect causality to the very possibility of logic and reason.

BERTRAND RUSSELL said "The law of causation, according to which later events can theoretically be predicted by means of earlier events, has often been held to be *a priori*, a necessity of thought, a category without which science would not be possible."[6] Although he felt some claims for causality might be excessive, Russell was unwilling to give up strict determinism, saying "Where determinism fails, science fails."[7] And, "what science cannot discover, mankind cannot know."

The great polymath HENRI POINCARÉ said

"Every phenomenon, however trifling it be, has a cause, and a mind infinitely powerful and infinitely well-informed concerning the laws of

Appendix D

---

5   "The Dilemma of Determinism," in *The Will to Believe*, 1897, p.155
6   *Our Knowledge of the External World*, p.179
7   *Determinism and Physics*, p.18

nature could have foreseen it from the beginning of the ages. If a being with such a mind existed, we could play no game of chance with him; we should always lose. For him, in fact, the word chance would have no meaning, or rather there would be no such thing as chance."

MAX PLANCK, along with Einstein, Schrödinger and others, opposed indeterminism. Einstein called chance a "weakness in the theory." Planck remained convinced that determinism and strict causality are essential requirements for physical science and so must be true.

> "Just as no physicist will in the last resort acknowledge the play of chance in human nature, so no physiologist will admit the play of chance in the absolute sense."

> "the assumption of chance in inorganic nature is incompatible with the working principle of natural science."

> "We must admit that the mind of each one of our greatest geniuses — Aristotle, Kant or Leonardo, Goethe or Beethoven, Dante or Shakespeare — even at the moment of its highest flights of thought or in the most profound inner workings of the soul, was subject to the causal fiat and was an instrument in the hands of an almighty law which governs the world."[8]

ERNEST RUTHERFORD studied the emission of particles from decaying radioactive atoms. He called them α and β rays. The alpha particles are helium nuclei stripped of electrons. The beta particles are electrons. It was NIELS BOHR who told Rutherford that the α and β rays were coming from the central nucleus that Rutherford had discovered in 1911, not from the surrounding electron cloud as had been thought.

Rutherford said the emission of rays is a chance process. There seemed to be no way to predict the time or direction of such events. He could only discover a characteristic time or "half-life" after which 50% of the original radioactive elements would be left.

When Bohr showed two years later that the electron cloud could be organized into circular orbits, and the electrons were jumping from one orbit to another with the emission or absorption of light quanta, Rutherford's question to Bohr was, "How do the electrons know which orbit they are going to jump to?" Bohr did not know.

Appendix D

---

8   *Where Is Science Going?*, pp.147, 154, 156

Einstein answered that question in 1916 when he showed it is purely a matter of chance. Einstein derived A and B coefficients describing the absorption, spontaneous emission, and (his newly predicted) stimulated emission of radiation. In two papers, "Emission and Absorption of Radiation in Quantum Theory," and "On the Quantum Theory of Radiation," he derived the Planck law (for Planck it was mostly a heuristic guess at the formula), he derived Planck's postulate $E = h\nu$, and he derived Bohr's second postulate $E_m - E_n = h\nu$. Einstein did this by exploiting the obvious relationship between the Maxwell-Boltzmann distribution of gas particle velocities and the distribution of radiation in Planck's law. He wrote:

> "The formal similarity between the chromatic distribution curve for thermal radiation and the Maxwell velocity-distribution law is too striking to have remained hidden for long. In fact, it was this similarity which led W. Wien, some time ago, to an extension of the radiation formula in his important theoretical paper, in which he derived his displacement law...Not long ago I discovered a derivation of Planck's formula which was closely related to Wien's original argument and which was based on the fundamental assumption of quantum theory. This derivation displays the relationship between Maxwell's curve and the chromatic distribution curve and deserves attention not only because of its simplicity, but especially because it seems to throw some light on the mechanism of emission and absorption of radiation by matter, a process which is still obscure to us."[9]

But the introduction of Maxwell-Boltzmann statistical mechanical thinking to electromagnetic theory produced what Einstein called a "weakness in the theory." It introduces the reality of irreducible objective chance!

If light quanta are particles with energy $E = h\nu$ traveling at the velocity of light c, then they should have a momentum $p = E/c = h\nu/c$. When light is absorbed by material particles, this momentum will clearly be transferred to the particle. But when light is emitted by an atom or molecule, a problem appears.

Appendix D

9   "On the Quantum Theory of Radiation," Sources of Quantum Mechanics, B. L. van der Waerden, Dover, 1967, p.63

The "statistical interpretation" of MAX BORN ("Born rule") tells us the outgoing wave is the probability amplitude wave function Ψ, whose absolute square is the probability of finding a light particle in an arbitrary direction.

Conservation of momentum requires that the momentum of the emitted particle will cause an atom to recoil with momentum hv/c in the opposite direction. However, the standard theory of spontaneous emission of radiation is that it produces a spherical wave going out in all directions. A spherically symmetric wave has no preferred direction. In which direction does the atom recoil?, Einstein asked:

> "Does the molecule receive an impulse when it absorbs or emits the energy ε? For example, let us look at emission from the point of view of classical electrodynamics. When a body emits the radiation ε it suffers a recoil (momentum) ε/c if the entire amount of radiation energy is emitted in the same direction. If, however, the emission is a spatially symmetric process, e.g., a spherical wave, no recoil at all occurs. This alternative also plays a role in the quantum theory of radiation. When a molecule absorbs or emits the energy ε in the form of radiation during the transition between quantum theoretically possible states, then this elementary process can be viewed either as a completely or partially directed one in space, or also as a symmetrical (nondirected) one. It turns out that we arrive at a theory that is free of contradictions, only if we interpret those elementary processes as completely directed processes."[10]

An outgoing light particle must impart momentum hv/c to the atom or molecule, but the direction of the momentum can not be predicted! Neither can the theory predict the time when the light quantum will be emitted. Einstein called this weakness by its German name - *Zufall* (chance).

He recalled that Rutherford's law for radioactive decay of unstable atomic nuclei could only give the probability of decay time. Einstein saw the connection with radiation emission:

> "It speaks in favor of the theory that the statistical law assumed for [spontaneous] emission is nothing but the Rutherford law of radioactive decay."[11]

---

10   On the Quantum Theory of Radiation, p.65
11   "Subtle is the Lord...", A. Pais, p.411

But the inability to predict both the time and direction of light particle emissions, said Einstein in 1917, is "*a weakness in the theory..., that it leaves time and direction of elementary processes to chance (Zufall, ibid.).*" It is only a weakness for Einstein, of course, because his God does not play dice.

Einstein clearly saw, as none of his contemporaries did, that since spontaneous emission is a statistical process, it cannot possibly be described with classical physics. Einstein had probably known this since 1905, but he deeply disliked the idea of chance in physics. But Einstein's dislike of quantum physics did not prevent him from seeing its necessity.

> "The properties of elementary processes required...make it seem almost inevitable to formulate a truly quantized theory of radiation."[12]

Einstein may not have liked this conceptual crisis, but his insights into the indeterminism involved in quantizing matter and energy were known, if largely ignored, over a decade before Heisenberg's quantum theory introduced his famous uncertainty principle in 1927. Heisenberg states that the exact position and momentum of an atomic particle can only be known within certain (sic) limits. The product of the position error and the momentum error is greater than or equal to Planck's constant $h/2\pi$.

$$\Delta p \Delta x \geq h/2\pi$$

Indeterminacy (*Unbestimmtheit*) was Heisenberg's original name for his principle. It is a better name than the more popular uncertainty, which connotes lack of knowledge. Quantum indeterminacy is ontological as well as epistemic lack of information.

Heisenberg declared that the new quantum theory disproved causality, using facts that were first described by Einstein years earlier. But Heisenberg did not reference Einstein's landmark 1916 work on the breakdown of causality.

---

12   Pais, ibid.

Heisenberg simply says:

> "We cannot - and here is where the causal law breaks down - explain why a particular atom will decay at one moment and not the next, or what causes it to emit an electron in this direction rather than that."

Indeed, Heisenberg (and possibly Bohr) were still not convinced about Einstein's light quanta as late this remark in 1926!

He told Einstein directly in a personal meeting,

> "Whether or not I should believe in light quanta, I cannot say at this stage. Radiation quite obviously involves the discontinuous elements to which you refer as light quanta. On the other hand, there is a continuous element, which appears, for instance, in interference phenomena, and which is much more simply described by the wave theory of light. But you are of course quite right to ask whether quantum mechanics has anything new to say on these terribly difficult problems. I believe that we may at least hope that it will one day."[13]

It is important to note that Einstein's indeterminism of time and direction is an intrinsic property of the interaction of radiation with matter. It does not depend on limits put on measurements, as Heisenberg's "uncertainty" suggested, nor on the presence of a conscious observer, as Bohr's Copenhagen Interpretation seems to imply. Where Bohr and Heisenberg describe *epistemic* limits to knowledge, Einstein's light quanta shows us an ontologically indeterministic world, independent of any observation or measurement. Einstein says:

> "If the molecule suffers a loss of energy in the amount of hv without external stimulation, i.e., by emitting the energy in the form of radiation (spontaneous emission), then this process too is a directional one. There is no emission of radiation in the form of spherical waves. The molecule suffers a recoil in the amount of hv/c during this elementary process of emission of radiation; the direction of the recoil is, at the present state of theory, determined by "chance"...

> "The weakness of the theory is, on the one hand, that it does not bring us closer to a link-up with the undulation theory; on the other hand, it also leaves time of occurrence and direction of the elementary processes a matter of "chance." Nevertheless, I fully trust in the reliability of the road taken."[14]

Appendix D

---

13   "Quantum Mechanics and a Talk with Einstein," *Physics and Beyond*, p.67
14   On the Quantum Theory of Radiation, p.76

Chance and Free Will

Our two-stage model for free will[15] sees a role for chance in the brain in the form of quantum level noise (as well as pre-quantal thermal noise). Noise can introduce random errors into stored memories. Noise can create random associations of ideas during memory recall. Many scientists have speculated that randomness in the brain may be driven by microscopic fluctuations that are amplified to the macroscopic level. This would not happen in some specific location in the brain. It is most likely a general property of all neurons.

We can distinguish seven increasingly sophisticated ideas about the role of chance and indeterminism in the question of free will. Many libertarians have accepted the first two. Determinist and compatibilist critics of free will make the third their central attack on chance, claiming that it denies moral responsibility. But very few thinkers appear to have considered all seven essential requirements for chance to contribute to libertarian free will.

• Chance exists in the universe. Quantum mechanics is correct. Indeterminism is true, etc.

• Chance is important for free will because it breaks the causal chain of determinism.

• But chance cannot directly cause our actions. We cannot be responsible for random actions.

• Chance can only generate random (unpredictable) alternative possibilities for action or thought. The choice or selection of one action must be adequately determined, so that we can take responsibility. And once we choose, the connection between mind/brain and motor control must be adequately determined to see that "our will be done."

• Chance, in the form of noise, both quantum and thermal noise, must always be present. The naive model of a single random microscopic event, amplified to affect the macroscopic brain, never made sense. Under what ad hoc circumstances, at what time, at what place in the brain, would it occur to affect a decision?

---

15   See chapter 4 for details.

• Chance must be overcome or suppressed by the adequately determined will when it decides to act, de-liberating the prior free options that "one could have done."

• To the extent that chance is not completely suppressed by the will, the resulting choice can be considered to have an element of randomness. The agent can still take responsibility for allowing the choice to be partially or completely random, the equivalent of flipping a mental coin, if no available option is clearly best.

Of those thinkers who have considered most of these aspects of chance, a small fraction have also seen the obvious parallel with biological evolution and natural selection, with its microscopic quantum accidents causing variations in the gene pool and macroscopic natural selection of fit genes by their reproductive success.

Our two-stage model of free will needs chance for the free generation of action items and thoughts in an agenda of alternative possibilities to be de-liberated by the will. Chance is the "free" in the first stage of free will and the source of human creativity. The adequately determined second stage is the "will" in free will that de-liberates, choosing actions for which we can be morally responsible.

Philosophy

Mind

Epistemology

Mind-Body

Metaphysics

Induction

Universals

Experience Recorder
and Reproducer

Self and Other M

Value

Mental Caus

Good and Evil

The

God and Immortality

Can Information Philosop

Appendix E

Experience Recorder and Reproducer

The *experience recorder and reproducer* (ERR) is our functional basis for an information mind model. The ERR is simpler, but superior to, computational models of the mind popular in today's neuroscience and cognitive science. Mind is *immaterial* information, software in the brain hardware. ERR provides deep insight into both the problem of "meaning" and the "hard problem" of consciousness.

Man is not a machine. And the mind is not a computer.

Our specific mind model grows out of the biological question of what sort of "mind" would provide the greatest survival value for the lowest (or the earliest) organisms that evolved mind-like capabilities.

We propose that a minimal primitive mind would need only to "play back" past experiences that resemble any part of current experience. Remembering past experiences has obvious relevance (survival value) for an organism. But beyond survival value, the ERR touches on the philosophical problem of "meaning." We suggest the epistemological "meaning" of information perceived is to be found in the past experiences that are reproduced automatically by the ERR.

The ERR reproduces the entire complex of the original sensations experienced, together with the emotional response to the original experience (pleasure, pain, fear, etc.). Playback is stimulated by anything in the current experience that resembles something in the past experiences, in the five dimensions of the senses (sound, sight, touch, smell and taste), as well as unique emotional experiences.

The ERR model stands in contrast to the popular cognitive science models of a mind as a digital computer with a "central processor" or even many "parallel processors." No algorithms or stored programs are needed for the ERR model. There is nothing comparable to the addresses and data buses used to stored and retrieve information in a digital computer.

An approximation might be a non-linear random-access data recorder, where data is stored using "content-addressable" memory (the memory address - a string of bits in a digital computer - would be the data content itself).

Much simpler than a computer with stored data structures, a better technological metaphor for ERR might be a multi-channel, multi-track analog video and sound recorder, enhanced with the ability to record smells, tastes, touches, and most important, feelings. Imagine one channel for each sense, one track for each neuron. But of course machines currently do not smell or taste and have no feelings, so could not reproduce them.

Although there is really no comparison between any current technology and the ERR, the closest thing in speed and completeness of recall, with the precision that recalled items are relevant, is state-of-the-art search and retrieval engines like that of Google.

But even Google pales in comparison with your ability to instantly recall the arrangement of rooms in your house when you were a teenager. You can visualize the surroundings of your home, maybe the color of the house, the direction to the nearest bus stop, etc.

And compared to the worldwide network of computers and databases that is Google, the biological and neurological basis for ERR is very straightforward.

No modern computer can surpass the amazing information storage capability and rapidity of search and retrieval of information as that of the human neocortex.

Unlike most of the brain, the neocortex randomly grows its over 10 billion axons, each with 10,000 dendritic connections.

As can be seen in RAMÓN Y CAJAL's drawings made at the end of the nineteenth century, the neocortex consists primarily of six horizontal layers segregated principally by cell type and neuronal connections.

The neurons are arranged in vertical structures called cortical columns, with a diameter of about *1mm*. A given column may respond to a sensory stimulus coming from a certain body part or region of sound or vision. These columns are similar, and can be thought of as the basic repeating functional units of the neocortex. In humans, a column contains approximately 70,000 neurons and the neocortex consists of about 500,000 columns.

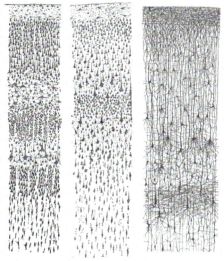

Figure 33-1. Cajal's extraordinary drawings.

The neuroscientist DONALD HEBB said in 1949 that "neurons that fire together wire together." Our ERR mind model is based on the simple extension of the Hebb idea to the notion that "*neurons that have been wired together will fire together.*"

• The ERR Recorder: Neurons become wired together (strengthening their synaptic connections to other neurons) during an organism's experiences, across multiple sensory and limbic systems.

• The ERR Reproducer: Later firing of even a part of the previously wired neurons stimulates firing of all or part of the original complex, thus "playing back" the original experience (including the emotional reaction to the experience).

The ERR mind model hypothesizes that related experiences are likely stored "nearby" (in the many "dimensions" of visual cortex, hearing pathways, olfactory nerves, etc., etc., plus the amygdala).

Appendix E

The ERR model might then nicely explain the philosophical notion of *association of ideas*. If it is neighboring neurons that fire, they will likely be closely related in some way (since they were stored based on the fundamental pattern of information in the experience). Similar experiences are likely stored in adjacent neurons. Note that a particular smell could cause the recall of experiences where that smell was present, and similarly for other senses.

The Binding Problem

Neuroscientists are investigating how diverse signals from multiple pathways can possibly be unified in the brain. The ERR model offers an extremely simple insight into this so-called "binding problem." There is an intrinsic binding of the multiple sensory and limbic systems present in the original wiring or "recording" of a complex experience. So the "binding" of all the original senses and emotion in each recalled thought or experience is simply the result of the Hebbian "wiring" of neurons during the original experience

We assume that whenever a particular experience plays back, it refreshes and strengthens the synaptic connections. It might also be the case that the current conditions can modify the connections somewhat, both slightly modifying the memories of the experience and the emotions associated with the experience. ERR might then become an explanatory basis for conditioning experiments, classical Pavlovian and operant conditioning, and in general a model for associative learning.

The capability of reproducing experiences is critical to learning from past experiences, so as to make them guides for action in future experiences. The ERR model is the minimal mind model that provides for such learning by living organisms. It is critical that the original emotions also play back, along with any differences from past emotions that are newly experienced during playback.

Speed and Power of the ERR

You might not normally notice the speed with which you can recall the name of a sixth-grade teacher or childhood friend that has not occurred to you for decades. Or that a few notes might bring back music and lyrics of a song not sung for many years. An odd smell might evoke memories of a foreign country. A taste might bring on feelings of nausea first experienced long ago. All the senses, not just visual stimulation, can replay complex, multi-sensory original events. How does it work so fast?

Sometimes when you consciously try to recall a particular name, it does not come immediately to mind, but you can feel it on "the tip of your tongue." Then hours, even days later the forgotten name just "pops into your head." It suggests unnoticeable "unconscious" information processing by the experience recorder and reproducer.

To make a crude estimate of the speed and power of the brain as a biological information processor, we can calculate the information creation going on in the body overall. Estimating how much power the body consumes (metabolizing of food as negative entropy), we can then use the fact that the brain uses about 20 percent of that energy.

We can take just one bodily process that is also vital to thought, the continuous replacement of red blood cells, which consumes a significant fraction of available energy. When 200 million of the 25 trillion red blood cells in the human body die each second, 300 million new hemoglobins must be assembled in each of 200 million new blood cells . With the order of a few thousand bytes of information in each hemoglobin, this is 10 thousand x 300 million x 200 million = 6×10^{20} bits of information per second, a million times more information processing than today's fastest computer CPU.

What is the brain doing with such immense power consumption and potential information generation. It could be the "blooming, buzzing, confusion" that WILLIAM JAMES imagined gong on just below his "stream of consciousness."

How can the mind "focus attention," as James put it? Think of how the eye can instantly be drawn to a tiny dark speck moving in our peripheral vision, or how quickly it can recall a specific fact not thought about for many years.

How the ERR works

The ERR's operation is nothing like the way a computer searches and retrieves information. ERR *does not decide what to search for* and then look systematically through all the information structures to find it.

We can compare Google's "distributed search" algorithms, which send a search phrase to hundreds of thousands of computers in centers around the world. After vast amounts of "parallel distributed processing," each computer returns its relevant pages within a fraction of a second. These are then assembled into the Google "results" pages.

By contrast, in the ERR, the current experience travels into the brain on neurons which process it in the normal way for storage, based on its analysis (breakdown) of the multi-sensory content of the image. At the same time, the neurons that are firing together are stimulating those nearby to fire, reproducing a vast number of past experiences that were (at least partially) recorded in neurons nearby the newly firing neurons.

It may sound absurd to suggest that the mind can pick anything useful out of such a cacophony. But it is precisely the past experiences found that provide the *context* for the current experience to be "meaningful." If there were nothing played back, like the infant brain, there would be no "meaning" in the experience. In the adult mind, a lifetime of experience is available, usually instantly played back unconsciously, without our ever having to consciously ask for it.

We can say that "what it's like to be" a certain animal depends entirely on what its ERR chooses to record and reproduce. A frog, for example, famously allows only the signals from certain shapes to go beyond the frog's eye to its brain. In our ERR model, the frog has no experience recorded of concave-shaped objects moving in its visual field. Such information then is literally "meaningless."

What would the neurophysiological evidence look like that could confirm or deny the ERR model?

In part, it will be the discovery by neuroscientists of the physical locations where memories are stored. ERIC KANDEL has spent decades in search of our memory systems.[1] Theories range from the relatively large synaptic structures that connect the neurons, to absurdly small sub-cellular components like the microtubules that form the cytoskeletal structures holding up the cell walls.

Better evidence will come from advances in the speed and resolution of tools that image brain activity. They are currently very slow, reacting to gross blood flows in the active areas. These will be combined with traditional studies of mental associations, presenting a subject with elemental experiences like images, sounds, and smells and watching where the brain is active as it elicits playback of important experiences.

The ERR and Consciousness

Humans are conscious of our experiences because they are recorded in (and reproduced on demand from) the information structures in our brains. Mental information houses the content of an individual character - the fabric of values, desires, and reasons used to evaluate alternatives for action and thus to make choices. The information in a human brain vastly exceeds our genetic information. Because humans store and retrieve information outside their minds, it has allowed human beings to dominate the planet. Animals may exceed us in strength and speed, but we have experience, memory, wisdom, and skills that have accumulated over thousands of generations.

The relatively small amount transmitted genetically is tiny compared to that stored in the experience recorder and reproducer of a single human mind. But even that enormous amount is being rivalled by the total knowledge stored externally (we call it the Sum)

---

1   Kandel, et al. 2012

now becoming available to all humans because it is being stored on the world-wide web and Internet.

Consciousness can be defined in information terms as a property of an entity (usually a living thing but we can also include artificially conscious machines or computers) that reacts appropriately to the information (and particularly to changes in the information) in its environment.

In the context of information philosophy, the experience recorder and reproducer can provide us with what we can define as information consciousness.

An animal in a deep sleep is not conscious because it ignores changes in its environment. By contrast, an inanimate robot may be conscious in our sense. Even the lowliest control system using negative feedback (a thermostat, for example) is in a minimal sense conscious of (aware of, exchanging information about) changes in its environment.

This definition of consciousness fits with our model of the mind as an experience recorder and reproducer (ERR). Can we say that an organism is "unconscious" If no past experiences are playing back during its current experiences? Can we say that a frog is "not conscious" of the concave objects flying by?

A conscious being is constantly recording information about its perceptions of the external world, and most importantly for ERR, it is simultaneously recording its feelings. Sensory data such as sights, sounds, smells, tastes, and tactile sensations are recorded in a sequence along with pleasure and pain states, fear and comfort levels, etc. We sometimes speak of a "heightened" consciousness that excels at this recording.

All these experiential and emotional data are recorded in association with one another. This means that when the experiences are reproduced (played back in a temporal sequence), the accompanying emotions are once again felt, in synchronization. Although past experiences played back internally are not the same as the current external, they can make us currently "conscious" of past pleasure and pain states, fear and comfort levels, and so forth.

Bernard Baars's Global Workspace Theory uses the metaphor of a "Theater of Consciousness," in which there is an audience of purposeful agents calling for the attention of the executive on stage.

In the ERR parallel, vast numbers of past experiences are clamoring for the attention of the conscious mind at all times, whenever anything in current experience has some resemblance to past experiences. If we define "current experience" as all afferent perceptions plus the current contents of consciousness itself, we get a dynamic self-referential system with plenty of opportunities for negative and positive feedback.

The "Blackboard model" of Allan Newell and Herbert Simon imagines pictures or words (concepts, say) being written on a mental blackboard by our current perceptions. Deep memory structures are watching what is written on the blackboard. They call up similar concepts by association and write them to the blackboard, which is visible to our conscious mind selecting the next things to think about. The ERR model clearly supports this view and explains the neural mechanism by which concepts (past experiences) are retrieved and come to the blackboard.

In Daniel Dennett's consciousness model, the mind is made up of innumerable functional homunculi, each with its own goals and purposes. Some of these homunculi are information structures in the genes, which transmit "learning" or "knowledge" from generation to generation by heredity alone. Others are environmentally and socially conditioned, or consciously learned through cultural transmission of information.

Four "Levels" of the ERR

We identify four evolutionary stages in the development of the experience recorder and reproducer.

• *Instinct*. These are animals with little or no learning capability. Reactions to environmental conditions have been transmitted genetically. Information about past experiences (by prior generations of the organism) is "built in" as inherited reactions.

Appendix E

• *Learning.* Here past experiences of animals guide their current choices. Conscious, but mostly habitual, reactions are developed through recorded experiences, including instruction by parents and peers.

• *Prediction.* - A Sequencer in the ERR system can play back beyond the current situation, allowing the organism to use imagination and foresight to evaluate the future consequences of its choices.

• *Reflection.* Here conscious deliberation about values influences the choice of behaviors. The ERR plays back a range of similar experiences including the reactions and feelings expressed by others to those experiences.

All four levels are *emergent*, in the sense that they did not exist in the lower, earlier levels of biological evolution.

Even the most primitive of biological systems are cognitive, in the sense that they use their internal information structure to guide their actions. Some of the simplest organisms can learn from experience. The most primitive minds are the earliest experience recorders. They reproduce past experiences as alternative possibilities for current actions.

In humans, the information-processing structures create new actionable information (knowledge) by consciously and unconsciously reworking the experiences stored in the mind.

Emergent higher mental levels exert downward causation on the contents of the lower bodily levels, ultimately supporting mental causation and free will.

What It's Like To Be A...

There are characteristic differences between the mental and the physical that modern science, even neuroscience, may never fully explain. The most important is the internal and private first-person point of view, the essential subjectivity, the "I" and the "eye" of the mind, its capability of introspection and reflection, its intentionality, its purposiveness, its consciousness. The mind records an individual's experiences as internal information structures and then can play back these recordings to compare them to new perceptions, new external events. The recordings include an individual's emotional reactions to past experiences, our feelings. The reproduction of recorded personal experiences, stimulated by similarities in current experience, provide the core of "what it's like to be" a specific individual.

The external and public physical world, by contrast, is studied from the third-person point of view. Although putatively "objective," science in fact is the composite "intersubjective" view of the "community of inquirers," as CHARLES SANDERS PEIRCE put it. Although this shared subjectivity can never directly experience what goes on in the mind of an individual member of the community, science is in some sense the *collective mind* of the physical world. It is a pale record of the world's experiences, because it lacks the emotional aspect of personal experience.

The world of chemistry and physics has no sense of its history. It does not introspect or reflect. It lacks an ERR and so lacks consciousness, that problem in philosophy of mind second only to the basic mind-body problem itself.

Mental States?

The ERR avoids the vague idea of a "mental state," whatever that may be. The ERR stores specific information in the brain's neural networks about all the perceptual elements (sight, sound, touch, taste, smell) of an experience, along with emotions felt during the experience. They automatically are stored in whichever neurons fire together.

Later, any new perceptual element that fires the some part of those neurons can activate the neural network to replay the original experience, complete with its emotional content. The unconscious mind is a "blooming, buzzing confusion" playing back many similar experiences, to some of which we focus our attention, as WILLIAM JAMES pointed out.

This rich spectrum of past experiences provides the "*alternative possibilities*" for action that James said was the first stage in his two-stage model of free will.

Appendix E

Instead of a general idea of a "mental state," ERR describes a mind full of many possible specific mental states simultaneously, any one of which may be focused on as the free thought that leads to the next action "self-determined" by the mind, brain, and body.

ERR finds support in the idea of *empathy* and the recent discoveries of "mirror neurons" in higher primates. Observing another being having an experience fires similar patterns of neurons that play back the observer's similar experiences, along with emotional reactions to those earlier experiences.

Different emotional reactions can explain how different individuals can be attracted to or repulsed by otherwise similar experiences.

Summary

The biological model for the experience recorder and reproducer is neurons that wire together during an animal's experiences, in multiple sensory and limbic systems, such that later firing of even a part of the wired neurons can stimulate firing of all or part of the original complex. Where Donald Hebb famously argued that "neurons that fire together wire together," our experience recorder and reproducer ERR model assumes that "neurons that have been wired together will fire together."

Neuroscientists are investigating how diverse signals from multiple pathways can be unified in the brain. We offer a simple insight into this "binding" problem. There is an intrinsic binding of the multiple sensory and limbic systems present in the original wiring or "recording" of a complex experience. So the "binding" of all the original senses and emotion in each new experience is partly the result of the *Hebbian* "wiring" of neurons during a similar original experience

Appendix E

Beyond the obvious relevance (survival value) for an organism of remembering past experiences, we suggest the "meaning" of information is found in the experiences reproduced by the ERR, when presented with that information.

A conscious being is constantly recording information about its perceptions of the external world, and most importantly for ERR, it is simultaneously recording its feelings. Sensory data such as sights, sounds, smells, tastes, and tactile sensations are recorded in a sequence along with pleasure and pain states, fear and comfort levels, etc.

All these experiential and emotional data are recorded in association with one another. This means that when the experiences are reproduced (played back in a temporal sequence), the accompanying emotions are once again felt, in synchronization.

The capability of reproducing experiences is critical to *learning* from past experiences, so as to make them guides for action in future experiences. The ERR is the minimal mind model that provides for such learning by living organisms.

Something like an ERR is obviously present in all the higher primates and it is unclear how primitive an animal must be before it cannot learn something from its experiences.

Philosophy

Mind

Epistemology

aphysics

Mind-Body

Universals

Cosmic Creation

ntology

Consciousn

Free Will

Meaning

Self and Othe

Value

Mental Causa

Good and Evil

God and Immortality

Can Information Philosoph

The Cosmic Creation Process

The Fundamental Question of Information Philosophy

Our fundamental philosophical question is cosmological and ultimately is profoundly metaphysical.

What are the processes that create emergent information structures in the universe?

Given the second law of thermodynamics, which says that any system will over time approach a thermodynamic equilibrium of maximum disorder or entropy, in which all information is lost, and given the best current model for the origin of the universe, which says everything began in a state of thermodynamic equilibrium some 13.75 billion years ago, how can it be that living beings are creating and communicating vast amounts of new information every day?

Why are we not still in that original state of equilibrium?

Broadly speaking, there are only four major phenomena or processes that can reduce the entropy locally, while of course increasing it globally to satisfy the second law of thermodynamics. Three of these do it "blindly," the fourth does it with a built-in "purpose," or telos."

- Universal Gravitation

- Quantum Cooperative Phenomena (e.g., crystallization, the formation of atoms and molecules)

- "Dissipative" Chaos (Non-linear Thermodynamics)

- Life

None of these processes can work unless they have a way to get rid of the positive entropy (disorder) and leave behind a pocket of negative entropy (order or information). The positive entropy is either conducted, convected, or radiated away as waste matter and energy, as heat, or as pure radiation. At the quantum level, it is always the result of interactions between matter and radiation (photons). Whenever photons interact with material particles, the outcomes are inherently unpredictable. As ALBERT EINSTEIN discovered ten years before the founding of quantum mechanics, these interactions involve irreducible ontological chance.

Appendix F

Information philosophy (actually information physics) has now identified the exact steps needed to create any new information structures in the universe. This includes the first matter - elementary particles like quarks, gluons, photons, and electrons. It also includes the first atoms and molecules (which did not appear until at least 380,000 years after the origin of the universe).

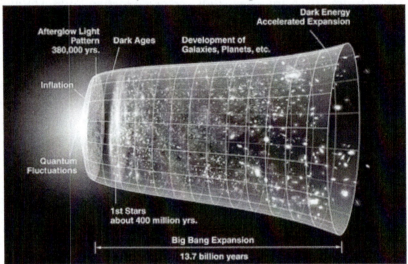

Figure 34-1. An artist's rendering of the cosmic expansion.

The very same steps are needed to form the galaxies, stars, and planets, which were starting to form about 400 million years after the origin. All these cosmic information structures are informationally passive. Their interactions follow the relatively simple laws of physics and chemistry. They do not process or communicate information.

Although we call it cosmic creation, the very same steps create all life on Earth. But biological structures are far from informationally passive. They have the extraordinary active and emergent capability of replicating, communicating, and processing information. They are cognitively aware of their environment. They exhibit purposeful, *teleonomic* behavior.

Finally, those same two steps are involved in our minds when we create a new idea! Information philosophy tells a story of cosmic and biological evolution that is one creation process all the way

Appendix F

from the original cosmic *material* to the *immaterial* minds that have now explained the creation process itself!

Sadly, cosmic creation is horrendously wasteful. In the existential balance between the forces of destruction and the forces of construction, there is no contest. The dark side is overwhelming. By quantitative physical measures of matter and energy content, there is far more chaos than cosmos in our universe. But it is the cosmos that we prize.

Information philosophy focuses on the qualitatively valuable information structures in the universe. The destructive forces are entropic, they increase the entropy and disorder. The constructive forces are anti-entropic. We call them ergodic. They increase the order and information.

By information we mean a quantity that can be understood mathematically and physically. It corresponds to the common-sense meaning of information, in the sense of communicating or informing. It also corresponds to the information stored in books and computers. But it also measures the information in any physical object, like a stone or a snowflake, in a production process like a recipe or formula, and the information in biological systems, including cell and organ structures and the genetic code.

The Two Steps in Cosmic Creation

For some years, we have argued that the creation of any new information structure requires two fundamental steps. The first involves quantum mechanics, the second thermodynamics. But the thermodynamics is not the usual entropy-producing kind. It must produce negative entropy, the "order out of chaos" that is new information. We call such a process *ergodic* and find that it works differently in the material, biological, and mental domains

Furthermore, the quantum mechanics of information creation raises metaphysical questions that suggest further analysis might be helpful. So we may have to break down each of these steps as needed for the best explanation.

The *first step* in the creation of new information needs the metaphysical existence of multiple future possibilities as a precondition. In a deterministic universe such possibilities do not exist. There is but one possible future. We thus need an ontological commitment to the existence of multiple possibilities, which like any "ideas" have questionable existential status.

For example, where do such possibilities go when one of them is actualized? When one "becomes" and now has "being," are the others destroyed? Have they become "nothingness," as existentialists claimed?

In a *deterministic* universe no new information is ever created. Information is a conserved quantity, like matter and energy, say many mathematical physicists and theologically minded philosophers, who think constant information fits well their idea of an omniscient god, for whom there is "nothing new under the sun."

Quantum physics provides us with a model for the first step. A quantum system has possible states. The wave function provides calculable probabilities for each state. And the wave function may "collapse," instantaneously and randomly, into one actual state if and when there is an interaction with another system. Some interactions may project the system into a different linear combination (a "superposition") of possible states, but we shall ignore that here.

Because the "collapse" is genuinely random, quantum physics is the origin of *ontological chance* in the universe, as first discovered by ALBERT EINSTEIN, many years before the "founders" of quantum mechanics and the "uncertainty principle."[1]

The inventor of the mathematical theory of the communication of information, CLAUDE SHANNON, explained how there would be no communication of new information without the existence of possible alternative messages.

A *deterministic* universe is one in which all messages from the past contain only the fixed totality of information in the past, nothing is ever "new." So the indeterminism of quantum mechanics opens possible futures and gives us humans the chance to be creative authors of our lives.

Appendix F

---

1   See Appendix D.

So why do we need a *second step* in the creation of information? The short answer is *irreversibility*.[2]

A quantum event may be reversible. It may not leave a permanent record in the universe.[3] Until it does, we have nothing new. For the many scientists and philosophers of science who deny the collapse of the quantum-mechanical wave function, the universe is left forever in a superposition of states. Nothing ever "happens." Claims of decoherence theorists that explain the *appearance* of something happening are *incoherent*.[4]

Making a quantum event irreversible is the job for thermodynamics in our second step. But thermodynamics is a two-edged sword. Every thermodynamic process is *irreversible*. Thermodynamicists invent hypothetical reversible processes to calculate the efficiency of engines, but in practice, as LUDWIG BOLTZMANN showed, there is always an increase in the entropy. So irreversibility alone cannot help us with the creation of information, which we identify with local *reductions* in the entropy. The creation of information requires the creation of local *negative* entropy, in the form of an information structure.

There are just a few natural processes that can create information structures. One is gravitation, which can attract matter from random distributions of dust and gas into structures with spherical or circular symmetry like planets, stars, and galaxies. Another is crystallization, when a snowflake with elaborate hexagonal symmetry forms from amorphous water vapor. But the most important ergodic processes are life and mind.

In order to satisfy the second law of thermodynamics, which demands that the overall entropy of the universe must increase, these anti-entropic or *ergodic* processes must transfer an amount of positive entropy (we can call Boltzmann entropy) away from the new information structure with local negative entropy (that we can also call Shannon entropy).[5]

---

2 See chapter 25.
3 See appendix C for a reversible quantum experiment.
4 See chapter 21.
5 See Appendix B for entropy and the second law.

Appendix F

Shannon's information is mathematically the negative of the Boltzmann formula for entropy. For Shannon it was the logarithm of the number of messages, weighted by their probabilities. For Boltzmann it was the logarithm of the number of possible distributions of gas particles in phase space.[6]

Should we consider the transfer away of positive entropy only a part of the second step? The means by which the transfer occurs is somewhat different in material, biological, and mental information processes.[7]

The Flatness Problem in Cosmology

The universe is very likely flat because it was created flat. A flat universe starts with minimal information, which is fine since our cosmic creation process can create all the information that we have today. Leibniz' question, "Why is there something rather than nothing?" might be "the universe is made out of something and the opposite of that something."

When I was a first-year graduate student in astrophysics at Harvard University in 1958, I encountered two problems that have remained with me all these years. One was the fundamental problem of information philosophy - *"What creates the information structures in the universe?"* The other was the flat universe.

At that time, the universe was thought to be positively curved. Edwin Hubble's red shifts of distant galaxies showed that they did not have enough kinetic energy to overcome the gravitational potential energy. Textbooks likened the universe to the surface of an expanding balloon decorated with galaxies moving away from one another.

That balloon popped for me when Walter Baade came to Harvard to describe his work at Mount Wilson. Baade took many images with long exposures of nearby galaxies and discovered there are two distinct populations of stars. And in each population there was a different kind of Cepheid variable star. The period of the

---

6   See appendix A for the mathematics.
7   See chapter 28.

Cepheid's curve of light variation indicated its absolute brightness, so they could be used as "standard candles" to find the distances to star clusters in the Milky Way.

Baade then realized that the Cepheids being used to calculate the distance to Andromeda were 1.6 magnitudes brighter than the ones used in our galaxy. Baade said Andromeda must be twice as far away as Hubble had thought.

As I listened to Baade, for me the universe went from being positively curved to negatively curved. It jumped right over the flat universe! I was struck that we seemed to be within observational error of being flat. Some day a physicist will find the reason for perfect flatness, I thought.

I used to draw a line with tick marks for powers of ten in density around the critical density ρ_c to show how close we are. Given so many orders of magnitude of possible densities, it seemed improbable that we were just close by accident. We could increase the density of the universe by thirty powers of ten before it would have the same density as the earth (way too dense!). But on the lighter side, there are an infinite number of powers of ten. We can't exclude a universe with average density zero, which still allows us to exist, but little else in the distance.

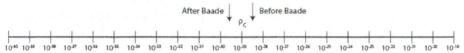

In the long run we are approaching a universe with average density zero. Some say all the non-gravitationally bound systems will slip over our light horizon as the expansion takes more and more of them faster than the velocity of light. At this time, galaxies with a redshift greater than $z = 1.8$ are already over our light horizon. We can never exchange signals with them.

But note that we may always be able to see back to the cosmic microwave background, all the same contents of the universe that we see today will always be visible, just extremely red-shifted!

What evidence could there be for a perfectly flat universe?

First, there is the problem of the "missing mass" needed to slow down the cosmic expansion so that it will never stop, except at an infinite time, when there will be no kinetic enrgy left over

Second, there is evidence for acceleration of the cosmic expansion. It depends on observations of a single kind of "standard candle," the type 1a supernovae.

It is essential that some other visible bodies at extreme redshifts can be used to show acceleration. The type 1a supernovae that exploded at the earliest times might have some systematic difference from those that exploded later.

Beyond any obdervations, there is pure theory. When Alan Guth presented his inflation thesis at Harvard in the 1980's, I asked him why not assume the universe has always been exactly flat. He replied, "That's too easy." The great cosmologist Steven Weinberg agrees that it is easy. He wrote

> "The simplest solution to the flatness problem is just that we are in a spatially flat universe, in which $K = 0$ and ρ is always precisely equal to ρ_{crit}." [8]

The Problem of Missing Mass

Given our assumption that the universe is exactly flat, the missing mass problem is that there is not enough observable material so that in Newtonian cosmology the gravitational binding energy can exactly balance the kinetic energy. The visible (luminous mass) accounts for only about 4-5 percent of the needed mass. Studying the rotation curves of galaxies and galaxy clusters reveals an invisible mass (called dark matter) contained inside the galaxies and clusters that amounts to perhaps 6 times the visible matter, which accounts for about 30 percent of the critical mass density needed to make the universe exactly flat. Current theory accounts for the balance by "dark energy," an interpretation of the cosmological constant Einstein considered adding to his equations as a pressure to keep it from collapsing (known as "vacuum energy"). But the miss-

Appendix F

---

8   *Cosmology*, p.39

ing mass could just be more dark matter between the galaxies and clusters. About three times their dark matter would do.

This much material can close the universe and explain its flatness. But it would not explain the apparent expansion acceleration seen in Type 1a supernovae. This might be an artifact of the assumption they are perfect "standard candles." Recent evidence suggests that distant Type 1a supernovae are in a different population than those nearby, something like Baade's two populations.

It seems a bit extravagant to assume the need for an exotic form of vacuum energy on the basis of observations that could have unknown but significant sources of error. And I am delighted that observations are within a factor of three of the critical density ρ_c.

When Baade showed the universe was open in the 1950's, we needed thirty times more matter for a flat universe. Now we need only three times more. More than ever, we are obviously flat!

The Horizon Problem

The horizon problem arises from the perfect synchronization of all the parts of our visible universe, when there may never have been a time in the early universe that they were close enough together to send synchronization signals.

We propose a solution to the horizon problem based on Einstein's insight that in the wave-function collapse of entangled particles, something is "traveling" faster than the speed of light. That something is *information about possibilities*. When the universal wave function Ψ collapsed at $t = 0$, parts of the universe that are outside our current light horizon may have been "informed" that it was time to start, no matter the physical distance.

This radical idea is consistent with RICHARD FEYNMAN's path integral (or "sum-over-histories") formulation of quantum mechanics. In calculating the probability of a quantum event, the path integral is computed over all the possible paths of virtual photons, many travelling faster than the speed of light.

Appendix F

Philosophy

Mind

Epistemology

aphysics

Mind-Body

Universals

ntology

Biosemiotics

onsciousr

Free Will

Meaning

Self and Oth

Value

Mental Caus

Good and Evil

God and Immortality

Can Information Philosop

This chapter on t
informationphilosopher.com/presentations/biose

Biosemiotics

Biosemiotics is the thesis that the essence of biology involves the creation, processing, and communication of information, in the form of a *language* that uses arbitrary symbols, inside cells, between cells, and between all organisms and their environment.

Information philosophy sees a continuous evolutionary development from the earliest communications inside cells over three billion years ago to the creation and communication of information by human beings today. When we say that information philosophy goes "beyond logic and language" we mean that many philosophical problems are not soluble with the particular human inventions of logic and languages today.

All life uses negative entropy for its maintenance and information as a guide to action, representing a repertoire of behaviors. All living things are communicating with signs. Biosemioticians believe that semiosis is coextensive with life.

We can define semiosis (Greek: σημείωσις, sēmeíōsis, from σημειῶ, sēmeiô, "to mark") as any form of activity, conduct, or process that involves signs, including the production of meaning.[1] The term was introduced by Charles Sanders Peirce to describe a process he called semiotics that *interprets* signs as referring to concepts and objects, about the same time that Gottlob Frege studied denotation and meaning.

We see this essential nesting of concepts.

Information>Biology>Communication>Language>Semiosis

In language we include syntax, semantics, pragmatics, morphology (graphology and phonology, but also smells, tastes, touches, as well as emotive expressions, body "language," sub-linguistic communications to the "mirror neurons" in others, etc.)

Even though intra- and inter-cellular communication using multiple molecules over diverse pathways is getting better and better understood, biologists have remained wary for decades of accepting the idea of "information" in biology, with its connotation

Appendix G

---

1   See chapter 11.

of a conscious intentional sender "informing" a conscious interpretational receiver. Quantum physics too is plagued by concerns over the role of "conscious observers." And of course philosophers do not yet use information as a tool for philosophical analysis. The philosophy of information is not information philosophy, just as the philosophy of language is not analytic language philosophy.

If we define "conscious" as being aware of incoming information and reacting to it with behaviors/actions that indicate the information is being interpreted and used correctly, we have a very broad definition of mindfulness that can apply to almost the whole of biology as well as to the computing and communicating machines that humans have built.[2]

Will Biologists Accept Biosemiotics?

Biosemiotics is as legitimate a science as bioethics, bioinformatics, biolinguistics, biomathics, and code biology, to name a few at the boundaries of biosemiotics. The established professional societies in each of these subdisciplines, with journals, international meetings, etc., are signs of a Peircean open community of inquirers that is the hallmark of a science.

The greatest barrier to acceptance of semiotics in biology may be the devotion of biosemioticians to the work of CHARLES SANDERS PEIRCE. Peirce's great contributions to logic and science are extraordinary, but he sometimes produced nonsense, wishful thinking that some of his ideals are actually in the world.

Peirce's greatest mistake was his triadic analysis of 1) thesis and firstness of Tychism/chance, setting it "over against" 2) the antithesis and secondness of Ananchism/necessity. The ultimate blow was his Hegel-inspired 3) *Aufhebung* and thirdness of Synechism/continuity, his perhaps deeply Christian hope for "evolutionary love" to blunt the "greedy" nature of chance in Darwin.

Biosemioticians need to decide between being disciples of Peirce or a subdiscipline of biology. FERDINAND DE SAUSSURE's dyadics may fall short of Peirce's interpretant, but as a linguist he was as great as Peirce and his move to synchronic structure as

Appendix G

---

2   See chapter 14 on consciousness.

a diagnostic tool to understand diachronic function and his great insistence that signs (symbols) are arbitrary inventions may be as important for communications in molecular biology as Peirce's insistence on interpretation.

Indeed, signaling in biology generally has very little interpretation in the sense of Shannon's entropy/uncertainty before a message is received, which becomes information after receipt. This is because evolution has for the most part reduced the message "possibilities," for example with an artful combination, perhaps left over from the RNA world, of editing in advance of protein creation (especially in eukaryotes) and aggressive "error" detection and correction afterwards. A major task for biosemiotics is to find specific examples in biology of signaling as signing, i.e. with interpretations of the sign. Examples in the case of a neurotransmitter being interpreted - in a *context*, which ROMAN JAKOBSON[3] added to Shannon's information communication - in more than one way. We can summarize the foundations of biosemiotics in the form of a flow chart.

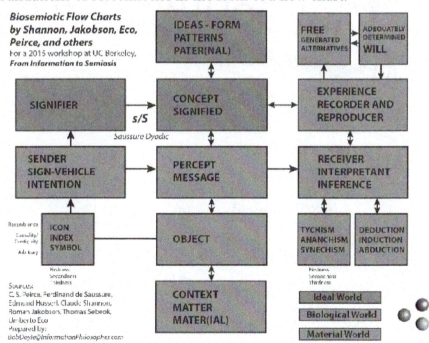

Biosemiotic Flow Charts by Shannon, Jakobson, Eco, Peirce, and others
For a 2015 workshop at UC Berkeley, *From Information to Semiosis*

---

3   "Linguistics and Poetics," in *Style in Language*, ed. T. Sebeok, 1960, p.350

Philosophy

Mind

Epistemology

physics

Mind-Body

Universals

tology

Bibliography

onsciousne

Free Will

Meaning

Self and Othe

Value

Mental Causa

Good and Evil

God and Immortality

Can Information Philosoph

Bibliography

Arrow of Time

Davies, P. C. W. *The Physics of Time Asymmetry*. Berkeley and Los Angeles: University of California Press, 1977.

Gold, Thomas, ed. *The Nature of Time*. First Edition edition. Cornell University Press, 1967.

Price, Huw. *Time's Arrow and Archimedes' Point: New Directions for the Physics of Time*. New York: Oxford Paperbacks, 1997.

Reichenbach, Hans. *The Direction of Time*. Mineola, N.Y: Dover Publications, 1999.

Zeh, H. Dieter. *The Physical Basis of The Direction of Time*. 5th edition. Springer, 2013.

Biology

Alberts, Bruce, Alexander Johnson, Julian Lewis, David Morgan, Martin Raff, Keith Roberts, and Peter Walter. *Molecular Biology of the Cell*. 6 edition. New York, NY: Garland Science, 2014.

Barbieri, Marcello. *Code Biology: A New Science of Life*. 2015 edition. New York, NY: Springer, 2015.

Brooks, Daniel R., and E. O. Wiley. *Evolution As Entropy: Toward a Unified Theory of Biology*. Second Edition edition. Chicago: University of Chicago Press, 1988.

Mayr, Ernst. *Toward a New Philosophy of Biology*: Observations of an Evolutionist. Reprint edition. Cambridge, Mass.: Harvard University Press, 1989.

Monod, Jacques. *Chance and Necessity*: An Essay on the Natural Philosophy of Modern Biology. Translated by Austryn Wainhouse. New York: Vintage Books, 1972.

Morowitz, Harold J. *Energy Flow in Biology*. Ox Bow Press, 1979.

Murphy, Kenneth. *Janeway's Immunobiology*. 8 edition. New York: Garland Science, 2011.

Schrodinger, Erwin. *What Is Life?*: With "Mind and Matter" and "Autobiographical Sketches." Cambridge University Press, 1992.

Smith, John, Szathmáry, Eörs Maynard. *The Major Transitions in Evolution* by Maynard Smith, John, Szathmáry, Eörs. Reprint edition. Oxford University Press, 1997.

Chance

Born, Max. *Natural Philosophy of Cause and Chance*. New York: Dover Publications, 1964.

Hacking, Ian. *The Emergence of Probability: A Philosophical Study of Early Ideas about Probability, Induction and Statistical Inference*. 2 edition. Cambridge ; New York: Cambridge University Press, 2006.

Lestienne, Remy, and E C Neher. *The Creative Power of Chance*. University of Illinois Press, 1998.

Lucretius, Titus, W. H. D. Rouse, and M. F. Smith. *De Rerum Natura: On the Nature of Things*. Cambridge, Mass: Harvard University Press, 1924.

Monod, Jacques. *Chance and Necessity: An Essay on the Natural Philosophy of Modern Biology*. Translated by Austryn Wainhouse. New York: Vintage Books, 1972.

Porter, Theodore M. *The Rise of Statistical Thinking, 1820-1900*. Princeton University Press, 1988.

Consciousness

Baars, Bernard J. *In the Theater of Consciousness: The Workspace of the Mind*. New York: Oxford University Press, 1997.

Chalmers, David J. *The Conscious Mind: In Search of a Fundamental Theory*. 1st ed. Oxford University Press, USA, 1997.

Dennett, Daniel C. *Consciousness Explained*. 1st ed. Back Bay Books, 1992.

Koch, Christof. *The Quest for Consciousness: A Neurobiological Approach*. 1 edition. Denver, Colo: Roberts & Company Publishers, 2004.

Koch, Christof, and Joel L. Davis, eds. *Large-Scale Neuronal Theories of the Brain*. 1 edition. Cambridge, Mass: A Bradford Book, 1994.

Nagel, Thomas. *Mortal Questions*. Cambridge [Eng.]: Cambridge University Press, 1979.

Searle, John R. *The Mystery of Consciousness*. 1st ed. New York Review Books, 1990.

Strawson, Galen, Peter Carruthers, Frank Jackson, William G. Lycan, Colin McGinn, David Papineau, Georges Rey, J. J. C. Smart, and et al. *Consciousness and Its Place in Nature: Does Physicalism Entail Panpsychism?* Edited by Anthony Freeman. Exeter, UK ; Charlottesville, Va: Imprint Academic, 2006.

Cosmology

Holt, Jim. *Why Does the World Exist?: An Existential Detective Story*. 1 edition. New York: Liveright, 2013.

Krauss, Lawrence M., and Richard Dawkins. *A Universe from Nothing: Why There Is Something Rather than Nothing*. New York: Atria Books, 2013.

Layzer, David. *Cosmogenesis: The Growth of Order in the Universe*. New York: Oxford University Press, 1991.

Liddle, Andrew. *An Introduction to Modern Cosmology.*Wiley, 2015.

Weinberg, Steven. *Cosmology*. OUP Oxford, 2008.

Weinberg, Steven. *The First Three Minutes: A Modern View Of The Origin Of The Universe*. New York: Basic Books, 1993.

Decoherence

Joos, Erich, H. Dieter Zeh, Claus Kiefer, Domenico J. W. Giulini, Joachim Kupsch, and Ion-Olimpiu Stamatescu. *Decoherence and the Appearance of a Classical World in Quantum Theory*. 2nd ed. 2003 edition. Berlin, Heidelberg: Springer, 2010.

Schlosshauer, Maximilian A. *Decoherence and the Quantum-to-Classical Transition*. Berlin ; London: Springer, 2008.

Tegmark, Max. *Our Mathematical Universe: My Quest for the Ultimate Nature of Reality*. New York: Vintage, 2015.

Einstein

Bernstein, Jeremy. *Einstein*. Penguin, 1979.

―――. *Secrets of the Old One: Einstein, 1905*. 2006 edition. New York: Copernicus, 2005.

Einstein, Albert. *Ideas And Opinions*New York: Broadway Books, 1995.

―――. *The Collected Papers of Albert Einstein, Volume 2: The Swiss Years: Writings, 1900-1909*. Edited by John Stachel, David C. Cassidy, Jürgen Renn, and Robert Schulmann. Princeton, NJ: Princeton University Press, 1990.

―――. *The Collected Papers of Albert Einstein, Volume 6: The Berlin Years: Writings, 1914-1917*. Edited by A. J. Kox, Martin J. Klein, and Robert Schulmann. Princeton, NJ: Princeton University Press, 1996.

Einstein, Albert, and Max Born. *The Born - Einstein Letters: Friendship, Politics and Physics in Uncertain Times*. Macmillan, 2005.

Einstein, Albert, and Roger Penrose. *Einstein's Miraculous Year: Five Papers That Changed the Face of Physics*. Edited by John Stachel. Princeton, NJ: Princeton University Press, 2005.

Frank, Philipp. *Einstein: His Life And Times*. Cambridge, Mass.: Da Capo Press: Da Capo Press, 2002.

Gamalath, Wijewardena. *Einstein: His Life and Works*. 1 edition. Oxford: Alpha Science International Ltd, 2012.

Isaacson, Walter. *Einstein: His Life and Universe*. New York, NY: Simon & Schuster, 2008.

Lanczos, Cornelius. *The Einstein Decade, 1905-1915*. New York: Academic Press, 1974.

Stachel, John. *Einstein from "B" to "Z."* Boston: Birkhäuser, 2001.

Emergence

Alexander, Samuel. *Space, Time, and Deity: The Gifford Lectures at Glasgow, 1916-1918*. HardPress Publishing, 2012.

Beckermann, Ansgar, Hans Flohr, and Jaegwon Kim, eds. *Emergence or Reduction?: Essays on the Prospects of Nonreductive Physicalism*. Berlin ; New York: de Gruyter, 1992.

Chaisson, Eric J. *Cosmic Evolution: The Rise of Complexity in Nature*. Cambridge, Mass.: Harvard University Press, 2002.

Clayton, Philip, and Paul Davies, eds. *The Re-Emergence of Emergence: The Emergentist Hypothesis from Science to Religion*. . Oxford: Oxford University Press, 2008.

Corradini, Antonella, and Timothy O'Connor, eds. *Emergence in Science and Philosophy*. New York: Routledge, 2013.

Holland, John H. *Emergence: From Chaos To Order*. Cambridge, Mass: Basic Books, 1999.

Koestler, Arthur, and J. R. Smythies. *Beyond Reductionism New Perspectives In The Life Sciences*. Boston: Houghton Mifflin Co, 1971.

Lewes, George Henry. *Problems of Life and Mind*. University of Toronto Libraries, 2011.

Mill, John Stuart. *A System of Logic*. CreateSpace Independent Publishing Platform, 2012.

Morgan, C. Lloyd. *Emergent Evolution*. Chandra Chakravarti Press, 2007.

Morowitz, Harold J. *The Emergence of Everything: How the World Became Complex*. New York: Oxford University Press, 2004.

Waldrop, M. Mitchell. *Complexity The Emerging Science at the Edge of Order and Chaos*. New York, NY: Simon & Schuster, 1992.

Zurek, Wojciech H., ed. *Complexity, Entropy and the Physics of Information*. Redwood City, Calif: Westview Press, 1990.

Entanglement

Gilder, Louisa. *The Age of Entanglement: When Quantum Physics Was Reborn*. 10.11.2009 edition. New York: Vintage, 2009.

Jaeger, Gregg. *Entanglement, Information, and the Interpretation of Quantum Mechanics*. 2009 edition. Berlin: Springer, 2009.

Epistemology

Almeder, Robert. *Harmless Naturalism: The Limits of Science and the Nature of Philosophy*. Chicago: Open Court, 1999.

Armstrong, D. M. *Belief, Truth and Knowledge*. London: Cambridge University Press, 1973.

Dancy, Jonathan, Ernest Sosa, and Matthias Steup, eds. *A Companion to Epistemology.*. Chichester, West Sussex, U.K. ; Malden, MA: Wiley-Blackwell, 2010.

Bibliography

Goldman, Alvin I. *Epistemology and Cognition*. Cambridge, Mass.: Harvard University Press, 1988.

Kornblith, Hilary, ed. *Naturalizing Epistemology*. Cambridge, Mass: MIT Press, 1985.

Popper, Karl. Evolutionary *Epistemology, Rationality, and the Sociology of Knowledge*. Edited by Gerard Radnitzky and W. W. Bartley. La Salle Ill.: Open Court Publishing Company, 1993.

Quine, W. V. *Ontological Relativity & Other Essays*. New York: Columbia University Press, 1969.

Russell, Bertrand. *Our Knowledge of the External World*. London ; New York: Routledge, 2009.

Sosa, Ernest, Jaegwon Kim, Jeremy Fantl, and Matthew McGrath, eds. *Epistemology: An Anthology*. . Malden, MA: Wiley-Blackwell, 2008.

Swinburne, Richard, ed. *Justification of Induction*. London: Oxford University Press, 1974.

Free Will

Dennett, Daniel C. *Brainstorms: Philosophical Essays on Mind and Psychology*. The MIT Press, 1981.

Doyle, Bob. *Free Will: The Scandal in Philosophy*. Cambridge, Mass.: Information Philosopher, 2011.

Fischer, John Martin, ed. *Free Will: Critical Concepts in Philosophy*. London ; New York: Routledge, 2005.

Gazzaniga, Michael S. *Who's in Charge?: Free Will and the Science of the Brain*. New York: Ecco, 2012.

Hobbes, Thomas, and John Bramhall. Hobbes and Bramhall on Liberty and Necessity. Edited by Vere Chappell. Cambridge University Press, 1999.

Honderich, Ted. *How Free Are You?: The Determinism Problem*. Oxford University Press, USA, 2002.

Inwagen, Peter Van. *An Essay on Free Will*. Oxford University Press, USA, 1983.

James, William. *The Will to Believe : And Other Essays in Popular Philosophy*,

Kane, Robert. *A Contemporary Introduction to Free Will*. Oxford University Press, USA, 2005.

———. *The Oxford Handbook of Free Will*. Oxford University Press, USA, 2005.

Murphy, Nancey C. *Did My Neurons Make Me Do It?: Philosophical and Neurobiological Perspectives on Moral Responsibility and Free Will*. Oxford: Oxford University Press, 2007.

Murphy, Nancey, George F. R. Ellis, and Timothy O'Connor, eds. *Downward Causation and the Neurobiology of Free Will*. 2009 edition. Berlin ;Heidelberg: Springer, 2009.

Searle, John R. *Freedom and Neurobiology: Reflections on Free Will, Language, and Political Power*. Columbia Themes in Philosophy. New York: Columbia University Press, 2007.

Swinburne, Richard, ed. *Free Will and Modern Science*. Oxford ; New York: British Academy, 2012.

Information in Biology

Avery, John. *Information Theory and Evolution*. World Scientific Publishing Company, 2003.

Campbell, Jeremy. Grammatical Man: *Information, Entropy,Language and Life*. Ward & Balkin Agency, Inc., 2012.

Gatlin, Lila L. *Information Theory and the Living System*. New York: Columbia University Press, 1973.

Quastler, Henry, Ed. *Information Theory in Biology*. University of Illinois Press, 1953.

Witzany, Guenther. *Biocommunication and Natural Genome Editing*. 2010 edition. Place of publication not identified: Springer, 2014.

Yockey, Hubert P. *Information Theory, Evolution, and The Origin of Life*. Cambridge University Press, 2005.

Information

Brillouin, Leon. *Science and Information Theory*: Second Edition. Mineola, New York: Dover Publications, 2013.

Chaitin, Gregory J. *Information Randomness and Incompleteness: Papers on Algorithmic Information Theory*. Singapore ; New Jersey: World Scientific Pub Co Inc, 1990.

Cover, Thomas M., and Joy A. Thomas. *Elements of Information Theory 2nd Edition*. Hoboken, N.J: Wiley-Interscience, 2006.

Davies, Paul, and Niels Henrik Gregersen. *Information and the Nature of Reality*. Cambridge University Press, 2011.

Newell, Allen. *Human Problem Solving*. Englewood Cliffs, N.J: Prentice Hall, 1972.

Reading, Anthony. *Meaningful Information: The Bridge Between Biology, Brain, and Behavior*. New York: Springer, 2011.

Roederer, Juan. *Information and Its Role in Nature*. Berlin: Springer, 2010.

Sebeok, Thomas. *Style in Language*. MIT Press, 1964.

Shannon, Claude E., and Warren Weaver. *The Mathematical Theory of Communication*. University of Illinois Press, 2015.

Weber, Bruce H., David J. Depew, and James D. Smith, eds. *Entropy, Information, and Evolution: New Perspectives on Physical and Biological Evolution*. Cambridge, Mass.: The MIT Press, 1988.

Wicken, Jeffrey S. *Evolution, Thermodynamics, and Information: Extending the Darwinian Program*. Oxford University Press, USA, 1987.

Meaning

Carnap, Rudolf. *Meaning and Necessity: A Study in Semantics and Modal Logic*. 1 edition. Chicago: University of Chicago Press, 1988.

Dreyfus, Hubert L., and Harrison Hall, eds. *Husserl, Intentionality, and Cognitive Science*. Cambridge, Mass.: The MIT Press, 1984.

Bibliography

Husserl, Edmund, and Dermot Moran. *Ideas: General Introduction to Pure Phenomenology.* London ; New York: Routledge, 2012.

MacKay, Donald M. *Information, Mechanism and Meaning.* Cambridge, Mass: The MIT Press, 1969.

Nagel, Ernest & Brandt, Richard B. *Meaning and Knowledge: Systematic Readings in Epistemology.* Harcourt, Brace & World, Inc., 1965.

Ogden, C. K., and I. A. Richards. *Meaning Of Meaning.* San Diego: Mariner Books, 1989.

Polanyi, Michael, and Harry Prosch. *Meaning.* Chicago: University Of Chicago Press, 1977.

Putnam, Hilary. *Meaning and the Moral Sciences.* London: Routledge, 2010.

Metaphysics

Chisholm, Roderick M. *On Metaphysics.* Minneapolis: University of Minnesota Press, 1989.

Lowe, E. J. *A Survey of Metaphysics.* Oxford ; New York: Oxford University Press, 2002.

Rea, Michael, ed. *Metaphysics.* London ; New York: Routledge, 2008.

Taylor, Richard. *Metaphysics.* Prentice-Hall Foundations of Philosophy Series. Englewood Cliffs, N.J: Prentice-Hall, 1963.

van Inwagen, Peter. *Metaphysics.* Fourth Edition, Boulder: Westview Press, 2014.

Mind

Andersen, Elizabeth A., Peder Voetmann Christiansen, Claus Emmeche, and Niels Ole Finnemann. *Downward Causation: Minds, Bodies and Matter.* Aarhus: Aarhus University Press, 2001.

Annas, Julia. *Hellenistic Philosophy of Mind.* Hellenistic Culture and Society 8. Berkeley: University of California Press, 1992.

Bechtel, William, and George Graham, eds. *A Companion to Cognitive Science.* Malden, Mass.: Wiley-Blackwell, 1999.

Chalmers, David J. *Philosophy of Mind: Classical and Contemporary Readings.* Oxford University Press, USA, 2002.

Churchland, Patricia Smith. *Neurophilosophy: Toward a Unified Science of the Mind-Brain.* The MIT Press, 1989.

Crick, Francis. *The Astonishing Hypothesis: The Scientific Search for the Soul.* Reprint edition. London: Scribner, 1995.

Damasio, Anthony. *Descartes' Error: Emotion, Reason, and the Human Brain.* Reprint edition. London: Penguin Books, 2005.

Damasio, Antonio. *Self Comes to Mind: Constructing the Conscious Brain.* Reprint edition. New York: Vintage, 2012.

Davidson, Donald. *Essays on Actions and Events.* Oxford : New York: Clarendon Press, 2001.

Delbruck, Max. *Mind from Matter?: An Essay on Evolutionary Epistemology.*

Blackwell Scientific Publications, 1986.

Descartes, René. *Meditations on First Philosophy*. Hackett Publishing, 1993.

Descartes, René. *Discourse on Method and Related Writings*. Translated by Desmond M. Clarke. London ; New York: Penguin Classics, 2000.

Donald, Merlin. *A Mind So Rare: The Evolution of Human Consciousness*. New York: W. W. Norton & Company, 2002.

Eccles, John C. *How the Self Controls Its Brain*. Springer-Verlag Telos, 1994.

Feigl, Herbert, Michael Scriven, and Grover Maxwell, eds. *Concepts, Theories, and the Mind-Body Problem*. Minnesota Archive Editions edition. Minneapolis: Univ Of Minnesota Press, 1958.

Flanagan, Owen. *The Problem Of The Soul: Two Visions Of Mind And How To Reconcile Them*. New York: Basic Books, 2003.

Foster, John. *The Immaterial Self: A Defence of the Cartesian Dualist Conception of the Mind*. London: Routledge, 1991.

Hasker, William. *The Emergent Self*. Ithaca, N.Y. ;London: Cornell University Press, 2001.

Hebb, D. O. *The Organization of Behavior: A Neuropsychological Theory*. Mahwah, N.J: Psychology Press, 2002.

Heil, John, ed. *Philosophy of Mind: A Guide and Anthology*. Oxford ; New York: Oxford University Press, 2004.

———, and Alfred Mele, *Mental Causation*. Oxford, England: Clarendon, 1993.

Kandel, Eric R., James H. Schwartz, Thomas M. Jessell, Steven A. Siegelbaum, and A. J. Hudspeth, eds. *Principles of Neural Science*, Fifth Edition. New York: McGraw-Hill Education / Medical, 2012.

Kim, Jaegwon. *Mind in a Physical World: An Essay on the Mind-Body Problem and Mental Causation*. Cambridge, Mass.: A Bradford Book, 2000.

———. *Philosophy of Mind*. Third Edition, Boulder, CO: Westview Press, 2010.

———. *Physicalism, or Something Near Enough*. Princeton: Princeton University Press, 2007.

Lange, Frederick Albert. *The History of Materialism*. Third edition. Humanities Press, 1950.

Libet, Benjamin. *Mind Time: The temporal factor in consciousness*. Harvard University Press, 2009.

Lowe, E. J. *An Introduction to the Philosophy of Mind*. Cambridge, U.K. ; New York: Cambridge University Press, 2000.

Moser, Paul K., and J. D. Trout, eds. *Contemporary Materialism: A Reader*. London ; New York: Routledge, 1995.

Nagel, Thomas. *Mind and Cosmos: Why the Materialist Neo-Darwinian Conception of Nature Is Almost Certainly False*. New York: Oxford University Press, 2012.

O'Connor, John. *Modern Materialism: Readings on Mind-Body Identity*. Harcourt, Brace, 1969.

O'Hear, Anthony. *Contemporary Issues in the Philosophy of Mind*. Cambridge, U.K. ; New York: Cambridge University Press, 1998.

Penrose, Roger. *The Emperor's New Mind: Concerning Computers, Minds, and the Laws of Physics*. New Ed. Oxford University Press, USA, 2002.

———. *The Large, the Small and the Human Mind*. 1st ed. Cambridge University Press, 2000.

Rosenthal, David M., ed. *Materialism and the Mind-Body Problem*. Englewood Cliffs, N.J.: Prentice Hall, 1971.

Ryle, Gilbert. *The Concept of Mind*. New York: Barnes & Noble, 1949.

Sayre, Kenneth M. Cybernetics and the Philosophy of Mind. Atlantic Highlands, N.J: Humanities Press, 1976.

Schilpp, Paul Arthur, ed. *The Philosophy of Karl Popper*. La Salle, Ill: Open Court Publishing Co ,U.S., 1977.

Searle, John. *Minds, Brains and Science*. Harvard University Press, 1986.

Searle, John R. *Intentionality: An Essay in the Philosophy of Mind*. Cambridge Cambridgeshire ; New York: Cambridge University Press, 1983.

Sellars, Wilfrid, and Richard Rorty. *Empiricism and the Philosophy of Mind*. Cambridge, Mass: Harvard University Press, 1997.

Stapp, Henry P. *Mindful Universe: Quantum Mechanics and the Participating Observer*. Berlin ; New York: Springer, 2011.

Strawson, Galen. *Real Materialism: And Other Essays*. Oxford University Press, USA, 2007.

Swinburne, Richard. *The Evolution of the Soul*. Oxford England : New York: Clarendon Press, 1997.

Thagard, Paul. *Mind: Introduction to Cognitive Science*, Cambridge, Mass: A Bradford Book, 2005.

Walter, Sven, and Heinz-Dieter Heckmann, eds. *Physicalism and Mental Causation*. Exeter, UK ; Charlottesville, VA: Imprint Academic, 2003.

Warner, Richard, and Tadeusz Szubka, eds. *The Mind-Body Problem: A Guide to the Current Debate*. Oxford, UK ; Cambridge, USA: Wiley-Blackwell, 1994.

Origin of Life

Cairns-Smith, A. G. *Seven Clues to the Origin of Life: A Scientific Detective Story*. New York: Cambridge University Press, 1990.

Cairns-Smith, Alexander Graham, and H. Hartman, eds. *Clay Minerals and the Origin of Life*. New York: Cambridge University Press, 1987.

Crick, Francis. *Life Itself: Its Origin and Nature*. New York: Touchstone, Simon & Schuster, 1982.

Dyson, Freeman. *Origins of Life*. Cambridge England ; New York: Cambridge University Press, 1999.

Eigen, Manfred. *The Hypercycle: A Principle of Natural Self Organization*. Berlin ; New York: Springer-Verlag, 1979.

Eigen, Manfred, and Ruthild Winkler-Oswatitsch. *Steps towards Life: A Perspective on Evolution*. New York: Oxford University Press, 1992.

Gregersen, Niels Henrik, ed. *From Complexity to Life: On The Emergence of Life and Meaning*. Oxford ; New York: Oxford University Press, 2002.

Hazen, Robert. Genesis: *The Scientific Quest for Life's Origins*. Joseph Henry Press, 2007.

Kauffman, Stuart. *At Home in the Universe: The Search for the Laws of Self-Organization and Complexity*. New York: Oxford University Press, 1996.

Küppers, Bernd-Olaf. *Information and the Origin of Life*. Cambridge, Mass: The MIT Press, 1990.

Luisi, Pier Luigi. *The Emergence of Life: From Chemical Origins to Synthetic Biology*. Cambridge: Cambridge University Press, 2010.

Morowitz, Harold J. *Beginnings of Cellular Life: Metabolism Recapitulates Biogenesis*. Yale University Press, 2004.

Oparin, A. I. *Life: Its Nature, Origin and Development*. Academic Press, 1961.

Orgel, Leslie E. Orgel: *The Origins of Life*. New York: John Wiley & Sons Inc, 1973.

Smith, John Maynard, and Eors Szathmary. *The Origins of Life: From the Birth of Life to the Origin of Language*. Oxford Paperbacks, 2000.

Philosophy

Ajdukiewicz, K. *Problems and Theories of Philosophy*. Cambridge: Cambridge University Press, 1975.

Ayer, A. J. *The Central Questions of Philosophy*. New York: W. Morrow, 1975.

Feinberg, Joel, and Russ Shafer-Landau. *Reason and Responsibility: Readings in Some Basic Problems of Philosophy*. Australia: Cengage Learning, 2013.

James, William. *Some Problems of Philosophy: A Beginning of an Introduction to Philosophy*. HardPress Publishing, 2013.

Locke, John. *An Essay Concerning Human Understanding*. New York: Oxford University Press, 1979.

Moore, George Edward. *Some Main Problems of Philosophy*. Routledge, 2015.

Rader, Melvin M., and Jerry H. Gill. *The Enduring Questions: Main Problems of Philosophy*. Fort Worth: Holt Rinehart and Winston, 1990.

Russell, Bertrand. *The Problems of Philosophy*. Radford, VA: Wilder Publications, 2009.

Stumpf, Samuel Enoch, and James Feiser. *Philosophy: History and Problems*: 6th Edition. McGraw-Hill Higher Education, 2003.

Wittgenstein, Ludwig, and Bertrand Russell. *Tractatus Logico-Philosophicus*: German and English. Translated by C. K. Ogden. New Ed edition. London ; New York: Routledge, 1981.

Bibliography

Physics

Bohm, David. *Quantum Theory*. Dover Publications, 1989.

Boltzmann, Ludwig. *Lectures on Gas Theory*. New York: Dover Publications, 2011.

Cassidy, David C. *Uncertainty: The Life and Science of Werner Heisenberg*. W. H. Freeman, 1993.

Cassirer, Ernst. *Determinism and Indeterminism in Modern Physics*. Yale, 1956.

Cercignani, Carlo, and Roger Penrose. *Ludwig Boltzmann: The Man Who Trusted Atoms*. Oxford: Oxford University Press, 2006.

Eddington, A. S. *The Nature of the Physical World*. Kessinger Publishing, LLC, 2005.

Eddington, Sir Arthur. *New Pathways In Science*. Frazer Press, 2007.

Einstein, Albert. *Ideas And Opinions*. New York: Broadway Books, 1995.

———. *The Collected Papers of Albert Einstein, Volume 2: The Swiss Years: Writings, 1900-1909*. Edited by John Stachel, David C. Cassidy, Jürgen Renn, and Robert Schulmann. Princeton, NJ: Princeton University Press, 1990.

———. *The Collected Papers of Albert Einstein, Volume 6: The Berlin Years: Writings, 1914-1917*. Edited by A. J. Kox, Martin J. Klein, and Robert Schulmann. Princeton, NJ: Princeton University Press, 1996.

Einstein, Albert, and Max Born. *The Born - Einstein Letters: Friendship, Politics and Physics in Uncertain Times*. Macmillan, 2005.

Greenspan, Nancy Thorndike. *The End of the Certain World: The Life and Science of Max Born*, 2005.

Lindley, David. *Boltzmanns Atom: The Great Debate That Launched A Revolution In Physics*. 1st ed. Free Press, 2001.

———. *Uncertainty Einstein Heisenberg Bohr And The Struggle For The Soul Of Science*. New York; Anchor Books:, Random House 2007

Moore, Walter J. *Schrödinger: Life and Thought*. Cambridge University Press, 1992.

Pais, Abraham. *Niels Bohr's Times,: In Physics, Philosophy, and Polity*. Oxford University Press, USA, 1994.

———. *Subtle Is the Lord: The Science and the Life of Albert Einstein*. Oxford University Press, USA, 2005.

Pauli, Wolfgang, L. Rosenfeld, and V. Weisskopf, eds. *Niels Bohr and the Development of Physics; Essays Dedicated to Niels Bohr on the Occasion of His Seventieth Birthday*. McGraw-Hill, 1955.

Planck, Max. *Where Is Science Going?* Ox Bow Press, 1981.

Prigogine, Ilya. *Order Out of Chaos*. Shambhala, 1984.

Reif, Frederick. *Fundamentals of Statistical and Thermal Physics*. McGraw-Hill Science/Engineering/Math, 1965.

Wigner, Eugene Paul. *Symmetries and Reflections*. Woodbridge, Conn.: Ox Bow Pr, 1979.

Psychology

Antonietti, Alessandro, Antonella Corradini, and E. Jonathan Lowe, eds. *Psycho-Physical Dualism Today: An Interdisciplinary Approach*. Lanham, MD: Lexington Books, 2008.

Brentano, Franz. *Psychology from An Empirical Standpoint*. Routledge, 2014.

James, William. *The Principles of Psychology*, New York: Dover Publications, 1950.

Roback, A. A. *A History of American Psychology*, New York: Collier Books, 1964.

Schacter, Daniel L., Daniel T. Gilbert, and Daniel M. Wegner. *Psychology*. New York: Worth Publishers, 2007.

Skinner, B. F. *Science And Human Behavior*. New York, NY: Free Press, 1965.

Watson, John B. *Behaviorism*. New York: W. W. Norton & Company, 1970.

Watson, John B., and William MacDougall. *The Battle Of Behaviorism: An Exposition And An Exposure*. Kessinger Publishing, LLC, 2010.

Quantum Mechanics

Bacciagaluppi, Guido, and Antony Valentini. *Quantum Theory at the Crossroads: Reconsidering the 1927 Solvay Conference*. Cambridge: Cambridge University Press, 2013.

Bell, J. S., and Alain Aspect. *Speakable and Unspeakable in Quantum Mechanics: Collected Papers on Quantum Philosophy*. Cambridge: Cambridge University Press, 2004.

Bohm, David. *Quantum Theory*. Dover Publications, 1989.

Bohr, Niels. *Atomic Physics and Human Knowledge*. Mineola, N.Y: Dover Publications, 2010.

Davies, P. C. W., and Julian R. Brown, eds. *The Ghost in the Atom: A Discussion of the Mysteries of Quantum Physics*. Cambridge: Cambridge University Press, 1993.

Dirac, Paul A. M. *Lectures on Quantum Mechanics*. 4th edition. New York: Clarendon Press, 1982

Jammer, Max. *The Conceptual Development of Quantum Mechanics*. McGraw Hill, 1966.

———. *The Philosophy of Quantum Mechanics: The Interpretations of Quantum Mechanics in Historical Perspective*. New York: Wiley, 1974.

Lifshitz, L. D. Landau and E. M. *Quantum Mechanics: Non-Relativistic Theory*. Addison-Wesley Publishing Company, 1958.

Mehra, Jagdish, and Helmut Rechenberg. *The Historical Development of Quantum Theory* Volumes 1-6. New York: Springer, 2001.

Neumann, John von. *Mathematical Foundations of Quantum Mechanics*. Princeton: Princeton University Press, 1996.

Pais, Abraham, Maurice Jacob, David I. Olive, and Michael F. Atiyah. *Paul Dirac: The Man and His Work*. Cambridge University Press, 2005.

van der Waerden, B. L., ed. *Sources of Quantum Mechanics*. New York, N.Y: Dover Publications, 1968.

Wheeler, John Archibald, and Wojciech Hubert Zurek. *Quantum Theory and Measurement*. Princeton Univ Pr, 1984.

Theology

Boyd, Gregory A., David Hunt, William Lane Craig, and Paul Helm. *Divine Foreknowledge: Four Views*. Edited by James K. Beilby and Paul R. Eddy. Downers Grove, Ill: IVP Academic, 2001.

Dawkins, Richard. *The God Delusion*. Mariner Books, 2008.

Dennett, Daniel C. *Breaking the Spell: Religion as a Natural Phenomenon*. Viking, 2007.

Flew, Antony G. *God, Freedom and Immortality*. Amherst, N.Y: Prometheus Books, 1984.

Hume, David, and Richard H. Popkin. *Dialogues Concerning Natural Religion: The Posthumous Essays of the Immortality of the Soul and of Suicide*. Hackett Pub Co, 1998.

Value

Nagel, Thomas. *The View from Nowhere*. New York: Oxford University Press, 1986.

Peirce, Charles. *Values in a Universe of Chance: Selected Writings of Charles S. Peirce*. Dover Publications, 1958.

Index

Index

Index

Index

Index

Image Credits

Some images are from websites with Creative Commons licenses or explicit permissions for non-profit and educational uses of their material, such as all the content of informationphilosopher.com and metaphysicist.com. We especially want to thank Drew Berry (the *Walter+Eliza Hall Insitute of Medical Research*), molecularmovies.com, and the *North Dakota State University* Virtual Cell Animation Collection on YouTube.

Books by Bob Doyle

Free Will: The Scandal in Philosophy (2011)

Great Problems in Philosophy and Physics Solved? (2016)

Metaphysics: Problems, Puzzles and Paradoxes, Solved? (2016)

My God, He Plays Dice! How Albert Einstein Invented Most of Quantum Mechanics (2017)

Mind: The Scandal in Psychology (2017)

Chance: The Scandal in Physics

Life: The Scandal in Biology

Value: The Scandal in Economics, Sociology, Politics, and Ethics

PDFs of all of Bob's books will be available for free on the I-Phi website, both complete books and as individual chapter PDFs for easy assignment to students.

Colophon

This book was created on the *Apple Mac Pro* using the desktop publishing program *Adobe InDesign CC 2015*, with Myriad Pro and Minion Pro fonts. The original illustrations were created in *Adobe Illustrator* and *Adobe Photoshop*.

The author developed the first desktop publishing program, *MacPublisher*, for the Macintosh, in 1984, the year of the Mac, intending to write some books on philosophy and physics. After many years of delay and further research, the books are finally in production, completing work, in his eighties, on ideas that first emerged in his twenties.

The index was edited by Heather Hedden, ASI.

Credits

Information Philosopher books are *bridges* from the information architecture of the printed page, from well before Gutenberg and his movable-type revolution, to the information architecture of the world-wide web, to a future of knowledge instantly available on demand anywhere it is needed in the world.

Information wants to be free. Information *can make you free.*

I-Phi printed books are still material, with their traditional costs of production and distribution. But they are physical pointers and travel guides to help you navigate the virtual world of information online, which of course still requires energy for its communication, and material devices for its storage and retrieval to displays.

But the online information itself is, like the knowledge in our collective minds, neither material nor energy, but pure information, pure ideas, the stuff of thought. It is as close as physical science comes to the notion of spirit, the ghost in the machine, the soul in the body.

Google It is this spirit that information philosophy wants to set free, with the help of Google and Wikipedia, Facebook and YouTube.

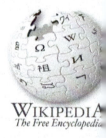

At a time when one in ten living persons have a presence on the web, when the work of past intellects has been captured by Google Scholar, we have entered the age of *Information Immortality.*

When you Google one of the concepts of information philosophy, the search results page will retrieve links to the latest versions of Information Philosopher pages online, and of course links to related pages in the Wikipedia, in the Stanford Encyclopedia of Philosophy, and links to YouTube lectures.

Thank you for purchasing this physical embodiment of our work. I-Phi Press hopes to put the means of intellectual production in the hands of the people.

CPSIA information can be obtained
at www.ICGtesting.com
Printed in the USA
LVOW13s1933020317
525948LV00012B/877/P